Political Theology after Metaphysics

SUNY series in Theology and Continental Thought
───────────
Douglas L. Donkel, editor

Political Theology after Metaphysics

DEREK BROWN

Cover: Monument to Che Guevara at the site of his death in Bolivia. Photograph by Augusto Starita. Courtesy Wikimedia Commons

Published by State University of New York Press, Albany

© 2023 State University of New York

All rights reserved

Printed in the United States of America

No part of this book may be used or reproduced in any manner whatsoever without written permission. No part of this book may be stored in a retrieval system or transmitted in any form or by any means including electronic, electrostatic, magnetic tape, mechanical, photocopying, recording, or otherwise without the prior permission in writing of the publisher.

For information, contact State University of New York Press, Albany, NY
www.sunypress.edu

Library of Congress Cataloging-in-Publication Data

Name: Brown, Derek, 1992– author.
Title: Political theology after metaphysics / Derek Brown.
Description: Albany, NY : State University of New York Press, [2023] | Series: SUNY series in theology and continental thought | Includes bibliographical references and index.
Identifiers: LCCN 2023015640 | ISBN 9781438495866 (hardcover : alk. paper) | ISBN 9781438495873 (ebook) | ISBN 9781438495859 (pbk. : alk. paper)
Subjects: LCSH: Political theology. | Social justice.
Classification: LCC BT83.59 .B769 2023 | DDC 261.7—dc23/eng/20230915
LC record available at https://lccn.loc.gov/2023015640

10 9 8 7 6 5 4 3 2 1

This book is dedicated to a scene from Ingmar Bergman's *The Seventh Seal.* Block broods. Mia offers a bowl of strawberries. Block says, "We worry about so much." Mia replies, "It's better to be two."

The world outside had its own rules, and those rules were not human.

—Michel Houellebecq, *The Elementary Particles*

And death, which I have always regarded as the greatest dimension of life, dark, compelling, was no more than a pipe that springs a leak, a branch that cracks in the wind, a jacket that slips off a clothes hanger and falls to the floor.

—Karl Ove Knausgaard, *My Struggle*

Contents

Acknowledgments		xi
Introduction		1
Chapter 1	Polemical Ontology: Carl Schmitt's "Decisionism" Is Not What It Seems	19
Chapter 2	Deconstructing Theology, Constructing Faith?	59
Chapter 3	Belonging to the World: Karl Ove Knausgaard's Secular Love	101
Chapter 4	Orthodoxy Is Orthopraxy: Kierkegaard's Relation to Marx Reconsidered	123
Chapter 5	God Is and Is Not Black: Black Theology, Marxism, and the Relationship between Race and Class	167
Conclusion: St. John Brown		219
Notes		229
Bibliography		263
Index		275

Acknowledgments

This project would not have been possible without the guidance and feedback I have received from peers at Boston College and elsewhere. Of these, I would like to thank most of all Andrew Prevot, my teacher and advisor, without whom I could not have written what I have. I am indebted also to Kevin Newmark, a reader of this project, whose rigor and kindness is remarkable, and from whom I have learned so much. Joerg Rieger has been helpful, encouraging, and demanding throughout, and I thank him for it. I would also like to thank Dan Horan, who introduced me to theology; Ronald Waite, who introduced me to philosophy; and Roos Slegers, who taught me how to think. Conversations with Steve Comery, my favorite worker on all of Wall Street, have undoubtedly improved this dissertation.

I would also like to thank my friends at SYF Brazilian Jiu Jitsu Academy, which is a home for me. Bruno Braz, Dan O'Neill, Andrew Low, and Edgardo Tormos Bilges, especially, are as responsible for this production as are my friends and mentors in academia.

A version of this manuscript was originally written as a dissertation, which was completed in November 2020. A large part of it was produced during a turbulent and unfortunate Democratic Party primary season, a deadly pandemic, and nationwide protest movements against racism and capitalism, which have by now all but fizzled. To that end, I would like to thank all those who don't know me, but who have nonetheless helped remind me that another world is possible: Jeremy Corbyn and Bernie Sanders; Cornel West and David Harvey; Michel Houellebecq and Karl Ove Knausgaard; Thomas Sankara and Che Guevara.

Above all, I thank Deniz Uyan.

Introduction

The Question and the Claim

My claim, which this book unfolds, is threefold. First: metaphysics has always been a political act. This is necessarily the case because metaphysics, as a discourse that hides its own production, is unavoidably ideological. Second: theology, which metaphysics secretly harbors as an authorizing force, has made possible metaphysics' ideological ruminations. Therefore, theology, too, has always been a political act. Third, and as a sort of normative complement to the first two: Theologians and religious believers should reject this ideological metaphysical discourse and instead preferentially pursue an orthopraxical and revolutionary political theology. It is now past time to recognize the unavoidability of the political and ensure that theology's underlying political commitments are revolutionary in general and anti-capitalist in particular.

On the one hand, the deconstruction of metaphysics—which, as Jacques Derrida demonstrates, and which I explore in detail in this text's second chapter—presents difficulties for the possibility of any theology, political or not: As will become clear, it is precisely theology that structurally articulates and defends the key metaphysical notion of the isomorphism of thinking and being. It is in this sense that metaphysics harbors theology as a sort of secret. And it is in this sense that one could even say, as Derrida does, that metaphysics *is* theology, and that, vice versa, theology is metaphysics. The deconstruction of metaphysics is the deconstruction of theology *tout court*.

But on the other hand, this book's argument concerns not theology in the abstract, but orthopraxical and revolutionary political theology in particular. The type of theologian in whom I am interested resembles John Brown more than Thomas Aquinas,[1] and, contra-continental philosophy's recent interest in St. Paul's alleged political universalism or messianism, the type of theology in which I am interested responds more to St. James's declaration that the rich have "fattened their hearts for the day of slaughter" (James 5:5) than it does Paul's claim that "if you confess with your mouth Jesus as Lord, and believe in your heart that God raised Him from the dead, you will be saved" (Romans 10:9).[2] As Jeffrey Robbins notes, the "philosophers' Paul" is a thinker seemingly devoid of particular political content.[3] And so my preference for James should be read as a materialist and praxis-oriented response to idealist formalisms and to the resurgence of political Platonism—most explicitly through Badiou—in contemporary continental philosophy.

Of course, given this emancipatory and material specification, the collapse of metaphysics might not so quickly sound theology's death knell. For while Derrida and a whole tradition of deconstructors have demonstrated the identity of metaphysics and what they call "infinitist" theology—which, as we will see, is quite different than demonstrating the identity of metaphysics and faith—Karl Marx and a whole tradition of anti-capitalist theorists have demonstrated if not the identity, at least the intimacy and complication of metaphysics and capitalism. Yes, metaphysics is theology. But capitalism also has a theology of its own, and, as I will argue and as Marx argued, the capitalist's theology is not so different from the theology of the metaphysicians.

Marx notes this entanglement of theology and capitalism in the famous commodity fetishism section of the first volume of *Capital*:

> A commodity appears, at first sight, a very trivial thing, and easily understood. Its analysis shows that it is, in reality, a very queer thing, abounding in metaphysical subtleties and theological niceties. So far as it is a value in use, there is nothing mysterious about it, whether we consider it from the point of view that by its properties it is capable of satisfying human wants, or from the point that those properties are the product of human labor. It is as clear as noon-day, that man, by his industry, changes the forms of the materials furnished by Nature, in such a way as to make them useful to him.

Yet when we look beyond this use value—when we dig beneath the surface appearance of the commodity—we discover a hidden infrastructural world of production: "The social character of men's labor appears to them as an objective character stamped upon the product of that labor; because the relation of the producers to the sum total of their own labor is presented to them as a social relation, existing not between themselves, but between the products of their labor. This is the reason why the products of labor become commodities, social things whose qualities are at the same time perceptible and imperceptible by the senses."

This ideological inversion, wherein the social relation between workers and owners is masked by the pseudo-objective exchange relation between buyer and seller, follows a logic recognizably religious: "In order, therefore, to find an analogy, we must have recourse to the mist-enveloped regions of the religious world. In that world the productions of the human brain appear as independent beings endowed with life, and entering into relation both with one another and the human race. So it is in the world of commodities with the products of men's hands."[4] Whereas capitalism masks workers' production of commodities, theology masks theologians' production of God. Marx sees clearly the similarity between these two ideological logics: they both mask the site (and sight) of production. But he less directly articulates their difference. In capitalism, the owner hides the proletariat's work. In theology, on the other hand, the theologian hides the work of his or herself: central to the theological gesture is the claim that the theologian responds to, but does not and cannot produce, God. For the theologian to maintain any sort of credibility, God cannot be a product of theology: God, as theology has always understood God, must be unproduced, outside of production, uncreated and unmoving, *sui generis*, not just substantial but supersubstantial, supereminent, outside of the text of metaphysics.

This brief turn to Marx, then, quickly brings us back to Derrida. Where Marx offers a political-economic critique of the ideological function of metaphysics, Derrida offers a deconstruction of the theoretical "grounding" of all metaphysical claims. Which is not to say that Marx is uninterested in philosophical critiques or Derrida in political ones. Indeed, and as will become apparent throughout this book, the line between Marxist critique and Derridean deconstruction is less opaque than either Marxist critics of "postmodernism" or post-structural critics of "metanarratives" might let on. In both, the Marxist critique of capitalism and the Derridean critique of metaphysics, the major point remains structurally analogous: An ideological-theological appearance obfuscates a hidden infrastructural reality. Or, what amounts to the same but in simpler terms: *The metaphysics of God and of commodities—metaphysics itself—is a lie that hides production.*

Because metaphysics is an ideology that hides, and because metaphysics is theology, all theology is necessarily political theology. This is true in a double sense. First, all theology is political because, as ideology, it necessarily obfuscates some underlying material reality. This process of obfuscation is unavoidably political. Second, all theology is political because the material reality that it hides is itself political. A dispute on this point is precisely why Marx left the Young Hegelians: For Marx, religion is worthy of critique not primarily because it is metaphysically incorrect, but because of the particular underlying material relations that particular religions obfuscate.[5] It is this attention to particularity—and not, contra Feuerbach, a psychological argument concerning fantasy projection—that leads Marx to write that Christianity, "especially in its more bourgeois developments, Protestantism and Deism," is "the most fitting form of religion" under capitalism (Marx, 51).

This discussion of theology's role in the ideological defense of capital is important for reminding us of the dangers of idealism. To say that theology is impossible—that is, to say that there is no metaphysical concept because there is no outside text, to say that theologians made God and that God did not make theologians—is not to say that theology does not actually exist. So long as universities have theology departments, so long as theologians exist, so too will theology. Theology's lack of metaphysical rigor is not an outright dismissal of the possibility of actually existing theology, in much the same way that the commodity's lack of ontological status within the productive processes does not mean that commodities do not exist as such. Ideologies can be effective with or without ontological ground or reality, and this is precisely the reason they must be fought not only in the intellectual realm, but also and predominantly in material actuality. To think the opposite—that a textual deconstruction of theology, or that a written critique of capitalism, amounts to an overcoming of theology or capitalism—is itself an idealist metaphysical gesture that assumes reality follows the mandates of logic. But reality does not do so.

That is, theology's actual possibility, the possibility of theology continuing to exist as a material actuality, has very little to do with the coherence of arguments concerning theology's theoretical impossibility or political danger. Ideologies simply do not need to make sense to function, and they certainly do not need to make sense to exist. Racism, which will receive extensive treatment throughout this project but especially in chapter five, is proof of this disconnect between the mandates of thought and the actuality of existence. And so the fall of metaphysics as a credible discourse in the twentieth and early twenty-first centuries will not lead to the necessary overcoming of theology any more than did Marx's critique of capital lead to the necessary overcoming of capitalism. Here, Derrida is perhaps more helpful than Marx: ideology might never be overcome, because there might not be a Truth, Logos, or God that or who could secure and determine non-ideological thought.

If theology and ideology mutually constitute each other, and if ideology is a perhaps unavoidable dimension of all thought, and if all theology is political in the double sense of ideologically obfuscating a particular political regime and, by the act of hiding, supporting said regime, then the question pertinent to theology is not "Will theology be political?" but is instead "What sort of politics will theology pursue and defend?" We can now understand my answer to this project's question—What kind of theology, if any, should one pursue after the deconstruction of metaphysics?—in some more detail. First, the question is not "What sort of theology is possible after metaphysics?" Theology is both impossible according to thinking and actual according to reality. This lack of identity between thinking and being—which will become important for this project beginning in its second chapter, and which grounds and defines all metaphysics as metaphysics—prevents any simple descriptive solution to the problem of theology's relation to ideology. Theology's relation to ideology—that is, to both metaphysics and politics, to both Derrida and Marx—will be determined and decided in material history and cannot be adequately described in ideal thought.

This book argues that theologians and religious believers should pursue an orthopraxical and revolutionary political theology over metaphysical alternatives. Specifically, theologians and religious believers should pursue an explicitly anti-capitalist theology. Metaphysical theologies are forced by their own ideological limitations to structurally deny their own political implications, and so should be treated critically as the reactionary theories that they always in fact have been. Idealist theologies that prioritize doxy over praxis, or thinking over being, should be treated in like manner. If the practice of doing theology demands an answer to the question "What political regime do you support?" then, as this book passionately argues, the practice of theology must always strive for the material emancipation of the poor, the oppressed, and the exploited. Such an emancipation demands not reform, aid, or structural readjustment, and certainly not a mere "rethinking" of the status quo or an "openness to dialogue," but instead an actual revolution of the entire global capitalist order. As I hope to demonstrate later, any theology that chooses otherwise is in fact a reactionary enemy of the sort of love promoted not only by Jesus Christ, but also by revolutionaries like John Brown, Fred Hampton, and Che Guevara—all of whom I consider saints. Theology must be political; it should be revolutionary.[6]

Clarification of Terms

Before outlining the book's trajectory in detail, it would be helpful to clarify a few terms and concepts upon which I have already relied.

First: *Metaphysics*. And relatedly, *deconstruction*. As I discuss in some detail in this text's second chapter, the critique of metaphysics—and so also its defense—has become something of a motif in analytical and continental philosophy, systematic and constructive theology, and in what has unhelpfully come to be known as "theory." As happens in philosophy, often these discussions turn into debates concerning the definition of metaphysics. For the purpose of this book, I intend the signifier "metaphysics" to refer to *any discourse that assumes or relies upon the philosopheme of the identity of thinking and being.* While the contemporary landscape does not offer any agreed upon sense of metaphysics, and so while my proposed heuristic definition above will not receive widespread acceptance in current academic literature, I do think there are good reasons to identify what has come to be thought of as metaphysics with this particular philosopheme.

We can turn, for example, to Parmenides, who wrote that "thinking and being are the same."[7] Another study could trace the iteration of this theme in Plato, Aristotle, and Plotinus, up through medieval debates concerning univocity, into the Renaissance's trust in soul, the Enlightenment's trust in reason, Spinozist monism and its later twentieth century reception in Deleuze,[8] through Kantian and Hegelian idealisms, into phenomenology, and, today, in the resurgence of realism in the forms of object oriented ontology, critical realism, and "new materialisms."[9] Indeed, as Philippe Lacoue-Labarthe has suggested, "the whole text of philosophy (metaphysics)" could be understood as beginning with Parmenides's claim and ending with Nietzsche's refutation: "Parmenides said: 'One cannot think of what is not.' We are at the other extreme, and say: 'What can be thought of must certainly be a fiction.' "[10]

As Lacoue-Labarthe notes, this reference to fiction brings us to Derrida, who (in)famously wrote and argued that there is no outside text.[11] As we will see, Derrida argues that metaphysical writing has always—and as a matter of structural necessity—relied upon, even as it produces, some transcendental Truth, God, or Logos that or who could secure the identity of thinking and being. That is, metaphysics, in its reliance on its own textual productions, has always looked to justify Parmenides's third fragment. This is what Derrida means by "the metaphysics of presence": the belief—and it is a belief—that the philosopher's text can and does refer to something outside of it, to another text, to an outside text. Deconstruction, then, is both a reading of the impossibility of this motif—thinking and being are not actually isomorphic, there is a necessary gap between thinking and being, there is, as Derrida says, no such thing as a metaphysical concept, only concepts about metaphysics—and a reading of its use and function in philosophical texts. In short: thinking and being are not the same, although philosophy thinks and requires that they are. Deconstruction reads the tension caused by this difference, which Derrida calls *différance*.

This double structure of metaphysics means that deconstructions of metaphysics are always a bit provisional and double themselves. An example: Michael Marder argues that Carl Schmitt is a post-metaphysical thinker of political ontology.[12] By this, Marder means that Schmitt is a "post-foundational" thinker reliant on a sort of Heideggerian existential ontology. And so for Marder, metaphysics means not a use of the philosopheme of the identity of thinking and being, but a reliance on epistemic foundationalism. I argue in the next chapter that Schmitt does rely on classically metaphysical concepts like substance and sovereignty. Yet, ultimately, and despite our disagreement on the extent to which Schmitt is a metaphysician, my argument is not that far from Marder's: Marder emphasizes the importance of "groundless" existential decision in Schmitt, and my reading agrees. Precisely because there are no metaphysical concepts, and precisely because thinking and being are not isomorphic, when I write that Schmitt is a metaphysician, or write that Schmitt is doing ontology, I am also writing that Schmitt is an ideologist. Schmitt relies on ostensibly ontological and metaphysical concepts to conceal his prior political decisions. Schmitt both is a metaphysician—he writes metaphysics—and is not a metaphysician—there is no such thing as metaphysics. This both/and structure is what led Derrida (and Heidegger) to occasionally write "Being" under erasure. And it is this both/and, this discursive concealing of political productions, that makes Schmitt ideological.

While I do believe I demonstrate that ideologists like Schmitt have relied upon this philosopheme, my goal is not and could not be to provide a thoroughly encyclopedic reading of the role of this philosopheme in the work of every self-proclaimed "metaphysician." It is possible that there are thinkers who think themselves metaphysicians who do not rely on or use this philosopheme. I do not know if such a person exists, but if he or she does, then he or she is not the object of my critique, of my deconstruction. Again: When I write *metaphysics*, I refer to the tradition of thought that assumes the identity of thinking and being. Sometimes *metaphysics* might not be the most readily available signifier to describe a particular thinker.

As Marder argues regarding Schmitt, *ontology* might be better. Or, as my discussion of metonym in chapter five suggests, sometimes the most appropriate word is *poetry*. I do believe that *metaphysics* is a generally historically appropriate word to signify the tradition of thought that assumes or uses the philosopheme of the identity of thinking and being, but it is not the only word that could be used to refer to this tradition. That is fine. The object of my critique is not the word *metaphysics* but the metaphysical/ontological/poetic/and so on use and abuse of the alleged identity of thinking and being. As this book demonstrates, this tradition is broad, hegemonic, and, ultimately, ideological.

To recapitulate and summarize the above: my critiques of metaphysics, ontology, and other discourses that use and assume an isomorphism of thinking and being should be understood as primarily political. My critique of the myth of ontological race, which appears in chapter one and receives extensive treatment in chapter five, does not deny that "race" "exists" within the frames of particular political or social ontologies, but instead critiques the belief that any ontological category necessarily coheres to a material or, in Kierkegaard's language, actual phenomenon. Whether or not something "exists" according to any *en vogue* ontology of the day—existential, hermeneutic, naturalist, dialectical, transcendental—is not my concern. Instead, I am concerned with the ways in which claims, concepts, and arguments—and they are usually metaphysical—are used to essentialize, reify, and substantialize historical, contingent, and political phenomena like race, private property, and so on. I am in particular concerned with the ways in which these reifications rely on the philosopheme of the identity of thinking and being.

And so my interest in metaphysics is ultimately inseparable from my interest in ideology. This relationship between metaphysics and ideology—and I argue that the relationship is a structurally necessary and intrinsic one—is what links the Derridean and the Marxist strands of this argument. Although a full exposition of Marxist political economy is well outside the scope of this book, a few guiding methodological notes will help situate Marx's role in this text.

In general, this book takes from Marx three primary concepts: Ideology, prescriptive materialism, and the critique of capitalist exploitation. Following Žižek, I understand the Marxist notion of ideology to refer to a discourse (or any "superstructural" phenomenon) that conceals its own political motivations or implications.[13] In this way, ideologies could be empirically accurate statements. For example, claims that the Taliban oppresses women are more or less empirically accurate. Yet, when these arguments are put forward by lobbyists and representatives of the military industrial complex, they function ideologically: These contractors and representatives use feminist arguments not to better the lives of women, but to better pursue their own financial and geopolitical interests.[14] As I argue, a similar pattern is at work throughout Schmitt's corpus, which uses truisms and apparently descriptive claims in order to ideologically advance a decisively anti-capitalist and antisemitic political program.

At the same time, sometimes ideological claims are self-evidently false. This is the case with all racist arguments. White supremacy is a patently ridiculous notion, and yet white supremacist claims and beliefs function in society. The point made by ideology critique is that we should not simply reject racist arguments at face value; more radically, the ideological premises that underly racist notions should be uncovered and critiqued. As mentioned above, the failure to advance to this second stage of critique is ultimately why Marx distanced himself from the Young Hegelians, who were myopically concerned with metaphysical arguments for atheism and not enough concerned with the ideological function of religion. In this case, Marx was aware that metaphysical and theological claims ideologically defend particular political-economic regimes. And so my argument that the deconstruction of metaphysics coheres with ideology critique could be taken as an elaboration of Marx on this point: As I will demonstrate through Derrida, a truly metaphysical claim regarding the nature of being, one that assumes thought has access to the presence of truth, is impossible. Yet, these claims are made all the time. The question, then, is what these metaphysical claims hide or elide. The tension between the impossibility of metaphysical concepts and their proliferation in philosophical and theological discourse is not only that which is read by deconstruction as *différance* but is also that which is read by Marx as ideology.

The second element of Marx's thought that this project takes up is his emphasis on prescriptive materialism. A traditional reading of Marx sees in him a rejection of idealism. In this rather simplistic view, idealists believe that ideas and concepts determine material reality, whereas Marx and other materialists believe that material reality (especially economic reality, the "base" of a society) determine ideas and concepts (which in part constitute a social "superstructure"). As should already be clear in regards to the material force of ideologies like racism and private property, and as contemporary theorists of "real abstractions" have argued,[15] such a view is inaccurate and politically unhelpful. But there is another sense of materialism that coheres more neatly not only with Marx's own arguments, but with James's, as referenced above. I call this a prescriptive materialism. By this I mean, as did Marx, that liberation is measured materially. Changes in hearts and minds alone do not do anything to alleviate the lived experiences of the oppressed and exploited. Or, in the words of James, faith without works is dead. This is the normative component of Marx's (and James's) thought that I accept: The work of an orthopraxical revolutionary political theology should be to improve the actual conditions in which the oppressed and exploited live. *Metaphysicians have merely described the world; the point is to change it.*

Which brings us to the third element of Marx's thought that this text employs: The actual conditions in which the oppressed and exploited live are those of late capitalism. This is not to deny that ostensibly non-economic forms of oppression like racism and sexism exist, but it is to deny that these forms of oppression are actually dissociable from political economy. The basic Marxist critique of the capitalist form of political economy, in its most simple form, is that there are two classes of people in capitalism: the proletariat, who trade their labor for money and then trade their money for commodities; and the capitalist class, who trade their money for commodities and then use those commodities to acquire more money. Workers work to live, and capitalists live off others' work.[16]

As I will discuss in much detail in chapters one and five, the ideologies of nationalism and racism (and, controversially, perhaps anti-racism) have functioned to create antagonisms within the proletariat, and so have functioned to secure the interests of capital. But as the proliferation of so-called corporate social responsibility has shown, capitalism does not need to rely on racisms and nationalisms to function. Capitalism is immensely flexible. In this way, the overcoming of racism—an undeniable good—would not necessarily lead to the overcoming of capital. Nor, however, do I naively argue that the overthrowing of capitalism would inevitably lead to the overcoming of racism. A communist can be a racist, even if racism works against his or her own class interests. Yet, it remains the case that, under capitalism, racial oppression leads to a stratified and so artificially divided working class, and so an anti-capitalist's interests should reside in overcoming the ideology of racism. The marginalized and oppressed are the "super exploited."[17] This super-exploitation, combined with the prescriptive materialism above, means that anti-capitalism is the best means we have at our disposal for improving the conditions of not only the working class in general, but of socially oppressed workers in particular. Of course, plenty of anti-racists—in this text, James Cone above all—have found Marxism lacking in its ability to overcome racism. Part of my intention in this book is to argue against that view by demonstrating that Marx does in fact provide us the critical means necessary for overcoming not only the ideology of racism but also the political-economic exploitation that feeds and feeds off of this ideology.

By emphasizing these three dimensions of Marx's thought, I do not mean to blindly countersign his entire project (which would be a task ripe with contradictions, as Marx himself developed throughout his life). For example, this project does not much care about whether or not Marx was right concerning the falling rate of profit, or that machines cannot produce value. These are tangential to Marx's emphasis on materialism and class struggle, and do not feature in my argument. Nor do I think that a simple re-reading of Marx is sufficient for my purposes. While I do believe that his central insights concerning materialism, ideology, and capital are correct and allow them to normatively work on my text, I also recognize the historical limitations of Marx. For example, Marx had very little to say about financial derivatives, yet we undeniably live in a time of finance capital. And while I argue against views that Marx did not account for race—he undeniably did—I do recognize, at the same time, that Marx is necessarily incapable of directly speaking of contemporary racial ideologies. For these reasons and others that will become apparent in time, I have found it necessary to rely on contemporary thinkers who are inspired by, but do much more than simply repeat, Marx, including David Harvey, Wolfgang Streeck, Claudia Jones, and, above all, Cornel West. Likewise, my use of Marx in conjunction with Derrida should reveal that I find Marx's critique of metaphysics less philosophically and theoretically compelling than the analysis offered by Derridean (and Kierkegaardian) deconstruction.

The Structure of the Argument

The project's first chapter begins by reviewing the recent attempt by some leftist political theorists, most notably Chantal Mouffe, to retrieve the reactionary political theologian Carl Schmitt for emancipatory purposes. For theorists like Mouffe, Schmitt offers a "post-Marxist" politics capable of re-politicizing liberal parliamentary democracy. These left-Schmittians argue that Schmitt's famous friend-enemy distinction is a useful heuristic by which the left can distinguish between emancipatory and reactionary figures and projects. More, they hold that Schmitt's formalism is sufficiently broad to redress Marxism's alleged economic reductionism, and so argue that a turn to Schmitt is a helpful way to advance beyond Marx. In all of these ways, left-Schmittians argue that Schmitt presents a decisionistic political theology that is useful for emancipatory politics.

Against these views, I argue that left-Schmittianism falls short in part because left-Schmittians do not engage with Schmitt's underlying theological and metaphysical commitments. While Schmitt alleges himself to promote decisionism, his political theology is so thoroughly embedded within an essentialist metaphysical paradigm as to render all decisions "decided" in advance. Indeed, for Schmitt, whether one is a "friend" or an "enemy" is an ontological-racial condition that has been decided in advance—has been decided since the beginning of time—by God. To this end, the problem with Schmitt's project is not only its obvious commitment to fascism, capitalism, and antisemitism, but is also its divinization and ontologization of these horrors. Moreover, and as the above suggests, this ontologization-divinization serves the ideological function of hiding the true location of decision in Schmitt's work. Where left-Schmittians applaud Schmitt's decisionism, the only decisions actually operative in Schmitt's works are his related decisions against Marxism and for antisemitism. In other words, Schmitt's text claims to offer a description of the reality of political theology, but actually offers a polemical defense of a particular fascist political theology. While I show in this chapter that the distinction between normative and descriptive registers is never clean—the description of a norm often descriptively countersigns a prior normative gesture, indeed, this is Schmitt's argument—it is the case that my project could be understood as an intentionally normative register. I recognize that theology is always normatively political, and that the denial of this normative dimension marks theology as ideological. In this way, by claiming my own normative commitments to a certain Marxist anti-capitalism, I look to avoid the ideological effects of the over-reliance on the normative/descriptive distinction.

The project then turns to Derridean deconstruction to argue that metaphysics as such, and so not just Schmitt's reactionary metaphysics, is a necessarily ideological discourse. While the relationship between theology and metaphysics has received significant scholarly attention, Derrida's direct contribution to this topic—which differs significantly from the projects of Jean-Luc Marion, Richard Kearney, and others—has not yet been fully appreciated. After briefly rehearsing Derrida's argument against metaphysics and metaphysics' implicit theology, the chapter adjudicates the debate between John Caputo and Martin Hägglund concerning Derrida's relationship to religion. Here, I argue that both Caputo and Hägglund offer correct but incomplete readings of Derrida. Specifically, neither explicitly account for

Derrida's primary contribution to the deconstruction of metaphysics: the deconstruction of the identity of thinking and being. It is within this identity that the theologic according to which God is truth and truth is the truth of God finds articulation. With this identity deconstructed, only a non-metaphysical religion remains theoretically possible. At the same time, it is only with this deconstruction of the identity of thinking and being that such a non-metaphysical religion becomes *possible*, because possibility requires that everything not be decided in advance. One possible manifestation of this form of non-metaphysical religion is exhibited in Derrida's lived encounters with Judaism. Derrida's non-metaphysical Judaism, I argue, demonstrates that the actual existence of a material and praxical religion does not contradict a deconstruction of theology.

Before analyzing two other materialist and praxical forms of religion—Søren Kierkegaard's and James Cone's—the project offers a brief interlude on the secularism of the Norwegian novelist and essayist Karl Ove Knausgaard. While Kierkegaard and Cone do demonstrate forms of religion responsive to the deconstructive critique of metaphysics, Derrida's deconstruction of theology prevents any sort of theistic methodological imperialism. That is, while Kierkegaard and Cone do offer credible responses to Derridean deconstruction, not all credible responses need to be religious. To this end, Knausgaard's secularism stands counter to some contemporary efforts in systematic theology to universalize both theological thinking and religious belief structures. The most prominent and influential of these views belongs to John Milbank and his "radical orthodoxy" school. For Milbank, the secular lacks the transcendent dimension that is both constitutive of and necessary for human flourishing. Moreover, Milbank argues that transcendence is simply ontologically the case, and so any secularism must be the result of a "violent" imposition. Such violence, according to Milbank, is reflected in the actual content of secular belief, which he holds to be "nihilistic." Against this position, Knausgaard embraces an immanent secularism that is intentionally antagonistic to religious interpretations. In doing so, Knausgaard's autofictional novels and essays demonstrate that a decision for the secular is not only intellectually defensible but is also morally and politically laudatory. Because he is interested in a secular peace and love, and he pursues such without any necessary reliance on theological structures or motifs, religious rejections of Knausgaard's position actually impose an imperialism and violence antithetical to the "ontological peace" allegedly defended by John Milbank and other radical orthodox theologians. Knausgaard's love for the world can and should be embraced without sublating it within some ostensibly higher religious frame. While more secular readers of this text might find this chapter a bit out of place, it serves an important function for the text's more religiously inclined readers: Although I suggest that a non-ideological theology is *possible* after the deconstruction of metaphysics, Knausgaard's project affirms that such a theology is in no way necessary.

After this engagement with Knausgaard, the project returns in its fourth chapter to the task of developing a political theology responsive to the deconstruction of metaphysics and does so through a constructive engagement with the Christian existentialism of Søren Kierkegaard. In particular, I argue that Kierkegaard's under-discussed political theology is both anti-metaphysical and, at least incipiently, anti-capitalist. The standard narrative, from both Marxists and Kierkegaardians, is that Kierkegaard and Marx agree that religion and politics are antithetical to each other. Given this opposition, Kierkegaard is held to side with religion against politics; Marx, with politics against religion. According to this accepted distinction, Kierkegaard is best understood as a philosopher of abstract inwardness unconcerned with, or even antithetical to, worldly political projects. For most Marxists who engage with Kierkegaard, Kierkegaard's relative popularity in the twentieth century is itself evidence of Kierkegaard's friendliness to capital: Kierkegaard, in this view, is a supremely bourgeois, idealist, and irrational philosopher who argues for everything a Marxist materialist would argue against.

I dispute this standard narrative by arguing that Kierkegaard is better understood as a dialectical materialist philosopher. The argument is made through a close reading of the Kierkegaardian distinction between "actuality" and "reality," which is analogous to Derrida's distinction between being and thinking. With this distinction, Kierkegaard resists philosophical idealism, which he associates with "reality," in favor of a materialist existentialism that requires actual praxis. For Kierkegaard, idealist philosophers deny or avoid the necessity of making existentially meaningful decisions, which, by definition, must happen in "actuality." Moreover, because Kierkegaard prioritizes materialist actuality over idealist reality, his understanding of truth is necessarily historical and social. For Kierkegaard, this privileging of historical actuality is marked of Christianity: Christianity divinizes actuality through Christ and so calls people to engagement with the actual world. All of this emphasis on actuality is entirely missed by Marxist critiques that portray Kierkegaard as an otherworldly philosopher.

After establishing Kierkegaard's philosophical materialism as found in the pseudonymous works, the chapter turns to Kierkegaard's later authorship to demonstrate that Kierkegaard populated this materialist structure with decidedly anti-capitalist content. For Kierkegaard, this socialist materialism is mandated by scripture and the Christian prophetic tradition. Kierkegaard does not argue against socialism in favor of religion, but more radically argues against any conception of religion—like Schmitt's—that is not itself socialist.

While Kierkegaard's historical materialist political theology is clearly aligned with socialist and emancipatory positions, Kierkegaard does not provide much by way of particular political content. In some ways, this lack of particularity and political analysis is itself part of Kierkegaard's project: The poor should not be poor, and Kierkegaard does not think much more analysis than that is necessary. While wanting to maintain Kierkegaard's sense of decisive urgency, the project's final chapter looks to James Cone as a source for providing a more analytically rigorous and politically specific form of orthopraxic revolutionary political theology. The introduction of Cone, and especially Cornel West's Marxist development and specification of Cone, provides just that political theology. In other words, while Kierkegaard provides an explicitly anti-metaphysical theology, it is only with Cone, helped by West, that we find a fully and explicitly anti-metaphysical, anti-racist, and anti-capitalist political theology.

The chapter begins by situating an anti-essentialist understanding of race—informed by the deconstructive and Marxist motifs articulated above—against current hegemonic "race relations" and "diversity" frameworks. I argue that these latter frameworks, wary of class reductionism, unhelpfully dissociate race from class and so are liable to create market-friendly anti-racisms. Moreover, these frameworks tend toward a fetishization of dialogue and conversation, and so idealistically misplace the actual site of racist oppression. In this sense, race-relations frameworks operate within the (ideological) realm of Kierkegaardian reality, but never address the (infrastructural, materialist) machinations of actuality. Against these approaches, Cone provides the intellectual framework for an explicitly anti-racist and anti-capitalist political theology. He does this primarily through an epistemological and moral privileging of "the oppressed." Cone, especially in his earlier works, radically orders all truth claims through reference to emancipation: something is only true to the extent that it supports the "truth" that the oppressed should be emancipated. If race relations frameworks do not actually produce the emancipation of the racially oppressed and economically exploited, then they are not "true" in Cone's sense.

Against such liberal idealism, for Cone, Marxism provides the best means by which one could understand and revolutionize racist and capitalist societies. Such a turn to Marxism as a source for anti-racism is especially important in the contemporary political climate, which seems to prefer to speak of socialism *or* anti-racism. Cone's position, and it is one supported not only by West but also by the entire trajectory of this project, is that this choice between anti-capitalism and anti-racism is a false one. However, and despite this embrace of a Marxist anti-racism, Cone was concerned that historical rifts and strategic disputes between Marxist anti-capitalists and black anti-racists would prevent the development of an emancipatory solidarity of anti-racists and anti-capitalists. In its conclusion, this chapter addresses Cone's concerns by turning to West, who articulates an explicitly anti-racist Marxism.

Finally, the project's conclusion begins by recapitulating the arguments made so far in a decidedly normative register: An orthopraxic and revolutionary political theology should reject both reactionary politics (contra Schmitt) and metaphysics (by way of Derrida), should leave open the possibility of embracing secularism (Knausgaard), employ a dialectical materialist philosophy (Kierkegaard), and establish the orthopraxic norms of anti-racist socialism (Cone and West). Then, in an effort to demonstrate the immediately political consequences of this sort of political theology, I provide a brief reading of the political theology of John Brown. While the majority of the project deals with texts, readings, theory, and intellectual positions, Brown demonstrates that such a decisive political theology is far from (only) an academic enterprise. Although existing before Derridean deconstructive, and likely oblivious to Marx's critiques of capital, Brown's religiously motivated lust for freedom demonstrates the sort of political theology—non-metaphysical, emancipatory, orthopraxical, revolutionary—for which this project argues. This turn to Brown, finally, brings the project full circle, back to the first chapter's critique of left-Schmittians. More than Schmitt, it is Brown and other revolutionaries who appear throughout the project—Che Guevara, Fred Hampton, anti-fascist French resistance fighters—who best actualize an emancipatory political theology responsive to the deconstruction of metaphysics.

While such is the book's main argument, and has been hinted at above, I intend this book to make at least three interventions in the literature concerning metaphysics, political theology, and ideology:

- First, the disparate discourses that have stemmed from Marx and Derrida should be brought together. While Marx has inspired a plethora of liberation theologians, and Derrida a plethora of "postmodern" ones, not enough has been done to recognize Derrida's debt to and clarification of Marx. This recognition can and will advance the discussion concerning theology and ideology.

- Second, the effects of the deconstruction of the identity of thinking and being have not been fully appreciated. While Derrida and Kierkegaard each imply this deconstruction, neither formulate nor thematize its effects in a thorough way. With thinking and being dissociated, we enter into a more wild and risky realm of action, one not motivated or measured by thought or logic. It is from out of these wild depths that saints like Brown, Hampton, and Guevara operate.

- Third, and as a result of the above, "truth" should no longer be considered a transcendental and primarily philosophical-theological category, but a political one. After the deconstructive and Marxist critiques of metaphysics, no one should naively interpret the measure of truth as the logos, the truth of being, or any other transcendental schema. As Cone argues and as I countersign, the "truth" is that the exploited should be freed. The orthopraxical adequacy of all other interpretations of truth is determined by those interpretations' allegiance to the emancipation of the exploited.

Above all, I intend this project as a work of ideology critique directed against reactionary metaphysicians and theologians—such as Carl Schmitt—and as an endorsement of revolutionary thinkers like Marx and Derrida, theologians like Kierkegaard and Cone, and saints like Brown and Guevara. May the fall of metaphysics lead to the rise of a new theology, an anti-metaphysical theology, an anti-capitalist theology, an orthopraxical and revolutionary theology.

Chapter One

Polemical Ontology

Carl Schmitt's "Decisionism" Is Not What It Seems

Introduction: Is There a Left Schmitt?

In 1987 *Telos,* an English language post-Marxist critical theory journal, published two special issues on the work of Carl Schmitt.[1] Featuring both original translations of Schmitt's work and commentaries on it, the issues helped inaugurate what is now known sometimes as "left-Schmittianism" and sometimes as "post-Marxist" Schmittianism. In general, post-Marxist Schmittians argue that (1) Marxist analyses of capitalism are insufficient for both analyzing and overcoming the totality of intersectional oppressions that currently plague the world, and (2) that Schmitt's political theorizing—especially his understanding of politics as antagonism and his critiques of liberalism—offers resources for addressing Marx's alleged shortcomings. Because this book argues that Marxist critiques of capitalism remain the most important tools that the proponent of total emancipation has at his or her disposal, and because it argues that Marxism and deconstructive political theology are convergent and mutually beneficial projects, a direct encounter with and critique of post-Marxist Schmittian political theology is unavoidable. In what follows, I argue that "post-Marxist" Schmittianism is better understood as a form of anti-democratic anti-Marxism, because proponents of left-Schmittianism do not grasp the depths of Schmitt's ideological commitments to antisemitism, reactionary political structures, anti-Marxism, and anti-democracy. These ideological commitments are not just existential accidents that reflect Schmitt's personal moral failings, but also inform and are inseparable from the general structure of Schmitt's political theology. Schmitt is a Christian fascist, and Schmittian political theology—"post-Marxist" or not—is the political theology of a Christian fascist. A turn from Marx to Schmitt—and for that matter, a turn from Derridean deconstruction to Schmittian reliance on metaphysical concepts like transcendence and unity—must be rejected by anyone interested in pursuing an orthopraxical revolutionary political theology.

Perhaps the most prominent contemporary proponent of "post-Marxist" Schmittianism, and its most articulate defender, is the Belgian political theorist Chantal Mouffe.[2] While Mouffe's particular reception of Schmitt is not exhaustive of the variations of left appropriations of Schmitt both critical and laudatory—see the above note—it remains the case that Mouffe, along with her partner Ernesto Laclau, have had the most prominent influence on contemporary theory's reception of Schmitt, and so Mouffe stands as something of a representative of post-Marxist Schmittians who find in Schmitt a resource for thinking through certain perceived anti-democratic and essentialist tendencies in Marx.

Mouffe's basic conceit is that Schmitt's generalization of political antagonism offers an important corrective to what she calls Marxism's "class essentialism" (*For a Left Populism [FLP]*, 2), which itself risks leading to anti-democratic totalitarianism.[3] Writing of the phenomenon in the past tense, Mouffe states that this "essentialist perspective dominant in left thinking" argued that "political identities were the expression of the position of the social agents in the relations of production and their interests were defined by this position" (*FLP*, 2). According to Mouffe, this class essentialism, which allegedly reduces all non-economic identity to superstructural expressions of an essentially economic infrastructural reality, could not account for democratic struggles that took place outside of an exclusively economic sphere. In Mouffe's anti-essentialist perspective, allegedly essentialist Marxism failed to offer a helpful analytic regime for understanding—or a helpful political regime for promoting—either the French unrest in May 1968 or the 1960s civil rights movements in America (*FLP*, 1). Indeed, this inability to engage democratic struggles without reducing them to epiphenomena of class "has always been . . . the fundamental mistake of the 'extreme left'" (*FLP*, 50).[4]

And so apparently unable to rely on Marxism either to explain or promote non-economic democratic struggles, Mouffe wishes to address the "need to take account of all the democratic struggles which have emerged in a variety of social relations and which could not be apprehended through the category of 'class'" (*On the Political [OTP]*, 53).[5] It is with Schmitt, and specifically with Schmitt's more generalized understanding of political antagonism, that

Mouffe finds the potential resources for just such an account. According to Mouffe, "antagonism, as Schmitt says, is an ever present possibility" (*OTP*, 16). That is, rather than result from a particular historical class struggle, political antagonism is an irreducible ontological fact: "the political belongs to our ontological condition" (*OTP*, 16). While class struggle might be one possible ontic manifestation of this ontological condition, it cannot, according to Mouffe, be raised to the ontological level of generalized antagonism. Such an elevation of class to an ontological level—and this is what Mouffe means by "class essentialism"—is what allegedly prevented Marxism from addressing other forms of democratic struggles. Marxists allegedly ontologize an ontic condition; they elevate one type of "politics" to the status of "the political" as such (*OTP*, 17). This ontologizing of class, according to Mouffe, in turn works to colonize and so reduce the inherently pluralistic "the political" to one particular form. In this reading, Marxism not only does not account for non-economic democratic struggles; more strongly, Mouffe suggests that a reductionist Marxist account of "the political" is itself antagonistic toward these struggles.[6] Schmitt's recognition of the unavoidability of antagonism, then, is held to prevent the sort of economic reduction of "the political" made possible by Marxist class essentialism.

Yet, Mouffe is aware of the fascist and violent contours of Schmitt's understanding of antagonistic politics. To this end, she offers no blind acceptance of Schmitt's program, but instead proposes "to think 'with Schmitt against Schmitt'" (*OTP*, 14). If Mouffe thinks "with Schmitt" by agreeing that political antagonism is an ontological fact, which is to say, she thinks "against Schmitt" by inscribing this antagonism not between the nation and the Jew—as does Schmitt—but instead more generally within any established political identity.[7] That is, whereas Schmitt conceives of antagonism as occurring between political peoples or identities, Mouffe argues that each and every political identity is always already marked by contradictions and antagonisms. In this way, Mouffe attempts to avoid reinscribing the fascism of Schmitt's political theology while accepting and building upon his central insight into the ontological nature of political antagonism. As we will see, though, this "thinking with Schmitt against Schmitt" raises an important—one could say, decisive—question: Why does Mouffe turn to Schmitt for a criticism of liberalism when other, more decidedly emancipatory, criticisms of liberalism already exist? In time, I will argue that this move to a Schmittian critique of liberalism serves the function not of complementing or supplementing Marx, but of more radically denying the basic Marxist insight into the unique structure of class antagonism.

In sum, Mouffe's appropriation of Schmitt is a "post-Marxist" one because she wishes to move beyond Marx's alleged class reductionism and toward a more expansive sense of radically pluralist democracy. This democratic pluralism recognizes, with Schmitt, the ontological fact of political antagonism. The question of how to peacefully and democratically reconcile this unavoidable antagonism is, for Mouffe, "the fundamental question for democratic politics" ("Post-Marxism: Identity and Democracy," 263).⁸ Given her acceptance of Schmitt's arguments concerning the ontological unavoidability of antagonism, Mouffe sees her political project as promoting not a totalitarianism that would squash all dissent and difference, but "a democratic society (that) makes room for the expression of conflicting interests and values" ("Post-Marxism: Identity and Democracy" ["PMID"], 263).⁹

But in what sense is antagonism ontologically constitutive of political identity? In a passage crucial for understanding the limitations of left or "post-Marxist" Schmittianism, Mouffe, in describing her and Laclau's *Hegemony and Socialist Strategy*, writes:

> One of the main theses of the book is that social objectivity is constituted through acts or power. This means that any social objectivity is ultimately political and that it has to show the traces of exclusion which governs its constitution; what, following Derrida, we have called its "constitutive outside." But, if an object has inscribed in its very being something other than itself; if as a result, everything is constructed as difference, its being cannot be conceived as pure "presence" or "objectivity." This indicates that the logics of the constitution of the social is incompatible with the objectivism and essentialism dominant in social sciences and liberal thought. ("PMID," 261)

The reference to Derrida is key. As we will see, Mouffe's claim that she and Laclau "follow" Derrida on the question of a "constitutive outside" constitutes a fundamental misreading of Derridean deconstruction. As I demonstrate below, Derrida is not primarily concerned with articulating the difference between two identities. Instead, and much more radically and deconstructively, Derrida is interested in the difference that is *internal* to any supposed substantive identity as such.¹⁰ Politically, Derrida—and this is where this project's reading of Schmitt radically differs from Mouffe's—is interested in the ways in which this internal differentiation is *ideologically* covered both through appeals to ideal substantive unity and through polemical attacks directed against an outside "other." As we will see, this ideological covering of internal differentiation through feigned antagonism directed toward external "existential threats" is precisely the fascist element of Schmitt's program.[11]

In short, and the rest of this chapter can be read as an unpacking of this claim, Schmitt is concerned with the antagonistic difference *between* the state and its enemies. Mouffe is also concerned with antagonistic difference but wishes to generalize and peacefully domesticate it within a program of pluralist democracy (and so she is concerned with racial difference, sexual difference, and so on). Mouffe's desire is to articulate a politics that allows for a peaceful working through of antagonisms. As noted above, she argues that the way to do this is to promote "a democratic society (that) makes room for the expression of conflicting interests and values." In what follows, I argue that the "expression of conflicting interests" is not an emancipatory goal. Indeed, the articulation of this goal might mark Mouffe's project as not "post-Marxist," but in an important sense as anti-Marxist: The prescriptive materialist goal of a Marxist-informed critique of late capitalism is not to allow for the conflict between capital and workers to "express" itself; instead, it is to eliminate capital's ownership of the means of production.

Yet, the fleshing out of that normative argument will come later in the text. In this chapter, my more immediate goal is to demonstrate that Schmitt's program is itself thoroughly antagonistic to Mouffe's desire for pluralist democracy. Following Derrida, I put forward a deconstructive reading of Schmitt that denies that "antagonism," especially of the allegedly ontological sort, exists fundamentally between identities. Instead, I argue, any alleged identity is always already internally differentiated. Schmitt's desire to defend the substantial unity of the state—of the "friend"—is an ideological attempt to deny and violently suppress the differentiations and conflicts, especially class conflicts, within the state itself.[12] And so Mouffe's acceptance of Schmitt's delineation of antagonism as existing between, as opposed to primarily within, identities—and her subsequent misattribution of this view to Derrida—leads us to two key reasons why Schmitt should be rejected, not "thought with," by anyone interested in emancipatory politics. First, Mouffe does not adequately address the extent to which Schmitt is a fundamentally anti-democratic thinker. Schmitt's entire articulation of both unity (which, we will see, is a crucial concept for Schmitt) and antagonism are ideologically aligned to suppress *democratic* differentiations within the state, with which Mouffe is concerned. Turning to the fundamentally anti-democratic Schmitt as a source for democratic theorizing is, as Mark Neocleous has put it, "an absurd position, made all the more so by being formed through a sympathetic critique of Schmitt, for it is the way of thinking about democracy that Schmitt most violently fought" (20).[13] Secondly, and as we will see shortly, Schmitt's fetishization of ontological unity serves not only an anti-democratic function, but also, and perhaps more immediately, an anti-Marxist one. The disruption of unity that most perturbs Schmitt is the Marxist one. Put otherwise, the "post-Marxist" democratic interpretation of Schmitt does not adequately enough consider the depth of Schmitt's ideological commitments to both anti-democracy and anti-Marxism; that is, Mouffe's reading is inattentive to the depth of Schmitt's Christian fascism.

The bridge that links Schmitt's politics and his theology—the device by which Schmitt articulates a fascist "political theology"—is his conceptualization of "decision" and "decisionism." This articulation follows a three-step process: First, Schmitt suggests and claims that the "decision" he is interested in is the sovereign's decision over the state of exception. Second, though, we see that the "sovereign" is not actually free to make political decisions as to the friend-enemy distinction, because these decisions have always been decided in advance by God. Third, and importantly for my project of ideology critique, this allegedly divine decision is proven a fake; that is, Schmitt's appeals to God only mask the actuality that all political decisions were Schmitt's. God did not make Schmitt an antisemite, but Schmitt did make God one. In a deconstructive voice, we could say that Schmitt himself, despite his rhetoric and his traditional reception, did not at all offer a theory of decisionism worthy of the name. Because of his ideological penchant for ontologization and metaphysics, the problem with Schmitt is not an excess of decisionism, but a dearth of it. Where Schmitt does make decisions in the strong sense of the term—deciding in an undecidable context—he decides for capitalism, fascism, the state, the law, and so on. He always defers his own responsibility for these decisions through appeals to a mythical ontological law.

And it is to this important category of decision that this chapter will now turn. Through a careful reading of Schmitt's use of the category in three major texts—*Dictatorship, The Concept of the Political,* and *Political Theology*—this chapter warns against a "post-Marxist" appropriation of Schmitt for all of the reasons gestured toward above: Where Schmitt makes decisions, they are bad ones; where Schmitt makes provocative and attractive moves—e.g., his insistence on politicization and antagonism—he does so for the sake of preserving markedly exploitative structures. Throughout, Schmitt's anti-decisionism is informed by a traditional metaphysics and a reactionary understanding of theology as ontologically aligned with fascistic capitalism. In the final analysis, an emancipatory political theology cannot credibly decide for Schmitt, because Schmitt has already decided against emancipation.

Decision in *Dictatorship*

The year 1922 saw the publication of the second edition of Oswald Spengler's *The Decline of the West*. In it, Spengler writes:

> The idealist of the early democracy regarded popular education as enlightenment pure and simple—but it is precisely this that smooths the path for the coming Caesars of the world. The last century was the winter of the West, the victory of materialism and skepticism, of socialism, parliamentarianism, and money. But in this century blood and instinct will regain their rights against the power of money and intellect. The era of individualism, liberalism and democracy, of humanitarianism and freedom, is nearing its end. The masses will accept with resignation the victory of the Caesars, the strong men, and will obey them. Life will descend to a level of general uniformity, a new kind of primitivism, and the world will be better for it. (395)[14]

The year also saw the publication of the second edition of Karl Barth's *The Epistle to the Romans*, a dialectical—and Kierkegaardian—assault on German liberal Protestantism. In it, Barth writes: "The Gospel is not a religious message to inform mankind of their divinity or to tell them how they may become divine. The Gospel proclaims a God utterly distinct from men. Salvation comes to them from Him, because they are, as men, incapable of knowing Him, and because they have no right to claim anything from Him" (28).[15] And also: "Religion is the possibility of the removal of every ground of confidence except confidence in God alone. Piety is the possibility of the removal of the last traces of a firm foundation upon which we can erect a system of thought" (88). Spengler's articulation of imminent epochal decline was grounded in race science and a mythology of archetypes. Barth's articulation of dialectical theology rejected any theology, especially those "natural theologies" with immanent and philosophical foundations, not grounded exclusively in God's unique and salvific decision for humanity.

In Spengler, Germany read about the decline of liberal parliamentarism. In Barth, the shortcomings and hubris of liberal Protestantism. In Spengler, the displacement of a culture. In Barth, the importance of radical decision.

Schmitt, a recently appointed professor in the law faculty, would have absorbed this postwar German intellectual climate in the small university town of Greifswald, eighty kilometers from the Polish border on the Baltic coast. Schmitt's experience in Greifswald was marked by a strong sense of provincial alienation:

> Greifswald was a particularly alienating environment for Schmitt: the university at the bottom of the hierarchy of German universities, the town a dreary and inclement cultural backwater. From his correspondence with Ernst Robertus Curtius, it is easy to discern that Schmitt was in a despairing mood during his brief stay, not knowing how brief it would be: "I keenly sympathize with your Greifswald situation . . . That you will be buried there seems highly unlikely. For both of us it is a matter of a short-term evil." (42)[16]

It was from out of this "short-term evil" that Schmitt published *Dictatorship: From the Beginning of the Modern Concept of Sovereignty to the Proletarian Class Struggle*.[17] In that text, relying on the thought of sixteenth-century French political theorist Jean Bodin, Schmitt delineates two types of dictatorship: commissarial and sovereign. The commissarial dictator is placed in dictatorial command by an agent of the state and for the purpose of reestablishing legal norms in exceptional times (188). The commissarial dictator responds to the command of a sovereign agent. That is, the commissarial dictator is granted permission to act lawlessly; but, precisely as granted, this lawless freedom operates from within an order carefully circumscribed by a sovereign "outside" and, in some sense, "above" the very order suspended. It is a lawlessness that preserves the foundations of law.

The primary difference between this commissarial type of dictatorship and the sovereign type is that the sovereign dictator does not rectify an already existing order but instead inaugurates a new one: "The entire existing order is a situation that dictatorship will resolve through its own actions. Dictatorship does not suspend an existing constitution through a law based on the constitution; rather, it seeks to create conditions in which a constitution—a constitution that it regards as the true one—is made possible" (189). That is, whereas the commissarial dictator responds to an emergency by rectifying the current order, the sovereign dictator responds to such an emergency by creating a new order. Both dictators respond to an emergency, but the one looks to rectify and the other looks to create. One is a "dictatorship of reformations" and the other a "dictatorship of revolutions" (xliv).

While Schmitt relies on Bodin's theorizing for articulating this "crucial distinction" conceptually or definitionally (xliv), he is not content with a purely structural distinction. To this end, Schmitt's historical argument is that the late eighteenth century—Schmitt has in mind the French Revolution—inaugurated a shift in the meaning of dictatorship from primarily commissarial to primarily sovereign. While Schmitt presents this development as primarily a change in the dominant meaning of dictatorship, or as a "transition" from one type of dictatorship to another, his ostensibly descriptive historical argument masks an implicit normative critique against, not this shift in the meaning of dictatorship, but more powerfully against the new form of sovereignty that such a shift implies. Specifically, Schmitt is worried that a sovereign dictatorship has actually, somewhat paradoxically, democratized sovereignty. In Schmitt's view, such a democratization ultimately leads to an undermining of not only the state, but also politics in the proper—that is, Euro-Christian—sense. The object of his descriptive historiography is "dictatorship," but the polemical target of his normative theorization is something like "mass sovereignty."

Despite its peculiarity, Schmitt's concern that sovereign dictatorship might democratize sovereignty does adhere to a certain logic. Noting the different structural locations of sovereignty in the two models of dictatorship points toward this logic. In the commissarial model of dictatorship, the sovereign—in the singular, a king or emperor, typically, or for Schmitt what amounts to the same, God—functions as an outside anchor of order, and the dictator as the sovereign's representative and carefully appointed tool. This ordering of representation, sovereignty, and utilization is upended in the sovereign model of dictatorship: the place once held by the outside sovereign is now held by the constituting power of the people, who, somewhat paradoxically, empower as their representative a sovereign dictator with total freedom to create a new legal order and regime. In the commissarial model, the sovereign operates from an as if untouchable outside. The sovereign creates, declares, suspends, and reimplements the legal order as he or she wishes. Dictatorship is constituted by and responsive to the sovereign, who, much like the Cartesian god, decides freely and without necessary consideration of the desires or arguments of the world over which he or she rules. In the sovereign dictatorship model, on the other hand, the dictator creates a new order with no regard for or loyalty to any preestablished outside location or anchor of sovereignty. With the old privileged position of transcendent sovereignty effaced, the sovereign dictatorship's political order operates with its own foundations, legitimations, and juridical norms.

For Schmitt, such a radical and revolutionary form of sovereignty undermines the ideality—the substantial continuity—of the state. The commissarial dictator preserves the state's identity by adhering to the commands of the sovereign, who transcends the accidental ebbs and flows of political variation. The sovereign dictator, however, does total violence to the state's identity in that this dictator entirely rejects the power and legitimacy of the old transcendent sovereign in favor of a new regime. And so the machinations of sovereign dictatorship lead to the decline of not only a particular state—for example, the Kingdom of France—but more radically to the rejection of the model of substantial statehood grounded in transcendent sovereignty. To the extent that such a statist model coheres with the European tradition of divine right, then sovereign dictatorship can also be read as a moment in the Spenglerian decline of the West.

And so Schmitt's critique of sovereign dictatorship and its commitment to mass democratic sovereignty is in part informed by a substance metaphysics: It is both the substance of the state and the fact that the state is a substance that must be defended. Here we see an early example of the confluence of Schmitt's metaphysical theology and his politics—that is, his political theology: for Schmitt, that the state is a substance is the allegedly Euro-Christian political-theological model of sovereignty. This is the theological and metaphysical dimension—indeed, for Schmitt, as for Derrida, *theology is metaphysics*—with which "post-Marxist" Schmittians typically do not critically engage.[18] This lack of engagement is unfortunate because, as is typical of Schmitt, these political-theological concerns are most clearly expressed in a polemic against Marxism.

First, Schmitt charges that Marxism, via its hope for the dictatorship of the proletariat, explicitly identifies sovereignty not with a single sovereign agent but with a collective: "In Marxism, where the agent of all real political activity is not an individual but a whole class, it is not difficult to define the proletariat as a collective entity—that is, the genuine agent—and therefore to see it as the subject of a dictatorship" (xxxix). Against the norms of Christian political theology grounded in a transcendent sovereign, atheist Marxism identifies sovereignty with the collective, not an individual.[19] Marxism indicates a grammatical shift from the singular concrete "the dictator" or "the sovereign" to the abstract collective "dictatorship" and "sovereignty." When Schmitt provides a historical account of European sovereignty, the dictator is a "he." When Schmitt provides an account of Marxist political theory, dictatorship is an "it." For Schmitt, this depersonalization is a retreat from politics proper into an impersonal Hegelian metaphysics of progress. The extent to which Schmitt's own political theory, his ideal politics proper, is too embedded in an impersonal metaphysical structure will become clear in time.

Second, Schmitt directly links this collectivization with an undermining of the state:

> From the perspective of a general theory of the state, the dictatorship of a proletariat identified with the people at large, in transition to an economic situation in which the state is "withering away," presupposes the concept of a sovereign dictatorship, just in the form it stands at the root of the theory and practice of the National Convention. What Engels required for his "praxis," in his address to the League of Communists in March 1850, also held for a political theory of the state of this transition to statelessness: it was the same situation "as in France 1793." (179)

In a defensible reading of Engels, Schmitt traces a line from the French Revolution to the specter of the dictatorship of the proletariat. For Schmitt, what links Robespierre to Marx is first and foremost their acceptance of the sovereign model of dictatorship—a model that explicitly rejects two tenets of, according to Schmitt, classical Euro-Christian culture: the identification of sovereignty with a transcendent agent and the substantial ideality of the state.[20]

Dictatorship, then, quietly constructs a reactionary conceptual matrix. On the one side, and valued positively, Schmitt associates concepts such as substance, exteriority/the outside, the transcendent sovereign, European monarchy, culture, and Christianity. On the other side, and valued negatively, stand concepts such as revolutionary change, immanence, collective sovereignty, anti-statism, "decline," and, perhaps, the Jewish atheism of Marx and the anti-Catholic deism of Robespierre. Schmitt opposes Marxism to what he considers to be Christian culture and theology. In other words, in Schmitt's text, there is a positive affinity between the theological motifs of transcendence, substance, and exteriority and the fascist motifs of the superiority of European culture, permanence, and fidelity to the state and the sovereign. Although published a year before the text titled *Political Theology*, *Dictatorship* has already constructed a political-theological hermeneutic.

Decision in *Political Theology*

"Sovereign is the one who decides on the exception."

So begins *Political Theology*. The goal of this section is to explicate the meaning of decision in this definition and to show that Schmitt has conceived of decision in a decidedly metaphysical, undemocratic, and anti-Marxist way. To start a reading of decision with this definition might seem misguided: the definition is not, at least not at first glance, a definition of decision, but of sovereignty. Schmitt is using the concept of decision to help define the concept of sovereignty; he is not, at least not explicitly or intentionally, defining decision through an appeal to sovereignty. Yet, my argument is that this appearance serves an ideological function: Schmitt ostensibly uses the concept of decision to inform a definitional understanding of sovereignty; yet Schmitt actually abuses the ambiguity of the concept of decision to reify a particular political-theological sense of sovereignty.

The opening of this ambiguity is the prepositional indeterminacy of "on." The definition states not only that "sovereign is the one who decides," but also more curiously that "sovereign is the one who decides on." What does *to decide on* mean? The German reads: *Souverän ist, wer über den Ausnahmezustand entscheidet.*[21] What is the meaning of *über*?

Schmitt's definition necessarily relies on this prepositional indeterminacy because he wants to emphasize the "exceptional" nature of sovereignty. The sovereign decides "on the"—that is, either whether or when there is an—exception. He is not concerned with quotidian decisions. Nor is he concerned with the sort of sovereignty one might expect to find in the home or workplace. For Schmitt, sovereignty is a high stakes game. It is a concept that associates with the highest and most dramatic moments of life and operates at the extreme limits of the already extreme "spheres" of theology and politics. It is a "borderline concept": "Only this definition can do justice to a borderline concept. Contrary to the imprecise terminology that is found in popular literature, a borderline concept is not a vague concept, but one pertaining to the outermost sphere. This definition of sovereignty must therefore be associated with a borderline case and not with routine" (*Political Theology [PT]*, 6). On the one hand, we read of borders and the outermost: the sovereign is found in the outermost border or sphere—and here the difference between residing on a border and residing within an outer sphere is curiously, and for Schmitt's purposes helpfully, elided. On the other hand, we see a rejection of vagueness, folk theorizing, and common or routine sense. It is a concept that is either on "the border" or "pertains" to "the outermost sphere," and does so with precision. That the appeal to precision occurs immediately after a declaration of liminality only further suggests that Schmitt does not succumb to as much as dominate and control semantic and logical play and indeterminacy. He defines the concept vaguely and declares that he has done so precisely.

These appeals to precision, specificity, and rigor feign an air of philosophical objectivity that obfuscates Schmitt's underlying polemical motivations: according to Schmitt, neither parliamentary democracy nor Marxism can account for sovereignty as a border concept. Schmitt's anti-parliamentarian polemic argues that this type of democracy rejects true sovereignty through a fetishization of proceduralism. For Schmitt, obsession with procedure immanentizes and democratizes, and ultimately permanently defers, real, which is to say "bloody," decision. Parliamentary democracy "discusses and negotiates every political detail" (*PT*, 64). Because of this fetish, the parliamentarian can only ever advocate for "a cautious half measure, in the hope that the definitive dispute, the decisive bloody battle, can be transformed into a parliamentary debate and permit the decision to be suspended forever in an everlasting discussion" (*PT*, 64). Devastatingly, and relying again on the counter-revolutionary Catholic Donoso Cortés, Schmitt says that parliamentary democracy exists "only in that short interim period in which it was possible to answer the question 'Christ or Barabbas?' with a proposal to adjourn or appoint a commission of investigation" (*PT*, 63).

The appeal to the Passover amnesty story is more than rhetorical flourish. The Gospel of Mark tells the story like this:

> Now at the feast he used to release for them any one prisoner whom they requested. The man named Barabbas had been imprisoned with the insurrectionists who had committed murder in the insurrection. The crowd went up and began asking him to do as he had been accustomed to do for them. Pilate answered them, saying, "Do you want me to release for you the King of the Jews?" For he was aware that the chief priests had handed Him over because of envy. But the chief priests stirred up the crowd to ask him to release Barabbas for them instead. Answering again, Pilate said to them, "Then what shall I do

with Him whom you call the King of the Jews?" They shouted back, "Crucify Him!" But Pilate said to them, "Why, what evil has He done?" But they shouted all the more, "Crucify Him!" Wishing to satisfy the crowd, Pilate released Barabbas for them, and after having Jesus scourged, he handed Him over to be crucified. (Mk 15:6–15)[22]

The importance of the reference hinges on the word *ochlos*, translated here as "crowd." In Matthew's more theologically motivated retelling of Mark's account, the crowd/mob/masses become identified with the Jews:

The governor said to them, "Which of the two do you want me to release for you?" And they said, "Barabbas." Pilate said to them, "Then what shall I do with Jesus who is called Christ?" They all said, "Crucify Him!" And he said, "Why, what evil has He done?" But they kept shouting all the more, saying, "Crucify Him!" When Pilate saw that he was accomplishing nothing, but rather that a riot was starting, he took water and washed his hands in front of the crowd, saying, "I am innocent of this Man's blood; see *to that* yourselves." And all the people said, "His blood shall be on us and on our children!" Then he released Barabbas for them; but after having Jesus scourged, he handed Him over to be crucified. (Mt 25:21–26)

Pope Benedict's exegesis of the passage argues that "Matthew, going beyond historical considerations, is attempting a theological etiology with which to account for the terrible fate of the people of Israel in the Jewish War, when land, city, and Temple were taken from them."[23] That is, the *ochlos* to whom Pilate's question is addressed is identified, at least in Matthew, with the Jews. And so the passage becomes important in antisemitic accusations of deicide.[24]

Schmitt's use of the passage might reinscribe this antisemitic trope—it would not be surprising—but the more immediate object of his critique is not the Jew, but the parliamentarian. Whereas the Jewish mob is accused of killing God, the parliamentarian is fantasized as not being able to do even that. For Schmitt, whereas the Jewish mob, precisely in their act of killing, is capable of some sort of political-theological decision, the parliamentarian cannot even reach the "outermost" level of sovereign decision, deicidal or not. According to Schmitt, the parliamentarian and the Jew are both enemies of

Christian political theology and sovereignty—if not the Christian God—but the parliamentarian's enmity is all the worse for his or her valorization of discussion in the face of the necessity of decision. Which is finally to say, the parliamentarian does not so much mount a political attack as he or she attacks politics itself: "Today nothing is more modern than the onslaught against the political . . . the political dissolves into the everlasting discussion of cultural and philosophical-historical commonplaces" (*PT*, 65). *Political Theology* begins and ends with this defense of sovereignty and the political against a perceived encroachment of the "popular" and the "common."

Important here is that Schmitt is not critiquing liberalism. Although it has become almost a trope to say that Schmitt is an anti-liberal—Mouffe, for example, writes that Schmitt "is one of the most brilliant and intransigent critics of liberalism" (*On the Political [OTP]*, 4)—his critique here is not aimed at liberalism as much as it is at democracy. It is the "democracy," rather than the "liberal," in "liberal democracy" that Schmitt takes as his object of critique. Here my argument supports the minority—but by no means nonexistent—reading of Schmitt that sees in him a type of liberal: namely, an "ordoliberal."[25] While "neoliberalism"—the faith in private market solutions to public problems—is currently the object of much critical discussion, Schmittian ordoliberalism, sometimes misleadingly referred to as "German neoliberalism" or less-misleadingly as "authoritarian liberalism," offers just as much cause for contemporary concern. Ordoliberals, as Schmitt decisively put it, argue for a "strong state and a free economy."[26] Whereas neoliberals argue that the state should use the capitalist market for the sake of addressing public problems—this looks like, for example, the reliance on public-private partnerships, the proliferation of NGOs, and the privatization of public good distribution through the implementation of austerity measures—ordoliberals argue that the state should interfere in the market only for the sake of preserving capitalism in the face of its internal contradictions. In practice, such an ordoliberal program might endorse anti-trust legislation, corruption regulation, and structural reforms necessary for the preservation of "free and fair" markets. That is, whereas neoliberals look to economize the state through privatization, ordoliberals recognize that the state must be kept free of capitalist influence for the sake of maintaining regulatory governance over capitalism, and this for the sake of saving capitalism from itself. As we will see in this chapter's next section, this ordering of political control over the economy only for the sake of preserving the integrity of the market economy totally coheres to Schmitt's dual efforts to defend both the purity and the supremacy of the political.

Of course, in addition to its own internal contradictions—the falling rate of profit, the necessary discrepancy between the appropriation of surplus value and the need for increasing aggregate demand, the tendency towards monopolizations and so towards non-competition, and so on—capitalism's security has also been threatened historically by mass democratic movements. Calls for and implementations of redistribution, nationalization, and other tools of democratic control over the market all chip away at *capital sovereignty*. In this way, the ordoliberal is faced not only with governing capitalists for the sake of securing the freedom of market against itself, but also with squashing democratic intrusions into the market. In smashing democratic control of the economy, the ordoliberal also secures the strength of the state against democracy—a democracy which, in this anti-capitalist trajectory, is starting to resemble a Marxist sovereign dictatorship of the proletariat more and more. That is, the ordoliberal mandate to protect the market economy from democratic control requires a state willing and able to protect itself from democratizations. For an ordoliberal, the worst-case political scenario would be a democratic takeover of the state for the sake of a democratizing of the market. Against this worst-case scenario, the ordoliberal argues for a state strong enough to suppress democracy in both the political and the economic spheres. A democratic political economy—a Marxist dictatorship of the proletariat—is this worst-case scenario.

The German sociologist Wolfgang Streeck puts Schmittian ordoliberalism's antagonism toward democracy like this:

> Schmitt's authoritarian state, as Heller rightly notes, was a liberal authoritarian state, one that was, in the classical liberal way, strong and weak at the same time: strong in its role of protector of "the market" and "the economy" from democratic claims for redistribution—to the point of being able to deploy the public power to suppress such claims—and weak in its relationship to the market as the designated site of capitalist profit-seeking, which government policy was to protect and if necessary expand without, however, entering it . . . Both Schmitt and the ordoliberals differ from Anglo-American liberalism in that they never believed in a market economy independent from state authority. (*How Will Capitalism End? [HWCE]*, 152–53)[27]

If liberalism implies individualism, then liberalism is not and never was Schmitt's object of critique. On the contrary, Schmitt defends a type of sovereign individualism—there is literally for Schmitt, one sovereign—that squashes collective democratic movements. This clarification on Schmitt's position regarding liberalism is important for evidencing the extent to which Schmitt's entire political-theological program is designed, from beginning to end, as a polemic against the democratic sovereignty of Marxism.

For an example of just how pervasive Schmitt's anti-democracy and anti-Marxism is, consider his arguments concerning the relationship between sovereignty, decision, and juridical theory. For Schmitt, every normal situation implies a prior abnormal, or exceptional, decision: "Every legal order is based on a decision, and also the concept of the legal order, which is applied as something self-evident, contains within it the contrast of the two distinct elements of the juristic—norm and decision. Like every other order, the legal order rests on a decision and not on a norm" (*PT*, 10). This specification of the legal order is important: Schmitt writes of "every order," but quickly narrows the discussion to "the legal order." He goes on to write of "decision in absolute purity" as "a specifically juristic element" (*PT*, 13), and to declare that sovereign is the one "who is entitled to decide those actions for which the constitution makes no provision; that is, who is competent to act when the legal system fails to answer the question of competence" (*PT*, 11). Legal orders, juristic elements, the constitution, and legal systems: Schmitt is clear in his desire to associate sovereignty not only with transcendence but also with the juridical as such. Working from within a long metaphysical theological tradition, Schmitt reveals that his concept of transcendent sovereign is also a concept of a transcendent lawgiver. And so another element of Schmitt's complicated political-theological matrix is established: the side of transcendence, Christianity, and Europe is also the side of the law and the side of legal norms.

Through this juridical reduction, Schmitt has effectively removed economics, and certainly any sort of economic populism à la Mouffe, from his account of sovereignty. Neither the market "laws" of ordoliberalism nor the class interests of Marxism, in Schmitt's account, rise to the level of exception and decision. The quotidian horrors of capitalism—the constitutive theft that is wage labor, the need to exchange labor time for necessary services, the need to let the market decide how this labor should be exchanged, the imposition of debt, the meaninglessness of work, the ritualized and normalized violence of the prison and military industrial complexes, and so on—are not exceptional, and so not worthy of political decision, because of their juridical normalcy. Schmitt is in favor of decisions constitutive of norms, so long as these decisions are made by the transcendent sovereign.

Decisions that the norm ought to be revolutionized, though, are dismissed as instances of sovereign dictatorship, that is, dismissed as the stirrings of the *ochlos*.

And so the sovereign, as the transcendent lawgiver, stands outside of both the legal order and the masses placed under control of this order.[28] Samuel Weber clarifies this relationship by stressing the importance of the decision's exteriority to norms, and so norms' dependence on decision:

> The sovereign decision marks the relationship of the order of the general—the law, the norm, the concept—to that which is radically heterogenous to all such generality. In this sense, the decision as such is sovereign, that is, independent of all possible derivation from or subsumption to a more general norm. It is a pure act, somewhat akin to the act of creation except that what it does is not so much to create as to interrupt and to suspend . . . The salient trait of (the legal order) is, as we have already seen, its dependence upon a certain transcendence, upon that which exceeds its self-identity, upon an irreducible alterity and exteriority: just as the miracle in Augustinian doctrine both exceeds and explains the created world. (10–11)[29]

Without doubt, this is one stream of decision in *Political Theology*. The decision is prior to, and so exterior to, the normal order that it inaugurates through its performance of deciding, where deciding is basically synonymous with creating. Such an account of decision as active is privileged in those moments in *Political Theology* where Schmitt describes the radically novel, non-derivable, and irreducible element of decision. The "decision in the true sense of the word" cannot be "derived from this (legal) norm" (6). "The decision frees itself from all normative ties" (12). A sovereign decision "should not be mixed up with calculability," nor should it be "derived from the necessity of judging a concrete fact" (30). The decision is "from the perspective of the content of the underlying norm, new and alien . . . Looked at normatively, it emanates from nothingness" (31).

This is a rather strong sense of decision opposed to calculation or deliberation. The motif might be borrowed from Kierkegaard (*PT*, 15), and will inform Derrida's later discussions of the indeterminacy of every decision "worthy of the name." Yet, we should not be too quick to read this understanding of sovereignty in a deconstructive register. It remains always polemical. Schmitt, whose interest remains in defending a strong sense of transcendent sovereignty, here relies on a sense of decision as radical for the sake of opposing both parliamentarian discussion and the democratic dictatorship of Marxism: He does not reject these democratic forms because of his notion of decision—which is flexible at best and equivocal at worst—but defines decision anti-democratically because he has always already rejected the *ochlos*.[30]

In other words, Schmitt's rejection of decision-as-calculation is not, as it will be with Derrida, a rejection of determining in advance, according to a strong teleological orientation, the effects of decision. Nor is it, as it will be with Kierkegaard, a rejection of quantifying a qualitative difference. Instead, it is a rejection of both political economy and an immanentism that Schmitt sees as constitutive of democracy in general and Marxism in particular. Echoing later critiques of class reductionism, including Mouffe's, Schmitt's argument here is that Marxist historical materialism reduces politics to an epiphenomenon derivative of infrastructural economic antagonisms:

> Instead of being conceived from the outside according to fantasies and splendid ideals, social and political reality was to be analyzed from within, according to its actual and correctly understood immanent circumstances . . . Convinced Marxism holds that it has found the true explanation for social, economic, and political life, and that a correct praxis follows from that knowledge; it follows that social life can be correctly grasped immanently in all of its objective necessity and thus controlled . . . Socialism retains the structure of Hegelian dialectics. (*Crisis in Parliamentary Democracy [CPD]*, 53, 60)

As in *Dictatorship,* the argument is one in favor of transcendence and against immanence: "The essential point (about Marxism) is that an exception never comes from outside into the immanence of development . . . the either/or of moral decision, the decisive and deciding disjunction, has no place in this system" (*CPD*, 63). Indeed, Schmitt's valorization of transcendence against Marxism is one of the reason his contemporary left readers—like Walter Benjamin and Jacob Taubes—ultimately diverged from Schmitt on the question of praxis, despite their shared critiques of liberal parliamentarianism. Whereas Benjamin, for example, advocated for a general strike—in his view the display of immanent power *par excellence*—Schmitt was critical of any attempt to establish sovereignty from an immanent, which is to say here explicitly proletarian, position.[31] Even the apparently decisive radicalness of the Bolsheviks is judged too immanent, if not, shockingly, too parliamentarian: "This vanguard does not wish to escape from the immanence of world-historical evolution at all, but is, according to the vulgar image, the midwife of coming things . . . Even the diktat of a dictator becomes a moment in the discussion and in the undisturbed development as (the immanent world spirit) moves further" (*CPD*, 56, 58). Without an outside point from which to judge and decide on immanent economic struggles, the Marxist—even Lenin—becomes structurally analogous to the fetishist of discussion, the parliamentarian. Schmitt's accusation that the vanguard "does not wish to escape from" immanence reveals the theological orientation of the critique: Schmitt is able to loosely identify bourgeois parliamentarianism and Marxism not because of economics—how could he?—but because of their apparently shared rejection of the transcendent, law-giving, Euro-Christian sovereign.

Slavoj Žižek, a contemporary Marxist who frequently engages critically with Schmitt, notes that such an emphasis on the exteriority of decision causes yet another problem for Schmitt: namely, substance-less formalism.[32] Žižek argues that Schmitt's emphasis on the exteriority and irreducible novelty of the decision leads Schmitt to valorize the pure form of decision: "The basic paradox of Carl Schmitt's political decisionism . . . is that his very polemics against liberal-democratic formalism inexorably gets caught in the formalist trap . . . There is no longer any positive content which could be presupposed as the universally accepted frame of reference" (*The Challenge of Carl Schmitt [CCS]*, 18, 19). My reading of Schmitt's anti-democratic and anti-Marxist polemics basically coheres with Žižek's critique. In those instances, Schmitt apparently offered no critique of the substance or content of Marxist or parliamentarian thought. Instead, he offered a critique only against the formal structures of these regimes. That is, Schmitt's critique focused on the immanence and indecisiveness of parliamentarianism and Marxism without arguing what this missing transcendent element should look like. What was important was the presence of an outside as such.

While accepting the thrust of Žižek's reading, it should be modified in at least two ways. First, we should not be too quick to accept that Schmitt's formalistic decisionism is actually without content, or that a too clean distinction between form and content is possible. Schmitt's apparently pure description of a pure outside is neither a pure description nor is it of a pure outside. Because of the political-theological matrix Schmitt has developed in both *Dictatorship* and *Political Theology*, we should read this "formalism" as not just an endorsement of an outside, but also more specifically of an endorsement of an outside associated with law, Europe, and Christianity. Complementarily, Schmitt's critiques of parliamentarianism and Marxism on these decisionistic grounds should not be understood as a critique of only a lack in those regimes—a lack of decision, or even, in this more expanded sense, of transcendent sovereignty, European culture, Christianity, and so on—but more directly a critique of a positive feature or identification, namely democratization. This distinction is important for understanding the privileged place of Schmitt's polemical articulation of sovereignty and for understanding the basically ideological character and function of all ostensibly metaphysical claims. On the one hand, Schmitt does critique democratic regimes for lacking a place for decision, or even for being intentionally antagonistic toward political decisions. On this account, Žižek's formalist critique works. But on the other hand, Schmitt does not simply critique Marxism for having no place for decision, but rather critiques Marxism for having an improper, because democratic and immanent, model of decision. Schmitt is against Marxism because it implies a democratic—and so, according to Schmitt, an anti-theological—sovereignty, not because it lacks the formal characteristic of pure decision. Schmitt's apparently formalist critique is actually an apologetic for the privileging of transcendent sovereignty, which is itself an ideological obfuscation of Schmitt's material commitments for capitalist markets against Marxism.

Consider the following passage from *Political Theology*, which makes precisely this anti-democratic argument: "In the struggle of opposing interests and coalitions, absolute monarchy made the decision and thereby created the unity of the state. The unity that a people represents does not possess this decisionist character; it is an organic unity, and with national consciousness the ideas of the state originated as an organic whole. The theistic as well as the deistic concepts of God become thus unintelligible for political metaphysics" (49). There are two things to note. The first is not new: Schmitt comes as close as possible to stating that democracy as such is antithetical to theology. For a properly theological politics, the "unity" of a people must be imposed from the outside position of the monarch. It should not arise "organically" through immanent processes, such as the constituent power of the dictatorship of the proletariat. The second point is that Schmitt's formal decisionism is not only an argument for an outside but is also, at the very same time, an argument for the unity and coherence of the "inside," of the state or people. Žižek does note this fascistic privileging of unity, but he does not consider that such a privileging belies—from within, as it were—Schmitt's alleged formalism.[33] Žižek notes that the decision that Schmitt privileges is "primarily the decision for the formal principle of order as such" (*CCS*, 18). In my view, such a decision for order is not without "any positive content." Instead, such a decision is a decision for a fascistic allegiance to unity grounded in the presence of a transcendent sovereign. This decision for unity is diametrically opposed to Mouffe's left-Schmittian hope for an agonistic politics.

Yet, at times, Žižek seems to realize the material political consequences of Schmitt's "formalism." For example, my political theological critique of Schmitt's project can fully endorse Žižek's reading when he writes: "Let us begin with a question: what is politics proper? Schmitt's well-known answer (a social situation which involves opposition between friend and enemy), radical as it may appear, is not radical enough, in so far as it already displaces the *inherent* antagonism constitutive of the political onto the *external* relationship between Us and Them" (*CCS*, 27). Such a critique correctly and helpfully presents Schmitt as a sort of nationalist anti-Marxist. Schmitt's emphasis on unity is a direct reproach against the Marxist slogan that all history is the history of class struggle. Whereas a Marxist approach views appeals to unity as ideological attempts to impose erasure on struggle and oppression, Schmitt's transcendent political theology views discourse on struggle and oppression as attempts to undermine unity.

And so my reading of Schmitt is close to Žižek's, but with the caveat that the primary critique is not a logical or philosophical one against the "paradox" of Schmitt's alleged formalism but, instead, is a Marxist and anti-metaphysical critique of Schmitt's fascist political theology. This distinction between a critique of Schmitt's formalism and a critique of Schmitt's reactionary apology for transcendently grounded unity is important for the advancement of my thesis: An orthopraxic and revolutionary political theology cannot satisfy itself with neutral critique or idealism. Pointing out Schmitt's inconsistencies and paradoxes is not difficult. Nor is it particularly meaningful to a leftist political theology. "No one has ever died from contradictions."[34] Rather than note the philosophical and logical problems with Schmitt's program—as if a correction of intellect will lead to a change in praxis, as if a contradiction in thinking will lead to a failure in being—an orthopraxic and revolutionary political theology should decide against Schmitt's identification of Christianity with a fascistic allegiance to a transcendent lawgiver and decide for an identification of Christianity with a left political praxis of total emancipation. The critical point is not that Schmitt was a formalist, but that he was a Christian fascist.

Schmitt explains that decisions create, and so in some sense stand outside of, legal norms and systems. This is the element of exteriority and novelty stressed by Weber and discussed above. In this model, the sovereign is the decider who freely and voluntarily—unbound by preexistent obligations or immanent logics—creates norms. Such a pure and creative exteriority gives the appearance of formalism, as if Schmitt's concern was to preserve a structure of transcendent sovereignty. Yet, I have just argued that Schmitt's concern was not to preserve a formal structure of transcendent sovereignty, but to preserve and defend a particular content: a political theology of transcendent sovereignty. Schmitt argues not on behalf of a structure of sovereignty but on behalf of the sovereign. Schmitt's alleged formalism is actually a material argument in favor of a fascist political theology that identifies form and content in the motif of unity.

It is only with such an a priori allegiance to a particular content that Schmitt can say: "Sovereign is the one who definitively decides whether this normal situation actually exists" (13). Which situation is this normal situation? The one wherein "the sovereign produces and guarantees the situation in its totality." The argument is entirely circular: "Sovereignty resides in determining definitively what constitutes public order and security, in determining when they are disturbed, and so on" (13). But, in making the sovereign decide such, the content of the public interest has been decided in advance: it is in the public interest to be ruled. The normal situation is the situation wherein the sovereign decides. Which is to say, the normal situation is the articulation of a fascist political theology of transcendent rule and unity.

Which is to say: The sovereign is now, as exterior and transcendent, *outside* of the political-theological-juridical norms *on* which he decides. Which is to say: The sovereign is now, as exterior and transcendent, an important and essential element *inside* the political-theological-juridical norms *on* which he has decided. Which is to say, about the sovereign: "Although he stands outside the normally valid legal system, he nevertheless belongs to it" (*PT*, 7). The "sovereign" is free, only truly sovereign, in so far as he rules from a position of simultaneous exteriority and interiority: in so far as he issues particular norms, the Euro-Christian norms of Schmitt's political theology, and, via his position as external lawgiver, follows them. In this sense, the political decision has been decided in advance: the sovereign makes decisions, and the sovereign must.

"Sovereign is he who decides on the exception," because otherwise the *ochlos* might decide to make an exception.

Decision in *The Concept of the Political*

First published in essay form in 1927,[35] and expanded in book form in 1932,[36] *The Concept of the Political* reinscribes, and sometimes intensifies, many of the structural features found in *Political Theology*: anti-democratic and anti-Marxist polemics, a strategically ordered internal incoherence, an emphasis on the relationship between decision and sovereignty, and so on. At the same time, the text relies on a couple of new motifs: namely, the purity and superiority of "the political" over other spheres of life. These new motifs intensify the ontologization of decision in Schmitt's text: as "the political," which largely does the work of "the sovereign" in *Political Theology*, becomes increasingly rarefied, decisions are rendered more and more passive. Eventually, as Derrida argues, "Everything seems to be decided where the decision does not take place" (*The Politics of Friendship [PF]*, 99).[37]

The Concept of the Political presents itself as an explication of the specificity of the political. Such an explication finds articulation in two complementary strategies or lines of thought. On the one hand, Schmitt is concerned with describing the purity of the political from other "realms." On the other, he is concerned with describing the supremacy of the political over those realms. Derrida describes these two "stratifications":

> Two stratifications of the political: sometimes the political is a particular and grounded stratum . . . sometimes the political, qua real possibility, invades the entire fundamental or grounding stratum of existence, whether individual or communal . . . This fundamentalist stratification makes the political at once both a regional stratum, a particular layer, however grounding the layer is, and the supplementary or overdetermining determination cutting through all other regions of the human world or of the cultural, symbolic, or spiritual community. (*PF*, 125)

At one time unique and underived ground, at another guiding and determining telos of all opposition: such is the duality of the Schmittian political. In this section I will read the moments in the text where these two stratifications are most clearly distinguished from each other. Yet, as has been one of my running arguments, I do not want to suggest that the presence of two competing understandings of the political undermines the philosophical legitimacy of Schmitt's text—at least not to the extent that we could dismiss Schmitt's arguments on grounds of contradiction. Above, I argued that the inconsistencies of *Political Theology* were the result of a polemical desire to preserve the transcendent sovereign and all that this sovereign stood for—especially in the face of the possibility of Marxist democratizations. Here, I argue in a similar way that the two stratifications of the political are moments in a polemical defense of the substantial unity of the state, which is to say moments in the articulation of Schmitt's political theology. On the one hand, purity. On the other, supremacy. Schmitt's concept of "the political" is a defense of the supremacy of purity and the purity of the supreme. Arguing at once for both of these stratifications is not an accidental trait in *The Concept of the Political;* rather, it is the point.

Schmitt most concisely describes the political as pure early in the text:

> The political must rest on its own ultimate distinctions, to which all action with a specifically political meaning can be traced. Let us assume that in the realm of morality the final distinctions are between good and evil, in aesthetics beautiful and ugly, in economics profitable and unprofitable. The question then is whether there is also a special distinction which can serve as a simple criterion of the political and of what it consists. The nature of such a political distinction is surely different from that of those others. It is independent of them and as such can speak clearly for itself. The specific political distinction to which political actions and motives can be reduced is that between friend and enemy. (26)

That is, the political is the "realm" defined by the distinction between friend and enemy. Inversely, the distinction between friend and enemy is the political distinction. Although one cannot help but see a flexible analogical structure at work—beautiful is to ugly as friend is to enemy, and so on—and although one cannot help but to read into this analogical structure the entire political theological matrix articulated in Schmitt's earlier works—which would now add "beautiful," "good," and "profitable" to the association of transcendence, unity, law, Christianity, Europe, and so on, and would add "ugly," "evil," and "unprofitable" to the other association—Schmitt's intention here is distinction. His argument is that, despite appearances—common, popular—the beautiful is not (always) the friend, and the friend is not (always) the good or the profitable.

The argument abounds: "If the antithesis of good and evil is not simply identical with that of beautiful and ugly, profitable and unprofitable, and cannot be directly reduced to the others, then the antithesis of friend and enemy must even less be confused with or mistaken for the others" (26). Once again, the political and politics are reduced to the political distinction of friend and enemy, and no other: "The specific political distinction to which political actions and motives can be reduced is that between friend and enemy" (26). And finally: "the inherently objective nature and autonomy of the political becomes evident by virtue of its being able to treat, distinguish, and comprehend the friend-enemy antithesis independently of other antitheses" (27).[38]

In these instances, Schmitt, by defining the purely political as nonderivable, is resisting what he sees as the simultaneous hyperpoliticization and depoliticization, or "neutralization," of nineteenth-century society. The argument is that parliamentarianism's fetishization of discussion and permanent deferral of decision results in a conception of politics as dialogical. The terms can easily invert, and "politics is dialogical" can become "dialogue is politics." Given such an inversion, anything that can be discussed can be discussed by parliament and/or civil society interest groups, and so the political has no object proper. In this sense, Schmitt preemptively critiques later feminist arguments that "the personal is the political," and later "poststructural" arguments that "everything is political." But Schmitt's point of contention here is not the expansion of the political into the "private" realm of performed identities and social scripts. Rather, he is concerned that this expansionist move results not in a strengthened, but rather in a neutered and abstract sense of politics. If the political is primarily dialogical or communicative, then, as Habermas will later argue in critique of Schmitt, political decisions will be made and judged by the norms of dialogue and communication. For Schmitt, such a dialogically normative ordering of the political is equivalent to replacing political norms with dialogical, which is to say, aesthetic, moral, or economic, ones.

On the one hand, Schmitt suggests, but only in an elliptical manner, that such attempts to "neutralize" politics are, in actuality, political attacks. Schmitt writes that "all the typical distinctions and depoliticizations characteristic of the liberal nineteenth century," for example the distinction between religion and politics that would result in an immanentization of sovereignty, are "thoroughly polemical and thereby again political antitheses" (*CP*, 23). The argument is philosophical and descriptive: attempts to order politics by dialogical norms are actually attempts to replace—fight, defeat—politics with dialogue. In this sense, the parliamentarian has made a friend out of dialogue and has made an enemy out of Schmittian political theology, and so has, despite pretenses to the contrary, performed a political act. Yet, such a descriptive and philosophical argument runs into the same problems as the "descriptions" offered in *Political Theology*. Namely: Schmitt's descriptions are always normatively and polemically guided by a prior commitment to a specific political theology of transcendent sovereignty. When Schmitt argues that liberal dialogue is a political attack against politics, then he is arguing that liberal dialogue is an attack on his fascist political theology.

On the other hand, Schmitt, echoing his treatment of the Barabbas story, argues that the democratic neutralization of politics enacts a cowardly evasion of true political decision. The argument is similar to, but differs slightly from, the one found in *Political Theology*: Where *Political Theology* was mostly concerned with securing the presence of a transcendent, anti-democratic lawgiver, *The Concept of the Political* raises the stakes: this transcendent sovereign does not give only law, but also gives life and has the authority to demand death. For Schmitt, the distinction between friend and enemy is an answer to the question of life and death. This is Schmitt at his most existential: the real enemy is the one who poses "an existential threat to one's own way of life" (*CP*, 49). In this view, the parliamentarian avoidance of political decision is now also an avoidance of recognizing friends and enemies—which is to say, an avoidance of fighting existential threats.

Here we see an instance of Schmitt's critique that is decidedly antiliberal, at least if liberalism is understood as a sort of libertarian individualism. Schmitt is concerned that liberalism's penchant for individualism will prevent the formation of friendship, by which Schmitt intends the patriotic "friendship" of state unity: "The question is whether a specific political idea can be derived from the pure and consequential concept of individualistic liberalism. This is to be denied" (*CP*, 70). The political potential of this sort of liberalism is to be denied because the individualist has no friend on whom he can call to help fight potential existential threats and has no friends who can call upon him to do the same: "In case of need, the political entity must demand the sacrifice of life. Such a demand is in no way justifiable by the individualism of liberal thought" (71).[39] If the enemy is the one who presents an existential threat, then the friend is the one who is willing to die to preserve "one's way of life." The liberal has no such friend. This liberal world, then, is a depoliticized world—which is now to say, a world without existential enemies or friends—that "might contain many very interesting antitheses and contrasts, competitions and intrigues of every kind" (35). However, this world would not contain "a meaningful antithesis whereby men could be required to sacrifice life, authorized to shed blood, and kill other human beings" (35). Without a strong sense of friends participating in a unified "way of life"—and without the identification of "existentially something different and alien" (26) as an "existential threat"—"men," individualist liberals, could not "be required to sacrifice life, authorized to shed blood." One might consider this depoliticized world without sacrifice or authorized bloodshed a promising one. That Schmitt does not consider it promising gives witness to the depth of his thought's fundamentally reactionary nature.

It is on these existential grounds that Schmitt distinguishes the political distinction from those of the "depoliticized" realms of life. The ugly, the evil, and the unprofitable might be offenses, and they might even be deeply hated, but they are not existential threats, and they are not grounds for political, which is to say sacrificial, friendship. At the same time—and despite the obvious analogical structuring that suggests otherwise—the existential, political enemy need not be ugly, evil, unprofitable, or deeply hated at all. Politics is a pure realm, unaffected by feeling or extra-political norms. Such norms do not, and by Schmitt's definition cannot, rise to the level of killing others or sacrificing oneself.

The immediate consequence of this constructed distinction between feelings of enmity (of which the parliamentarian, the liberal, and the Marxist are all capable) and the political declaration of enmity (of which they are not) is that the political actor can kill without regard for morality. In fact, such an actor can only kill amorally: "If such physical destruction of human life is not motivated by an existential threat to one's own way of life, then it cannot be justified. Just as little can war be justified by ethical and juristic norms. If there really are enemies in the existential sense as meant here, then it is justified, but only politically, to repel and fight them physically" (*CP*, 49). If an enemy cannot be killed for non-political means, and if political means are their own criteria, then such a limitation of the "physical destruction" of enemies to political norms thoroughly ontologizes the enemy. That is: Schmitt says that the enemy is the one who poses an existential risk to one's way of life, but this risk is determined as if by transcendent sovereign decision, not by particular circumstances. Whether or not one is a "threat" has nothing to do with economics, morality, aesthetics, or anything else. Whether or not one is a threat is, instead, decided. In his private writings, Schmitt acknowledges that even the aforementioned reactionary appeal to the threateningness of otherness is, in the final analysis, irrelevant to the political decision of enmity: "Jews always remain Jews . . . Just the assimilated Jew is the true enemy."[40] Schmitt identifies the Jew as the enemy, especially after assimilation. For him, conforming and assimilating have no bearing on the Jew's ontological status as a political threat.[41]

Such an ontologizing of enmity serves the ideological function of basically absolving Schmitt, or any political actor, of responsible agency. The Jew is a raced-other-enemy, and this has been decided as if transcendentally, ontologically, and not, therefore, by Schmitt or indeed anyone in particular. Whatever the Jew does or does not do, and whatever Schmitt feels, wishes, or does, the Jew will remain an enemy, and Schmitt will be "justified" in "physically destroying" the Jew. In this sense, "Everything seems to be decided where the decision does not take place, precisely in that place where the decision does not take place qua decision, where it will have been carried away, where it will have got carried away in what has always-already taken place: at birth, in other words the day before birth" (*PF*, 99).

This horrible politics is, however, and as we should now expect of Schmitt, not actually the result or effect of a logical or philosophical deduction. Antisemitism is not the necessary conclusion of Schmitt's distinguishing the private and the political. The opposite might always be the case, and, as we will see shortly, Schmitt's private writings provide good reason for thinking that the opposite *is* the case: Antisemitism and the fascism of which it is a part is prior to and motivating of Schmitt's distinction between personal feelings of enmity and political declarations of it. Schmitt uses the distinction between private and political for the sake of defending Jew-hatred. He argues: Hating the Jew does not make one ugly or evil; nor does hating the Jew imply a judgment of the Jew's ugliness or evil. Schmittian antisemitism depends upon no psychological ill will, unconscious bias, or anything of the sort. One is to hate the Jew because he is ontologically a Jew, not because of anything the Jew has or has not done. By Schmitt's reasoning, one could quite like a Jew but also be politically obligated to kill him. Indeed, to hate the Jew for anything less than ontological reasons is, Schmitt says, unjustified.

When Schmitt does act as if this distinction is natural or axiomatic, he is led to incoherence. This is most apparent in Schmitt's eisegesis of Jesus's command to love one's enemies. The passage in Matthew, part of the Sermon on the Mount, reads:

> You have heard that it was said, "You shall love your neighbor and hate your enemy." But I say to you, love your enemies and pray for those who persecute you, so that you may be sons of your Father who is in heaven; for He causes His sun to rise on *the* evil and *the* good, and sends rain on *the* righteous and *the*

unrighteous. For if you love those who love you, what reward do you have? Do not even the tax collectors do the same? If you greet only your brothers, what more are you doing *than others*? Do not even the Gentiles do the same? (Mt 5:43–47)

In response to which Schmitt, in a rhetorical feat, writes:

> The enemy is "hostis," not "inimicus" in the broader sense; "πόλεμος (polemios)," not "ἐχθρούς (echthrous)" (sic). As German and other languages do not distinguish between the private and the political enemy, many misconceptions and falsifications are possible. The often quoted "love your enemy" (Matt 5:44; Luke 6:27) reads "diligite hostes vestros, agapate tous ekhthrous umon" and not "diligite inimicus vestros." No mention is made of the political enemy. Never in the thousand-year struggle between Christians and Muslims did it occur to a Christian to surrender rather than defend Europe out of love toward the Saracens or Turks. The enemy in the political sense need not be hated personally, and in the private sphere only does it make sense to love one's enemy, i.e., one's adversary. The Bible quotation touches the political antithesis even less than it intends to dissolve, for example, the antithesis of good and evil or beautiful and ugly. It certainly does not mean that one should love and support the enemies of one's own people. (*CP*, 29)

The most charitable reading could not help but find this "it certainly does not" absurd, and not only because of the incredible hermeneutic that interprets "love your enemies" as "certainly not" meaning "love your enemies." More structurally, the entirety of the eisegesis rests on Schmitt's distinction between private and political enmity, which he finds in the Greek *ekthros* and *polemios* and in the Latin *hostis* and *inimicus*. As an exegetical heuristic, the distinction is specious for several reasons.

First problem: Schmitt's German reads: "Feind ist *hostis*, nicht *inimicus* im weiteren Sinne; 'πόλεμος,' nicht 'ἐχθρούς' (*CP*, 29)." This is wrong. Matthew and Luke use ἐχθρούς, not πόλεμος, for enemy.[42] Granted, a few sentences later Schmitt correctly writes: "Die viel zitierte Stelle 'Liebet eure Feinde' heisst 'diligite inimicos vestros,' ἀγαπᾶτε τοὺς ἐχθροὺς ὑμῶν . . . (*CP*, 29)." This correction—which now has ἐχθροὺς despite Schmitt's earlier claim that the gospels used πόλεμος—might be evidence that the mistake was a copy error. Yet, the sloppiness with which Schmitt appeals to Greek points toward the dilettantish—that is, not rigorous, not precise—nature of Schmitt's interdisciplinary endeavors. The jurist is not a biblical scholar.

Second problem: If Schmitt were a biblical scholar, his position on this question would be a minority one. Schmitt relies on a distinction between a personal foe—toward whom one has enmity grounded in non- or a-political reasons—and a political enemy. Schmitt's claim is that Jesus instructs the disciples to love their personal foes, not their political enemies. The distinction is an imposition onto the meaning of ἐχθροὺς. Warren Carter argues that the word refers, sometimes more and sometimes less explicitly, to both "types" of enemies: The Hebrew Bible speaks of enemies as sometimes recognizably private—Psalm 18, 31, and 41; Sirach 6, 12, 17—and sometimes explicitly political—Deuteronomy 20. More troublingly for Schmitt, Carter also notes that the distinction between personal and political is an anachronistic imposition onto the biblical text. Early Christians would have struggled to cleanly delineate between personally and politically despising an enemy: "Enemies include those who persecute followers of Jesus, opponents of God's purposes enacted in Jesus and his people" (155). Given the nation status of the Jewish people, it is not at all clear if such persecutors of God and God's followers would be considered personal or political enemies. Carter concludes: "Enemy is not limited to national opponents and foreigners but includes personal foes" (154).[43]

Beyond these problems of translation and semantics, Schmitt's myopic interpretation can also be critiqued for ignoring the love command's immediate context. According to Ulrich Luz, Jesus's sermon distinguishes the hyperbole of Christian morality from an alleged formalism of Platonic ethics. Jesus does not command a love of the Platonic form of humanity, but more specifically and radically a command to love each person in their particularity. On this front, the semantic range of ἐχθροὺς cannot be reduced without doing violence to the hyperbole of the love command:

> Jesus speaks explicitly of the love of enemies. The hyperbolic imperatives cannot be seen as extreme cases of a general commandment of love of human beings. Jesus speaks emphatically of the enemy in all his or her maliciousness . . . It is inappropriate to limit the enemy to the sense of personal enemy, the Greek ἐχθροὺς is a comprehensive word for enemy on the basis of the LXX. The intensification which lies in the three examples of Luke

6:27 speaks in favor of including even quite extreme types of enmity. Jesus' demand is a demand of contrast."[44]

That is, ἐχθροὺς must refer to the most extreme types of enmity or else the command to love would lose its contrastive and hyperbolic force.

Granted, both Carter and Luz are aware of Schmitt's interpretation, and are potentially reacting against it. Gerhard Kittel, a fellow Nazi and avowed antisemite, though, would have no such interest in using the occasion of interpretation as an opportunity to criticize Schmitt. He writes: "In the NT ἐχθροὺς is used for personal enemies in the various relationships of everyday life. More important is the use which follows the OT and the LXX. Thus ἐχθροὺς can be used for the foes of Israel . . . ἐχθροὺς is particularly used, however, for what is hostile to God and His Christ" (813).[45] Kittel might agree with Schmitt's view that ἐχθροὺς, in the New Testament, means something like personal enemies, and so the command to love ἐχθροὺς would be a command to love personal, not political, enemies. However, such a reading would overlook the distinction Kittel makes between the sense of "enemy" in the Hebrew Bible and "enemy" in the New Testament. According to Kittel, the Hebrew Bible typically speaks of enemies in precisely the national or political sense of existential threat intended by Schmitt. Moreover, the Hebrew Bible, in Kittel's reading, advocates not for love of these enemies, but for violence: "There are many commands to hate national enemies in the OT, e.g., the command to exterminate the Canaanites as well as passages like Ps. 31:6. It is the widespread view of Rabbinic Judaism that the enemy, i.e., the ungodly, the Epicurean or whoever else it might be, is to be hated, and this is in keeping with OT teaching" (814). And so Kittel argues that the Hebrew Bible interprets enemies as national enemies and advocates their destruction. Thus, Schmitt's politics would be Jewish. The properly Christian view, according to Kittel, is to consider the enemy all those who are hostile to "God and His Christ." Kittel's reference to "personal enemies in the various relationships of everyday life" refers, then, to the Christian's daily struggle against the enemies of God. At this point, Schmitt could argue that the specification of enmity to daily relationships coheres with his view that ἐχθροὺς refers to personal enemies—indeed, Kittel uses the word. The problem with such an argument is that Schmitt's entire political theological matrix is a polemic against precisely these enemies of God. Kittel's use of "personal" implies a distinction between the theological difficulties of the Christian and the national political difficulties of the Jew. But because it has identified the theological and the political,

Schmitt's program cannot make sense of this distinction: For Schmitt, the enemy of God is the political enemy. *The Concept of the Political* wants to purify the political of the other "realms" of life, yet *Political Theology* has already inscribed a specific religious content within the structure of politics. By insisting on a "political theology," Schmitt has foreclosed in advance the possibility of Kittel's distinction between the theological enmity toward God's enemies and the political enmity toward threatening nations. All of which is to say: When Jesus commands to love the enemy, he commands to love the enemy of God. When Schmitt argues for the physical destruction of the anti-Christian forces of democracy and Marxism, he argues for killing the enemy of God. Unless Schmitt wants to argue that loving and killing are interchangeable—or perhaps especially if he wants to argue this—he has lost control of his argument to the point of absurdity. To this point, Derrida writes: "Killing would be an affair of love . . . To love in love or friendship would always mean: I can kill you, you can kill me, we can kill ourselves" (*PF*, 122).

So much for the purity of the political, which is not so much a philosophical argument for conceptual rigor as it is a political argument for the killing of the impure, of the enemies of God, of the enemies of Schmitt's political theology. The other "stratification of the political" in *The Concept of the Political* concerns not the political's purity from other realms, but rather its supremacy over them. In this argument, any distinction that rises to the level of killing and sacrificing becomes, by definition, political. If an originally non-political distinction becomes intense to the point of killing or sacrificing, "then the relevant antithesis is no longer purely religious, economic, or moral, but political" (*CP*, 36). Again: "That grouping is always political which orients itself toward this most extreme possibility" (*CP*, 38). One might despise a religious other, an economic oppressor (although Schmitt does not speak of economic oppressors, only, in a thoroughly capitalist mode, competitors), or an evil actor, but such an other, oppressor, or actor is not an enemy in the political sense of the word. If, however, one decided that "physically destroying" such a person is justified, and acts on this justification, then one is acting politically.

The distinction is terminological, and so reads with a certain artifice: an antithesis becomes political when it induces or justifies a friend-enemy distinction, thus any friend-enemy distinction is a political one. Granted, Schmitt seems to think that this terminological distinction reflects at least some aspect of social reality: "To demand seriously of human beings that they kill others and be prepared to die themselves so that trade and industry may flourish for the survivors or that the purchasing power of grandchildren may grow is sinister and crazy" (*CP*, 48). To kill for nonpolitical reasons, and perhaps especially for economic reasons, is immoral or insane. It is a judgment that reintroduces or reveals a certain ethics and logic within the realm of the "purely" political: if nonpolitical killing or sacrificing is immoral and insane, then, Schmitt suggests, political killing and sacrificing is, at least potentially, moral and sane. The dismissal of nonpolitical killing and sacrificing on these ethical and psychological grounds is only another instance of the allegedly pure political's impurity.

At other moments in the text, Schmitt is less satisfied with presenting the relationship between the political and other realms as one of binary opposition (either political or not, either willing to die and to kill, or not). In these moments he writes of the political as the—sometimes necessary or unavoidable—intensification of any antithetical relationship: "every concrete antagonism becomes that much more political the closer it approaches the most extreme point, that of the friend-enemy grouping" (*CP*, 29); "religious, moral, and other antitheses can intensify to political ones and can bring about the decisive friend-enemy constellation" (*CP*, 36). Any antithesis can intensify—and in both directions, friendship and enmity, at once—until the antithesis takes on the political form of the friend-enemy distinction: "The real friend-enemy grouping is existentially so strong and decisive that the nonpolitical antithesis, at precisely the moment at which it becomes political, pushes aside and subordinates its hitherto purely religious, purely economic, purely cultural criteria and motives to the conditions and conclusions of the political situation at hand" (*CP*, 38). The argument is that all antitheses or oppositions are weakened forms of politics that can take on a properly political form if given enough intensity. All antitheses are potentially political, but the political is not potentially other than itself—indeed, the political is the actualization of the potential hostility embedded in any other antithesis. Such an asymmetrical articulation of actualization and potential—which is classically metaphysical—clarifies Schmitt's earlier suggestion that not all realms are pure in purely the same way. There, Schmitt described the political as the least derivable, or most independent realm. The political was the most pure of the pure realms, because its content was also one of purity. The other realms were structurally and formally independent, but contained democratic, immanent, and so in some sense inferior, contents. It was the political, and the political only, that was pure in both content and form: Schmitt's politics is, allegedly, a pure politics of purity.

"Allegedly," because what could a pure content be? For Schmitt, as we have seen, the hyperpurity of the political is a claim to the ontological status of friend and enemy. The enemy, the Jew, is pure enemy. And so on the one hand we have an ontologization of content—the ontologization of Jew-as-enemy. In this sense, the "intensification" of antitheses into a political mode is not quite the actualization of dormant political potential, but is the realization or revealing of the ontological enemy who was always already there. On the other hand, the actualization of potential enmity happens as "intensity" increases, making opponents or competitors quantitatively more hostile, until eventually the decisive moment takes place, and the qualitative move—leap, Kierkegaard might say—from economic, moral, or religious to political, that is, to life and death, happens. In either case all of the antitheses of "human endeavor" increase in intensity, and so lose their particular content, on the path toward pure, ontological politics. The only subtlety is that Schmitt sometimes describes this as a fulfillment of a teleological ordering (the actualization of potential) and sometimes as the revelation of an original arche (the Jew as eternal real enemy). In either case, though, the purity of the political is made possible by its inscription in a thoroughly metaphysical regime. In either case, this metaphysical regime supports Schmitt's ordoliberal, that is anti-Marxist, interests: the realms are kept pure from each other, economics stays out of the state, and the state keeps out of the economy unless to preserve economic purity.

And so Schmitt has the antitheses of every "realm" intensify until the realm cedes its own content in a process of becoming political. Religion, aesthetics, morality, and economics, and especially economics, lose the specificity and purity of their contents when they become more antagonistic, which is to say, either more final or more original, more metaphysical, more political:

> A class in the Marxian sense ceases to be something purely economic and becomes a political factor when it reaches this decisive point, for example, when Marxists approach the class struggle seriously and treat the class adversary as a real enemy and fights him either in the form of a war of state against state or in a civil war within a state. The real battle is then of necessity no longer fought according to economic laws but has—next to the fighting methods in the narrowest technical sense—its political necessities and orientations, coalitions and compromises, and so on. (*CP*, 37)

The serious Marxist has nothing to do with dialectical materialism, political economy, or international class struggle, and certainly has nothing to do with the working day, wages, or rent. In other words, the serious Marxist is not a Marxist in any recognizable sense. Instead, the serious Marxist "fights" according to political, not economic, "orientations, coalitions, compromises, and so on." These "compromises and so on" are not only vague but are also seemingly impossible. What compromises could the Jew—the assimilated, that is, the compromising, Jew—offer to overcome his or her status as ontological, "real enemy"? The "intensification" of all antitheses that results in a qualitative shift is an ideological reduction of all political-historical content to ostensibly ontological content. It is Schmitt, not the nineteenth-century parliamentarian or the Marxist, who, by constructing a political theology of ontological enmity, has neutralized politics in any historical material sense.

It is a teleology and an archeology. In the end, there is the fulfillment of pure hostility and pure friendship, killing enemies and dying for friends. In the beginning, there are the antitheses whose potential will be fulfilled in the end, the already politically oriented antitheses of ostensibly apolitical realms, the eternal enemy and eternal friend, the potential and promise of killing and dying, of a time where "I can kill you, you can kill me, we can kill ourselves." Schmitt's archeo-teleo-onto-theologico politics imagines an ontological narrative wherein true enemies are locked in perpetual warfare, where the lack or absence of war is only a temporary and weakened condition. In the beginning and the end are the Jew and the Aryan. All history, all economics, all aesthetics, all morality, even, sometimes, all religion, all non-ontological-racial content of every kind, all are nothing but attempts, and in the twentieth century, Jewish Bolshevik attempts, to displace this pure field of political battle.

Before concluding, it is worth clarifying that, despite appearances, Schmitt does not view this ontological metanarrative as one of struggle or violence, but instead as one of friendship and peace. Indeed, much has been made of the ontologization and privileging of *enmity* that this structure apparently involves, that in the beginning and the end is the Jew as enemy, that all politics involve an enemy decision, and so on. Derrida, for one, seems to make the point throughout *The Politics of Friendship:* "Politics could never be thought without knowing what enemy means, nor a decision made without knowing who the enemy is" (106); "the major moments of political decision are those of the response to the question: who is the enemy?" (125). Derrida argues that this privileging of the enemy question is not accidental but is a constitutive structural element of Schmitt's thought: "What is said of the enemy is not symmetrical and cannot be said of the friend, even under the heading of structural or shared conditions of possibility. Friendship would consist in the suspension of this structure of possibility" (122). But Derrida's point here is not just that Schmitt has privileged enmity over friendship, but more that Schmitt has conceived difference itself as antagonistic: the difference between friend and enemy is a difference of enmity; the one term of the pair comes to dominate and determine the internal relation of the two terms; there is no pure difference, but only the structural dominance of enmity; there is no difference between friendship and enmity, there is only enmity, and so on.

There is a subtle but important difference between the reading that critiques Schmitt for privileging enmity over friendship and the one that critiques Schmitt for inscribing enmity into the structure of difference. Derrida argues the latter but has been read as arguing the former. For example, Jeffrey Robbins speaks of Derrida's "deconstruction of the concept of the political itself" as "the basis for what Derrida calls 'the politics of friendship'" (111)[46]—as if "the politics of friendship" were a concept in the regulatory Kantian sense or as if "the politics of friendship" were a norm upheld by Derrida. Such readings are misguided: "the politics of friendship" is not Derrida's political program but is the object of Derrida's deconstructive critique. In this sense, the political problem with Schmitt's text is not just in the way that he figures the enemy but also in the way in which he figures the friend.

For Schmitt, the friend is self-same, uniform, not "existentially alien and other." Fighting against the enemy is only possible given the unity of a friendship formed by the transcendent sovereign. Only such a friendship—a friendship that is not an association of singularities but is an ontologically uniform and substantial entity—is capable of fighting the enemy. As it is "crazy" to kill for economic reasons, it is "in no way justifiable" to ask a non-uniform individual to die for me. One can only ask this of the friend: "The political entity must demand the sacrifice of life. Such a demand is in no way justifiable by the individualism of liberal thought. No consistent individualism can entrust to someone other than to the individual himself the right to dispose of the physical life of the individual. An individualism in which anyone other than the free individual himself were to decide upon the substance and dimension of his freedom would be only an empty phrase" (*CP*, 71). This political entity is never more than one: "In reality there exists no political society or association but only one political entity—one political community" (*CP*, 45). It cannot be more than one, because difference is thought of as antagonistic. Any internal difference is the mark of the enemy and must be physically destroyed. For Schmitt, the noting of any internal difference that denies the state's ontological unity, such as a Marxist analysis of class stratification, perverts or weakens the substantial, ontological identity of the nationalist friend group. Precisely this threat to the unity of friendship—this threat to a substantial metaphysical racism—is the threat posed by Marxism. Schmitt is concerned with "international movements, for example, the Third International," which "transcend the borders of states and ignore the territorial integrity, impenetrability, and impermeability of existing states" (56). Such international movements undermine the unity of a people and so undermine friendship. They look to create transnational and transracial economic friendships; but, in doing so, they undermine the truly political friendship of national and racial unity. In this sense, Mouffe and other "post-Marxist" Schmittians who turn to Schmitt for a model of agonistic politics are misguided. In an effort at "post-Marxism," they decide for Schmitt against Marx for the sake of intersectional and pluralistic democratic struggles. But as is now clear, Schmitt himself decided against Marxism because Marxism—not Schmittianism—promoted just these intersectional and pluralistic struggles. Marxism, not Schmittian political theology, disrupts fascistic nationalism and ontological racism from within.[47] Marxism, not Schmittian political theology, finds a friend in the exploited everywhere and an enemy in the exploiter anywhere.

Mouffe and other "post-Marxist" Schmittians have relied on Schmitt as a source for re-politicizing, through a strong decisionism regarding friendship and enmity realigned as a democratic agonistic politics, the post-political status quo. This project is misguided not only because of its decision for Schmitt over a misconstrued and reductionist Marx, but also because the decisionistic Schmitt in whom it finds an ally is imaginary: Schmitt's decisionism is a fake twice over. First, all relevant decisions as to friend—the nation—and enemy—the Jew, the Communist—are made in advance. This is why Schmitt can coherently write that the real "decision" is to "clearly evaluate" and "distinguish correctly the real friend and the real enemy" (*CP*, 37). The political consists not in forging friendships and enmities, but in "being able to treat, distinguish, and comprehend the friend-enemy antithesis" (*CP*, 27). The distinctions have been drawn in advance, as if by God. The political decision, then, is not to enact a state of exception, nor to make friends or enemies. The political decision is, for Schmitt, entirely reactionary, entirely determined in advance by the material content of his fascist political theology, which creates ontological races of friend and enemy. The decision is not: There are two sides, friend and enemy, on which side will you align? But is: You are either a friend or an enemy already, will you recognize it, will you assume your role? And either way—does it matter?

Second, Schmitt believes or pretends to believe—either way, writes—that the side of right and friendship is also the side of the transcendent sovereign. Indeed, that there is a transcendent sovereign—and not a democratic dictatorship of the proletariat or a conversing parliament—is what marks this side as right. Whether descriptively or prescriptively, it is not clear, but it is the argument: This order is grounded in the transcendent sovereign. But I have argued that Schmitt's sovereignty is rooted not in the transcendent but in the particular and pathetic nationalisms and racisms of a twentieth-century Spenglerian ideologue. The appeal to the outside is an appeal to ontologize and naturalize the national friendship, forged in blood and soil, over the international friendship of the proletariat.

On both counts, Schmitt's project is plagued by a fascistic and reactionary political theology that associates the transcendent, ontology, theology, sovereignty, racial superiority, the good, the beautiful, order, law, capital, and the friend. Against this association stands another of immanence, history, Judaism, weakness, inferiority, evil, ugliness, chaos, anarchy, socialism, and the enemy. Schmitt would like us to believe that the most relevant political decision is to decide for the first association. In actuality, the matrix has been so constructed as to have been decided as if in advance, by God, to predestine our fates, Of course, this matrix was not decided in advance by anyone but Schmitt in his own historical attachment to Christian fascism and capitalism. The task of a contemporary political theology is first and foremost to decide against this associative matrix, to reject its false claims to both formal, sovereign transcendence and its polemical, material content.

Each of the next four chapters will contribute to that project. Among other resistances: Derrida will reject the possibility of grounding any order or law, or anything, in an outside. Knausgaard will reject the opposition between immanence and love. Kierkegaard will lampoon the notions of both a metaphysical and a capitalist Christian. Cone will reject the opposition between Marxism and Christianity, indeed, will demonstrate their near total convergence. Schmitt's political theology operates through ideological appeals to the transcendent and pure outside. An orthopraxical and revolutionary political theology cannot do so.

Chapter Two

Deconstructing Theology, Constructing Faith?

Introduction

Throughout the previous chapter, I argued that Carl Schmitt's alleged decisionism is an ideological obfuscation of his prior political commitments. Schmitt's constant appeals to and reliance on the metaphysical categories of substance, identity, transcendence, truth, and law—all of which inform his equally metaphysical understanding of race—undermine his purported decisionism. For Schmitt the metaphysician, everything is decided ontologically in advance; the truth of things is ontologically secured a priori through its subjection to sovereign transcendence. Which is to say, the alleged political decisions that Schmitt calls for are only ever fakes, because one can only ever decide to assent to an ontological order that is always already present.

At the same time, though, I argued that this ontological foundation was itself a fake. Schmitt's appeals to transcendent sovereignty did not, in actuality, appeal to an already existent outside, but instead produced this alleged outside as an authority and ground of argumentation in the very process of appeal. Schmitt's discourse produces its own God, and so cannot possibly be an earnest response to this God. Rather than theologically informed, then, Schmitt's decisionism proves itself ideological in the sense of hiding the real decisions at work in Schmitt's project: Schmitt decides for fascism and capitalism but claims that he has decided for God. Only in this ideological sense is Schmitt a decisionist: Schmitt *does* perform a decisionism, but not in the sense in which he claims; indeed, Schmitt claims metaphysical decision in order to hide and reify his actual political decisions.

It should be uncontroversial to argue that these commitments to fascism and capitalism run contrary to the goals of any emancipatory political theology. By definition, neither the fascist nor the capitalist can inspire or support an emancipatory program. Yet, Schmitt's reactionary commitments have not prevented certain "post-Marxist" Schmittians, most notably Chantal Mouffe, from attempting an appropriation of his thought. Such an appropriation requires that Schmitt's particular political commitments can be somehow detached from his general program, that Schmitt can be read against himself, and that his project's potentially revolutionary form can be purified of its decidedly reactionary content. But as I argued in the previous chapter, such a separation of form and content is impossible because Schmitt identifies the two through a deep ontologization of his most important categories: for Schmitt, God chose Europe, unity, and capitalism, and any disturbance to this order is a direct attack on the theological truth of the political as such. The ontologization of Euro-Christian-fascist-capitalist supremacy *is* Schmitt's project, and so a failure to engage with this metaphysical dimension is a failure to engage with Schmitt.

The task of this chapter is to argue that all metaphysics—and not just Schmitt's—must necessarily follow the ideological structure that Schmitt exemplified. As ideological, all metaphysical gestures follow a doubly obfuscating structure. First, any apparently metaphysical decision will prove a lie because metaphysics—again in the sense outlined in the introduction, which is to say all thinking that assumes an isomorphism between thinking and being—is incapable of making actual reference to, description of, or in any way engaging with the truth of being. Instead, metaphysical texts can only ever be just that: texts. Second, this necessary failure of metaphysics to perform its goal must mean that any alleged metaphysical decision or deduction is actually informed by some other and prior non-metaphysical decision. That is, and importantly for my Marxist-aligned reading of Derrida, all metaphysical gestures that claim access to some transcendental truth must, in actuality, refer to some prior and basic material reality and commitment. Metaphysics is not and can never be about truth understood as the truth of truth, the truth of being, logos, and so on, because these transcendental signifieds are simply textual—that is, earthly, material—productions. This ideological structure of metaphysical claims makes metaphysics an incredible discourse both politically and theoretically—and "incredible" in the strongest sense, meaning not only that metaphysics is currently unpopular and unattractive as a narrative style, but more directly that metaphysical discourses are ultimately epistemologically incoherent, theoretically indefensible, and politically suspect for the simple fact of their necessary elision of their own motivating decision.

Relying on primarily the work of the twentieth-century philosopher Jacques Derrida, this chapter explicates and defends this claim as to metaphysics' necessarily ideological structure. This critique of metaphysics in general is different than the previous chapter's critique of the particular metaphysics of Schmitt. In other words, and to momentarily stay with Schmitt for the sake of clarification, this critique of the fact of metaphysics in Schmitt's work is a critique on a different order than the (political) critique of the particular contents ontologized in Schmitt's work. While Schmitt's particular commitments are reprehensible from an emancipatory political perspective, my claim is decidedly not that Schmitt could have saved the theoretical credibility of his program by plugging in more acceptable political content: the theoretical problem with Schmitt is not that he did metaphysics wrong; but, is rather that he did metaphysics at all. In arguing this, my intention is not, as it is with some commentators, idolatry critique. Such a critique would argue that Schmitt's failure lies not in the fact of his metaphysical appeal to a transcendent outside, but instead in his particular interpretation of this outside. It would argue that if only Schmitt had referred to the outside properly, which is to say non-idolatrously, then his project of political theology would have found success.[1] While the charge that Schmitt has idolatrously identified God with the German state is plausible—although, as the next chapter will argue, we should be careful of any such charge of idolatry, not only because of the potential imperialism implicit in any accusation of idolatry but also because of its possible figuration of Christianity as a primarily doctrinal and orthodoxical affair—my immediate concerns are more theoretic and general. It is not as though a better interpretation of God-as-transcendent-sovereign would have saved Schmitt's formal structure, because any and all attempts to metaphysically refer to God-as-transcendent are theoretically indefensible and politically reactionary as such.

The distancing from idolatry critique also means that, against especially some streams of contemporary Catholic systematic philosophy, I am not arguing that the metaphysical treatment of God is itself idolatrous. This is the approach taken, for example, by Jean-Luc Marion, for whom "only an idol could be identified with the concept" (75).[2] Marion's concerns with conceptual idolatry—the reduction of God to "God," to a concept of God—are related to but ultimately differ from my own Derridean-inspired deconstruction of metaphysics. While Derrida would certainly agree with Marion that no metaphysical concept can be identified with God—indeed, for Derrida, "there is no such thing as a metaphysical concept" (*Dissemination [D]*, 6)[3]—Derrida would just as certainly disagree with Marion that metaphysical treatments of God should be avoided for the sake of preserving a properly religious distance from God. To this end, the two are critical of metaphysics for essentially diametrically opposed reasons: whereas Marion is worried that metaphysics reduces God to "God," Derrida argues that there is only ever "God," that the quotation marks that allow for citation are essential to "God" as God, and, moreover, that "God" is the metaphysical signifier *par excellence*. While a precise adjudication of this debate is just outside the scope of this chapter—which is primarily concerned not with conceptual idolatry but with metaphysical ideology—I hope to demonstrate that Derrida has good and compelling reason to argue his position that the dichotomy of God and "God" is always already metaphysically, which is to say textually, inscribed. Moreover, this impossibility of non-textual metaphysics is antithetical to Marion's project, as Marion's anti-idolatry framing seems to suggest that a non-idolatrous metaphysics is possible. This, indeed, is the argument he makes in his essay "Thomas Aquinas and Onto-Theo-Logy," wherein Aquinas's analogical metaphysics are saved from the Heideggerian critique that ontotheology reduces Being to a being (and, in parallel for Marion, God to "God") by virtue of this metaphysics' apophatic commitments.[4]

And so neither arguing for a particular metaphysics over another nor that metaphysics (particularly or in general) is idolatrous, this chapter makes the more general critique that all metaphysical discourse is theoretically indefensible and politically ideological. Indeed, it is because metaphysics is theoretically indefensible—because, as Derrida says, there is no such thing as a metaphysical concept—that metaphysics can only ever presuppose, hide, and derive itself from a prior non-metaphysical decision. Metaphysics as such cannot be decisive, because there is no such thing as metaphysics as such, but only ever a textual production that calls itself metaphysical for the sake of displacing the real site of decision.

This turn to a Derridean critique of metaphysics might seem old, stale, or otherwise repetitive. Indeed, the relationships between the three terms Derrida, metaphysics, and theology invoke at least two substantial bodies of pre-existing literature: that of post-metaphysical theology, on the one hand, and the related set of discourses that more directly relate Derrida to theology on the other. A complete bibliographic treatment of these literatures is impossible, but a few comments to distinguish my argument from ones commonly found in this space should be made. First, the general conversation concerning the relationship between theology and metaphysics more typically engages Heideggerian "destruction" than it does Derridean "deconstruction." That is, with some notable exceptions—Richard Kearney and John Caputo being perhaps exemplary here—theologians receptive to a critique of metaphysics seem in general responsive to Martin Heidegger's arguments concerning ontotheology.[5] This is certainly the case with the aforementioned Marion, for whom Heidegger stands as a primary interlocutor.[6] Likewise, Jason Alvis's recently published *The Inconspicuous God: Heidegger, French Phenomenology, and the Theological Turn* not only associates the French theological turn with the German Heidegger, but also mentions Derrida only once in passing—and this to note that Jean-Luc Nancy offers a philosophy that is "reflective of Derrida's deconstruction" (147).[7] Kevin Hector's *Theology without Metaphysics: God, Language and the Spirit of Recognition*, which sets itself up as a response to Heidegger's critique of ontotheology, likewise mentions Derrida only sparingly—and once to note that Heidegger "anticipated" Derrida (15).[8] More examples could be given interminably.

Undoubtedly, this attention given to Heidegger and the Heideggerian critique of ontotheology reflects a real and important development in a critical understanding of theology's relationship to metaphysics. Heidegger is an important figure in twentieth-century continental philosophy and the critique of ontotheology deserves serious engagement. That does not mean, however, that engagement with Heidegger's critique of metaphysics can stand in for an engagement with Derrida's. As I will demonstrate in this chapter, Derrida's critique of metaphysics offers a unique and marked challenge of its own. Importantly, Derrida is able to offer this challenge without explicit reliance on the apparently metaphysical categories of Being, being, concealment, truth, and so on that occupy Heidegger. As my distinction from Marion suggested, Derrida's main concern is not that Being is reduced to a being or that metaphysics will lead to conceptual idolatry, because Derrida does not believe metaphysics is possible.

At the same time, and again with a couple of notable exceptions, those theologians and philosophers of religion who do engage Derrida typically do not focus on Derrida's critique of metaphysics. The standard narrative informing this lacuna is that Derrida's early work—where the critique of metaphysics is most explicit—differs radically from his later works, which more explicitly engage topics of religion and politics.[9] Recently, Clayton Crockett has argued that Derrida's early texts on "writing" need to be surpassed or put behind in order to engage more explicitly with Derrida the religious thinker: "To read and think about Derrida beyond the motor scheme of writing is to engage with the religious and political significance of his later work."[10] And so theologians generously treat Derrida on topics such as hospitality,[11] the gift,[12] apophasis,[13] the secret,[14] animality,[15] and so on, but spend comparatively little time wrestling with motifs like the trace, citation, dissemination, and the supplement.[16] The reception of this gap has led to several unfortunate misleading interpretations. In my view, the discursive force and even semantic intention of Derrida's "religious" motifs typically treated by theologians cannot adequately be captured without a prior coming to terms with Derrida's radically anti-metaphysical and anti-theological arguments.[17] And so it is to a reading of these anti-metaphysical and anti-theological arguments—sidestepped both by theologians overtly concerned with the Heideggerian critique of metaphysics and by those who are concerned only with the "later" Derrida—that this chapter will offer.

In the chapter's first section, I will argue that all appeals to an "outside"—and so not just Schmitt's—will necessarily fail. Relying on a close reading of Derrida's arguments concerning "writing" found especially but not only in *Of Grammatology*, I argue that rejecting the possibility of an outside text—"text" understood in the general sense that will be developed shortly—implies and requires a concomitant rejection of any discourse that structurally relies on such an outside. This rejection of all outside-oriented metaphysics—and it is Derrida's argument that all metaphysics in the classical and strong sense do structurally rely on an outside—is why I can claim that all metaphysics necessarily follow a basically ideological structure: metaphysics must rely on an outside but cannot actually do so. Metaphysical theologies that think of God as self-fulfilled and transcendent truth—theologies that identify God and truth through an identification of God as truth and God as the God of truth—will be particularly vulnerable to this critique precisely because of their interest in divinizing the outside.

Beginning with Aristotle and extending especially but not only to the transcendental Thomisms inspired by or reliant on him, these theologies all translate the identity of God and truth into a coincidence—even if sometimes "hyperbolic"—of being and thought. This coincidence is held together by the "logos," which is then read back into the structure that produced it in order to secure the (actually presupposed) identity of God and truth. Such is the formal model of all metaphysics and theologies: two identities, God is Truth and Being is Thought, inform and reinforce each other. To this end, the chapter's first section argues that Derridean deconstruction, through a reading of textuality and the textual production of philosophy, radically dissociates this alleged coincidence of thought and being. In so doing, deconstruction presents a real challenge to the credibility of any theology that takes *logy* in a sense that harbors or grounds this coincidence. The problem with metaphysics, then, turns out to be more basically the problem of all metaphysics' implicit reliance on theology. Notably, this locating of metaphysics' problem in its implicit theology is what makes Derrida's project fundamentally different from Marion's, which argues that metaphysics is not theological enough.

The chapter then turns to consider two competing responses to Derrida's critique of theology. If theology is the reason metaphysics should be rejected, then it would seem that no Derridean theology is possible. This is the position taken by Martin Hägglund, who argues that Derridean deconstruction articulates a "radical atheism" that not only argues against the existence of God, but also argues that God is an undesirable reality. Against this interpretation, John Caputo argues that deconstruction is "structured like a religion." After adjudicating this debate—and challenging the extent to which Hägglund and Caputo actually disagree with each other—I suggest that neither Hägglund nor Caputo adequately account for the dissociation of being and thought suggested above. Despite their "radical" intentions—Hägglund writes of a radical atheism and Caputo of a radical hermeneutics—both ultimately imply a metaphysical philosophy that obscures the truly radical potential of Derridean deconstruction. In the final analysis, I agree with Hägglund that Derrida's work offers a sustained critique of theology. Yet, contrary to Hägglund, I argue that such a posture precludes, rather than requires, a radical atheism. If Derrida has convincingly critiqued the identity of God and truth that secures the coincidence of being and thought, Hägglund has unconvincingly articulated a new identity of "no-God" and truth. Caputo, despite the tone of his "poetics," risks the same. Rather than displace the logic of identity thinking, Hägglund and Caputo have each reinscribed the structure with new terms. Thus, whereas I ultimately side with Hägglund over Caputo that Derridean deconstruction precludes theism, I argue that it is a mistake—and one ultimately grounded in metaphysical thinking and the principle of noncontradiction—to assume that a critique of theism implies atheism.

In other words, and like Schmitt, both Hägglund and Caputo have offered a theory of decision wherein all "decisions" are decided in advance. For Hägglund, a decision for religious faith is a priori precluded by "deconstructive" philosophy. For Caputo, a decision for religion, albeit a curious "religion without religion," is demanded by it. Both positions avoid an understanding of decision as aporetic. This aporetic understanding, which is Derrida's, argues that decision is possible only in undecidable situations. The chapter's third and final section returns to Derrida's generalized account of writing to show the ways in which he has made religious decision—for or against, Caputo or Hägglund—impossible, because any framing of the question of religious decision must itself already imply a theologically informed metaphysics. However, and at the very same time, because the metaphysical thinking that secures the coincidence of thought and being has been rejected, the logical and philosophical impossibility of theology does not imply the actual, existential impossibility of God or of faith in God.[18] In other words, deconstruction makes theology impossible by critiquing the identity of thought and being, but this very critique makes possible a decision against the mandates of a priori philosophical and structural barriers. More strongly, this critique reveals that a decision against—or at least not reliant on—philosophical reasoning is unavoidable: as the ideological structure of metaphysics has shown, a non-philosophical decision, including the decision for or against God, has always been at work in every metaphysics.

Before beginning in earnest, it is worth briefly posing a couple of questions that this chapter will never attempt to answer. For a Derridean, appeals to biography must necessarily fall short: as we will see in reference to Jean-Jacques Rousseau and his mother, the meaning and play of a text cannot be reduced biographical or psychoanalytic determination. However, given the current suspicion that "high theory" in general and "French theory" in particular are abstract discourses with no practical or pragmatic considerations—that is, given the suspicion that theory is a pastime for the privileged and the comfortable at best and a white bourgeois tool of obfuscation and canonical imperialism at worst—it is perhaps worthwhile here to point out that Jacques Derrida was an Algerian Jew who spent his formative high school years under Nazi occupation. Derrida the name might now be associated with the comforts of academia, but Derrida the person, "a little black and a very Arab Jew," was not.[19] And so the unanswerable, at least for me, question is this: Why is it that an Algerian Jew would be so interested in showing the violence inherent in the Western philosophical condition? And, complementarily, what is there to be lost—or, perhaps, who is to be lost—if this violence, grounded in theology, witnessed to and critiqued by a victim of fascism, is not fought?

While these questions point toward the inseparability of the political critique and theoretical deconstruction of metaphysics—indeed, it is because metaphysics denies and obfuscates its own theoretical impossibility that it must be primarily political, and this because all metaphysicians must be guilty of producing the ostensibly external transcendental signified that they claim guides their projects—this chapter is primarily concerned with demonstrating Derrida's theoretical problematization of metaphysics. The full political effects of this theoretical destabilization—which is ultimately a radical deconstruction of all idealisms, and so is an heir to, as Derrida says, "a certain spirit of Marx"—will become apparent in the coming chapters.

Writing Theology

The task of this section is to explicate Derrida's argument concerning the deconstructive relationship between writing and theology. In brief, Derrida argues that all classical metaphysics rely on theology, and especially on the theologeme of the coincidence of thinking and being. This reliance on theology should not be read in the Radical Orthodox sense by which theology is the secret *truth* of all secular philosophy. On the contrary, theology's involvement with philosophy is the reason Derrida theoretically problematizes philosophy's claims as to its own knowledge. In the final analysis, according to Derrida, theology, and so all philosophy that depends on theology, is impossible because all theology depends on an impossible transcendental signified. Which is to say, theology depends on something outside of writing. As itself writing, theology cannot do so. As I hope to show, this critique of the coincidence of thinking and being because of the impossibility of theology is a much more subtle and rigorous critique than is sometimes granted. John Milbank, for example, describes Derrida's argument like this: "Derrida's critique of metaphysics is centered around an assault on the notion of a 'meaning' that can be separated from the play of signs and referred to the original 'presence' of a thing or a thought. Signs do not denote pre-existing realities but are caught up in a chain of connotations that can be infinitely extended. Hence the transcendental premise of all language is a logic of 'supplementation' and of 'deferral' " (310).[20] While Milbank is correct that Derrida argues that "signs do not denote pre-existing realities," this is not because signs are "caught up in a chain of connotations" but because signs, understood as the unity of signifier and signified, do not exist. Whereas Milbank is suggesting that Derrida thinks of meaning as always deferred through "a chain of connotations," Derrida's more immediate point, as I show below, is that the intelligible and secured meaning of something called a "sign," which is to say the sign itself, is always already a chimera, a fake, an ideological obfuscation. There is no sign, and so no meaning of the sign, because there is never a signified. Derrida locates the indeterminacy of meaning not in the relationship *between* signs, as Milbank suggests and as his later affirmative gestures toward Hans Georg Gadamer's hermeneutics confirm (*TST*, 312), but rather *within* the sign itself.[21] It is this destabilization of the possibility of signification, more than the deferral of meaning, that poses a problem for theology. And it is this mislocating of the site of indeterminacy—Milbank's thinking of difference as between two signs, as opposed to Derrida's thinking of difference as productive and disruptive of any "sign" as such—that ultimately leads Milbank to accuse Derrida of being a "nihilist" who promotes "red-guard politics of ceaseless negativity" wherein "only a fascistic politics remains viable" (*TST*, 319).[22] Given the previous chapter's discussion of the relationship between unity and fascism, the accusation that an attention to difference leads to fascism can only be read as misplaced. What fascism has ever privileged difference? There have been none, by definition. Ultimately, the trope that Milbank is reiterating here—that Derrida's "assault" on metaphysics is that meaning is deferred—basically misreads Derrida's fundamental point: all philosophical and theological structures that ground themselves in something outside themselves do so through their own textual inventions. The textual invention that most occupies me in this section is the invention of the theologeme of the coincidence of thinking and being. In this way, Derrida is not critiquing metaphysics by "assaulting" something called "meaning" as much as he is demonstrating that the metaphysical conception of meaning is always already theological—a point on which Milbank would vigorously agree—and that this theological formation is precisely the problem for metaphysics.

The argument might begin with Aristotle, who writes that "spoken words are the symbols of mental experience and written words are the symbols of spoken words."[23] That is, according to Aristotle—but not only Aristotle—there exists first a mental content to which every person has direct intuition. This content is then represented by verbal speech, which is in turn represented by writing. Writing, now twice removed from the pure realm of pure content, is a representation of a representation, a sign of a sign. The same derivative structure is found wherever writing is held to represent something that comes before it or something that exists outside it. What is writing according to philosophy? " 'Sign of a sign,' said Aristotle, Rousseau, and Hegel" (*Of Grammatology [OG]*, 29). And so the classical model of writing claims to adhere to the following generic structure: a prelinguistic content is represented by first a verbal and then a written sign.

Such a structure provides a sort of mirror inverse of Schmitt's decisionism. Whereas Schmitt claimed that he was making political decisions but was actually doing indecisive metaphysics (even as his metaphysics was actually hiding other political decisions), Aristotle and the philosophers of writing claim to not make any decision. They accept that, for metaphysics, all is decided in advance, that all that is left to do is the inscription and communication of content: the philosopher writes that writing is non-necessary and external to the truth that it represents. Philosophical texts, then, at least insofar as they adhere to the idealist structure identified by Derrida, present themselves as representing their own other, as representing some truth that is pre- or non-philosophical.

The basic deconstructive critique is that this self-presentation does not account for the philosophy already inscribed within this allegedly pre-philosophical structure. That is, the appearance of the classical model of writing is that philosophy relates to some outside content as an exterior and non-necessary inscription. We have, according to this appearance, a relationship between philosophy and its other. Like Schmitt's relationship between friend and enemy, the classical model of writing is presented as a relationship of both alleged difference and alleged equality: philosophy and its other are different, because without difference no inscription would be possible; but philosophy and its other are the same, because nothing essential is changed or lost in this process of transcription. Yet, also like Schmitt's relationship between friend and enemy, this appearance of difference and equality is actually the elision of a more fundamental dominance by one term over the other. Derrida demonstrates that philosophy dominates—or at least secretly tries to dominate, for actually non-philosophical decisions are always at work—its relationship to its other. More specifically, the structure that is said to relate philosophy-as-external to pre-philosophical content already relies in its own articulation upon several discrete and identifiable philosopheme: namely, content, structure, relation, difference, and expression. Or, closer to Aristotle's description, the structure that allegedly relates philosophy to its other relies on the philosophemes of symbol, mind, and word: "spoken *words* are the *symbols* of *mental experience* and written *words* are the *symbols* of spoken *words*" (*The Basic Works of Aristotle*). What is a symbol, what is an experience, what is the mental, and what is a word that does not already involve within itself an entire philosophy? Which is to say: the philosophic model reads itself into what is allegedly before or outside itself. Philosophy must refer to particular philosophic concepts—including the concept of the concept—in order to provide itself an allegedly pre-philosophical ground that it claims to find in intuitive mental experience. Moreover, this reliance on a cluster of philosophemes means not only that the allegedly pre-philosophical structural relationship between philosophy and its other calls upon and relies on philosophy, but that this structure itself articulates an entire philosophical theory of truth, expression, and being. That is, philosophy is not one part of this structure that relates philosophy to its other but is instead itself articulated in this presentation of philosophy's relation to its other. Philosophy *appears* to be an element in a more general and encompassing structure, but philosophy is *actually* the control that this structure displays over what it calls philosophy and what it calls truth. Or as Derrida puts it, in the classical model of writing, "not only is a philosophy implied, but also a conceptual network in which philosophy itself has been constituted" (*Margins of Philosophy [MP]*, 230).

Aristotle continues: "Just as all men have not the same writing, so all men have not the same speech sounds, but the mental experiences, which these directly symbolize, are the same for all, as also are those things of which our experiences are the images. This matter has, however, been discussed in my treatise about the soul" (*On Interpretation [OI]*, 1.1). Here, Aristotle accords temporal and logical priority to "mental experience" over the "speech sounds" that express them—and so twice over the "written words" that express the speech sounds. Without this pre-philosophical mental experience—the existence of which we have already questioned—translation and interpretation would be impossible, because "men" would be confined to speak and listen to only those with the same speech sounds. Between groups with different speech sounds, according to Aristotle, mental experience works as a sort of transcendent and mediating term. In other words, the "sameness" of mental content that allows its identical representation in different languages refers to the content's exteriority to its allegedly subsequent and unnecessary inscription. Structurally, this exteriority of writing makes of it a transport of something other and higher than itself, and writing becomes a transport of meaning and truth. This pre-inscribed content of mental experience, which writing transports and communicates, is given as intuitively true, as immediately present to the mind of either the philosopher or God or both. Derrida describes the structure like this: "All signifiers, and first and foremost the written signifier, are derivative with regard to what would wed the voice indissolubly to the mind or to the thought of the signified sense, indeed to the thing itself (whether it is done in the Aristotelian manner that we have just indicated or in the manner of medieval theology, determining the res as a thing created from its eidos, from its sense thought in the logos or in the infinite understanding of God)" (*OG*, 11). In the pages immediately following this claim, Derrida will speak of this "signified sense" as also "presence," "substance," "the proper," "the primary," and "the transcendental signified." In each case, some element—the transcendental signified—is presented as outside of language in general and of writing in particular. That this element is given intuitively in mental experience can only mean that its subsequent inscription is only a temporary pedagogic detour: one writes in order to express an intuition so as to help others reach the same intuition. More precisely, in such a scheme, that which the other reaches is not the object of writing but is the intuitive truth of which writing is a representation twice removed. In this sense, writing effaces itself in its process of pedagogical communication—philosophers write in order that writing will not be necessary; complementarily, intelligible writing is possible only because it is unnecessary.

Derrida detects in this philosophical structure a theological moralism of sin and of purity: Morally, writing—and so communication and pedagogy—are thought according to a model of the fall. It is only when one falls from direct intuition of the truth that writing becomes necessary. Only as fallen and removed from truth, only when truth is absent, is one forced to momentarily use the material things of the world, and this only for the sake of once again transcending these things. Derrida notes that philosophers as methodologically diverse as Hegel, Saussure, Levi-Strauss, and Husserl all employ some variation of this analogy of writing and sin.[24] For them, writing "always seem(s) to make an apparent, provisional, and derivative notch in the system of first and last presence . . . The sign is always a sign of the Fall. Absence always relates to distancing from God" (*OG*, 283).[25] The human person would then need to purify him or herself of this sinful character of writing in order to return to God. All writing would be done only for the sake of overcoming itself. Such a self-overcoming is possible only because the difference between immediate intuition of truth and writing as removed from truth has no essential effect on truth as such: this is a truth that does not depend upon closeness or proximity, and this is a fall with no noetic consequence.[26]

Importantly, this self-overcoming done in an effort to achieve moral purity structurally resembles Schmitt's model of the purification of "realms" as they become more and more political. Recall that for Schmitt the realms of economics, ethics, aesthetics, and so on, all denude themselves of particular content as their inherent antagonisms intensify into their properly ontological-political condition. The proletariat only becomes political when it stops engaging economics and starts living out is divinely-ordained ontological position. And so with Schmitt in the last chapter and Aristotle in this one, we have two discrete instances of the complication of a transcendental signified—the sovereign, direct intuition of being—with the structure said signified is meant to authorize and guide. Derrida's argument in *Of Grammatology* is that such a complication is not an empirical accident particular to these or any other writers but is a structural effect of writing. As soon as the element allegedly outside the structure, the transcendental signified, relates to the structure in any way—including the very basic relational position of *being outside*—it cannot help but refer to elements "within" the structure. In other words, in order for the transcendental signified to represent the truth available to writing, it must use the conceptual resources—above all, the concept of truth—of said writing. There is no entity in autochthonous isolation, there is no determination of meaning outside of reference to a received conceptual apparatus, be it scientific, philosophical, theological, or whatever else. There is no non-philosophical structure that relates philosophy to its other.

Because of these necessary problems—this impossibility—of grounding a discourse of truth in a truth that resides outside of discourse, Derrida argues that reading "cannot legitimately transgress the text toward something other than it, toward a referent (a reality that is metaphysical, historical, psychobiographical, etc.) or toward a signified outside the text whose content could take place, could have taken place outside of language, that is to say, in the sense that we give here to that word, outside of writing in general" (*OG*, 158). Neither reading nor writing can any longer be thought on the model of a detour ordered toward a transcendental truth, meaning, or signified. This impossibility of leaving the text and finding rest in its transcendental referent—a model followed by both Aristotle and Schmitt—is not an empirical effect of language's imperfectability. Derrida is not arguing that there is a transcendent being, truth, or reality that we cannot "reach" because of our fallen state. Such is precisely the "theological" structure that he critiqued in Saussure, Hegel, and Husserl.[27] Rather, Derrida is generalizing the critique of the transcendental signified and making of it a "quasi-transcendental" condition of all reading and writing: every alleged signified is a signifier, every signified is part of the chain of associations, differences, and deferrals that constitute text.[28] If this were not the case, if there were to be a self-present and absolute transcendental signified, then signification would be impossible. We would not even have the "direct symbols" that

Aristotle thought he found in speech, for, as Derrida has demonstrated, such symbolizations immediately open syntactical relations between signifiers; that is, symbolization always articulates text. Such a plentitude without signifying would be an absolute presence without difference or movement, it would be "another name for death" (*OG*, 71).[29]

And so the rejection of the transcendental signified immediately becomes a rejection of the possibility of the signified as such: the full presence of any signified anywhere would absolutely cease the movement of signification and would thus be "another name for death."[30] That is, without the absolute signified that would arrest movement and signifying, we come to see that any alleged signified is "always already in the position of a signifier" (*OG*, 73). Geoffrey Bennington puts it like this: "Without a transcendental signified, the difference between signifier and signified cannot be rigorous. A 'signified' is just a signifier positioned by other signifiers as a signified" (97).[31] If writing is the sign of a sign—"said Aristotle, Rousseau, and Hegel," said Derrida—then every signified, precisely as a signifier, that is, as a sign of other signs, is writing. It is this generalized sense of writing that leads Derrida to write that "one cannot abstract from the written text to rush to the signified it would mean, since the signified is here the text itself" (*OG*, 150). And it is in this sense of a generalized writing that allows us to read the infamous claim that "there is no outside text" (*OG*, 158).[32]

Gayatri Chakravorty Spivak's translation, of course, offers "there is nothing outside the text."[33] Derrida, for his part, wrote: "*Il n'y a pas de hors-texte.*" The problem with Spivak's preferred translation, as I see it, is her use of the definite article. Derrida's sentence occurs in a larger discussion of Jean-Jacques Rousseau's *Confessions*. In it, Derrida is arguing that the "meaning" of Rousseau's text cannot be determined through reference to any transcendental signified. This for the reasons discussed above; namely, that any alleged transcendental signified will itself be found to be a signifier of something else, which itself will be a signifier, and so on, endlessly. Even psychoanalytic and pseudo-psychoanalytic discourses that would argue that Rousseau's text is "about" his mother would fail to make non- or pre-textual reference, precisely because Rousseau's mother herself functions within a series of substitutions and references. This is not to say that Rousseau's text invents his mother in any vulgar sense, or that Rousseau has no mother, but is to understand text and writing in the generalized sense articulated above: Rousseau's mother is not present to herself. The claim "this text is about Rousseau's mother" can always be questioned: "And who is Rousseau's mother? What is she about?" This sense of generalized writing is lost, or possibly lost, in Spivak's use of the definite article: where, in this generalized sense, does Derrida write about "the" text? "The" text implies Rousseau's *Confessions*. Derrida does not say that Rousseau's mother does not exist outside of *Confessions*, but that there is no "outside text" which somehow articulates or contains the full "meaning" of Rousseau's mother.

That Derrida does not argue that there is nothing outside of "the" text, *Confessions*, is important in order to grasp the generality of his critique of all structures of knowing grounded in the truth of a transcendental signified: these transcendental signifieds—the sovereign, being as directly intuited, the inexpressible God, Rousseau's mother—are not only held to be outside the texts that they direct, but more importantly function to secure the intelligibility of text as such. That is, they function to secure the coincidence of the knowledge articulated in text and the being outside of text with which said knowledge coincides—it is a coincidence implied in every model of writing that holds on to the difference/equality structure displayed in Aristotle's classical discussion of writing. In this authorizing and securing sense, all transcendental signifieds are simultaneously the content to be communicated and the guarantee that communication is possible. They are simultaneously the truth which writing represents and the promise that the truth can be represented. They claim: the truth is, being can be known.

And so Derrida has seemingly articulated two competing and antagonistic models of writing: on the one hand, we have the philosophic model, which argues for a direct coincidence between the knowledge given by writing and the being that exists in full presence outside of writing. On the other hand, we have not logocentrism and the metaphysics of presence, but grammatology: a reading of the writing—the interminable deferral of the truth and meaning, and so the impossibility of determined meaning—of all transcendental signifieds.

Throughout *Of Grammatology*, Derrida clearly associates theology—and not only "ontotheology"—with the metaphysics of presence. Indeed, it is the "logos" of metaphysical logocentrism that, as alleged pure and absolute ground of purity and the absolute, is held to be the most pernicious of all theologemes. Echoing Marx, for whom religion is the archetype of all ideology,[34] Derrida argues that theology is primarily responsible for the promotion of all transcendental signifieds: "God is the name and the element of that which makes possible an absolutely pure and absolutely self-present self-knowledge" (*OG*, 98). This concept of the absolute, which is another name for the self-presence of truth, wherever it is found, "always leads to an infinitist theology and to the logos or the infinite understanding of

God" (*OG*, 78). And reversing the causal arrow, relating not logocentrism to theology but theology to logocentrism: "Infinitist theologies are always logocentrisms" (*OG*, 71). "The age of the sign," that is, the age of the coincidence of the knowing signifier and the being signified, which is critiqued by deconstruction, "is essentially theological" (*OG*, 14). "The intelligible face of the sign remains turned toward the word and the face of God" (*OG*, 13). Finally, Derrida tells us plainly, this theology constitutes "the major obstacle to all grammatology" (*OG*, 76).

If theology's "theo" names God as transcendental signified, if theology's "logy" secures the isomorphism of its own discourse with its own exteriority, and if it then follows that "theology" means the truth of God—where the genitive is double, truth about God and God's truth, which would be identical—then theology is, without doubt, the major obstacle to all grammatology. Which is the same as saying that all deconstructive readings that dissociate God and truth, and so undermine the theological coincidence of thought and being, render theology impossible. Philosophy and theology become partners in the ideological structure of all metaphysical claims: philosophy presents itself as responding to and recovering direct intuition of an immediate and present truth; this presentation, though, masks its own prior and pre-philosophical reliance on the theological security of the identity of truth and God, of thought and being. That is, theology is nothing more than philosophy's secret attempt to hide its own inability to know.

"Radical Atheism" or "Religion without Religion"

The previous section argued that Derrida's generalization of writing—the argument that all signifieds are signifiers—undermines all structures of truth that are grounded in a notion of truth as exterior to writing. Such an exteriority of truth marks a simultaneous difference and coincidence between being, which is outside of writing, and thinking, which isomorphically represents being. As theology is the discourse that most explicitly affirms the authority of a transcendental signified, grammatology deconstructs theology. As "the outside" is a theologeme upon which all metaphysical structures of truth depend, theology is "the major obstacle" to grammatology.

In his book *Radical Atheism: Derrida and the Time of Life*, Martin Hägglund argues that Derrida critiques not only theological discourse and the theological element of all discourse, but more strongly critiques the possibility of theism in general. Hägglund's book makes primarily two arguments, which are related. The first, from which Hägglund will eventually distance himself, concerns the impossibility of God's existence. This anti-theist argument is meant to be descriptive and value neutral. The second argument concerns not the nonexistence of God, but the undesirability of God. It is this second argument that most occupies Hägglund, and, in his view, is what marks Derrida's atheism as "radical."

Concerning the nonexistence of God, Hägglund precedes from an argument about the necessity of temporality and the consequent impossibility of eternity: "The temporal can never be in itself but is always disjoined between being no longer and being not yet. Thus, time itself is constitutively out of joint. Or more exactly: time itself is the impossibility of any 'itself' . . . To think the tracing of time as the condition for life in general is to think a constitutive finitude, which from the very beginning exposes life to death, memory to forgetting, identity to alterity, and so on" (*Radical Atheism [RA]*, 79). Hägglund's argument here is that every "now" is only possible as the passing of a "past" and the coming of a "future." This passing and coming are not accidents that affect the present from without, but are rather constitutive elements of all temporality that give rise to the phenomenon of the present. Rather than think of the past as a past present, as if yesterday is gone because we are no longer present to it and it no longer present to us, and rather than think of the future as a future present, as if tomorrow will be soon present to us as a "now," Hägglund wants to think all time as constantly passing and coming, constantly "out of joint." Any sense of immediacy and presence is a derived effect of this originary "out of joint" temporality.

For Hägglund, identity is an effect of this out of joint temporality, of this necessary passing and coming of time. To reach this conclusion, Hägglund argues that one's spatial continuity through time—the "spatialization of time"—allows for a sense of identity as that which repeats in space at different temporal moments. In other words, identity arises as a means by which one can secure and explain a sense of spatial continuity through temporal difference: there is an identity between the "I" that I now am, the "I" who I was as a child, and the "I" that I will be in the future precisely because there is an irreducible difference between these moments. Without this difference, the repetition through time that constitutes the "I" would not be possible; there would be only unchanging plentitude, no temporal difference by which spatial continuity could be measured. The upshot of this argument is that identity, "I," comes about after the fact of difference. Identity does not precede difference but follows it. Difference "itself," the spatialization of time and the temporalization of space, is both ontologically and logically prior to identity.

Implementing a classic Derridean motif, Hägglund then argues that these conditions that allow for identity also make for the impossibility of identity. In the sense that identity is an effect of difference understood as temporalization and spatialization, difference functions as the condition of possibility for identity. Yet, precisely because difference is prior, temporalization and spatialization also function as the conditions of impossibility of any identity understood as consummated or eternal self-presence. Everything that "is," "is" only to the extent that it "is" its own passing and coming: "No moment is given in itself but is superseded by another moment in its very event and can never be consummated in a positive infinity" (*RA*, 3).

Hägglund applies this quasi-transcendental condition of difference as temporalization—the "ultratranscendental condition from which nothing can be exempt" (*RA*, 19)—to God, and does so for the sake of rendering God impossible. For Hägglund, and for Hägglund's Derrida, temporalization "entails that nothing—including whatever is posited as 'God'—can be exempt from temporal finitude" (*RA*, 142). Because temporalization is an "ultratranscendental" condition for anything to be, God could only ever arise as an effect of difference. Because God would then be subject to the higher laws of temporality, God would not be God in any theologically recognizable sense. God would be one fleeting and temporary signifier on par with any and all other so-called identities. God would only ever be "God."

In his response to Hägglund's text, Caputo criticizes this temporalization argument against God:

> (Hägglund) simply uses *différance* to stipulate that life is mortal and that being is spatio-temporal but he offers no non-circular argument that there is no life or being outside space and time. He simply assumes the conditions of space and time and then complains that eternity does not meet them. His objection to eternity is that it does not abide by the conditions of space and time. But that is not an objection to eternity; it is the definition of eternity.[35]

In my view, Hägglund does more than merely "stipulate" that life is mortal: Hägglund presents an a priori argument for the priority of difference over identity by demonstrating identity's logical and ontological dependence on difference. Yet, Caputo's point that Hägglund has not so much criticized "eternity" as he has described it is well taken and seems to cause Hägglund to distance himself from this ontological version of his anti-theist argument. Indeed, in his response to Caputo, Hägglund claims that "radical atheism does not dispute the existence but rather the desirability of God and eternity . . . Whether or not such a state can exist is not decided by radical atheism and nothing in my argument depends on deciding it" ("The Radical Evil of Deconstruction" ["RED"], 134).[36]

While contradicting his earlier claim that "the absolute being of God is unattainable" (*RA*, 111), the move to desire is helpful in understanding what is at stake between Hägglund's and Caputo's respective interpretations of deconstruction. This help is welcome because the difference between the two is not always clear. About *Radical Atheism*'s critique, Caputo writes that he "would say that it is a perfect misunderstanding of my work but for the fact that nothing is perfect" ("The Return of Anti-Religion" ["RAR"], 42). Yet, in the same essay, Caputo claims that "Hägglund describes quite felicitously what is in fact my present project" ("RAR," 111). Both accuse the other of articulating a "systematic misreading of everything I say" ("RAR," 36 / *RA*, 120). Yet, both are quick to clarify that neither believes that God "exists," and both are, at least ostensibly, avoiding any sort of "metaphysical" commitment. Neither believes that Derrida believed in God. Both are critical of religion's influence on culture and politics (although Hägglund, the professed atheist, less so: "There are any number of situations in which the given structure of a society makes religious discourse the most powerful tool for mobilizing a struggle against injustice" ["RED," 149]). At one curious point in his text, Caputo seems to agree that deconstruction makes "the case for atheism," and note the definite article, but denies that this atheism is "a case against religion" ("RAR," 47). This turn from theism to "religion" is muddled when Caputo, again and again, assures Hägglund that his "religion" is "only structured like a religion," that it is properly "without religion" and "without the God of classical religion" ("RAR," 35). Yet, if Caputo's religion is without God and without religion, Hägglund's atheism is not without faith: in *This Life*, his follow-up to *Radical Atheism*, Hägglund speaks of a "secular faith . . . in the future and in those on whom I depend" (47). Indeed, his life's "commitments" are "sustained by faith" (197).[37] Parsing the debate, one gets the sense that each is eager to prove their atheist bonafides to the other.

Apparently, then, the dispute between Hägglund and Caputo is not primarily about personal religious belief or practice. Neither believe God exists; both are comfortable with the language of faith; both demur when tasked with making metaphysical commitments. What is at stake, instead, is the question of how best to read and understand Derrida. On this front, both Hägglund and Caputo offer coherent, if incomplete, readings of some Derridean motifs. Neither, however, address the issue with which this chapter has been occupied: the deconstructive critique of the coincidence of thought and being. Indeed, both offer examples of precisely this coincidental thinking.

Throughout his corpus, Caputo's master-signifier for interpreting deconstruction as religious, as "structured like a religion," is "the impossible." Both deconstruction and religion are, for Caputo, structurally related to "the impossible" in that both demonstrate a "passion for the impossible." In both cases, deconstruction and religion, Caputo speaks of a "passion" that is "evoked or provoked" "when the tensions of the impossible are raised to their highest pitch, when the easy routine of the possible is shattered by the impossible" ("Looking the Impossible in the Eye" ["LI"], 4).[38] By so closely defining the two, Caputo renders deconstruction and religion convertible: Caputo can and does speak of both religion as deconstructive and deconstruction as "structured like" a religion.

Caputo holds that this "passion" is the originating and driving motivation of both deconstruction and religion, and thus speaks of an "axiom of impossibility" from which both discourses operate ("LI," 3). It is an axiom that produces two discourses that are more than analogically associated. The liberality with which Caputo transitions between the two is most clear when he associates Derrida with Kierkegaard and the Kierkegaardian pseudonyms:

> The rule is that only the impossible will do, and anything less will result in a mediocre fellow; only the impossible will produce results that are truly worth the effort. A passion or a desire is maximized, reaches what Climacus calls "the ultimate potentiation," only *in extremis,* under the harshest, the most inhospitable and impossible conditions. It is only when a passion is pushed beyond itself, to the breaking point, that it is moved to make a radically new move, impelled to another plane or register. This paradoxical movement constitutes, if this is possible, a certain "law" of the impossible, which must mean a certain outlaw, an archic rule without rule, an auto-interrupting law, or perhaps a "logic" of the impossible, which would only be a paralogic or a paradoxical logic. We can thus identify a certain quasi-method

to the sublime madness of Derrida and de Silentio, Climacus and Constantin, who are, I would say, kindred poets, pranksters and paralogicians *extra ordinaire*, transgressors and trespassers *sensu eminentiore*. ("LI," 4)

Besides the circular reference to "inhospitable and impossible conditions," Caputo does little here to provide any semantic determination of "the impossible." Instead, Caputo offers a few heuristics by which one might be able to recognize or describe the impossible: the impossible will be without rule, self-interrupting, and so on. A couple of pages later, Caputo will write of the impossible as "representing" "an absolute interruption in the regime of the possible, an exposure to and an opening upon an absolute heterogeneity, a wholly other" ("LI," 6). The subtle shift to representational language, where the impossible is no longer that which "evokes or provokes" passion but is instead a *representation* of that which "evokes or provokes" passion, further distances Caputo from any determination of content. Granted, a refusal to define the impossible makes some degree of sense, and certainly Caputo would dismiss any demand to do so. After all, defining the impossible would be to render it, in some semantic sense at least, possible. But this move to representation has evoked a familiar pattern: "the impossible" is now, as representational, a signifier. Religious passion, in this register, is not impassioned by "the impossible" as an outside inbreaking of "the wholly other" as much as it is part of a chain of substitutions and significations—that is, writing.

On the one hand, Caputo has found himself treating "the impossible" in a fairly equivocal manner. It is sometimes the unknown and unpredictable that can break into our quotidian existence, and, in doing so, create unprogrammable and anarchic effects. The impossible is "a wholly other" that or who provokes a religious passionate response. It is in this sense that the impossible most closely resembles the "God of classical religion." It is Caputo not as a postmodern Catholic, but as a Barthian. On the other hand, "the impossible" is not God, but is a *sign* of something that might perhaps be God—but, Caputo assures us, not the God of religion at all. We have in this sense not a wholly other breaking in from afar, but a sort of auto-deconstructive play constitutive of any alleged identity. It is in this sense that the impossible most closely resembles the Derridean motifs of khora and *différance*, and, incidentally, most closely resembles Hägglund's notion of difference-as-temporalization.

Caputo treats both deconstruction and religion as "passions for the impossible," and so grants himself some degree of leniency in liberally translating one into and out of the other. Yet, such a posture of translation elides an underlying equivocation: Caputo has not so much rendered God and khora translatable as he has made "the impossible" equivocally refer to both. In Caputo, "the impossible" is the transcendental signified that harbors the translatability of God and khora. As the previous section's critique of all transcendental signifieds makes clear, this structure is impossible in a sense much more straightforward than Caputo's.

Such an equivalency seems to have been critiqued in advance by Derrida himself. In "Sauf le nom," Derrida discusses the relationship between khora, understood as "the barren, radically nonhuman and atheological" nonplace that allows for the possibility of spatialization and temporalization, and God. Whether khora precedes God or God precedes khora is, Derrida says, ultimately and necessarily undecidable:

> It remains to be known if this nonsensible (invisible and inaudible) place is opened by God, by the name of God (which would again be some other thing, perhaps), or if it is "older" than the time of creation, than time itself, than history, narrative, word, etc. It remains to be known (beyond knowing) if the place is opened by appeal . . . or if it remains impassively foreign, like Khora, to everything that takes its place and replaces itself and plays within this place, including what is named God. (76)[39]

To this extent, Caputo might be in agreement. However, this undecidability does not mean that the two possibilities are equivalent or interchangeable, indeed, they are exclusive of one another. Derrida clarifies this antagonism:

> But it is true that these two "places," these two experiences of place, these two ways are no doubt of an absolute heterogeneity. One place excludes the other, one (sur)passes the other, one does without the other, one is, absolute, *without* the other . . . on one side, on one way, a profound and abyssal eternity, fundamental but accessible to messianism in general, to the teleo-eschatological narrative and to a certain experience or historical revelation; on the other side, on the other way, the nontemporality of an abyss without bottom or surface, an absolute impassability (neither life

nor death) that gives rise to everything that it is not. ("Sauf le nom," 77)

In reference to this antagonism—even if an antagonism with something of a supplemental structure—Kearney notes that Caputo distances himself from Derrida, even if trying to appeal to him: "I suspect that Caputo thinks that we don't have to choose—since the issue remains radically undecidable. But I would like to disagree and suggest that we do whenever we opt to believe in God or not believe. A religious belief, I submit, is hardly worthy of the name unless it calls for a choice. And Derrida himself, it seems, has little hesitation about declaring his own personal option, namely, for atheism" (*Strangers, Gods, and Monsters [SGM]*, 201).[40] Whether or not Derrida "has little hesitation about declaring his own personal option" is not of particular importance for this project.[41] Indeed, a concern with Derrida's personal religious or atheistic conviction might be one of the problems with Caputo's treatment of deconstruction and Derrida—it is a treatment that, as Graham Ward argues, often borders on hagiography.[42] What is more immediately important is Caputo's treatment of decision in relation to this equivocal notion of "the impossible": Kearney suggests, and my reading has agreed with his suggestion, that Caputo *decides to not decide* between khora and God. As I will argue in this chapter's final section, Derrida performs a similar decision-to-not-decide in terms of faith. But there is a decisive distinction between Derrida's refusal to decide and Caputo's: Caputo's non-decision is actually a plethora of mutually exclusive decisions. Faced with the undecidable choice between khora and God, Caputo collapses the distinction in equivocation. Caputo chooses, or wants to choose, both. The disjunctive "or" in the question "God or khora" becomes, in Caputo's work, conjunctive. It is a conjunctive hidden in the equivocation harbored by "the impossible": God and khora are both the impossible

Is such an equivocation and such a conjunction *possible?* Above, Derrida argued that it is not: God and khora exclude each other. And so the reader of Caputo is faced with a choice: either Derrida is wrong that God and khora exclude each other, in which case Caputo's deconstruction disagrees with Derrida's on this important point, or Derrida is right and Caputo's equivocation is actually only in appearance. In this latter case, Caputo's apparent indecision masks a prior decision for either God or khora.

There is good reason to choose the latter option. Consider Caputo's treatment of the Christian doctrine of the incarnation as it functions for Kierkegaard: "That is precisely the point where, much as I love him, I jump the Kierkegaardian ship—where Kierkegaard *identifies* the 'Paradox,' which is a structure of passion, desire, existence, and temporality, with the Christian doctrine of Incarnation. That would be like the Messiah actually showing up (which in fact it precisely is) and that would ruin everything. For me, the truest form of Christianity is the one in which the Messiah can as a structural matter never show up" ("RAR," 36). Which is to say, the "truest form of Christianity"—and why this introduction of truth as a measure?—would be a structural atheism. As Hägglund also posits an a priori, structural argument against the possibility of a messiah, Caputo and Hägglund are in complete agreement. The only difference here is that Caputo wants to call this structural atheism a religion, and Hägglund, more plausibly, does not.

I see little reason to side with Caputo over Hägglund on this point—and not just because of Caputo's reliance on equivocation, wherein the "without religion" so far overpowers the "religion" in the phrase "religion without religion" as to render the phrase's tension resolved. More troublesome for Caputo's entire argument is his apparent dismissal of the *possibility* of incarnation. It is a dismissal with which Caputo seems to find pleasure, especially as it distances him from "the Christian right." Because Caputo strongly distinguishes between the "specific messianisms" of particular religions and the structure of "the messianic," which allows for the possibility of such messianisms, he forecloses in advance the possibility of deciding in favor of any messianism. For Caputo, such messianisms are not only always violent, "bloody," but are to be excluded a priori because they would materially determine the promise of "the messianic," which is always, for Caputo, open-ended and without fulfillment. At its extreme, this rejection of any particular messianism is, according to Caputo, also a rejection of any particular faith: "deconstruction keeps a safe distance from any 'determinable faith,' even if it is not fundamentalist or even religious in the conventional form" (*The Prayers and Tears of Jacques Derrida [PTJD]*, 150).[43] By so removing the possibility of coincidence of the particular and the universal, though, Caputo has seemingly opted for a Kantian-esque religion within the boundaries of reason alone. Caputo's religion is never particular, material, or historical—and so never materially or orthopraxically revolutionary—but is only ever formal and determined by the "law without law" of "the impossible."

This a priori privileging of the formal over the material undermines Caputo's commitment to his two primary motifs: passion and the impossible. Caputo has rendered the Incarnation impossible. And he has rejected it on those grounds. "The impossible," then, turns out to be that which is possible within the a priori structural confines of a rational formalism. Is not such a reduction of the impossible also a foreclosure of passion? Caputo explicitly rejects Kierkegaard precisely at his most passionate: at the moment when Kierkegaard finds faith in the passionate and existential commitment to the objective absurdity of the incarnation. Quite literally, Caputo's faith is without Passion.[44]

Caputo's project ought to be subjected to one more turn of the screw. By now, we are aware that any allegedly pure transcendental signified will prove itself to be a signifier of some other specific and material inscription. To this point, Caputo has gone to great lengths to purify his transcendental signified, "the impossible." The impossible is pure of religion, of God, of the Incarnation. It is even, in a move that associates Caputo with Schmitt's distaste for the ochlos, pure of "ordinary fellows." But if, for example, the Incarnation is not "the impossible," and precisely because it is impossible, then what, for Caputo, is? The question can always be asked: what is this transcendental signified about? When Caputo writes of a passion for the impossible that separates "saints" from "ordinary fellows," what does he have in mind? Responding to Žižek, a frequent critic of Caputo despite being a fellow partisan of the impossible, Caputo writes:

> I would be perfectly happy if the far left politicians in the United States were able to reform the system by providing universal health care, effectively redistributing wealth more equitably with a revised IRS code, effectively restricting campaign financing, enfranchising all voters, treating migrant workers humanely, and effecting a multilateral foreign policy that would integrate American power within the international community, etc., i.e., intervene upon capitalism by means of serious and far-reaching reforms . . . If after doing all that Badiou and Žižek complained that some Monster called Capital still stalks us, I would be inclined to greet that Monster with a yawn. (*After the Death of God* [*ADG*], 124)[45]

Caputo would be perfectly happy if the "far left" revised tax codes, among a few other reforms. Apparently, for Caputo, the political partner of deconstruction's passion for the impossible is a program of bureaucratic structural readjustment. Religion's passion for the impossible is "evoked or provoked" by a structural atheism with mildly social-democratic aspirations.

In response, Žižek, the affirmed Marxist, notes precisely what I am suggesting here: that Caputo's theology, for all of its presumed and announced radicalness, articulates a fundamentally conservative gesture. Comparing Caputo's "impossible" to J. J. Altizer's conception of the death of God, Žižek writes:

> [Caputo's] "religion without religion" appears much too aseptic, lifeless, bloodless, lacking the properly religious passion . . . in comparison with someone like Altizer, whose vision of the death of God retains a properly apocalyptic shattering power. Caputo's reading of the death of God reduces it to a happy "deconstructive" event: the God who dies is the onto-theological Master of creation, the supreme Entity, and the field is thereby open for the (re)assertion of the true abyss of Divinity . . . For Altizer, on the contrary, what "dies" on the Cross is not just the false (positive, ontic) envelope of Divinity, which was obfuscating its eventual core; what dies is God himself, the structuring principle of our entire universe, its life-giving force, the guarantee of its meaning. The death of God thus equals the end of the world, the experience of "darkness at noon."[46]

That is, Žižek detects in death of God theology a commitment to apocalypse missing in Caputo's deconstructive theology. In this rendering, Caputo's deconstructive gesture is guilty of the aforementioned charge that Derrida elsewhere levies against negative theology: namely, that by claiming to deny ontic affirmations, negative theology in fact creates a bulwark defending an ever-more-pure God from truly atheistic critique. Žižek suggests, as does my reading, that the pretense of radical deconstruction in fact serves to conserve a particular, center-left politics and, in doing so, occlude the possibility of a truly revolutionary praxis.[47]

Hägglund also critiques Caputo's use of "the impossible," but for a different reason than the one I have articulated here. Where I argue that Caputo's use of "the impossible" seemingly equivocates between referring to God and khora but actually functions as an a priori reduction of the possible to exclude both material religious beliefs and radical politics, Hägglund opts to take Caputo at his word. The result of doing so is that Hägglund believes that Caputo conceives of the impossible as an inbreaking of the wholly other. The model of inbreaking, though, proves no more convincing as a deconstructive reading:

> According to Caputo, "the impossible, being impassioned by the impossible, is the religious, is religious passion," since "our hearts are burning with the desire to go where we cannot go, to the impossible." It is easy to see how misleading this argument is once we realize that the impossible for Derrida is not somewhere we can never go—or something we can never reach—but rather where we always find ourselves to be. The impossible is what happens all the time, since it designates the impossibility of being in itself that is the condition of temporality. ("RED," 141)

According to Hägglund, Caputo's distinction—as opposed to equivocation—of the possible from the impossible constitutes "the matrix for Caputo's misunderstanding of Derrida" ("RED," 136). Such a distinction relies on and introduces a series of binary oppositions—"inventive or uninventive, exceptional or routinized, generous or mundane, surprising or preprogrammed, unexpected or predictable, excessive or merely normative," and I would add the binary of heroic or ordinary—that are "utterly deconstructible" ("RED," 144).

Hägglund's critique of Caputo's reliance on binary distinctions is not an a priori or dogmatic dismissal of binary thinking. Indeed, Hägglund himself sometimes relies on such distinctions, even if only for the sake of deconstructing them—such as the dichotomy between eternity and temporality, or that between identity and alterity. Hägglund's real concern here is that Caputo has, much like Schmitt, constituted an oppositional matrix wherein each side offers an associative cluster of analogous terms. Each cluster takes as its master signifier either the impossible or the possible; that is, these two terms function as a master binary by which all other antagonisms make sense. And so the inventive, the exceptional, the generous, the surprising, the unexpected, the excessive, and the heroic are all associated together as having something to do with "the impossible"; whereas the uninventive, the routinized, the mundane, the preprogrammed, the predictable, the merely normative, and the ordinary are all governed by "the possible."

For Hägglund—and it is a point to which I subscribe, although I question if it takes Caputo too literally—such a structure undermines the necessary complication of the possible and the impossible. Hägglund argues for this complication because, unlike Caputo, Hägglund does not identify the impossible with a permanently futural alterity or with a series of center-left reforms. Instead, Hägglund argues that "the impossible" in Derrida primarily refers to the impossibility of identity and plentitude. Here, Hägglund is consistently implementing his critique of temporalization: the passing and coming of time makes any "in-itself" impossible. Against Caputo, then, Hägglund argues that the impossible is not that which will (never) come, but is that which happens, quite literally, *all the time*. Indeed, anything that happens only happens within this context of the temporal impossibility of identity. The possible and impossible are not bipoles constituting an antagonistic binary, but are each other's supplemental pair. Each is the condition of possibility, and so impossibility, of the other.

By arguing that the impossible happens—indeed, happens all the time—Hägglund presents a thoroughly non-ontological understanding of the impossible. It is one that coheres with an argumentative structure common in Derrida's texts: the conditions of possibility of a phenomenon are also found to be said phenomenon's conditions of impossibility. Examples—instances of deconstruction—abound: Derrida will write of the im/possible conditions of giving gifts (a gift must be given outside of conditions of exchange, but precisely this is to say that gifts must be given without being given),[48] of signing signatures (each signature must mark a unique event and unique commitment, but must also be infinitely repeatable and tied to the signatory),[49] of offering hospitality (one cannot offer hospitality to the other with conditions, for to do so would be to domesticate the other, yet such an unconditional hospitality necessarily risks its own demise as the other could be a monster),[50] of implementing and defending democracy (unconditional democracy necessarily makes possible democracy's undoing),[51] of asking forgiveness (one must consider oneself unforgivable in order to ask for forgiveness),[52] and countless other autoimmune and auto-deconstructive structures, commitments, or events. In each case, the coincidence of possibility and impossibility marks an initial destabilization or deconstruction of the metaphysical principle of noncontradiction—according to Aristotle, the "most certain of all principles," and one which "a man must know if he knows anything."[53] Granted, precisely: it is this possibility of *knowing* anything, and especially anything grounded in a metaphysical axiom held to be self-evident and undeniable, that is at stake in the deconstructive gesture.

Which is not to say that a deconstruction of the metaphysical determination of the meaning or possibility of, say, forgiveness, implies a denial of the fact of forgiveness. This is where Hägglund is especially helpful. These deconstructive conditions of impossibility are peculiar: these structural impossibilities do not determine whether or not something *happens*. Regarding signatures, for example, Derrida asks: "Does the absolute singularity of an event of the signature ever occur? Are there signatures?" And answers: "Yes, of course, every day" ("Signature Event Context" ["SEC"], 328). And on the im/possibility of forgiveness? "God forgives Noah" (*The Gift of Death & Literature in Secret [GD]*, 150). Gifts are given, democracies run, and hospitality is offered. As Hägglund has it, the impossible happens all the time.

What all these arguments concerning transcendental possibilities and impossibilities articulate, when faced with the undeniable fact of happenings, is a dissociation of knowledge from being. That one cannot know if forgiveness is possible—even if one knows that it is impossible, at the same time that one knows it is possible—does not mean one cannot forgive. Which is to say, with a slightly different emphasis, the critical object of this thinking of the indissociability of possibility and impossibility is a metaphysics of truth grounded in the coincidence of being and thought. Derrida is attempting to articulate a "logic" without reference to truth understood as the transcendental content of thought, a logic without reference to truth as available in plentitude and self-identity, a logic without reference to "Being qua Being," that is, without "qua," without metaphysics. It is an im/possible task, and one whose effects should not be underestimated. This is not wordplay, which is sometimes the impression effected by Derrida's reflections on the impossibility of forgiveness, gifts, and so on. Instead, this total solicitation of fundamental metaphysical axioms—noncontradiction, the coincidence of thought and being—induces the terrifying possibility of a thinking without security, without truth. Not wordplay, but a rejection of the Aristotelian myth—which has been carried through the history of metaphysical thinking—of the unity of word and thing. That which cannot happen does, that which should happen does not, and knowledge has no governance over either case.

While I reject that Caputo's texts actually perform an understanding of the impossible as a futural exteriority—that is the gesture of the text, but a reading of the letter demonstrates that Caputo's equivocal play masks an underlying univocity between the possible and the impossible, wherein "the impossible" is a euphemism for the very possible—Hägglund's criticism is compelling on Caputo's terms. And to the extent that Hägglund has made explicit the complication of the possible and the impossible, he has contributed a positive development in the generalization of Derrida's specific arguments concerning hospitality, the gift, and so on. However, when arguing his case for radical atheism, Hägglund does not pursue this line of inquiry, and instead opts for a re-ontologization of deconstruction through a reinscription of a sharp distinction between the possible and impossible.

The problem arises when Hägglund makes his second argument for atheism. What makes his atheism radical, Hägglund says, is that it not only denies God's existence—which, as we have seen, is a claim on which Hägglund vacillates—but that it denies that God is desirable. For Hägglund, the two arguments are related in that the argument from desire follows the argument from temporalization. Hägglund argues that if everything that happens only happens insofar as it is subject to temporalization, then temporalization is the "ultratranscendental" condition for anything to happen. To desire a cessation of temporalization—to desire eternity—would be to deny and reject life, which can only be temporal: "Radical atheism proceeds from the argument that everything that can be desired is mortal in its essence . . . The absolute being of God is not only unattainable but undesirable, since it would annul the mortality that is integral to whatever one desires" (RA, 111). In *This Life (TL)*, Hägglund presents a version of this same argument, but now concerned more with "care" than "desire." Here, the argument is not only that to desire eternity is to desire death, but also that care is only possible given mortality: "Absolution is not only impossible to attain but also not a goal worthy of our striving, since it would remove the care that animates our lives" (TL, 47). If one were immortal, then there would be no need to take care to preserve life. It is for this reason that one can neither care for nor be cared for by an immortal God: if nothing happens to an immortal or eternal being, then such a being cannot care about what happens. Hägglund then proceeds to argue that such care, which is only possible given finitude, is that which motivates existential projects and commitments. Pursuing and preserving these commitments in the face of mortality is what Hägglund means by "secular faith": "Secular faith is a necessary uncertainty. In being committed to someone or something, I must have faith in the future and in those on whom I depend" (TL, 50). And so not only is desire possible only given mortality, but so too are care and faith.

An effect of the argument is a demonstration of the credibility of secular living. Hägglund makes this element of his argument explicit only once: "I take issue with the idea that there is an essential human need for something called 'religion' or 'the religious,' which a secular life will try in vain to fulfill" (TL, 55). By demonstrating a secular logic of desire, care, and faith, Hägglund has convincingly argued that these activities need not presuppose a prior religious orientation or commitment. This project's final chapter will argue for the possibility of convergence between secular and religious political projects, and this argument against the need for religious orientation will prove important to that effort. Hägglund's argument for the non-necessity of "religion" also functions as a welcome curb to the colonizing tendencies of apologetic theologies that seek to unveil the religious commitments of secular morality or that argue against the possibility of nonreligious morality.[54] Such a curbing will also be necessary for my later argument that Marx's atheism does not foreclose the possibility of a Marxist political theology.

Unfortunately, this strength is undermined when Hägglund ontologizes his argument. There is a difference in content and tone between an argument defending secularism and one advocating for atheism. While *This Life* tends to speak of the former, both it and *Radical Atheism* ultimately argue for a thoroughly ontologized atheism. Even the arguments concerning care, desire, and faith—which are apparently more existential than the obviously ontological argument concerning temporalization—presuppose the authority, the sovereignty, of temporalization: ultimately for Hägglund, desire for God is impossible because God is impossible because time does not allow God. In Hägglund's project, there is no time for God. This is subtly but crucially different from arguing against a need for religion, and it is with this move from a critique of religion to a critique of God that Hägglund reintroduces an "utterly deconstructible" ontology. Rather than dogmatically argue for theism against atheism, or even argue for the impossibility of atheism, as Marion has done, my concern is that such an ontologization undermines that which is truly radical in any deconstructive project: the dissociation of knowing and being.

Both of Hägglund's atheist arguments—from time and from care—are metaphysical in that they cohere to a logic of identity and imply a coincidence between knowing and being. Each version of the argument ultimately claims that desire is determined by knowledge. The argument from time runs like this: we can only desire what happens, and happening is made possible by temporalization. God, who would be eternal, cannot be—nothing eternal can be. Thus, God, who does not exist, cannot be desired. Hägglund's argument from care subtly differs but relies on the same basic logic: we cannot care about God because we cannot care for an eternal being, who would be free from vulnerability and lack. Thus, on the one hand, we cannot desire God because God does not exist. On the other hand, even if God did exist, we could not desire God, because God would be outside of the temporal structure of desire. Such an argument could be disputed on theological grounds—and grounds on which one might find Derrida, at least insofar as the aforementioned claim that "God forgives Noah" might be read as an attempt to temporalize God. Indeed, the possibility of God acting in and through history will be a major topic of the coming discussion concerning James Cone, and the possibility of understanding "eternity" differently than Hägglund will feature prominently in the discussion concerning Kierkegaard. These approaches will challenge Hägglund's understanding of theology as necessarily a metaphysics of the eternal.[55] For now, though, Hägglund's arguments can also be critiqued on his own deconstructive terms.

In both versions of his argument—time and care—Hägglund determines the possibility of desire by its adherence to a prior and exterior philosophical judgment. Either we cannot desire God because temporalization forbids it, or we cannot desire God because to do so would result in definitional absurdity. Implicit in both claims is the impossibility of desiring against knowledge: we cannot philosophically authorize desire, and so desire is rendered impossible. In this sense, Hägglund's logic of desire is traditional and metaphysical, it must cohere to independent philosophical judgment. For Hägglund, only the philosophically possible can be desired. Indeed, for Hägglund, such a qualifier is unnecessary: the philosophically possible—that which coheres to a philosophical argument concerning time or care—*is* the possible. Which is to say, there is no longer a gap in Hägglund's argument between thinking and being: desire cannot *be* if *thinking* shows it impossible.

What is lost in this reduction of the object of desire to the possible-as-determined-by-thought is Hägglund's earlier thinking concerning the coincidence of the possible and the impossible. In response to *Radical Atheism*, Naas asks if it might "not make more sense to talk about an aporia or denegation of desire" ("AA," 61). That is, wouldn't it make more sense—at least, wouldn't it be more consistent with Hägglund's own deconstructive project—to speak of a coincidence of the desirable and the undesirable? Much as how the only true gift is the gift that isn't, might not the only true object of desire be that which is, fully and completely, undesirable?

The argument is Derrida's. If the debate between Hägglund and Caputo ultimately concerns how to best read Derrida on the related questions of desire, impossibility, and God, then it would perhaps be helpful to read Derrida on the matter:

> What I am interested in is the experience of the desire for the impossible. That is, the impossible as the condition of desire. Desire is not perhaps the best word. I mean this quest in which we want to give, even when we realize, when we agree, if we

> agree, that the gift, that giving, is impossible, that it is a process of reappropriation and self-destruction. Nevertheless, we do not give up the dream of the pure gift . . . We continue to desire, to dream, through the impossible. The impossible for me is not a negative concept." ("On the Gift" ["OTG"], 72)[56]

Derrida is clear here that there is no opposition between desire and the impossible. Against Hägglund's interpretation, the knowledge of impossibility does not prevent the desire of being: we know that a gift is impossible, yet we still desire one. While Derrida is circumspect concerning the possibility of real gifts given, his comments on the reality of forgiveness, signatures, and hospitalities suggest that these comments could be extended: not only is desire of the impossible possible, but so too is an impossible desire possible. Derrida's argument here is not the basic phenomenological or anthropological one that people *do* desire God or pure gifts. To this point, Hägglund argues that such purported desires for eternity are actually dissimulated desires for survival.[57] Derrida might well share these suspicions about purported desire for God. As the previous section argued, such desires would be subject to deconstructive (and Augustinian) solicitations of the referent of desire: one could always ask, "What does 'God' mean when you say you desire God?" To this extent, a Derridean critique of transcendental signifieds would also suggest Hägglund's conclusions concerning dissimulation. However, this is not what Derrida is doing here: he is arguing that the impossible makes desire possible. Derrida speaks of desire, which is "perhaps not the best word" for what he is after, as occurring "through" the impossible. Such an understanding of desire as occurring through and made possible by the impossible also implicitly critiques Caputo's project, where desire is primarily *for* the impossible—at least, ostensibly. This desire-made-possible-by-the-impossible brings us closer to Kierkegaard's absurd faith than it does either Hägglund's secular faith or Caputo's religious atheism.

Such a faith is absurd in that it is a faith without reference to truth, perhaps without a referent at all. Still on the topic of the gift, Derrida writes:

> The gift is totally foreign to the horizon of economy, ontology, knowledge, constative statements, and theoretical determination and judgment . . . The gift, I would claim, I would argue, as such cannot be known; as soon as you know it, you destroy it. So the gift as such is impossible. I insist on the "as such." I will explain why in a moment. The gift as such cannot be known, but it can be thought of. We can think what we cannot know.

Perhaps thinking is not the right word. But there is something in excess of knowledge. ("OTG," 60)

And elsewhere, in a discussion explicitly about Caputo's work, Derrida grants that whether or not God or khora is prior is ultimately undecidable, but argues that this undecidability is of a certain type:

> To be in undecidability does not mean simply that I don't know. It means, firstly, that it does not belong to the order of knowledge and, secondly, that I don't want to know. I know that I should not know. If I could rely on this translatability there would be no God anymore. Now, when the God comes, when the Messiah comes, we will see! But I cannot foresee and program this. That is why I am an atheist in a certain way—a faithful one! I am faithful to this sort of atheism. So I agree with Jack Caputo when he says there is this undecidability, but to say that there is such undecidability doesn't mean that the two terms are replaceable one for the other. ("The Becoming Possible of the Impossible" ["BPI"], 50)

The claim disputes Hägglund's account on two points. First, Hägglund does not argue that whether or not God or khora is prior is an undecidable question. For Hägglund, khora—which he thinks of as temporalization—must always be prior. God is only ever an effect, only ever "God." Second, Derrida displaces the privileged place that Hägglund accords to knowledge. Whereas Hägglund determines the question of God on the grounds of knowing, Derrida claims that the question "does not belong to the order of knowledge." This critique of knowledge is consistent with the previous citation, wherein Derrida associates knowledge with "the as such"—indeed, it is a point on which he "insists." The "as such," the possibility of a signified, the possibility of knowledge, the coincidence of thinking and being, all effaced by Derrida's account of generalized writing, all of this does not belong to the question.

The Decision of the Other

So far, I have argued that Derrida's account of generalized writing renders theology not only impossible, but also antagonistic to the deconstructive project. This impossibility and this antagonism are the effect of the critique of the theological structure of truth that harbors a coincidence of thinking and being in the assured self-presence of a transcendental signified. Rejecting the possibility of any transcendental signified, then, also affects a rejection of any structure of truth that depends on the theologeme of the logos as exteriority of truth.

Hägglund and Caputo then offer two competing—at least, allegedly competing—responses to this critique of theology. Hägglund looks to radicalize the critique of theology by making of it a critique also of God. Caputo, on the other hand, believes that deconstruction is motivated by the same passion for the impossible as religion, and so argues that deconstruction is "structured like a religion." The disputed point in this debate was found to be the interpretation of "the impossible." For Hägglund, God is impossible because all that is is subject to the laws of temporalization. In this sense, the impossible *happens,* because it is constantly governing the possible. For Caputo, on the other hand, the impossible is that which deconstruction/religion strive for and are motivated by.

Each of these understandings of the impossible ultimately fails because it presupposes a coincidence between thinking and being. For Hägglund, that which is possible is determined by philosophical argumentation. His is an idealism that ignores the possibility of not only desiring the impossible, but also the possibility of impossible desire. If thinking knows something to be impossible, then it cannot be. For Caputo, the impossible—for all of its "poetic" charge—turns out to obey a priori considerations of both philosophy (there can be no incarnation) and politics (the reference to tax codes). By equivocating between "God" and "khora" as respective referents of "the impossible," but also simultaneously rendering the impossible an object of rationalist bourgeois reflection, Caputo rewrites religion as a structural atheism devoid of any radical political potential. For Caputo, the impossible is only that which thought renders possible.

And so each response shirks the theoretically and politically radical consequences of dissociating thinking and being. From the moment he denies the possibility of a transcendental signified, this dissociation is implicit in Derrida's work. The effects of such a dissociation are perhaps most pronounced in precisely the place Hägglund and Caputo ignore them: religion. Whereas Hägglund prioritizes khora—or *différance,* or temporalization—over God, and whereas Caputo renders the terms interchangeable, although in an interchangeability governed by the privilege of khora, Derrida insists that the question as to the priority of God or khora remains necessarily undecidable. The answer to the question cannot be known because knowledge itself imposes a theological regime of truth. Knowing and truth beg the question: to speak of knowing the answer to this question, to even speak of knowing the question, to speak of the truth of God or the truth of atheism, is already to stack the deck with theologemes.

In this sense, Derrida is in agreement with the transcendental theologians who speak of knowing as constitutively ordered toward God. But this is, for Derrida, all the more problematic for theology and for knowledge. Indeed, it is with this recognition of the theological structure of truth that Derrida presents theology with its biggest challenge. The question of whether or not this ordering toward God is an effect of language or an effect of God is ultimately undecidable. More precisely, every possible answer to this question, and indeed even the structure of the question itself, is "undecidable" in that the meaning and intention of every question and every answer is ultimately indeterminable. Before deciding whether or not God or *différance* is prior, one would have to determine what is meant by God and by *différance*. But this is precisely the impossibility articulated by Derrida's generalized account of writing. One cannot determine the relative privilege of God or *différance* not only because to do so would be to claim direct access to the truth of being, but also more immediately because to do so would be to impossibly determine the meaning of God and *différance*, it would be to make of them transcendental signifieds, that is, ideological gestures.

Of course, while rendering both God and *différance* undecidable and indeterminable, Derrida has also brought the two unimaginably close together. The gap between God and khora is as small as the gap that constitutes itself in the repetition of the same. This is difference at its most basic: the difference constitutive of any identity. It is the recognition of both this non-dialectical, irreducible difference and this amazing proximity between God and khora that leads Kearney to write:

> There is, after all, a fundamental decision to be made between reading the desert place as khora or as God. Even if that choice is never final or assured. For if the theist does choose God it is always in fear and trembling and can never be more than a hair's breadth from the underlying, undecidable abyss of khora—a common pre-original void from which faith issues and from which it is never definitively removed, to its dying day. Indeed, were it so definitively removed it would no longer be faith. (*SGM*, 210)

And it is what leads Derrida to write that "sometimes you have to be an atheist of this sort," the sort outlined here, the sort that cannot determine what it means by atheism and what it means by the "theism" of its own atheism, "if one is to be true to faith" (12).[58] Faith and atheism become not only undecidable, but also now indissociable. The dissociation of thinking and being affects the indissociability of atheism and faith. Derrida, then, helps us rigorously think the conditions of im/possibility of religious decision. God or khora—it is radically undecidable. At the same time, it is with the dissociation of thinking and being—that is, it is with the making impossible of theology—that the possibility of religious decision is freed from the very a priori metaphysical determination that renders decision impossible by ideologically deciding everything in advance.

And so a careful following of the effects of deconstruction leads to a perhaps surprising result, which is all the more surprising when juxtaposed with Schmitt's political theology. Schmitt claims to be a theorist of decision, and is, but only in the sense that his true decision is not theological nor metaphysical, but rather political. Wherever Schmitt writes metaphysics—which is everywhere he pretends to describe the natural order of things—one should only ever read an ideological obfuscation of fascism. Schmitt identifies thinking and being, and so the product of his thought is identified with the ontological truth that is always ostensibly decided in advance without concern for actual decisions—at least, this holds until a further turn of the screw is applied and Schmitt's ontology is itself found out to hide his real decisions. Derrida, on the other hand, shows the ways in which metaphysics always harbors the theological motif of truth as guarantor of the identity of thinking and being, and demonstrates that this theologeme is always an actual impossibility. There is no outside text, there is no and has never been any transcendental signified, all metaphysics is a fake. In this sense, Derrida makes a religious decision entirely impossible. Yet, the impossible is no longer governed by the metaphysical law of noncontradiction. The relationship between the possible and the impossible is no longer one of antagonism, but is rather, more strongly, one of mutual constitution. In terms of religious decision, this mutuality of possibility and impossibility has the following effect: a decision for God is only possible when God, theology, and truth are rendered impossible, because without this impossibility the ontological identity of thought and being decides everything in advance and so renders decision impossible. Thus, the Derridean discourse concerning religion is neither affirmative as Caputo has it, nor prohibitive as Hägglund has it, but instead reveals the ways in which affirmation and prohibition mutually and paradoxically inform and make each other possible, even as, and only as, they render each other impossible. A decision for God requires that God no longer secures the truth of thought—such a decision for the transcendent and sovereign truth can only ever follow the ideological structure of metaphysical decision; that is, it can only ever be an obfuscation of some prior material commitment. For Caputo, this commitment is to a certain left-of-center bourgeois rationalism. For Hägglund, an Enlightenment-era fidelity to the governing power of philosophy, and so, ultimately, to the entire history of idealist political philosophy that attempts to dictate being by the mandates of thought.

None of which answers the question as to what a religion without the (false, ideological) security of metaphysics and truth could or might look like. For that, the project's next three chapters offer various possibilities. In each case, the sort of ideological decisionism demonstrated by Schmitt will be avoided and the sort of groundless decision without truth effected by deconstruction will be promoted. With Karl Ove Knausgaard, we will see that the question of religious decision, so long as religion is to remain actually possible, can always earnestly and coherently be answered in the negative; that is, God can actually be rejected. With Kierkegaard, we will see the articulation of a different sort of truth, one not grounded in ontological identity but in orthopraxic actuality. Finally, with Cone, we will see that this orthopraxic actuality—and the revolutionary impulse that Cone receives from the prophetic Christian tradition—itself becomes the measure of truth: truth, in this non-metaphysical sense, is primarily a political, not philosophical, gesture. Importantly, in all these cases religious decision is affirmed or denied in actual, material reality. The paradox that possibility and impossibility are mutually constitutive and not mutually exclusive of one another is basic, and no further epistemic, ontological, metaphysical, or logical synthesis of these two positions is possible. Paradox, especially understood in this Derridean sense of the priority of difference over identity, is fundamental and not derivative of self-same substance. And so any political-theological engagement response to the deconstruction of metaphysics cannot look to resolve this paradox into more basic components, because these more basic components do not exist. Instead, a political theology responsive to this Derridean deconstruction must take place in lived reality, in text, not outside of it. In other words, that meaning and truth cannot be known does not mean that decisions are avoidable—indeed, they are unavoidable.

And while this chapter has not been concerned with Derrida's biographical choice for or against God but with the effects of his critique of metaphysics for political theology, it is the case that Jacques Derrida the person subscribed to some form of this materialist response to the aporetics of non-metaphysical decision. In his haunting essay "A Silkworm of One's Own (Points of View Stitched on the Other Veil)," Derrida develops a relationship to religion that is not ordered on the logic of "the veil," the metaphysical (and Heideggerian) logic of veiling and unveiling truth, but instead of "the shawl," a *textile*: "My reference cloth was neither a veil nor a canvas, but a shawl. A prayer shawl I like to touch more than to see, to caress every day, to kiss without even opening my eyes or even when it remains wrapped in a paper bag into which I stick my hand at night, eyes closed . . . It veils or hides nothing, it shows or announces no Thing, it promises the intuition of nothing" (19).[59] The shawl is "without truth, or veracity, or veridicity, without the slightest promised reappropriation" (48). No Aristotelian return to unity, no Schmittian God of the transcendent, but a thing in a bag that he touches darkly. The rest of Derrida's discussion deserves to be quoted at length:

> Mine was white first, completely white, only white, virgin and without those black or blue stripes that are printed, it seems to me, on almost all the talliths in the world. It was in any case the only white tallith in my family. It was given to me by my mother's father, Moses. Like a sign of having been chosen. But why? I say it was white because with time it is going a little yellow. I do not know why, but after I left the house in El Biar where I had left it, my father borrowed it from me for a few years. It is true that he still had reason to wear it, and he took it across the Mediterranean at the time of the exodus. After his death, I took it back as though I were inheriting it a second time. I hardly ever wear it (is wear the right word? Do you wear this thing? Does it need it? Does it not carry off before being worn?) So I no longer wear it. I simply place my fingers or lips on it, almost every evening, except when I'm traveling to the ends of the earth, because like an animal it waits for me, well hidden in its hiding place, at home, it never travels. I touch it without knowing what I am doing or asking in so doing, especially not knowing into whose hands I am entrusting myself, to whom I'm rendering thanks . . . What will become of the one my grandfather had given me if he did not know what he was doing when he chose a white one, and if he chose

me for the choice of this white tallith? The decision is not yet taken, and will not be mine: ashes after fire? Earth? Virgin soil with a burial in the white tallith? I ought to have pretended to dictate this decision, but I have suspended it designedly. I have decided that the decision would not be mine, I have decided to dictate nothing as to my death. Giving myself up thus to the truth of the decision: a verdict is always of the other. Life will have been so short and someone is saying to me, close to me, inside me, something like: "It is forbidden to be old." (19/20)

And so Derrida relates to his shawl with neither theological affirmation nor atheistic prohibition but with a recognition of ignorance, and a faith in, a "giving myself up" to, a senseless materiality. His tallith, we are told, is yellow with age. It was only ever white, "pure," according to the witness of Moses. He does not know why he touches it, he does not know to whom his touch is addressed—Moses, God, nobody at all—he does not even know if he wears it, this animal thing that was given to him from before his birth, by someone who "did not know what he was doing." The tallith is not the source of intelligible theologizing, it grounds no identity between thinking and being because it cannot be thought and the "truth" of its being is permanently indeterminable—which is to say, not deferred, but more simply not. The tallith is a stained thing of which Derrida cannot be rid. Without knowledge, without identity, without truth, Derrida's tallith is with him, unavoidably, inexplicably, until the end.

Chapter Three

Belonging to the World
Karl Ove Knausgaard's Secular Love

Introduction

And so the possibility that Martin Hägglund is right—that there is no God and that there can be no God, that deconstruction requires atheism, that the deconstruction of the transcendental signified is the deconstruction of God—must be defended from a religious point of view: without an atheist deconstruction of theology and metaphysics (the two are the same), no religious faith is possible. Indeed, as the previous chapter suggested, anyone interested in believing in God should *hope* that Hägglund is right. If theology is not deconstructed, then it remains metaphysical. But if theology remains metaphysical, then any theological decision can only ever be ideological: there is no metaphysical decision because there is no metaphysics. On the other hand, the deconstruction of metaphysics, in its very rendering impossible of theology, frees us from the fetters of the (theo)logic that identifies thinking and being. Now thought of as modes of difference and not as concepts situated within a transcendental schema, possibility and impossibility show themselves to mutually constitute, not mutually exclude, each other. And so the impossibility of theology—which effects the impossibility of metaphysics—becomes a necessary condition for the possibility of faith, which is only possible without the ontological necessities of metaphysics.

But any talk of conditions of possibility should be immediately restrained by the complete impossibility of theology—which means that theology's impossibility should be taken in the strongest sense possible.

Elsewise, there is a risk of a sort of conceptual imperialism in the claim that the deconstruction of theology becomes a condition for the possibility of faith. Without a strong—or as Hägglund would have it, a radical—commitment to the impossibility of theology, all of the deconstructive insights effected by the critique of theology are lost. If the "impossibility" of theology is interpreted and sublated by a "higher" theologizing hermeneutic, then theology is "impossible" only in the sense that it is necessary, and so has nothing to do with possibility at all. This reinscription of theology as always already overcoming and sublating its own negation, perhaps Christianized by a metaphorical reading of the death and resurrection of Jesus as the death and resurrection of ontotheology, would reassert a higher metaphysics on the back of the discourse, deconstruction, that renders metaphysics obsolete.

Which is to say, faith must recognize the *necessary possibility* that Hägglund is right—that there is no God, that deconstruction is the deconstruction of God, and that the absolute annihilation brought by death is the inescapable and mute horizon of life. Right without qualification: theology is impossible and metaphysics is only ever a textual invention with no ontological relationship to its own object of study, Being, at all. More materially, this philosophical recognition implies the concomitant existential recognition that one can always decide against God and against religion. With thinking and being dissociated, the actual, existential decision for or against God cannot be grounded in ontological truth claims, because the truth of metaphysics and the actuality of being have nothing to do with each other. As an irreducible and basic option, then, the decision against God can only be prevented or occluded through violence.

Anglican theologian John Milbank's "radical orthodoxy" project risks this violence. Whereas the debate between Hägglund and Caputo concerned the difference between theism and atheism, Milbank's concern maps more neatly onto the distinction between religion and secularism. His basic argument is that "secular reason" is not a neutral procedure that has freed itself from religious contamination. Rather, Milbank argues, contemporary secularism is itself a type of explicitly anti-Christian, and so heretical, theology. Although his genealogy is complex, Milbank typically claims that medieval nominalism—especially as found in Duns Scotus's conceptualization of the univocity of being—is responsible for a "horizontal" leveling of the "vertical" difference between God and humans. This leveling then made possible the secular rejection of transcendence. Secular reason sees this rejection of transcendence as both a mature and an emancipatory act: the secular person—and Milbank's *Theology and Social Theory* provides intricate readings of many such or allegedly secular social theorists and philosophers, including Weber, Durkheim, Kant, Hegel, Marx, and Derrida—maturely rejects the juvenile myths of the divine and, in doing so, reveals that humankind is not hierarchically subservient to a transcendent divine master. Milbank argues that this emancipatory argument relies on a sometimes implicit and sometimes explicit identification of difference and violence.

According to Milbank, the notion that a rejection of hierarchical difference is itself emancipatory is only sensible if hierarchical difference is thought of as oppressive or violent. But, according to Milbank, this identification of transcendence with violence and the subsequent rejection of transcendence can only ever lead to nihilism. Although he occasionally states and appears to endorse the point, Milbank's general argument here is not simply that immanentism necessarily leads to nihilism because it lacks the semantic security of a transcendental signified. More subtly, Milbank argues that the secular and "postmodern"—he reads figures as diverse as Deleuze, Derrida, Baudrillard, and Lacan as "neo-Nietzschean" "postmoderns"—identification of difference with violence is itself nihilistic because it accepts violence as primordially and necessarily the case. It is only theology, and specifically only Christian Trinitarian theology with its conceptualization of difference as peaceful, loving, and harmonious, that can offer an alternative to secular nihilism: "Only Christian theology now offers a discourse able to position and overcome nihilism itself. This is why it is so important to reassert theology as a master discourse; theology, alone, remains the discourse of non-mastery" (*Theology and Social Theory [TST]*, 6).[1]

The upshot of Milbank's argument is that secularism, in its alleged attempts to present an "autonomous secular realm, completely transparent to rational understanding" (*TST*, 1), has come into conflict with "the critical non-avoidability of the theological and the metaphysical" (*TST*, 2). For Milbank, there is no such thing as the non-theological, there are only good and bad theologies. In other words, theological and metaphysical thinking are unavoidable, and so any attempt to avoid the two can only lead to "violence." Of course, part of Milbank's argument is that secularism considers violence a basic phenomenon, and so an accusation of violence would not be troubling to a secular theorist. Because of this, Milbank describes his task as one of constructing a Christian "metanarrative" that is "persuasive" to secular people. Secularism, for Milbank, "is only a mythos, and therefore cannot be refuted, but only out-narrated, if we can persuade people—for reasons of 'literary taste'—that Christianity offers a much better story" (*TST*, 331).

Milbank's presentation leaves much to be desired. It has been critiqued for its Islamophobia,[2] its cultural imperialism,[3] its interpretation of its own major theological antagonist,[4] and its interpretations of its own major sociological antagonists.[5] More directly, *Theology and Social Theory* has failed on its own grounds. If Milbank wished to "persuade" social theorists of their implicit heretical theology and so convince them of the superiority of orthodox Christian theology, then he has unquestionably failed. *Theology and Social Theory* has never been reviewed in any of the American Sociological Association's several journals. Nor does Milbank's name appear as a serious interlocutor in the work of any contemporary social theorist or in any standard handbook.[6] If persuasion is Milbank's measure of success, and if "this book is addressed to both social theorists and theologians" (*TST*, 1), then the book has succeeded in neither convincing of its argumentative goal nor in reaching its desired audience.

For these reasons, and others, it might be time to finally let go of Milbank's theological project. Indeed, he himself seems to have let go of the necessity to theologically situate every discourse. Milbank's recent critiques of capital, for example, do not feign any theological grounding.[7] However, Milbank's argument concerning the Christianly informed nature of secularism—unintentionally bolstered by Charles Taylor's *A Secular Age*, which also finds in secularism a sort of perverted theology—is still influential in theological discourses of "post-secularism"[8] and "political Augustinianism."[9] And more to the point of this project, Milbank's rendering universal of theology—both secularism and religion are theological—makes theology metaphysically necessary; which is to say, Milbank renders theology entirely ideological.

Against Milbank, this chapter defends secularism as a credible and relatively independent discourse and way of life. Its independence is only relative because, as Milbank demonstrates, secularism *does* draw from theological language and religious practice. But a non-imperial response to these moments should be: so what? Europe in many ways evolved with Christianities (as well as Islams, of course), and so it is not surprising that ideas common in Europe today were articulated by Christians in years past.[10] This is not an argument for the unavoidability of theology or the universality of Christian truth. It is only evidence of some bare minimal continuity of culture.[11] To most social scientists, of course, this claim—that one does not need to believe in God and that theology is not necessary—is not controversial. But Milbank is clear that social scientific arguments do not hold sway over his program. Instead, he is interested in constructing a narrative with high "literary taste." And so it is to the work of contemporary Norwegian novelist and essayist Karl Ove Knausgaard, who does have high literary taste, that this chapter turns. Knausgaard offers a response to Milbank on at least two fronts. First, Knausgaard provides a compelling "narrative" of secular life that is aware of its own Christian heritage while remaining decisively atheistic. Second, Knausgaard performs a critique of Milbank's identification of secularism with nihilism and violence; indeed, it is precisely because there is no God that, for Knausgaard, this life has meaning at all.

Knausgaard is primarily known for his six-volume autofictional novel *My Struggle* (*Min kamp*—the reason for the proximity to Hitler's *Mein Kampf* is not addressed until volume six and will be discussed toward the end of this chapter).[12] The novel, which is over 3,600 pages long, has drawn comparisons to Proust's *À la recherche du temps perdu*,[13] and has been translated into at least thirty-five languages. Knausgaard has followed *My Struggle* with his Seasons Quartet, four texts—*Autumn, Winter, Spring,* and *Summer*—that stray from *My Struggle* in both form and content.[14] Knausgaard's "struggle" in *My Struggle* is multiple—the death of his father, parenting, love, childhood, sexuality, writing—but typically concerns Knausgaard's psyche. They are, he says, books about the inner life. It is this Knausgaard—Knausgaard as keen observer of himself—that has solicited the comparison with Proust. In the Seasons Quartet, on the other hand, Knausgaard turns his gaze outward: with the exception of *Spring*, each of these novels consist of short reflections not (immediately or obviously) on himself but on "objects" Knausgaard encounters in his daily life—winter boots, coins, the brain, labia, but also fainting, intelligence, Vincent van Gogh, and so on. More recently, Knausgaard has produced works on the twentieth-century Norwegian painter Edvard Munch[15] and on soccer.[16] The two sets of texts—*My Struggle* on the one hand, the Seasons Quartet, Munch, and soccer on the other—relate to each other, Knausgaard says, like Dostoevsky to Tolstoy.

Despite their differences, these two sets are each occupied by the im/possibility of belonging to the world. That is, Knausgaard, in nearly every text, describes himself as outside of life, as outside of the world. In doing so, Knausgaard articulates a structure that is near opposite to what is classically considered the religious problem. Knausgaard does not find himself stuck in the world and hoping to transcend it. Rather, he finds himself stuck in the world as always already a bit out of the world. Although not widely celebrated, the theme of permanent exile is a Derridean one,[17] and so Knausgaard can be read as pursuing a strand of Derridean thought radically other to those pursued by either Hägglund or Caputo. In that Knausgaard resists a religious interpretation of this development, he can also be read as pursuing a Derridean response to Milbank's categorization of Derrida as violent nihilist.

Nature, Society, Infancy, and Walpurgis Night

This desire to be in the midst of the world is expressed throughout his oeuvre, but is perhaps nowhere articulated as well as when Knausgaard recalls a recent Walpurgis Night celebration. The cathartic passage comes toward the end of *Spring*, which is written as an extended note to his newborn daughter and is primarily about her mother's debilitating depression. Here, the existential themes of *My Struggle* and the phenomenological reflections of the Season Quartet collide, and Knausgaard comes to find the two strands inseparable:

> One moment I saw the flag, heard the march, saw the little parade of people, all of it gathered into one whole beneath the darkening sky in an agricultural landscape that opened up in every direction, while the sun hung like a reddish ball behind a veil of haze in the west, and then it felt as if something lifted inside me, a feeling that we were here, now, that this was our time. Then, in the next instant, I saw the idiotic handcart with its ugly sound system, the tracksuit bottoms, the all-weather jackets, the heads that seemed shrunken inside their caps, big nodes, little eyes, fat cheeks, the old people trying to keep time to the music with stiff, faintly dragging steps, the smell of fertilizer, which was really the smell of shit, the hair of the woman in front of me, which a breath of wind flung across her face and which she couldn't quite get back into place, she tried once, but it blew back, and then again with an annoyed jerk of her hand, the father who shouted a reprimand to his daughter. (*Spring*, 174)

The unity and cohesion that Knausgaard initially describes—and it is a unity not only with his fellow celebrants, but more strongly is also that between nature and society, where the landscape and the parade seem to reinforce each other—leads to what will become one of his favorite motifs: the replacement of the "I" with the "we." The "something" that "lifted inside *me,*" is a "feeling" that "this was *our* time." This collapse of the self into the community and of the community into nature, which is an experience for which Knausgaard longs, though, immediately gives way to distance. The "idiotic handcart" pulls Knausgaard out of his immersion, and he resorts to description of—as opposed to identification with—those around him. He retreats from participant to spectator.

The turn from participation to description undoes both senses of unity mentioned above. Not only is Knausgaard removed from those around him, but he also no longer sees natural and social phenomena as convergent: "The triviality of the ketchup and mustard bottles, the blackened hot dogs, the camping table where the soft drinks were lined up, was almost inconceivable there beneath the stars, in the dancing light of the bonfire. It was as if I was standing in a banal world and gazing into a magical one, as if our lives played out in the borderland between two parallel realities" (174). This is a sense of "borderland" is radically opposed to Schmitt's. Whereas Schmitt spoke of the border as the place that separated the pure from the impure and the sovereign from his subjects, and so spoke of the border as a place worth defending, Knausgaard laments his border position. The border becomes a place of separation, and it is a separation that Knausgaard continually longs to overcome. Although Knausgaard's brief valorization of "the flag" might imply a nationalism at home with Schmitt, this impression is misleading: the celebration is taking place in Sweden, and so the flag is foreign to, not representative of, the Norwegian Knausgaard. The reverence for this foreign flag suggests that Knausgaard's true desire is not national belonging, but rather a desire for the quotidian and familial belonging made possible by this Swedish celebration. That is, the "we" that lifts inside him is not a national collective, but is the very particular and irreplaceable "collective" of him and his daughter, and of all the other families and irreplaceable bonds around him. Such an embrace of quotidian and common familial love could not be further from Schmitt's project, which explicitly rejects the common.

So far, Knausgaard could be read as a sort of romantic writer: he wishes for unity and belonging, valorizes the sublimity of nature, and bemoans his distance from it. This romanticism would be accented only by an equal longing for and valorization of immediate quotidian experience (and so Knausgaard would be a romantic with a Scandinavian accent). But Knausgaard is not a romantic. After noting the gap between himself and others, and noting the gap between nature and society, Knausgaard makes the dialectical move of including this gap into the thing itself:

> We come from far away, from terrifying beauty, for a newborn child who opens its eyes for the first time is like a star, is like a sun, but we live our lives amid pettiness and stupidity, in the world of burned hot dogs and wobbly camping tables. The great and terrifying beauty does not abandon us, it is there all the time, in everything that is always the same, in the sun and the stars, in the bonfire and the darkness, in the blue carpet of flowers beneath the tree. It is of no use to us, it is too big for us, but we can look at it, and we can bow before it. (*Spring*, 175)

The beauty that he longs for as distant from daily life is not, in fact, distant. This beauty "does not abandon us" but is "there all the time." What has changed in the move from unity to distance is not an ontological adjustment in the status of the presence of beauty, but instead the mode in which beauty presents itself. At first, Knausgaard experiences a unity with beauty—and it is a unity both within the social realm and between the social and the natural. Then, these unities are undone by the gritty banality of daily life: hot dogs, camping tables, and angry fathers. However, Knausgaard does not read this distancing in a Kantian manner, wherein the thing itself—social unity, natural beauty—would be kept off limits due to Knausgaard's particular apperceptive limits. Rather, Knausgaard makes the more Hegelian move of sublating this distance and otherness into the thing itself: distance and otherness do not prevent experience of the beauty of nature and of social belonging; rather, distance and otherness are constitutive of any experience of the beauty of nature and of social belonging. To experience social belonging as fleeting is to experience social belonging; to experience the beauty of nature as alien is to experience the beauty of nature—and so, contra Milbank, an entirely immanent difference is read not as violent, but as constitutive of beauty.

Which is not to say that this incorporation of difference means that longing for immediacy is negated. The longing remains, but Knausgaard recognizes that the immediacy for which he longs—to be in the world, to be present to himself—is not a longing for a return to an originary state. After declaring that one could bow to the inaccessible and terrifying beauty that is both set off against and always found concomitantly with daily life, Knausgaard does not bow to the heavens, but to his daughter: "I stood there for a long time, looking at all the people standing about in the dusk, talking and laughing, the children scampering between them, the orange flames of the bonfire stretching into the darkness. When I bent down over you, tears were running down my cheeks. You smiled as you saw my face approaching, because you didn't know what tears were either" (*Spring*, 175). This is Knausgaard at the height of his artistic struggle. In mere moments—and surely, as is typically the case with Knausgaard, the act of reading must take more time than had elapsed in the "original" experience of which Knausgaard writes, and this temporal asymmetry must imply that Knausgaard's memorialization of the phenomena is adding more noematic content than was originally intuited—Knausgaard has approached a romantic unity both within the social order and between society and nature, has found this unity effaced by the grittiness of a burnt hot dog, has sublated this effacement into nature itself, and then, finally, has turned, with tears, away from it all, toward his daughter.

What makes Knausgaard's work so fascinating—and that his often meandering and unstylish prose has no apparent right to fascinate has been commented on at length—is precisely this tearful turn to his daughter. To read this turn as Knausgaard giving up on his dream of belonging—or as a conservative turn toward the familial and quotidian and away from the theoretical and utopian—would be a mistake. Knausgaard never stops desiring immediate belonging. What Knausgaard describes is a desire for the banal and the magical to cohere. He wants to not "stand there for a long time, looking at the people talking and laughing," but wants to be one of the people talking and laughing, absorbing and belonging to the night immediately. To share this absorption with his daughter—for him and his daughter to experience the night together as a "we"—is an irreplaceable part of this desire. Knausgaard wants nothing more than to laugh with his child. That he discovers a constitutive gap in experience, and so discovers the impossibility of immediacy, does not diminish Knausgaard's desire: he turns to her and cries because there is a permanent distance, which he will never stop wanting to overcome.

Crucial here is that Knausgaard does not fantasize that his daughter reinscribes some state of fullness or completion. Her lack of knowledge prevents this. On the one hand, the daughter's ignorance—that she does not know what tears are—saves her from sharing her father's realization that simple unity and belonging are impossible, that to belong is always also to not belong, or that to belong is to belong as not belonging. On the other hand, the very thing that saves her is that which makes it impossible for her to recognize her own salvation. Her ignorance is bliss, but this is a bliss that doesn't know its own father. Much as he sublated the gap between culture and nature into culture and nature themselves, Knausgaard here makes ignorance of salvation constitutive of salvation itself. His daughter is saved from tears, but only because she does not know them. To be saved is to not know it; to be is not to know.

Materialism, Life, and Death

This turn to his daughter is just one of the ways that Knausgaard responds to his desire for belonging. As a solution to a problem, the appeal fails: if what Knausgaard wants is immediate belonging, he cannot find it through children. He is not a child and they themselves present an immediate belonging only of an unknowing kind: to belong in this infantile sense would not satisfy any desire for belonging, precisely because such a belonging would efface knowledge and so also knowledge of the desire as such. As Hägglund argued relative to God in the last chapter, this belonging would be indistinguishable from death—which does not mean that Knausgaard does not desire it. Unlike Hägglund, though, Knausgaard does not operate from within a strict distinction of finitude on the one hand and infinitude/death on the other. Whereas Hägglund opposes death to life on the grounds of desire—recall that, for Hägglund, we can only desire the mortal, finite, and living—Knausgaard is quick to describe the immanence of death to life. This immanence is not meant to be figurative. Knausgaard does not argue that death and finitude give meaning to life, that life would be without struggle and purpose if it did not expire, but more radically that life and death are modes of the same material substrate. The two are indissociable in a very real sense:

> The abyss is inside us. I saw it the first time I stood in front of a dead body. I didn't understand it, but I saw it and knew. Death is not the abyss, but exists in the living, in the space between our thoughts and the flesh through which they pass. In the flesh, thoughts are a kind of intruder, conquerors of a foreign land, who leave it just as quickly again the moment it becomes inhospitable, which is to say when all movements cease and all warmth seeps away, as it does in death. (*My Struggle [MS]*, 6:177)

Knausgaard here reflects on a new type of belonging: a mute materialism. Whereas infantile belonging is without both existence and nonexistence, and so is ontologically indeterminate, flesh is here conceived as being without thought. Even to speak of flesh is misleading: Knausgaard's argument is that the matter of living beings and the matter of inanimate objects is the same. The difference between the two—that which makes matter flesh—is the fleeting and ephemeral "warmth" of life, which temporarily colonizes matter as a conqueror. What these passages articulate is not just that flesh once was and once will be again dead matter, but that life is always already composed of mute, nonliving matter.[18] Even those organs that are essential for life are themselves quite unknown and alien to this very life that they allow: "the dismal gray twins that are these lungs, we are unthinkable without them, yet they live within themselves and do not know us, for they know no one, and the muscles cannot tell if their twitching occurs in someone dead or someone alive" (*MS*, 6:702). Muscle is muscle with or without the life that it animates and that animates it. Complementarily, this life can seemingly persist with or without any particular organ. Particularity does not matter, the body is not jealous: "We may feel the heart to be ours, but if our heart should falter, it has been shown that we can insert a new one, from a dead person, and go on living" (*MS*, 6:702). And not only can the body's alien inside be replaced, but the body can also internalize what is foreign, and make its own what is typically thought of as its other: "Nothing that enters the baby, mostly milk but also a little mashed banana and potato, bears the slightest resemblance to teeth, which in contrast to the food are hard. Yet this must be what happens—that certain substances are extracted from this partly liquid, partly soft nourishment and transported to the jaws, where they are assembled into the material used to make teeth" (*Autumn*, 23). Knausgaard's point here, as elsewhere, is that a sort of belonging is possible if the authority of knowledge is undermined. As the muscle does not know if it is living or dead, the substances that make the tooth do not know if they are soft potatoes or hard teeth. Lungs, muscles, teeth, bananas, potatoes, milk—these all belong together and in some sense are interchangeable with each other, but only in a non-cognizant way. It is a belonging without the experience or knowledge of belonging.

This discussion of teeth—and Knausgaard is frequently interested in the ways in which the body is open to and sometimes indistinguishable from its other—is important for radicalizing his sense of materialist belonging. Once the living and the dead are considered not hierarchically, but as different modes of matter, and once this matter is freed from any scientific or philosophic presupposition that determines its status in advance, the subject, the human person, loses its perceived ontological privilege.[19] This, perhaps, is the grand thesis of the Seasons Quartet, a phenomenology of objects: not just the body, but the person, too, is an object among others. With death, the object that the person is will lose its pretense of privilege and will "take the final step into the world of things, becoming a thing among other things, like a fallen leaf, a stick, a mound" (*Inadvertent,* 31).

Or like a table. The dead body referenced above, the first one Knausgaard ever saw, is his father's. At the end of the first volume of *My Struggle,* Knausgaard elaborates on this realization of the shared matter of the living and the dead:

> There was no longer any difference between what once had been my father and the table he was lying on, or the floor on which the table stood, or the wall socket beneath the window, or the cable running to the lamp beside him. For humans are merely one form among many, which the world produces over and over again, not only in everything that lives but also in everything that does not live, drawn in sand, stone, and water. (*MS,* 1:441)

The person is a form of the world's productive processes and has no necessary privilege over any other. This is a leveling of not only the binary of life and death, which are made mutually constitutive of each other, but of the living-dead person and all other phenomenal objects. Perhaps echoing Ecclesiastes, Knausgaard argues that all is always already drawn in sand, stone, and water, as if all came from and return to dust. Unlike Milbank, though, Knausgaard alludes to scripture for the sake of describing a fundamentally atheistic world of the mute and purely material living dead.

And so Knausgaard's materialism offers another way of belonging not to God, but to the world. It is a belonging that emphasizes the shared origin and fate of all—not just all people or all creatures, but of everything that is and could be. This material sense of belonging differs from Knausgaard's pseudo-romantic and infantile senses in that Knausgaard seems to think that this description is apodictically the case. Whereas Knausgaard permanently longs for the impossible romantic unity of society and nature, and whereas the immediate belonging of infancy is no longer possible, and in any case was never experienced as such, Knausgaard does believe that this understanding of a shared material origin and fate is actually the case. Whether we want it or know it to be so, our teeth belong to the same material world as the potatoes, bananas, and milk that made them. Granted, it is a belonging that suffers the same problem of unthinking as that of infantile belonging. A muscle does not know if it twitches in a living or a dead body, and the matter of the soft potato and the hard tooth knows nothing, either. And so the recognition of this material belonging, despite being the case, does not satisfy a longing to experience belonging: it is but it is not thought, and so whatever belonging it offers cannot be experienced or known. Knausgaard's dead father does not and cannot know that he is exactly like the table on which "he" "lies."

Literature Against Fiction

The passage about his father's body continues: "And death, which I have always regarded as the greatest dimension of life, dark, compelling, was no more than a pipe that springs a leak, a branch that cracks in the wind, a jacket that slips off a clothes hanger and falls to the floor" (*MS*, 1:441). Later, in the sixth volume, Knausgaard reflects on this passage: "I wrote, 'And death . . .' That was beautiful, it was something, whereas what it described was nothing, empty, neutral, as hopeless as it was merciless" (*MS*, 6:177). Knausgaard is worried that his description of the materiality of death articulates a poeticism that undermines the very point he wants to make: that matter is unknowing, uncaring, more silent than silence. The concern brings Knausgaard close to reinscribing the Aristotelian model of writing, wherein his words would temporally and logically follow a prelinguistic experience. If this were the case, then Knausgaard would be arguing that his written words do not live up to the full significance of the experience that they represent. Indeed, Knausgaard occasionally writes of the artist as grasping for an external and prelinguistic truth, and in doing so seems to adhere to this model. But this Aristotelian proximity and those comments concerning truth betray, in my reading, that which is more fundamental to Knausgaard's project: he wants to experience belonging. The problem is that the methods of belonging so far described—romanticism, infancy, and now materialism—preclude, for the reasons already explained, experience. There is no experience of belonging, although Knausgaard wishes that there were. Recognizing this impossibility of experiencing belonging, Knausgaard's comments about the failure of writing should not be understood in an Aristotelian way. Knausgaard cannot be maintaining that his words fail to live up to the experience of belonging because he maintains that there is no experience of belonging.

If not a discrepancy between word and experience, what, then, is Knausgaard's complaint with his own description of his father's death? The concern that his language is too "beautiful" betrays a more fundamental concern that his writing does not accurately reflect his life. Knausgaard's concern, after all, is not that his writing is beautiful but that the beauty of the text does not cohere with the nothingness that it attempts to describe. That no text—ugly, beautiful, figurative, literal, or whatever—could cohere with nothingness means that Knausgaard's concern here is less with his own idiosyncratic style than it is with the formal and structural relationship between life and text.

In the second volume of *My Struggle,* Knausgaard reveals his project's aim: "The idea was to get as close as possible to my life" (*MS*, 2:582). Fredric Jameson has called the style of writing that Knausgaard uses to pursue this aim "itemisation," by which he means a type of writing that is primarily a reporting of life without privilege for the exciting over the mundane.[20] It is this desire to report the quotidian that leads Knausgaard to write about "things (that) happen all the time, every single day, and everyone knows they do: alcoholism, infidelity, mental illness, and masturbation" (*MS*, 6:1007).

While admitting that he is attracted to this style of writing because it comes easy to him, Knausgaard is also motivated by ethical concerns, which do not feature in Jameson's depiction.[21] Namely, Knausgaard's concern for the quotidian serves the function of specifying what kind of belonging—fascist—he is not interested in. In volume six, Knausgaard differentiates his *My Struggle* from Hitler's:

> It is not his father's life as such that is significant to him, the person he was in real life, the man whose smell could be described in such and such a way, who walked and stood and sat like this or like that, who expressed himself in this way rather than that and who filled a room with his very own presence, but rather what he in his life represented . . . Hitler turns his problematic social background to his advantage, at the same time as he keeps private that which would ruin the trajectory, the striving to surmount, that which takes place in the material world among real people, who not only belong to a lineage, but also belch and shit and yell and lash out, and with a certain regularity drink themselves senseless; who slurp and spit and reek of piss and sweat, who drag their sons here and there by their hair. (*MS*, 6:511)

Coming at the end of the novel, the passage winks at the reader, who by now knows that Knausgaard's own father was prone to belch and shit and yell and lash out, and with a certain regularity drink himself senseless. Knausgaard wants to report these sometimes-embarrassing phenomena because to do otherwise would not respect the irreplaceable particularity of his father. Whereas Hitler made his abusive father into a sort of plot device, Knausgaard wishes to preserve the irreplaceability of his father. In terms of belonging, Knausgaard does not want to make his father belong to a constructed fiction, but aims to make himself belong to the world of which his father is a part. The treatment of his father's particularity is governed by the same desire that Knausgaard felt on Walpurgis Night: Knausgaard wants to belong to the world of grittiness and particularity, of burnt hot dogs and abusive fathers. In his reflections on Hitler, Walpurgis Night celebrations, the body, and death, Knausgaard always demonstrates a deep desire to belong "in the material world among real people."

Among "real people," that is, with "the concrete, singular life. That's the only thing that really exists" ("Karl Ove Knausgaard Looks Back" ["KOKLB"]). The world to which Knausgaard longs to belong is this world of real, concrete people. In this sense, he articulates a desire for belonging antithetical to the Schmittian belonging to ontological metanarratives that racially classify individuals. Such metanarratives—which Knausgaard shows serve a fundamental role for Hitler as well as Schmitt—rely, Knausgaard says, not on the "I" and the "you," but on the "we." The belonging implied by this metanarratalogical "we" is the opposite of the belonging—particular, individual, real, material—for which Knausgaard longs and about which his project writes: "That 'we' is general—it doesn't really exist, it's a fiction. So the duty of literature is to fight fiction. It's to find a way into the world as it is" ("KOKLB"). The fleeting "we" that Knausgaard experienced at Walpurgis Night is contraposed to the "we" of Schmitt and Hitler as literature is to fiction, as mute materialism is to ontological narrative, as the quotidian is to the grand, and as his daughter below is to the heavens above.

Yet, it is one thing to reject an explicitly fascist metanarrative of explicit ontological war. It might be another to reject Milbank's Christian metanarrative of ontological peace. For while Milbank also preserves the privilege of a "we"—Christians—and although Milbank also interprets all of material history as scenes in the higher Christian drama of salvation, his argument is not in favor of the formal structure of metanarratives as such. Rather, Milbank argues in favor of the unique peacefulness and unique credibility of the Christian, and by this he ultimately means Augustinian, metanarrative. The question would then concern not the credibility of metanarratives as such—Milbank knows the arguments against metanarratives and rejects them *on faith*—but instead would concern the particular attractiveness of Milbank's Augustinian metanarrative. In other words, and using Knausgaard's distinction, it remains to be seen, for now, whether Milbank's metanarrative is fiction or literature.

God and Belonging

And so Knausgaard searches for belonging through quotidian existence, mute materialism, and literature. In each case, he finds that belonging entails an openness and an alienation that Knausgaard once thought would be overcome by belonging to the world. He still wants to belong in the naive sense: he never stops writing literature in the hope of dispelling fiction. This is the tension that animates Knausgaard's whole project: on the one hand, the recognition that "belonging" is possible only if belonging is understood in a rather alienating sense; on the other hand, the unceasing hope to experience full belonging in the world anyway.

As we would expect, though, Knausgaard submits this tension to one further turn of the dialectical screw. In 2018, an interviewer with the *New Yorker* asked Knausgaard what "spiritual possibilities" his sense of materialism allowed. Knausgaard responds: "A friend of mine has wood pigeons who build a nest, lay eggs, have chicks, and there's a hawk that comes and takes them. That's happened four years in a row. But the pigeons still go to the same place because, for them, the future doesn't exist. Maybe they're in what Kierkegaard would say is the kingdom of God." His friend's pigeons seem to experience the sort of unreflective and immediate belonging for which Knausgaard apparently longs. In Knausgaard, the lilies of the field and the birds of the air become the burnt hot dogs of the pushcart and the pigeons of the hawk's dinner. Lilies and birds belong to the kingdom of God, but Knausgaard has trouble enough belonging to the gritty, material, and uncaring world that he has described. So far, everything runs as expected: Knausgaard resists a too-easy acceptance of belonging that does not account for the particularity and materiality of the world.

Knausgaard continues this reflection on his friend's pigeons by noting the difference between them and us humans. Unlike the pigeons, "we're not in the world—we're looking at the world, longing for it." At this point, the familiar reader would expect Knausgaard to say that he longs to be like the pigeon, even if doing so would fundamentally alter his understanding of himself and would rob himself of the possibility of ever experiencing the belonging for which he longs. But this is not what happens. Instead, Knausgaard puts the whole project into question. He continues: "Do we want in there? Is that where God is?"

In the sixth volume of *My Struggle,* Knausgaard straightforwardly declares that he does "not believe there to be a God, nor that Jesus was the son of that God" (*MS*, 6:639). Given this apparent atheism, and it is a specifically anti-Christian atheism, Knausgaard's question can be interpreted in a variety of ways. First, the question could be meant as a simple profession of a philosophical position. Knausgaard, who does not seem to think that experiencing belonging to the world is humanly possible, asks if God is in this belonging and means by this that there is neither belonging nor God. But Knausgaard's question might be more straightforwardly earnest: we cannot experience belonging, but there is belonging—the pigeons belong to the world—and, perhaps, God is in this inaccessible, non-experiential place. That he does not believe there to be a God would not, in this register, imply an ontological judgment concerning the impossibility of God.

But a third interpretation is more fitting. I read Knausgaard as saying: if God is there, then all the better for God, but I live here; perhaps I want to belong there, perhaps I want that more than everything, but I want that and burnt hot dogs, that and my daughter. This reading is consistent with Knausgaard's emphasis on desiring the quotidian and the common: he does not want to enter the kingdom of God if doing so means leaving behind all that he loves. When Knausgaard recognized the possibility of bowing to the sublime heavens above but immediately turns instead to his daughter below, he raised this question: "Do we want in there?" And answered it: no; at least, not without this, too.

This is the question with which Knausgaard's project confronts the reader: where do you want to belong? Understood in this manner, Knausgaard's repeated dialectical troubling of ways of belonging read less as descriptions or "itemizations" of the world as they do defenses of it. Knausgaard wants to belong in the world. He wants this so much that he is skeptical of any belonging that might elide the world's particularities: in each case of potential belonging, Knausgaard worries that the world might slip, that a hot dog will go unaccounted for, that his daughter won't recognize him. Which is not to say that Knausgaard is merely inventing trouble for himself and sabotaging the fulfillment of his own desire. I am not providing a psychoanalytic reading of Knausgaard. The dialectics of belonging that Knausgaard describes are real: the world is, his writing convincingly shows, mute, alienating, and ruptured from within. It is also full of irreplaceable others, laughing children, and love. And it is precisely the reality of all of this that Knausgaard wants to save, and it is to this that Knausgaard wishes to belong.

As Marx thought of religion as providing the structural prototype for all ideology, as Derrida thought of theology as providing safe harbor for the metaphysical coincidence of thinking and being, so does Knausgaard think of religion as providing the highest means of effacing the world by belonging to its outside. The logic is different than that articulated in this project's first two chapters and differs from what is usually considered religion's postmodern difficulty: for Knausgaard, the religious problem is not the problem of finding the outside despite our epistemological limits. Unlike Hägglund's, Knausgaard's atheism is not grounded in the philosophical impossibility of God. Rather, for Knausgaard, the religious problem is the problem of rejecting the religious temptation of leaving the world. Unlike Hägglund's, Knausgaard's atheism is an ethical choice against belonging to a world other than this one—really, it is a choice against his own desire for such a belonging.

For Knausgaard, to believe in God would be to belong to the world in a way that would efface his fleeting attachments to those he loves in this world. To belong to the world would be to lose the world. This world is fleeting and unknowing, offers little by way of comfort, and does not offer any hospitality and does not ask us to belong. Looking at the world he loves, Knausgaard sees almost nothing:

—"There's almost nothing there?"

—"Yes."

—"But it's good anyway?"

—"In a way." (*So Much Longing in So Little Space* [*SML*], 169)

In a way, the world is good. In the ways it is not good, we can, as political people, improve things: "Humanity requires at least some minimum of material comforts. As Mackie Messer says in Bertolt Brecht's *Threepenny Opera, erst kommt das Fressen, dann kommt die Moral*" (*MS*, 6:585); "Economic inequality: That is what we should talk about, nothing else" ("KOKLB"). Granted, Knausgaard, now an economically and culturally wealthy cosmopolitan European, spends relatively little ink discussing this necessity of material comfort. Indeed, his desire for the world in all of its grittiness might well display a material privilege that affords him some safety from a grittiness too gritty. Yet, in a more profound sense Knausgaard's desire to belong to the world in its entirety and his position against inequality are not at all antithetical: Knausgaard's position is that life is hard enough, that people are dying and in a sense dead already, that belonging is impossible—one certainly does not need poverty on top of it all. The complexity and particularities of the world can be appreciated, can be held on to, without also accepting exploitation and dispossession. In fact, such exploitation might impede the possibility of choosing to belong to the world by impeding choice as such. In this sense, Knausgaard's argument against religion is totally consistent with the standard Marxist argument: a turn to the heavens is a fictive, not literary, flight from difficulties here below. Which is to say, that which all political regimes and all literary projects must care for is this world, and no other. For Knausgaard, bowing to the heavens belongs to fiction—and bowing to this world belongs to literature.

Of course, there is a long tradition for which this turn to the world would be sympathetic with, not antipathetic to, religion. A religious struggle to embrace and correct the world will be found in this project's next two chapters. But Knausgaard's decision is clear: he decides against God. To dispute Knausgaard's minor premises—to argue, as indeed the next chapters will risk doing, that a decision for faith is also a decision for, not against, the world—in order to sublate his thought into an allegedly higher religious metanarrative would be an entirely unnecessary and violent imposition. This imposed sublation would be violent not only because it would be unwelcome, but also more fundamentally because to do so would reinscribe a basic identity between thought and being: to demonstrate theoretically that Knausgaard has misread religion's relationship with the world, and to do so for the sake of religious apologetics, would imply that a theoretical construction can and should dictate both desire and praxis. Knausgaard has already recognized that one can bow to the heavens. And he has chosen not to do so. A reinscription of a metaphysical logic in order to argue against this decision would undermine, not fortify, the possibility of religious decision as such: to argue that his turn to his daughter masks some underlying religiosity or that he has described himself as secular only because he misunderstands religion would serve to make religious decision impossible by rendering it necessary. If religious decision is to be a true decision and not an ideological obfuscation—and so not rendered necessary, not observing the iron metaphysical laws of noncontradiction, not determining an outcome in advance—then Knausgaard's decision against religion has to be not only respected but also more strongly affirmed as necessarily possibly correct.

In addition to these deconstructive reasons, there are more obviously theological reasons to not only respect, but also more strongly valorize Knausgaard's secular decision. And Knausgaard reminds us of them, via a note to his daughter, which comes at the beginning of *Spring*:

> I want you to know this—that you were born into love, and that it will envelop you, no matter what happens, as long as your mother and I are alive. It may happen that you don't want anything to do with it. It may happen that you turn away from it. And one day you will understand that it doesn't matter, that it doesn't change anything, that unconditional love is the only love that doesn't bind you but sets you free. (*Spring*, 4)

The passage echoes Paul's from Corinthians, and so can be read as a message to his religious readers. In this case, what matters is the content of Paul's—and Knausgaard's, the question of authorial ownership here is complex at least—claim concerning the liberating function of love. Knausgaard appeals to religious discourse for the sake of telling religion: set me free. It is as if he were saying, if you care for love, then do not bind me. Again, the argument concerns belonging: Knausgaard wants to belong to the world; to force him to belong to religion is, then, an unloving imposition of inclusion. Not all welcomings are welcome.

Surely this is the place where Milbank could respond that Knausgaard's secularism is inextricably bound to Christian theology. Not only is Knausgaard here responding—consciously or not—to Paul, and not only did he earlier allude to Ecclesiastes, and not only was his discussion of Walpurgis Night a necessary reference to Saint Walpurga, but also more generally Knausgaard's commitment to matter and the world is itself a reflection of the Christian motif of incarnation. Milbank could claim that Knausgaard's ethical positions are grounded not in immanent secularism, but in a higher mysticism of love, and that it is only because of this "vertical" integration that Knausgaard is able to do anything like ethics at all.[22] In all of these instances, Milbank could argue that where Knausgaard argues against religion, he must use religious arguments and the material given him by religious traditions. Knausgaard would only ever be a theologian.

But in what sense would any of these claims theologically position Knausgaard's secularism? The case of Walpurgis Night is especially illuminating. Walpurgis Night is celebrated on the eve of the feast day of Saint Walpurga, niece of Saint Boniface. In Sweden, where Knausgaard celebrated, the night is now associated with the pagan ritualistic welcoming of spring, typically through song and the lighting of bonfires. Milbank's metanarrative could interpret this bonfire celebration as a heretical and pagan derivation from the primary and orthodox significance of the saint's feast day. But bonfires and song long pre-existed Christianity, and they certainly pre-exist the feast of Saint Walpurga. And so a plausible interpretation could the opposite of what I am imagining Milbank's to be: the pagan celebration of which Knausgaard took part is not a heretical derivation of Christianity; rather, the feast of Saint Walpurga, a saint celebrated for, among other things, warding off witchcraft, was a temporary and fleeting colonization of local pagan traditions. Where Milbank's metanarrative requires a heretical deviation from truth, the phenomenal reality suggests an inescapable inextricability of pagan, secular, and formally religious dimensions. In a limited sense, Milbank's narrative does recognize this inextricability. He does not argue that Christianity is a distinct and discreet way of life superior to an antagonistic totally atheistic and totally secular way of life. Instead, Milbank is quick to point out the religious allusions and implied theology of secularism—indeed, this is his argument. What Knausgaard's Walpurgis Night celebration shows, though, is that "the religious" is likewise full of secular information and sedimentations. If there is an implied theology in "the secular," then this is only because there is also an implied secular philosophy in "the religious"—as Milbank's Platonism confirms.

Importantly, this recognition of the inextricability of the religious and the secular—which is opposed to the Schmittian logic of the purity and supremacy of one "realm" over all others, which appears to be Milbank's logic—is not an argument for the superiority of a secular metanarrative. Knausgaard decides against God, but he does not look to situate or position religious belief within some higher metanarrative. There is no apology for any metanarrative in Knausgaard. If he is suspicious of God and religion—and he is—then his is a suspicion that does not look to "master" religious discourse, because it holds that mastery is itself one form of religious discourse. And so there are narratives in Knausgaard—many thousands of pages of narratives—but there is no desire to efface the antagonisms and irreducible differences between these narratives. Knausgaard presents a "literary" description of life as cold and violent, but also as warm and loving. It is a complexity and antagonism that is more reflective of quotidian experience than is the mythical ontological peace preached by Milbank. To this end, as descriptions of reality, Knausgaard's multiple secular narratives are entirely more "persuasive" than Milbank's universalizing and rigidly orthodox metanarrative. Indeed, part of the literary value of Knausgaard's project is found in the ways in which he slides in and out of religious praxis—his children are baptized—and makes use of religious motifs. But this always as a sort of bricoleur, not an engineer of a dominant master metanarrative. In this secular recognition of irreducible difference, and it is only with irreducible difference that a truly multiple bricolage is possible, Milbank detects a violence and a nihilism. As I have tried to show, the violence that a Milbankian metanarrative detects is the violence it imposes by subjecting Knausgaard's secular love for the world to a mythically pure and allegedly superior theological regime. Mastery and violence are produced, not uncovered, by radical orthodoxy's Christian metanarrative.

Applauding Knausgaard's secularism for its attachment to the world resists Milbank's pseudo-religious colonization of love as always a religious, and so not also a secular, phenomenon. Knausgaard, because of and not in spite of his secular love for the secular world, is an ally to the left political theology this project develops. Which does not require incorporating him into a Christian metanarrative. Indeed, it requires a refusal to incorporate at all. Contra Milbank, a truly peaceful conceptualization of difference recognizes the irreducible doctrinal and creedal difference between Knausgaard's secularism and Christian orthodoxy, and yet recognizes the possibility of political and praxical convergences anyway. A theological interpretation should not be imposed, because imposing it might force Knausgaard to walk away:

> We continued drinking in Peter's room. He tore the phone loose and used it as a window stopper, so we could smoke without being fined, and handed me his book with photos of the wars in Afghanistan and Iraq, which he had covered for a decade, and of the lives of the veterans back in the U.S. I leafed through it while I tried to come up with something to say to him. I ended up saying that he sought complexity, not the iconic, and that this gave his photos enormous distinction. The expression on his face didn't change when I said it, so it was impossible to tell whether I had pleased or insulted him.
>
> He put the book on the bed and opened a new beer.
> "So what's your position on the question of God?" he asked.
> I got up, put out my cigarette and set the half-empty beer can on the coffee table.
> "I think I'll go to bed now," I said. "It's been a long day."[23]

Chapter Four

Orthodoxy Is Orthopraxy

Kierkegaard's Relation to Marx Reconsidered

Introduction

To review, this project's first chapter argued that Carl Schmitt provides a compelling critique of the conversational and basically apolitical nature of modern liberal democracy, but does so by relying on an ontologized political theology that undermines any possibility of real decision. Moreover, Schmitt conflates liberalism and Marxism as versions of the same neutralization of politics and the same rejection of (Christian) political theology. This rejection of Marxism and dialectical materialism, in turn, serves to bolster Schmitt's preference for ontology. That is, Schmitt critiques Marxism through a retreat to ontology. The project's second chapter turned to Jacques Derrida, who was found to convincingly critique the very ontological political theology offered by Schmitt. Because of the relationship between Schmitt's anti-Marxism and his metaphysics, Derrida's critique of metaphysical political theology suggests the possibility of a materialist alternative. Such an alternative might be the only hope for political theology responsive to the fall of metaphysics, because, after Derrida, any theology, including any political theology, that grounds itself in a metaphysical or logocentric discourse of truth must be dismissed as ideological; that is, as theoretically dubious and politically reactionary.

Finding these critiques of liberalism and metaphysics basically convincing—although marked by a deep and clear rejection of Schmitt's anti-Marxist fascism and ontologization of theology, both of which are anyway undermined by Derrida's critique of logocentrism—my commitments are to a political theology both deconstructive and Marxist. This chapter argues that Søren Kierkegaard's Christian existentialism provides material for just that. Specifically, Kierkegaard, (1) offers an existentialist alternative to the metaphysical theologies critiqued by Derrida, and (2) offers a dialectical-materialist alternative to Schmitt's ontological politics.

These two strands find common articulation in Kierkegaard's conception of decision: for Kierkegaard the existentialist, any decision worthy of the name does not take place in the ideal realm of philosophical deduction, but in the material realm of actual existence. That these existential decisions cannot be grounded in the ideal metaphysical identity of thinking and being makes Kierkegaard's project a deconstructive one. That such decisions ought to be guided by the explicit norms established by Jesus and recorded in scripture makes his project not only deconstructive, but also Christian.[1] That these norms are clearly, for Kierkegaard, a critique of private property and the political-economic regime secured by the right of private property—that is, capitalism—and that these norms clearly demand a political privileging of the poor, makes his project not only deconstructive and Christian, but also socialist. All of which is to say, the three traditions that primarily inform this project—Derridean deconstruction, political theology, and Marxist critique—find coherence in a Kierkegaardian political theology.

While there might be tensions between deconstruction's anti-theological position and Kierkegaard's Christianity—and these tensions will be explored through reference to the work of not only Derrida, but also contemporary deconstructive theorists Caputo, Hägglund, Bennington, and Agacinski, all of whom write extensively about Kierkegaard—it is the association of Kierkegaard with Marxism that is most nearly novel, if not controversial, in my argument.[2] Indeed, the relationship between Marxists and professional Kierkegaardians could reasonably be described as often hostile—and this from both parties.

The suspicion of Kierkegaard in Marxist circles begins with the Hungarian philosopher György Lukács, who made Kierkegaard a prominent antagonist in his 1954 text *Die Zerstörung der Vernunft*.[3] Importantly, Lukács confines his study to only Kierkegaard's pseudonymous works, which he holds as "the only crucial ones philosophically." In reading these texts, Lukács argues that Kierkegaard responded to the limitations of Hegelian idealism—and Lukács is clear that Kierkegaard's critiques on this front are compelling—not by turning to the materialist dialectics of Marx, but through "the construction of a subjectivist pseudo-dialectic" (*Die Zerstörung der Vernunft*, 250). With this charge of a "subjectivist pseudo-dialectic,"

Lukács issues his two primary critiques. First, in critiquing Hegel's introduction of movement into logic—and this introduction is an object of critique for Lukács, too—Kierkegaard falls into irrationalism: "In that the leap is divided from the transition of quantity, its irrational character comes about as a matter of necessity" (252). That is, Lukács holds that the Kierkegaardian category of the leap, upon which Kierkegaard relies in his critique of Hegelian logic, is a basically irrational, and so not properly dialectical, category. Second, Lukács depiction of Kierkegaard's dialectic as "subjectivist" is meant to critique Kierkegaard's alleged anti-Marxist use of abstraction: here, the argument is that Kierkegaard's "single individual" is only ever an abstraction from the particularities of real people in the midst of class struggle. This alleged abstraction from socio-economic reality is read as a retreat into idealism: "idealist dialectics . . . became with Kierkegaard the cornerstone of the most highly advanced irrationalist philosophy which had hitherto existed" (256). In the final analysis, Kierkegaard's subjectivist/idealist pseudo-dialectic, in its withdrawal from material reality, is held to support capital's ideological machinery: Kierkegaardian philosophy is popularized in the twentieth century in order to support "the imperialist bourgeoisie's increasingly reactionary needs," and Kierkegaard himself is proven to only ever have been a "pure apologist of bourgeois decadence, and nothing else" (296).

Eight years after Lukács's work, Theodor Adorno published his *Kierkegaard: Konstruktion des Asthetischen*.[4] Adorno's engagement with Kierkegaard is more subtle and more careful than is Lukács's, but ultimately Adorno, too, finds in Kierkegaard an idealist opponent to anti-capitalist struggle. An early work, this text was written before Adorno's later turn to a more conventionally Marxist position. Yet even here, Adorno makes some of the same critiques as Lukács; namely, that Kierkegaardian inwardness is a retreat from material reality. Adorno writes that Kierkegaard has a "lack of any developed concept of praxis," and that, without such a concept, Kierkegaard positions himself at a distance from "the external world," which is "condemned in general as 'the external world,' and not as a specifically capitalist world" (*Kierkegaard: Konstruktion des Asthetischen*, 49). This removal from the specifically capitalist world is, according to Adorno and echoing Lukács, at least partially the result of Kierkegaard's idealism. According to Adorno, Kierkegaardian idealism is grounded in the identity—and "identity" is the catchword for idealism in all of Adorno—"of truth and person" (49). Such an idealism occludes the possibility of rational, scientific critique of the capitalist world, and so "in Kierkegaard's philosophy the knowing subject can no more reach its objective correlative than, in a society dominated by exchange-value, things are 'immediately' accessible to the person" (39). That is, Adorno is in agreement with Lukács in that Kierkegaard presents an idealist and irrational alternative to Hegel's idealism: "Reason, which in Hegel as infinite reason produces actuality out of itself, is in Kierkegaard, again as infinite reason, the negation of all finite knowledge: if the former is mythical by its claim to universal sovereignty, the latter becomes mythical through universal annihilation" (119).[5]

Finally, this Marxist of Kierkegaard as an anti-worldly irrationalist is perhaps most succinctly articulated by George Novack, who, in his *Understanding History*, confidently states that, "Søren Kierkegaard did contend that it was neither possible nor desirable to think systematically about the reality of life."[6] Like Lukács and Adorno, Novack credits Kierkegaard with responding to a real problem, but opting for an unreal solution: "It must be said that the heresies of the existentialists do not always succeed in shedding completely the values of the society they rebel against. Kierkegaard assailed the sluggishness and self-deception of the smug citizens around him only to embrace the Christian God with more passionate intensity." It is easy to see how this structure, wherein religion ideologically operates as an ideal response to material injustice, has found favor in Marxist interpretations of Kierkegaard. Eventually, I will attempt to show that this reading of Kierkegaardian religion is misplaced: far from otherworldly and subservient to the demands of capitalism, Kierkegaard's political theology requires critical engagement precisely with capitalist structures of oppression. These readings, in short, read a bourgeois understanding of religion into Kierkegaard.

This classic Marxist characterization of Kierkegaard remains largely unchallenged by contemporary Marxist theorists. Tom Carter, writing for the Trotskyist International Committee for the Fourth International, states that "Kierkegaard's thinking, as it emerged in the arena of philosophy, took on a truly reactionary and backward form."[7] Even Marxists comfortable in continental philosophy and theory—Fredric Jameson, Antonio Negri, Michael Hardt—rarely, if ever, engage Kierkegaard as a serious political thinker.[8]

In the rare occasion when a contemporary Marxist does engage positively with Kierkegaard, the engagement is largely treated with suspicion from within the Kierkegaard scholarly community. Consider the case of Slavoj Žižek, who is perhaps the only committed contemporary Marxist theorist who positively engages Kierkegaard's work. For Žižek, unlike Adorno, Lukács, and Novack, there is "only a thin, almost imperceptible line that separates Kierkegaard from dialectical materialism proper" (*The Parallax View [PV]*,

75).⁹ Žižek holds that Kierkegaard's philosophical and theological projects, insofar as they relate to immanence, are materialist in method and scope. This materialism is only prevented from being "dialectical materialism proper" by Kierkegaard's theological commitments: for Žižek's Kierkegaard, God is a transcendent spectator who possesses final knowledge of all human history. In this transcendent perspective, history and truth are identified in the person of God. Such a posited identity, which is totally removed from existence from our human perspective, is the "thin, almost imperceptible line" that prevents Kierkegaard from adopting a fully (atheist) Marxist materialism. But this lingering idealism, Žižek argues, is not a reason for Marxists to dismiss Kierkegaard. Indeed, by placing the identitarian thought of idealism in such a transcendent—and so removed—position, Kierkegaard has freed actual human history from idealist baggage. Where Lukács, Adorno, and Novack see a withdrawal from the world, Žižek sees a freeing of the world: with no prior ideal philosophical or theoretical commitments, the political actor is free to truly decide how to proceed, is free to leap into the future: "In the last resort there is no theory, just a fundamental practico-ethical decision about what kind of life one wants to commit oneself to" (*PV*, 75). Žižek sees this emphasis on decision as a corrective toward deterministic tendencies in some forms of Marxist theorizing. Žižek is arguing Kierkegaard is right, movement does not come about on its own, but must be forced. It is for this reason that Žižek is able to read certain leftist revolutionaries—most notably Robespierre, Guevara, and, above all, Lenin—as enacting "works of love in the strictest Kierkegaardian sense of the term" (*The Puppet and the Dwarf [PD]*, 30).¹⁰

One would think, then, that Kierkegaardians might be interested in engaging with Žižek on this point—after all, Žižek is elevating Kierkegaard to a central role within a philosophical program typically resistant to Kierkegaard. However, Žižek has mostly been met by this community with suspicion—if not scorn. In his "Risible Christianity? Kierkegaard vs. Žižek," Leo Stan, a contributor to Jon Stewart's *Kierkegaard: Sources and Reception* series,¹¹ describes Žižek as a "cultural critic" primarily interested in "pop culture, classical opera, smut, revolutionary Marxism,¹² cyberspace, and Hitchcock's films."¹³ According to Stan, Žižek's program is both a "challenge to" and a "deconstruction of" Christianity. It is both of these things because Žižek "puts forward a secularistic reading of Christian theology in accord with the demythologizing hermeneutic of psychoanalysis. This approach is rooted in a violent, immanentist, and narcissistic ontology of the void." Throughout this same article, Žižek's "hermeneutic" is held to be "aggressive," "groundless," "unwarranted," "unjustifiable," and "quite erratic." As I hope to demonstrate shortly, several of these negatively charged adjectives might actually receive a positive valence in Kierkegaard's work, and so Žižek's unwarranted, groundless, and so on reading of Kierkegaard might not be as "arbitrary" as Stan thinks. Regardless, Stan's major critique of Žižek is that his "secularizing" reading is a "reductionistic" one. From Stan's perspective, Žižek's secularized, materialist, and heterodox interpretation of Christianity can only ever be a challenge to and deconstruction of Christianity, because Christianity is essentially not secular, materialist, or heterodox. This chapter will challenge each of these associations, especially in their ideological—and Schmittian—use.

As noted above, Stan's view, taken as a rejection of a Marxist Kierkegaard on the grounds that Marxism is antithetical to either Christianity in general or Kierkegaardian Christianity in particular, or both, is widespread in the Kierkegaardian academic community. Saitya Brata Das's recent manuscript *The Political Theology of Kierkegaard* approvingly cites Karl Lowith's claim that Kierkegaard wrote *Two Ages* as an "anti-communist manifesto."[14] For Brata Das, who is inadvertently echoing the early communist critiques of Kierkegaard, Kierkegaard and Marx are each responding to the same problem of a tyrannical "world order." Yet, "while for Marx the 'outside' of the system is in the world, for Kierkegaard the 'outside' of the system is the 'outside' of the world" (*The Political Theology of Kierkegaard*, 33). Kierkegaard's position here as other-worldly, in turn, is meant to radicalize the critique of immanent worldly powers. Kierkegaard's other-worldly political theology delegitimizes by contextualizing all earthly claims to power; that is, his political theology is "an eschatological delegitimation of the worldly power on theological foundation" (*The Political Theology of Kierkegaard*, 75). Unfortunately, Brata Das is here reinscribing Kierkegaard within the very idealist paradigm that served as an object of critique for the early Marxists. Especially after Derrida's critique of such transcendental structures, a responsible political theology must side with the Marxists in this debate. That is, reinscribing Kierkegaard within an idealist paradigm, and so reinscribing the Marx/Kierkegaard relationship as one of antagonism, should be resisted if Kierkegaard is to function as a credibly emancipatory thinker after the fall of metaphysical claims.

Citations of this kind could be given interminably. For example, George Pattison writes that "Marx and Kierkegaard may be representatives of two essentially irreconcilable positions. They can scarcely both be right in their radically divergent accounts of what is truly human in our humanity" (31).[15]

And Jacob Taubes, neither a Marxist nor a Kierkegaardian, writes: "Kierkegaard aims at essentially the same relationship between religion and politics as Marx, though admittedly in inverse valuation" (173).[16] The recently published volume of the 2018 annual meeting of the Søren Kierkegaard Society, the theme of which was "Kierkegaard and Political Theology," mentions Marx only once, and that to note that Marx had not elsewhere appeared in the volume.[17] Needless to say, the standard narrative, from Marxists, Kierkegaardians, and the political-philosophical literature in general, is that Marx and Kierkegaard articulate basically incompatible philosophical, political, and (a)theological programs. The two are said to be in agreement that religion and politics exist in a confrontational and basically competitive relationship. Marx, the story goes, sides with politics; Kierkegaard, with religion. When a partisan attempts bipartisanship, as with the case of Žižek, he or she is more often scorned than appreciated. My position is that this standard narrative is not only unhelpful, but that, more straightforwardly, it offers an incorrect view of Kierkegaard's political theology. In short, I am arguing here that both the Marxists (except Žižek) and the Kierkegaardians have gotten Kierkegaard wrong: his political theology is a dialectical materialist one, and his explicit political sympathies are socialist. If it is correct, then the ramifications of my argument are this: for the Kierkegaardians, a deep reevaluation of their own biases against Marxist political economy and secular political projects in general; for the Marxists, a deep reevaluation of their own biases against religion and religious thinkers as essentially other-worldly, idealist, and so on. Again, my sympathies are with a deconstructive and Marxist political theology. This is only anti-religious if religion, as Schmitt had it, is fundamentally metaphysical and anti-Marxist. As Kierkegaard shows, it is neither.

The chapter moves in two parts.

First, relying primarily but not only on Kierkegaard's *Concluding Unscientific Postscript to Philosophical Fragments* (CUP),[18] I will explicate Kierkegaard's theoretical critique of the identity of thinking and being. This critique relies on a distinction between "reality" (*realitet*) and "actuality" (*virkelighed*). For Kierkegaard, thinking is identical to being if and only if being is thought of as an ideal thought content. In this idealist sense, thinking has "reality." However, such an ideal reality is not actual if it is not actualized in existence. And so the Kierkegaardian version of the critique of the identity of thinking and being is more properly a critique of the identity of thinking and actuality. The possibility of this identity is judged not in ideal thought, but only in actual existence. This privileging actual existence over ideal thought is one of the senses in which I consider Kierkegaard a materialist: the privileging of existence means that all truth—far from the metaphysics critiqued by Derrida and employed by Schmitt—must be actualized in the world. Here, truth is not an objective content secured by the identity of thinking and being. Nor is truth an intellectual coherence secured by a transcendental signified. Kierkegaard, then, is not an other-worldly idealist, but is instead a materialist who is himself critical of ideal attempts—like the ideal identity of thinking and being—to undermine the importance of actual existence.

In the chapter's second section, I develop Kierkegaard's critique of the identity of thinking and actuality along politically materialist lines. If the first section demonstrates that Kierkegaard is a dialectical materialist—that is, that he employs a materialist and not an idealist dialectic, and that such a dialectic is at least partially constituted by his existential privileging of actual existence—then this second section demonstrates that this dialectical materialism coheres explicitly with a leftist material politics. This is done by arguing that Kierkegaard uses a materialist understanding of truth to destabilize the religious privileging of orthodoxy over orthopraxy. More specifically, Kierkegaard reinscribes orthodoxy as itself a type of orthopraxy: to be a Christian, for Kierkegaard, is to belong to an orthopraxic community concerned with improving the actual, material conditions of the poor and dispossessed. Far from Christianity and Marxism representing antithetical programs, for Kierkegaard, and for me, a credible Christian political theology suggests that orthodoxy is demonstrated by one's enactment of the political praxis elaborated by both Marx and the prophetic Christian tradition, beginning most of all with the Gospels. This reinscription of orthodoxy along the lines of orthopraxy is important for this project in general in that it helps articulate the ways in which religious and secular political projects can align in the struggle for political emancipation.

Thinking and Being:
"The identity of thinking and being is won in pure thinking."[19]

Kierkegaard writes the sentence that names this section about halfway through *Concluding Unscientific Postscript to Philosophical Fragments (CUP)*.[20] The book, published in 1846, is written as a "postscript" to Kierkegaard's much shorter 1844 text, *Philosophical Fragments (PF)*.[21] In *Fragments*, Kierkegaard, writing under the pseudonym Johannes Climacus, responds to the question of how the eternal relates to the temporal. More specifically, *Fragments* asks how eternal happiness, which Christianity promises, can be grounded in an historical event, which Christianity is. My presentation of this argument involves two parts. First, the actual written argument should be rehearsed and its logic understood. This involves a rather straightforward exposition. Second, and more intricately, the argument must be placed within Kierkegaard's larger political-theological project. That is, not only what the argument says, but what it does, how it functions in and what it is doing for Kierkegaard, will prove important. These two readings, which also resemble the deconstructive distinction between saying and wanting to say, could be described as addressing first Climacus and second Kierkegaard.

In terms of exposition, Climacus's argument runs like this: according to Climacus, the elevation of the historical to an essential, as opposed to accidental, element of eternal salvation is what most marks Christianity as different from philosophy. For philosophy, "any point of departure in time is *eo ipso* something accidental, a vanishing point, an occasion" (*PF*, 11). In contradistinction, and as is "well known," "Christianity is the only historical phenomenon that despite the historical—indeed, precisely by means of the historical—has wanted to be the single individual's point of departure for his eternal consciousness, has wanted to interest him otherwise than merely historically, has wanted to base his happiness on his relation to something historical . . . no philosophy has ever had this idea" (*PF*, 109). The majority of the rest of *Fragments* goes on to discuss and embrace this paradoxical nature of Christianity. In brief, the explicit philosophical argument—which, again, is not the only argument—goes like this: that an eternal decision is based on a temporal moment is absurd. It is absurd because historical knowledge can only ever be an approximate knowledge, and so only ever a knowledge subject to interminable revision. An eternal decision, by nature of its eternity, must not deal with calculations, approximations, and revisions. As revision is a change, and as time is marked by change, and as eternity is timeless, so an eternal decision cannot, strictly speaking, have anything to do with an historical event that can only ever be known in approximation.

Climacus's move is to render the absurd in general, and this paradoxical relationship between the eternal and the temporal in particular, constitutive of faith. It is only an absurdity that can truly be held in faith. Historical knowledge, for instance, could not be held as an object of faith. The distinction here is between, on the one hand, faith as an existential, subjective, and passionate commitment—and to just what this is a commitment will become clear shortly—and, on the other hand, a tentative or provisional acceptance of objective knowledge as the result of calculations and approximations.

This rejection of historical and calculable knowledge does not mean that faith should turn to its opposite, to allegedly eternal truth. For Climacus, where historical knowledge appears as somehow below faith, eternal knowledge appears as somehow higher than or above faith. This argument against eternal knowledge is made through a proxy argument with the Socratic theory of recollection, which is formulated as a response to the problem of acquiring knowledge in time. Climacus states the problem like this: "A person cannot possibly seek what he knows, and, just as impossibly, he cannot seek what he does not know, for what he knows he cannot seek, since he knows it, and what he does not know he cannot seek, because, after all, he does not even know what he is supposed to seek" (*PF*, 9). What is Socrates's solution to this problem? "Socrates thinks through the difficulty by means that all learning and seeking are but recollecting" (*PF*, 9). That is, the Socratic theory of learning posits that all knowledge exists somehow within each person, and merely needs to be recalled or recollected in order to be "learned." Socratic pedagogy, then, becomes a strategy for bringing the learner to a place of recollection. In *Fragments*, Climacus critiques this theory on two fronts.

First, Christian salvation, which elevates a historical moment to the status of an essential occasion for salvation (and this notion of an "essential occasion" is precisely the absurd that philosophy cannot accept), is a repudiation of the Socratic theory of recollection's implicit pedagogy: for Socrates, the teacher is a self-erasing mediator between the learner and that which the learner has forgotten that he or she already knows. For Christianity, on the other hand, the teacher is not self-erasing, but is the object of knowledge. The Christian teacher is not the Socratic ironist, but is Christ, the eternal God become person in time. Christ does not remind the learner of what he or she already always knows but presents the disciple with the absurd offer of eternal salvation in time. That this offer is an offer of the teacher's self, and so that the teacher becomes not the tool of learning but the object of it, is incompatible with, and an offense to, the Socratic theory.

Second, Climacus argues that this reliance on the eternal nature of knowledge precludes the possibility of faith. In the Socratic view, the recollection of knowledge is held as sufficient means for the appropriation of knowledge. The Socratic problem is phrased in terms of overcoming a logical paradox. Such a phrasing, for Climacus, elides the more fundamental and actual problem: the problem of knowledge is not how it is logically possible, but how it is actually appropriated as true. By positing the eternal nature of truth, the Socratic method precludes this possibility of appropriation:

as always and everywhere true, knowledge would exist objectively without regard for the subject. Insofar as it is purely objective, such a knowledge would resemble more the approximations of historical knowledge than it would the passionate commitments of faith. In both cases, the subject is held to have an exterior and accidental relationship to knowledge. The subject approaches knowledge as a spectator, either of the objective calculations and approximations of history or of the eternal necessities of ideal truths. In both cases, the subject's decision is irrelevant. In both cases, faith is impossible.

This line of critique, which is a theological critique of both scientific positivism and philosophic idealism, is continued in *CUP,* especially in the first section of the book's second part, titled "Something about Lessing." It is in engaging with Lessing's "ugly broad ditch" between "contingent historical truths" and "eternal truths of reason" that Climacus formulates his much-discussed notion of the leap of faith.[22] This leaping Kierkegaard is the Kierkegaard who valorizes decision as constitutive of subjectivity, truth, and faith. It is the Kierkegaard who critiques history and Platonic metaphysics as indecisive. It is the ostensibly radical fundamentalist Kierkegaard of *Fear and Trembling*.[23] And it is the Kierkegaard of Carl Schmitt, who praises this Kierkegaard when he writes of "a Protestant theologian who demonstrated the vital intensity possible in theological reflection in the nineteenth century" (*PT,* 15)[24]. It is also, importantly, the Kierkegaard who leaps out of the world; that is, the Kierkegaard rejected by Marxists like Lukács, Adorno, and Novack.

This is the Kierkegaard who wrote not under his own name, but as Johannes Climacus, in the case of *Fragments* and *CUP,* and as Johannes de Silentio, in the case of *Fear and Trembling*. A reading of this decision[25] to sign these particular texts under a pseudonym will help us transition from a rehearsal of the philosophical argument concerning time and eternity to a reading of the role that this particular argument plays within Kierkegaard's general project. The choice of Johannes Climacus is especially relevant here: "Johannes Climacus" is an ironic pseudonym that refers to a sixth-century Christian monk who lived twenty years as an ascetic hermit at the foot of Mount Sinai. Certainly, the philosophic arguments rehearsed above, the ones given by Climacus, are not without merit. Indeed, certain of Climacus's motifs—the relationship between eternity and the temporal, the necessity of decision—recur throughout Kierkegaard's corpus, both his "first authorship" of the pseudonyms and his "second authorship," which consists of works typically signed in his own name. But a too myopic view of these arguments decontextualized from their function within Kierkegaard's larger project might well lead, and have indeed led, to the fascistic Kierkegaard in whom Schmitt imagines, or finds, an ally.

Given Climacus's reliance on the category of the leap, it is perhaps important to note that Climacus the monk's only surviving text, *The Ladder of Divine Ascent,* describes a program by which one can raise one's soul to God through a series of increasingly stringent ascetic rituals.[26] Needless to say, to climb a ladder is not to leap. Further, Kierkegaard writes under the name of a monk but has this "monk" write that "the monastic movement itself was an enormous abstraction, monastic life a continued abstraction" (*CUP*, 401). But to concretely live life, to not abstract from life, Kierkegaard tells us in this very same text, "is the task" of the Christian (*CUP*, 164). I suggest that these cracks in the text ought to be read as moments of what Derrida calls auto-deconstruction: moments in text where what one says somehow runs away from what one wants to say. Here, Climacus wants to present some philosophical arguments concerning the relationship between time and eternity. Yet, what Kierkegaard actually writes reveals that what Climacus wants to say is not the whole story: these little slips and cracks that emerge in the text call into question "Climacus's" control over his apparently very controlled arguments. The text, operating as "merely a kind of lunacy" (*CUP*, 17), undoes itself, loses control of its play. Toward the end of *CUP,* Kierkegaard has Climacus write about using reason "in order then to lose the last foothold of immanence, and to exist, situated at the edge of existence, by virtue of the absurd" (*CUP*, 569). Such a deconstructive use of reason is, I argue, precisely what Kierkegaard, via Climacus, is up to in the above arguments: Climacus uses reason to argue against reason; Climacus uses philosophy to argue against itself. Climacus is reasonable through and through, but, precisely by maintaining such reasonableness, never quite reaches these absurd edges of existence.

Climacus's *thought* is internally coherent, but he makes little effort to apply this thought to *actuality.* In my reading, this distinction between thought and actuality—or as it is rendered in Derrida, this distinction between thinking and being—is Kierkegaard's most important contribution to an emancipatory political theology. It is hard to connect the formal and philosophical arguments of Climacus with the political critiques signed elsewhere in Kierkegaard's own name. Yet, this is precisely what Kierkegaard's use of the name of Johannes Climacus suggests would happen: these are the arguments of a hermit, of one who has abstracted from life. In this view, the apparent discrepancy, or at least lack of an intrinsic relation, between Climacus's philosophical arguments and Kierkegaard's political arguments would be precisely Kierkegaard's point: the logic of philosophy does not identify with the actuality of existence.

The critique does receive a few moments of explicit formulation in *CUP*. Typically, these elaborations rely on a distinction between reality (*realitet*) and actuality (*virkelighed*).[27] The distinction is operative in the following passage, which is one of the most clear in all of Kierkegaard's corpus on the difference between reality and actuality: "Greek philosophy assumed as a matter of course that thinking has reality. In reflecting upon it, one must come to the same result, but why is thought reality confused with actuality? Thought reality is possibility, and thinking needs only to reject any further questioning about whether it is actual" (*CUP*, 328). The argument here seems to be that thinking produces a real content that is entirely detached from actual existence—the "abstractions" of philosophical thought are real insofar as they are really thought, and perhaps they are even real insofar as they cohere to universal laws and necessities, as with mathematical thought, but they are not actual in the sense of finding concrete articulation in existence. Put another way, thinking is always ideal, and so universal: it can only use received and communicable general concepts. Existence, though, contains something irreducibly particular and incommunicable. This incommunicability of subjective experience is what later analytic philosophers of mind will call *qualia*, and it is also what contemporary phenomenologists and post-phenomenological continental philosophers might refer to as simply the "secret." In each instance—Greek philosophy, analytic philosophy, continental philosophy—the same basic tenet holds, and this whether any particular philosopher or religious believer wishes it to be the case or not: "the particular cannot be thought, but only the universal" (*CUP, 326)*.[28]

Because it does not account for existence, which cannot be thought as such, the identity of thinking and being is only ever an invention or product of thought, not a feature of existence; hence the sentence that names this section: "The identity of thinking and being is won in pure thinking" (*CUP*, 335). That is, the identity of thinking and being is a philosopheme. In its more expanded form, Kierkegaard frames the argument like this: "The philosophical thesis of the identity of thinking and being is just the opposite of what it seems to be; it expresses that thinking has completely abandoned existence, that it has emigrated and found a sixth continent where it is absolutely sufficient unto itself in the absolute identity of thinking and being" (*CUP*, 328). The proposition of the identity of thinking and being seems to imply a sort of equality between thinking and being. Thinking and being, identical, would be both isomorphic to and equal with one another. There appears to be no privileged place within this identity. Such an understanding of equality, we should note, is the very understanding employed by Schmitt, wherein difference is disruptive, chaotic, troublesome. In this logic—which, Kierkegaard is saying, is *the* philosophical logic—equality is only possible amongst isomorphic equals. Yet, as my previous engagement with Schmitt demonstrated, such claims to equality and identity should be treated with suspicion. A binary relation given as equal often elides a more fundamental privileging of one term over the other. In the case of Schmitt, enmity was found to control and dominate the binary of friend and enemy, because the relation that linked friends and enemies was itself one of enmity. Here, Kierkegaard argues, the term "thinking" is actually dominating the allegedly equal partnership of thinking and being: the relationship is thought, it is not being. Or, in a shorter hand, the relationship is thought and it *is* not: "This pure relation between thinking and being, this pure identity, indeed this tautology . . . does not mean that the thinking person is, but basically only that he is a thinker" (*CUP*, 123).

The recognition that the identity of thinking and being is a philosopheme—a "philosophical thesis"—allows Kierkegaard to reintroduce into the identity, in order to destabilize it, his existential category of actuality. A rethinking of thinking along the lines that this category suggests will demonstrate the ways in which the Kierkegaardian critique of the identity of thinking and being is important for his understanding of decision in general and religious decision in particular: the privileging of actuality (*virkelighed*) over reality (*realitet*) informs the way in which Kierkegaard thinks—*actually* thinks—of religious belief, which will prove inseparable from religious praxis. Before tracing this line of argument, though, I think it is important to once again address the Marxist charge that Kierkegaard ignores worldly struggle in favor over an idealist escapism. More provocatively, I want to suggest that Kierkegaard, even when he operates in an apparently deconstructive and highly theoretical register, as he does here by demonstrating the philosophical control of difference within the philosophical thesis of the identity of thinking and being, is fundamentally a dialectical-materialist thinker. Consider the following passage, which is somewhat awkwardly placed in the middle of a lengthy and rather byzantine discussion of the paradoxical nature of Christian truth: "Suppose the speculative thinker is the restless resident who, although it is obvious he is a renter, yet in view of the abstract truth that, eternally and divinely perceived, all property is in common, wants to be the owner, so that there is nothing to do except to send for a police officer, who would presumably say, just as the subpoena servers say to Gert

Westphaler: We are sorry to have come on this errand" (*CUP*, 214). Gert Westphaler is the title character of Norwegian playwright Ludvig Holberg's 1722 five-act play *Gert Westphaler*, or *The Loquacious Barber*. The reference to this play is important for several reasons. The first concerns its plot: in the play, Gert Westphaler, the loquacious barber, is seen losing customers because of his insatiable appetite for conversation. Westphaler talks until his customers leave—and even this does not stop him. That is, Kierkegaard refers to a play about a worker who loses money because of a penchant for talking. Svend Kragh-Jacobsen, in this introduction to Holberg's collected plays, notes that this is a motif of Holberg's:

> The play ("Gert Westphaler, ir, the Loquacious Barber") is a comedy of character, closely related to the first, and one of the most famous, of Holberg's comedies of character, "Den politiske Kandestøber" ("The Political Tinker"). The talkative Master Gert is a spiritual cousin of the politically eloquent Master Hermann; both are workers, and—when they do not abandon their trades in order to talk—good workers, but they are both possessed by fixed ideas. In the barber comedy there is a suggestion that Master Gert was a politician, but Holberg has stressed his loquacity and reserved the satire of the ignorant but conceited amateur politicians for the play about the tinker. (7)[29]

Holberg's plays are about workers and politicians who fail to improve material conditions because they talk too much, because they are "possessed by fixed ideas." And so the reference to Gert Westphaler helps us understand the first part of the above passage from Kierkegaard: Westphaler, like any speculative thinker, is under the impression that they do not have to pay rent because they are aware of the eternal truth that private property is a lie. Of course, Kierkegaard is saying, such knowledge of eternal truth has little to do with police action. In actuality, owners own and renters rent, and this despite whatever eternal philosophy has to say. Ideal truth claims do not affect material emancipation.

According to Kragh-Jacobsen, "Gert Westphaler" was originally performed in five acts. However, the loquacious barber proved too loquacious not only for his clients, but also for the actual audience of the play: fed up with Westphaler's chattiness, audiences frequently left the theatre before the show's conclusion. And so Holberg, apparently interested in the plight of the working class, sees his political performance undermined in the very same way that he describes: Westphaler talks too much and loses clients; Holberg, via Westphaler, talks too much and loses audience. Is Kierkegaard, who is also "talking" quite a bit through a loquacious author in Johannes Climacus, using this reference as a means of critiquing the project of enacting political change through interminable philosophical meditations—even true, undeniably true, meditations? It seems to me that Kierkegaard's acknowledgement that the text is "merely a kind of lunacy" suggests so. The philosophical critique of idealism always points to its own limit: rent is a lie, but the police, who have internalized this lie, are actual. More generally, this recognition of loquacious philosophy's political limits articulates an explicitly existentialist critique of ideology: The actual functioning of ideology does not depend upon logical or philosophical coherence, because actuality does not depend upon thinking. If existentialism is to overcome the limits of idealism, it cannot rely on only deconstructively pointing out the tensions and philosophical contradictions of idealist claims. The struggle for emancipation needs to occur not in the ideal realm of thought, which is where the elites would prefer it to happen, but in actuality.

Of course, Gert Westphaler was *actually* loquacious—this was precisely his problem—and so this privileging of "actuality" should be further specified. If thinking is real but not actual, and if existence is actual, then existence must have some content that is independent of thinking. Existence, then, not only resists conceptualization but also places a sort of outer limit on it: because of their radical incompatibility, thinking can never appropriate the actuality of existence.

That thinking and existence stand in this asymmetrical nonrelation—that actuality is not identical to thinking; that the reality of thought is different from the actuality of existence—is crucial for a project of an orthopraxical and revolutionary political theology: if existence and actuality are basically unattainable in thought, then the measures by which existence and actuality are judged cannot be found in the categories of thought. This incompatibility between the actualities of political existence and the calculations of reason and thinking suggests that a political theology responsive to Kierkegaardian existentialism cannot ground itself in the sort of statistical programs—Caputo's tax code readjustments, for example—that have become standard operating procedure in neoliberal regimes: a political program that is oriented by statistical or even logical arguments will always risk deep disappointment when applied to actuality. This inability to govern actuality by thought, and this inability to measure the truth of an actual program according to the measures of thought, implies a strong materialism not only in Kierkegaard's program, but indeed in any program—such as Derrida's—that rejects the (actual) identity of thinking and being.[30]

And so from an existentialist critique of the identity of thinking and being, Kierkegaard articulates the basic groundwork for any materialist understanding of the relationship between ideas—or, as Kierkegaard and Derrida would each sometimes have it, between philosophy as such—and material actuality. Once this materialism is established, it becomes easier to reread Kierkegaardian arguments as not ideal, as his Marxist critics have it, but more strongly as dialectical-material, as his Marxist critics would want it. For example, Kierkegaard writes that "the logical system must not be a mystification, a ventriloquism, in which the content of existence emerges cunningly and surreptitiously" (*CUP*, 111). Targeting Hegel's argument concerning the identity of the history of philosophy with the philosophy of history, Kierkegaard is here arguing that a philosophical system cannot, in actuality, deduce the events, both mundane and world historical, that constitute actual existence. Things do not do what thinking says they should do. And so any confluence between historical events and speculative philosophy—and again Kierkegaard is thinking of the Hegelian metanarrative of the development of world spirit—is a sign that the philosopher has smuggled in empirical actuality under the appearance of pure rationality. Europe, for example, was not the site of the pinnacle of philosophical achievement because the world spirit rose with the sun in the east and hit a high point over Europe in the center, which is what Hegel argues. Instead, Europe seemed to be the pinnacle of philosophical achievement because of Hegel's own Eurocentric geographical, political, and historical location. And so Hegel's particular existence becomes the impetus for a philosophical rationalization of its own supremacy. Which is to say, Hegel, according to Kierkegaard, has reverted to a pre-Lessing and pre-critical understanding of the relationship between the accidental truths of history and the eternal truths of reason: where Lessing saw a ditch, Hegel saw perfect identity.

This line of critique is materialist in that it rejects the reduction of actuality to ideal categories. The critique applies to both those idealist tendencies that think of ideas as productive of or identical to reality (Hegel) and those idealist tendencies that substitute actual action with intellectual activity (Gert Westphaler, liberals). In much the same way that knowing the truth of (the lie of) private property does not lead to an emancipation from private property, neither does knowing a philosophical program lead to "knowing" actual existence. The argument is most compelling when applied to those who think of ethics in terms of cognition and not action: "Am I the good because I think it or am I good because I think the good? Not at all" (*CUP*, 330). And again: "To have thought something good that one wants to do, is that to have done it? Not at all" (*CUP*, 339). These passages show the incoherence of an ethics that privileges knowing and thinking over actuality: the very question "Am I the good?" reveals the absurdity of identifying as an individual with an abstract category of thought. The question confuses genera, and the thinker begins to abstract from his or herself in the very moment—an interrogation of what is good—that most requires concreteness, particularity, and actual action.[31]

And so thinking cannot substitute for actual action because thinking and actuality do not relate. The argument is similar to Marx's critique of Pierre-Joseph Proudhon, the nineteenth-century French anarchist theorist. In a letter dated December 28, 1846, Marx writes the following about Proudhon:

> He (Proudhon) fails to see that economic categories are but abstractions of those real relations, that they are truths only in so far as those relations continue to exist. Thus he falls into the error of bourgeois economists who regard those economic categories as eternal laws and not as historical laws which are laws only for a given historical development, a specific development of the productive forces. Thus, instead of regarding politico-economic categories as abstractions of actual social relations that are transitory and historical, Mr. Proudhon, by a mystical inversion, sees in the real relations only the embodiment of those abstractions. Those abstractions are themselves formulas which have been slumbering in the bosom of God the Father since the beginning of the world.[32]

Marx's critique of Proudhon is structurally analogous to Kierkegaard's (and Marx's) critique of Hegel. Proudhon, according to Marx, has devised a link between allegedly eternal economic laws and particular historical circumstances. Likewise, Hegel, according to Kierkegaard, has devised a link between eternal philosophical truths and his own particular circumstances. In each case, the critique is more subtle than might first appear. On one level, Hegel and Proudhon are each critiqued for inverting the relationship between the historical and the eternal: they write as if historical events and circumstances were manifestations of eternal, God-given truths. As I have argued throughout this text, and as is becoming more clear here, any attempt to legitimate historical circumstances through an appeal to divine truth can only reify an ideological conception of God. I take both Kierkegaard and Marx to subscribe to such a critique of the ideological use of God. But their critiques are operating on another level, too. Here, the concern is not that of an ideological inversion of the particular and the universal, but of the construction of the universal as such. For Marx, economic "laws" are better thought of as descriptions of contingent historical truths. Indeed, the very notion of universal law implies an entire essentialist ontology to which neither Marx nor Kierkegaard subscribe. And so, from this perspective, the act of "inverting" the relationship between the particular and the universal is better understood as the process by which the universal is created as such. The myth of an eternal law is created in the act of abstracting from the particular. An ideal authority is invented for the sake of securing the intelligibility and credibility of the material order. This, in brief, is the materialist critique of ideology as deployed by both Marx and Kierkegaard.

According to Marx, Proudhon, by inventing an eternal law, displaces the site of actual political struggle. In the idealist view, social and political change occurs by way of changing our relation to the eternal. This is the inverse of Marx's materialist conception of political struggle, according to which our relation to the eternal—which is only ever an invention of thought—is changed by changing material conditions. Simplified, for Proudhon, according to Marx, one must change ideas in order to change actual material relations; whereas for Marx, one must change actual material relations in order to change ideas. Marx continues:

> Still less does Mr. Proudhon understand that those who produce social relations in conformity with their material productivity also produce the *ideas, categories,* i.e., the ideal abstract expressions of those same social relations. Indeed, the categories are no more eternal than the relations they express. They are historical and transitory products. To Mr. Proudhon, on the contrary, the prime cause consists in abstractions and categories. According to him it is these and not men which make history. (Marx, Letter to Pavel Annenkov)

And so the ideological creation of eternal laws and the concomitant inversion of the concrete with the general denies the agentic power of human activity in political emancipation. Concepts and ideal categories, not people, become political actors. For Marx, every ideological distortion adheres to this general structure: whereas people create ideas, ideology says that ideas create people. This ideological apparatus suggests that any successful act of liberation would have to take place on the level of ideas—liberation would become a matter of talking, and Gert Westphaler would be a revolutionary. But this notion of a loquacious revolutionary is precisely the ideological distortion imposed on the oppressed by the oppressors for the sake of undermining the possibility of actual revolution: the ideological understanding of oppression is that the oppressors are suffering an intellectual flaw, that they have misunderstood the truth, that they need some epistemological clarification on the truth content of eternity. In reality, say Marx and Kierkegaard, the oppressors are acting out of self-interest and power, and the correction of injustice must be fought on this level of actuality, not ideality: "It is only possible to achieve real liberation in the real world and by employing real means . . . people cannot be liberated as long as they are unable to obtain food and drink, housing and clothing in adequate quality and quantity. *Liberation is a historical and not a mental act.*"[33] That liberation is a historical—that is, actual, existing—and not a mental act is the materialist presupposition of Marx's critique of political economy and the materialist conclusion of Kierkegaard's critique of the identity of thinking and actuality.[34] Life, and so emancipation, is lived actually, not ideally.

So far, I have suggested that Kierkegaard's materialism is implied by his existentialism: because existence separates thinking from actuality, any attempted liberation or emancipation of existing individuals must take place not ideally in thought but materially in actuality. Yet, to speak of Kierkegaard as belonging to the same tradition as avowed atheists Jean-Paul Sartre (for whom atheism is a precondition for existentialism, because it is the lack of God that assures that human existence precedes essence)[35] and Albert Camus (who explicitly critiques Kierkegaard throughout *The Myth of Sisyphus*),[36] not to mention Marx, seems to miss something central to Kierkegaard's project, or at least something central to Kierkegaard's own self-understanding: Christianity.

What is the relationship between Kierkegaard's Christianity and his existentialism? Importantly for this project—which is interested in defending the convergence of religious and secular political projects—does Kierkegaard's Christianity mark a substantial enough difference as to render his project fundamentally different or even opposed to those thinkers named above? How can Kierkegaard, who claims to first and always seek the kingdom of God, be squared so neatly with Marx, for whom the emancipation of the proletariat implies the abolition of religion?

Any squaring between the two—and any convergence between secular and religious political projects—cannot be defended on grounds of orthodoxy, at least if orthodoxy is understood as an intellectual commitment to propositional truth claims. That is, and again echoing Derrida's critique of theology, if theology means metaphysical speculation and the affirmation of propositional truth claims, then theology can never have anything to do with the atheist or secular left. In such a case, theology would make an enemy of this left because of its own prior metaphysical positions. And if a left political project strives above all for the emancipation of the oppressed—and this is how I understand it—then such a theology would have to be rejected as not only reactionary, but also as unloving, that is, as an anti-Christ.

But as Kierkegaard's emphasis on actuality demonstrates, there is another way of understanding both religion and theology. In this view, orthodoxy loses its privileged position over orthopraxy. Which is not to say that a loss for orthodoxy implies a symmetrical gain for orthopraxy: Kierkegaard does not reverse a hierarchy, but instead displaces the hierarchical relationship altogether. Echoing Marx's critique of Proudhon, the content of proper praxis would no longer be considered deducible from the eternal truths of orthodoxy, because orthodoxy would no longer be described as a set of eternal truths. Instead, and more radically, orthodoxy would be re-signified as a type of actually existing political-theological project: to be a Christian and to believe the truths of Christianity would require the decision to act as a Christian.

In other words, if theology is not to be antithetical to emancipation, then truth cannot be thought metaphysically. This non-metaphysical truth is articulated in Kierkegaard's oft-quoted claim, which risks becoming a slogan, that "subjectivity is truth." At first blush, the claim might be read as a reduction of truth to inwardness, as if the rejection of objective criteria meant the valorization of an internal state or condition. In such a view, what would determine veracity or falsity would not be the measure of some objective content, but instead the mode by which a person relates to objectivity. Truth would be dispositional, a psychological effect or mood. Indeed, Kierkegaard sometimes comes close to saying just this: "Objectively the emphasis is on what is said; subjectively the emphasis is on how it is said . . . At its maximum, this 'how' is the passion of the infinite, and the passion of the infinite is the very truth. But the passion of the infinite is precisely subjectivity, and thus subjectivity is truth . . . The passion of the infinite, not its content, is the deciding factor, for its content is precisely itself. In this way the subjective how and subjectivity are the truth" (*CUP*, 202/203). Here, Kierkegaard seems to be—and is—distinguishing between an objective what and a subjective how, and is using this distinction to help articulate his theory of truth. Similar passages are found in *Fear and Trembling*, in which Kierkegaard, via his pseudonym Johannes de Silentio, spends comparatively more ink applauding Abraham's dispositional passionate faith than he does explicitly critiquing the content of this faith—filicide. Such an emphasis on disposition at the expense of content leads Caputo, whose complicated relationship to Kierkegaard was discussed two chapters ago, to argue that "in *Fear and Trembling* we see the first signs of a distorted conception of religion that emerges in the last years of his life, where the demands of God above are so overwhelming that they can completely annul the significance of life on earth" (*How to Read Kierkegaard [HK]*, 52).[37] This conception of religion is "distorted," according to Caputo, because,

> It is one thing if the absurd simply means a marvel that exceeds human reason, something of which an omnipotent God is capable but which is beyond our understanding, like making Sarah pregnant again at an advanced age. But it is quite another thing (and this is the problem with *Fear and Trembling*) to approve of a divine command to kill an innocent child, which seems to be absurd in a stronger sense, not simply exceeding reason but flatly contradicting all reason. (*HK*, 53)

That is, according to Caputo, Kierkegaard has improperly transposed the transcendent category of the absurd into an immanent ethics: Kierkegaard is on solid ground when he speaks of the absurd as synonymous with the unknowability of God, but goes too far when he suggests that the absurd is precisely to know something about God—here, for example, to know that God has demanded filicide. In other words, Caputo criticizes Kierkegaard for not being ideal enough—for letting religion say too much about worldly affairs.

Hägglund makes a similar critique of Kierkegaard giving too much credence to the "demands of God" in especially *Fear and Trembling*. According to Hägglund, Kierkegaard argues that "To prove your religious commitment, you must be able to renounce your secular devotion to any form of living on—including the living on of your most beloved child—by virtue of your complete faith in the eternal" (*TL*, 128).[38] While Caputo sees Abraham's planned filicide, and Kierkegaard's seeming endorsement of it, as a distortion of religion, and while Hägglund sees it as the logical and terrible fulfillment of religion, both Caputo and Hägglund are in agreement that Kierkegaard has ethically gone too far, that his emphasis on passion and inwardness has dangerously removed consideration of the well-being of others from political decision making. This is a sort of terrorist Kierkegaard willing to do anything to anyone for the sake of pleasing his God.

Certainly, Caputo's and Hägglund's concerns are justifiable: nobody can credibly argue that an emancipatory political theology should endorse filicide. At the least, such a program would not be particularly emancipatory for Isaac. In the next section, I will more closely demonstrate that Kierkegaard's political theology is guided by fairly straightforward and clear norms: none of which could possibly be construed to endorse filicide. For now, three responses can briefly be offered.

First, the most honest response should be to accept these obvious and justifiable concerns with Kierkegaard's apparently terrorist and homicidal inclinations, but to note that they are not, in the most literal analysis, Kierkegaard's at all: *Fear and Trembling* was written by Johannes de Silentio, and, as my treatment of Johannes Climacus argued, one cannot quickly identify the pseudonym's words with what Kierkegaard wants to say. In this reading, one should accept that Johannes de Silentio has described an absolutely terrifying and irresponsible type of religion. For what purpose would Kierkegaard have de Silentio do this? Perhaps, as George Pattison has suggested, to demonstrate that the decision for religion is not easy, not even sane.[39] Here, rather than read Kierkegaard's famous "three stages of existence" as a progression from the aesthetic, through the ethical, and to the religious, we would read all three spheres as ultimately indefensible. This would be Kierkegaard as deconstructionist: the religious sphere is not the telos of human living, but is another internally contradictory and ultimately indefensible way of life.

The second response is to also accept that nobody should endorse filicide, but to more clearly situate de Silentio against other of Kierkegaard's works. For example, is this terrifying Kierkegaard the same Kierkegaard who writes, in his own name, that "the beggar is infinitely more important than the king, infinitely more important, because the Gospel is preached to the poor" (*The Moment [TM]*, 44)?[40] Or is it the Kierkegaard who writes that "faith turns its back on the eternal in order to have it at its side this very day" (*Spiritual Writings [SW]*, 156)?[41] Putting the various positions in such a direct confrontation—they do not cohere—at the least suggests that there is more to the story than the simple read whereby Kierkegaard conceives of religion by way of blind willingness to kill.

But there is a third option—and this is the possibility that is at the heart of Caputo's and Hägglund's concerns. Putting aside the question of Kierkegaard's endorsement or criticism of filicide, *Fear and Trembling* can also be read as confronting the reader with the wildness of faith after metaphysical surety. As is a theme both for Kierkegaard and Derrida, faith can never be grounded in knowledge. The opposite is the case: faith is only possible after the deconstruction of the identity of thinking and being. In this way, Abraham's faith in God is concomitant with the empirical fact that Abraham did not know if it was God who commanded filicide. As I will argue shortly, the reader of *CUP* can never be sure that the text is not lunacy—indeed, the text forbids this surety. Likewise, Abraham could never be sure that his experience of theophany was not actually an experience of lunacy—or even that theophany and lunacy are separable categories. The possibility of an irreducible lunacy will become important in this book's conclusionary reflections on John Brown, for instance. Abraham as knight of faith—if he is one, and this is never established and could not ever be established—should, in this reading, be understood in its full deconstructive indeterminacy: without the sure ground of metaphysical knowledge, we each find ourselves on Moriah, wondering if we are experiencing lunacy or God, wondering if God is a lunatic, wondering what to decide, and knowing that knowledge will not provide the answer. This reading of *Fear and Trembling* is much more troubling than is the one concerned with Kierkegaard's potential endorsement of religious fundamentalism. As articulated above, I believe Kierkegaard himself provides plenty of good reason to deny this terroristic reading. But this, the text might suggest, if no solace at all. The authority of Kierkegaard—the knowledge that Kierkegaard did not endorse the killing of children—does not shield anyone from facing the fear and trembling found on Moriah, and a myopic focus on Kierkegaard the individual can only serve as a retreat from these potentially radical heights.

We will return to those heights later, where we will find not only Abraham (who, in fact, did descend), but also Che Guevara, Fred Hampton, and John Brown. For now, the immediate concern is to situate Caputo's and Hägglund's concerns within Kierkegaard's broader political theology. With Caputo's and Hägglund's concerns, we have the opposite problem of relation as that between Marx and Kierkegaard. With Marx, the question was how to square Kierkegaard's Christian commitments with an apparently secular political program. Now, the problem raised by Caputo's and Hägglund's readings is how to square the emancipatory potential of Kierkegaard's political program with his apparent religious fundamentalism and its apparently murderous sympathies. Although approached from differing and antagonistic angles—Kierkegaard is here too religious, there too worldly—the basic problem is the same: how to relate Kierkegaard's politics with his theology?

This question of the relationship of politics and theology, the question of political theology, seems to be the crux of the issue: for Marxists and Kierkegaardians, and for deconstructive Kierkegaardians like Caputo as well as for deconstructive anti-Kierkegaardians like Hägglund, Kierkegaard's religious commitments seem antithetical or at least in tension with a leftist political program. To address this question, we have to return to—or, in Kierkegaardian language, repeat—the topic with which this chapter opened: the Christian paradoxical relation of the eternal and the temporal. There, it was seen that the Christian conception of truth is paradoxical because it holds that neither eternal truths nor historical approximations are grounds for faith commitments, yet precisely the combination of the two—that the eternal is given in, as, and through time—is both the content of truth and the absurd ground of faith. Neither the one nor the other on their own are the content of faith, yet the two together become precisely that. Such was the argument of *Philosophical Fragments,* and it seemed to demonstrate that Christianity is a theological response to the limits of philosophical—specifically Socratic and Lessingian—thinking. Now, though, after this analysis of the divergence between thinking and actuality, we are able to repeat this account of Christian truth in a way that is more explicitly political.

Kierkegaard himself, via Climacus, gestures toward this political repetition. The account is given in *Philosophical Fragments* and happens quickly over the course of a couple of important and dense pages. In these pages, we see Kierkegaard at the height of his speculative and theoretic powers. That he uses reaching these heights as an occasion for arguing the privilege of existence and actuality over speculation is, for Kierkegaard, what makes his thought Christian: at the highest high there is ultimately found "the poor and despised" (*Journals and Papers Volume 3 [JP]*, 232, entry 2793).[42] Here is the important passage wherein Kierkegaard begins to articulate this theological epistemic privilege of the poor: "The paradox came into existence through the relating of the eternal, essential truth to the existing person. Let us now go further; let us assume that the eternal, essential truth is itself the paradox. How does the paradox emerge? By placing the eternal, essential truth together with existing. Consequently, if we place it together in the truth itself, the truth becomes a paradox. The eternal truth has come into existence in time. That is the paradox" (*CUP*, 209). The passage demands some clarification. Kierkegaard begins by repeating his position from *Philosophical Fragments* that "the paradox" is that the eternal can and does relate to the existing, and so temporal, person. However, he quickly looks to "go further" by assuming "that the eternal, essential truth is itself the paradox." What does this mean? Kierkegaard here is clarifying his position by specifying the content of "the eternal." It is one thing to say that something called the eternal structurally relates to something called the temporal, as if "the eternal" and "the temporal" were abstract and contentless philosophemes. But such a reliance on empty categories of thought is not what Kierkegaard is doing. This passage begins to fill in some of that missing content by "assuming" that the eternal is "itself the paradox." On the one hand, then, "paradox" in Kierkegaard's text means that the eternal exists in, through, and as the temporal. But this position leaves the semantic intention of its terms empty: what do the eternal and the temporal signify? Kierkegaard is attempting an answer to those questions by "assuming" that, on the other hand, "the eternal" that relates to the temporal in such a way is, precisely, "the paradox."

I suggest that this passage demonstrates Kierkegaard struggling to articulate an existentialist and materialist notion of truth. What he is not doing—or is no longer doing—is thinking of paradox as the extrinsic relation between the eternal and the temporal. Instead, he is arguing that the eternal truth itself is precisely this paradoxical involvement with its other. This can be clarified again through analogy with Marx. Above, we saw that Marx critiqued bourgeois economics for acting as if material circumstances are particular manifestations of ideal laws. According to such a view, the eternal law of exchange exists in God's mind, and particular circumstances come about accidentally and according to these eternal laws. The Marxist critique demonstrates that such a program is an ideological obfuscation of the invention of such eternal laws: whereas the bourgeois economist wants to give the impression that he or she is appealing to eternal truths in order to deduce particular circumstances, Marx argues that such an economist is actually producing these laws in the very act of appealing to them. In much the same way, Kierkegaard is here providing an ideology critique of the category of eternity as such: it is not as if the eternal exists independently and above the temporal, dictating and producing accidental manifestations of eternal law along the way. Rather, what is called the eternal has only ever existed in, as, and through its manifestation in the temporal. That there appears an other to the temporal—and we call this other the eternal—is precisely what the eternal is. That is: "the paradox" is not that two distinct realms, the eternal and the temporal, have come into contact. Rather, "the paradox" is that the eternal *is* only insofar as it exists always already in, as, and through the temporal. The eternal is the appearance of itself in the temporal, and there might not ever be anything "behind" this appearance.

Such a complication of the relationship between these three terms—paradox, eternal, temporal—is important for Kierkegaard's project because it affirms the privileged place accorded to existence in Kierkegaard's understanding of truth. In this complication, Kierkegaard existentially specifies the philosophical problem of the relation of eternity to time as posed by both Socrates and Lessing. The categories of the eternal and the temporal are actual only if they *exist*. "The eternal," understood as an ideal philosopheme, has reality or thought-content insofar as and whenever it is thought. But such reality is not actual if the eternal does not exist: without existence, there is no actuality, only thinking. *There is actually nothing outside existence.*

But, according to Kierkegaard, if the truth exists in actuality, and if every single individual also only exists in actuality, then every single individual finds him or herself in a position of necessary confrontation with the truth. Actual existence becomes the place where each person must decide how he or she is to actually relate to the truth. That is, existence becomes "the time of decision" (*CUP*, 212). Here, by framing existence as the time and place of deciding how to relate to the truth, which has already been understood as the passionate commitment to live according to thought content, Kierkegaard advances his position another step: not only would a speculative retreat from existence be a retreat from truth, but such a retreat is also actually impossible. No single individual has the ability to stave off engagement with existence. Idealism is an intellectual effort to sublate the particularities and actualities of existence into the allegedly higher ideal realm of pure thought, but such attempts can never succeed in removing the thinker from existence: "The fraud of speculative thought in wanting to recollect itself out of existence has been made impossible. This is the only point to be comprehended here . . . The individual can thrust all this (the necessity of actually engaging with existence) away and resort to speculation, but to accept it (existence) and then want to cancel it through speculation is impossible, because it (existence) is specifically designed to prevent speculation" (*CUP,* 209). That is, the speculative thinker, by relying on a coherence of thinking and being that elides actuality, removes him or herself from decisively engaging with truth in existence: idealism has reality, but not actuality.

So far, these meditations have situated a few important Kierkegaardian concepts in a dialectical, as opposed to static, relationship with each other.

The temporal, the eternal, passion, existence, truth, actuality, paradox: these concepts cannot be defined without reliance on each other. Indeed, in some cases, such as with the Kierkegaardian understanding of paradox, the concepts' relations with each other and even with themselves *are* the semantic definition of the concept. Always privileging actuality, Kierkegaard understands concepts by their actual, dynamic relations in existence. Importantly, this lack of structural simplicity—as our understanding of paradox changes, for example, so must our understanding of the eternal, which in turn affects an understanding of what counts as actual, which is now read back on our understanding of paradox, and so on—prevents the transmission of simple propositional truth claims: no single proposition can be communicated without a dynamic reference to other propositions.

Kierkegaard is aware of the befuddling effect that such an incommunicability will have, and, for this reason, writes that "lunacy and truth are ultimately indistinguishable" (*CUP*, 194). Why indistinguishable? Because whether or not these dialectical—and, admittedly, highly theoretical—meditations have any actual relationship with actual existence cannot be proven by the content of the meditations themselves. Truth cannot be propositionally communicated, but only existentially actualized. It will always remain possible that Kierkegaard has only ever invented a more subtly idealist system, or even a highly sophisticated ironic fictional production. Whether *CUP* is a theoretical treatise that captures something of actuality or is a purely fictional novel cannot be decided by the content explicated within *CUP*'s pages.

Paradoxically enough, that the decision as to *CUP*'s plausibility or credibility cannot be determined only by referencing the content of the text is exactly what the content of the text argues. As Boris Groys points out, this textual resistance to the easy appropriation of a text's truth is a motif of Kierkegaard's: "A philosophical text is first and foremost a thing, an object among many other objects, which, by virtue of its objectivity, remains separated from the subjectivity of the reader—and likewise from the subjectivity of its author—by an unbridgeable gulf. The reader has to leap over this gulf in order to identify himself with the text, but no one and nothing can force him to make such a leap" (*Introduction to Antiphilosophy [IA]*, 2).[43] Because truth is no longer thought of as an objective content but as an actual relation the existing individual takes towards any objectivity, the reader of *CUP* can only accept *CUP*'s truth through a leap of appropriation. Indeed, the necessity of a leap is exactly the truth content of the book. Once that leap is made, and so once the book's ideal content is confirmed as true through actuality, then the reader engages the text not as a spectator approaching an objective content, but as an engaged—"infinitely interested," is Kierkegaard's phrase—participant. Deciding to participate with any objective content will always involve a high degree of risk: the content might be wrong, misleading, dangerous. *CUP* could always be only lunacy.

This relationship to the truth differs from the metaphysical religious understanding—which is Schmitt's understanding—in that it does not hold truth to be a transcendent mystery overpowering our limited epistemic powers. This metaphysical regime of transcendent and mysterious truth is "paradoxical" only in the first sense described above—that the eternal as transcendent could relate to the temporal as immanent. But such an understanding does not think the eternal itself according to this logic of paradox, and so still maintains a representative structure of truth as coherence between objectivity (even if transcendent) and subjectivity. Truth is not yet action, and passionate commitment to action is not yet possible. That is, faith is not yet possible:

> When the eternal truth relates itself to an existing person, it becomes the paradox. Through the objective uncertainty and ignorance, the paradox thrusts away in the inwardness of the existing person. But since the paradox is not in itself the paradox, it does not thrust away intensely enough, for without risk, no faith; the more risk, the more faith; the more objective reliability, the less inwardness; the less objective reliability, the deeper is the possible inwardness. When the paradox itself is the paradox, it thrusts away by virtue of the absurd, and the corresponding passion of inwardness is faith. (*CUP*, 209)

"When the paradox itself is the paradox," that is, when truth is understood as the actualization of itself in existence, only then is faith possible. Any structure that makes mystery, transcendence, historical approximations, or eternal laws the object of knowledge—any system that posits a transcendental term of knowing—cannot offer faith, because any such structure understands truth as the (even asymmetrical) coherence of thinking and being and not as the passionate actualizing of thinking in existence. Kierkegaard is not arguing that the objective truth is uncertain and interminable, and so can never be known. More radically, Kierkegaard is arguing that the objective truth is the absurd, paradoxical truth that objectivity is only ever actualized in existence. This actualization is faith: "Instead of the objective uncertainty, there is here the certainty that, viewed objectively, it is the absurd, and this absurdity, held fast in the passion of inwardness, is faith" (*CUP*, 210).

And so faith is, as of this moment in the text, a passionate holding fast of the absurd. What happens next in *CUP* is more than an example of a leap. Indeed, for Kierkegaard, what happens next is *the* leap—absurd, paradoxical, and intellectually offensive as it is: "What, then, is the absurd? The absurd is that the eternal truth has come into existence in time, that God has come into existence exactly as an individual human being, indistinguishable from any other human being" (*CUP*, 210). A comma separates, on the one hand, "the eternal truth" and "existence," and, on the other hand, "God" and "an individual human being," Jesus Christ. By a leap marked by a comma, Kierkegaard moves from the "eternal" to "God," from "existence" as a category to Jesus as an individual, actual human being. Kierkegaard spends no time defending this leap. He only marks it with a comma. Indeed, he spends much time lamenting and lampooning it: to leap from the eternal as a philosopheme to God as an individual person is absurd, an offense, a "crucifixion of the understanding" (*CUP*, 564). Precisely for these reasons is faith a necessarily passionate act.

Nowhere does Kierkegaard defend the decision to leap. And he certainly does not attempt to convince anyone else to make the leap. However, while Kierkegaard does not argue for the leap, he does argue that one must choose whether to leap or not. The reason for the leap can only come about through the leap—the eternal happiness offered by Christianity is found only in the leap, and so cannot be a reason to leap. There is no good reason, and plenty of bad, according to Kierkegaard, to be a Christian. But, if one does decide in passionate freedom to make the leap to become a Christian, then, Kierkegaard's arguments concerning actuality and truth say, one must act like it.

Christian praxis: "Christianly understood, truth is obviously not to know the truth but to be the truth."[44]

The emphasis on truth as action is emphasized in Kierkegaard's retelling of Pontius Pilate's questioning of Jesus. The Gospel of John tells the story like this:

> So Pilate entered his headquarters again and called Jesus and said to him, "Are you the King of the Jews?" Jesus answered, "Do you say this of your own accord, or did others say it to you about me?" Pilate answered, "Am I a Jew? Your own nation and the chief priests have delivered you over to me. What have you done?" Jesus answered, "My kingdom is not of this world. If my kingdom were of this world, my servants would have been

fighting, that I might not be delivered over to the Jews. But my kingdom is not from the world." Then Pilate said to him, "So you are a king?" Jesus answered, "You say that I am a king. For this purpose I was born and for this purpose I have come into the world—to bear witness to the truth. Everyone who is of the truth listens to my voice." Pilate said to him, "What is truth?"

After he had said this, he went back outside to the Jews and told them, "I find no guilt in him. (Jn 18:33–38)

And Kierkegaard's interpretation "If Pilate had not asked objectively what truth is, he would never have let Christ be crucified. If he had asked the question subjectively, then the passion of inwardness regarding what he in truth had to do about the decision facing him would have prevented him from doing an injustice" (*CUP*, 229). Pilate, by framing the question of truth ontologically—"what *is* truth"—is presupposing an understanding of truth as ideal and not as actual. That is, Pilate's questioning implies that the content of truth is a proposition that Jesus can deliver in response to an inquiry—as if truth was something to be communicated in speech. Such a questioning, though, obfuscates the actual structure of truth. Asking the question subjectively would entail not asking for an ontological ideal content, but would instead entail asking about the action required by a commitment to truth. According to Kierkegaard, Pilate's question to Jesus, if Pilate was actually interested in the truth, should have been, "What should I do?" Instead, Pilate asks an ontological question and so rejects his possible role in the actualization of truth: "When a person has before his eyes something as immensely big as the objective truth, he can easily cross out his fragment of subjectivity and what he as a subjective individual has to do. Then the approximation-process of objective truth is symbolically expressed by washing one's hands, because objectively there is no decision" (*CUP*, 230). Which is to say, Pilate's recourse to ontology shields Pilate from the necessity of making a decision. In much the same way that Schmitt's appeals to ontological antisemitism attempted to shield him from the embarrassment of actual antisemitism—remember that, according to Schmitt, proper Jew-hatred has nothing to do with personal feelings of animus toward any actual Jew—Pilate here is appealing to Jesus's silence on ontological matters as a way of "washing his hands" of responsibility. Of course, to avoid making a decision in this way is itself a type of decision. Schmitt did not appeal to ontological truths but decided to construct said truths as a way of ideologically masking his decisive role in their very construction; likewise, Pilate decides to ask about ontology and not praxis as a way to ideologically mask his own decision to hand Jesus over for crucifixion. In both cases, the appearance of metaphysics is ideological.

And so Kierkegaard's treatment of Pilate's questioning demonstrates the privileged place of praxis in Kierkegaard's political theology: each individual is faced with the necessity of making a decision as to whether or not he or she will accept the responsibility of his or her own action, his or her actual existence. In the first instance, Kierkegaardian decision is not what to do, but whether or not one will accept responsibility as such. The various attempts to identify being with thinking that have been discussed so far are but various means of rejecting this primordial decision; that is, to argue ontologically that everything has been decided in advance is but one way of washing one's hands of the need to make actual decisions.

The potential problem, as I see it, is that Kierkegaard has heightened the tension of praxical decision to such a degree that Pilate's actions seem reasonable. Or rather, since Kierkegaard did not place Pilate in front of Jesus, the truth of the difficulty of opting for praxis—the difficulty of asking Jesus what to do—is such that Pilate's ideological decision to abrogate his authority appears reasonable. Apparently, with neither ontological nor historical grounding, the individual existing person looking to make such a decision can rely only on his or her own dogged faith. Such a reasonless faith, which leaps over any philosophical or historical ground offered to it, becomes an act of extreme difficulty. Indeed, the absolute difficulty of faith constitutes faith's specific difference from other forms of assent—say, historical or philosophical knowing. In those epistemic discourses, one is never completely responsible: historical authorities, the objective truths of logic, etc., all serve to reduce personal liability in that these factors operate as objective determinants of future actions. One can always defend an action by claiming that it was done according to the best evidence available at the time and so on.[45] But faith commitments and praxical decisions, which are decisions for which the single individual is entirely responsible, foreclose the possibility of appeals to objective authorities of this kind. This lack of external authority puts the faithful in a rather precarious and terrifying situation.

It is not surprising, then, that Kierkegaard himself never claimed to have made such a leap into Christian praxis. Indeed, he questioned whether it wouldn't be better to prevent anyone from making such a leap. In his own name, he writes:

> I want honesty. If this, then, is what the generation or the contemporaries want, if they want straightforwardly, honestly,

> candidly, openly, directly to rebel against Christianity and say to God, "We cannot, we will not submit to this power"—but, please note, this is to be done straightforwardly, honestly, candidly, openly, directly-well, then strange as it might seem, I go along with it, because I want honesty. Wherever there is honesty, I am able to go along with it; an honest rebellion against Christianity can be made only if one honestly acknowledges what Christianity is and how one relates oneself to it . . . I do not dare to call myself a Christian; but I want honesty, and to that end I will venture. (*TM*, 48/49)

Clearly, Kierkegaard is not acting as an apologist for Christianity. In these texts signed in his name, Kierkegaard is critical not only of the Christendom of the state church of Denmark, but perhaps even of Christianity as such. At least, Kierkegaard is open to an honest criticism of Christianity—and even an honest rebellion against God. Such an openness to rebellion is far from the unquestioning faith of Abraham found in *Fear and Trembling*, and again suggests that the pseudonymous texts should be read as ironic representations of positions with which Kierkegaard himself does not necessarily agree. In this view, it is Knausgaard and Derrida, the one rejecting God and the other clinging to his tallith, and not Schmitt, who aggressively and unquestioningly decides in favor of (a violent, antisemitic, and deeply metaphysical) Christianity, who are actually aligned with Kierkegaard. On this matter of not necessarily aligning with those who profess to share one's religious commitments, Kierkegaard writes:

> If someone who lives in the midst of Christianity enters, with knowledge of the true idea of God, the house of God, the house of the true God, and prays, but prays in untruth, and if someone lives in an idolatrous land but prays with all the passion of infinity, although his eyes are resting upon the image of an idol—where, then, is there more truth? The one prays in truth to God although he is worshipping an idol; the other prays in untruth to the true God and is therefore in truth worshipping an idol. (*CUP*, 201)

This passage, which seems to suggest that the truth of faith is not determined by professed belief in God but by passion, comes only a few pages before the aforementioned important discussion of the paradoxical nature of truth. By foregrounding that discussion of truth with this recognition that an "idol" might be more "true" than the "true God," Kierkegaard is preparing the reader to give up any a priori conception of religious truth. It is as if he is saying: I am about to speak of eternity and of eternal truth, but do not think that by this I necessarily mean the Christian God that is prayed to in our Danish churches.

On the one hand, such an openness to rebellion against God and such a destabilization of the God/idol binary should be read as a critique of any reified understanding of Christianity as a set of objective doctrinal truths. According to Kierkegaard, any religion that identifies itself with the preservation and communication of a set of doctrinal truth claims has nothing to do with the actual truth. In that it would look to communicate the eternal truth, which would be held to exist objectively and independently of existing individuals, a regime that showed myopic concern with doctrinal and orthodoxical purity would be a variation of the Socratic theory of pedagogy, and so would encounter all of the already discussed problems that face this theory.

In this sense, the desire to protect and preserve a Christian doctrine becomes a means of undermining the actual truth of Christianity. Kierkegaard articulates this argument in more explicitly political terms toward the end of *CUP*:

> The Church theory assumes that we are Christians, but now we must in a purely objective way have it made sure what the essentially Christian is in order to secure it against the Turk and the Russian and the Roman yoke, and valiantly battle Christianity forward by having our age form a bridge, as it were, to a matchless future, which is already glimpsed. This is sheer aestheticism. Christianity is an existence communication. The task is to become a Christian or to continue to be a Christian, and the most dangerous illusion of all is to become so sure of being one that all Christendom must be defended against the Turk—instead of defending the faith within oneself against the illusion about the Turk. (*CUP*, 608)

That is, obsessions with defining the difference between Christianity and its others—especially when these obsessions are pursued for the sake of defending an alleged supremacy or purity of the Christian, as with Schmitt—are not instances of defending the faith but are instead instances of undermining faith via a displacement of existential responsibility onto objective criteria: faith becomes not a project of materially actualizing existential truth, but instead an ideological project of demarcating and defending hierarchical ontological categories. This resistance to Christian xenophobia stands in stark contrast to Schmitt, who unbelievably claimed that "never in the thousand year struggle between Christians and Muslims did it occur to a Christian to surrender rather than defend Europe out of love toward the Saracens or Turks" (*The Concept of the Political [CP]*, 29).[46] In Kierkegaard's view, the privileging of a European over a Turk on the grounds of professed religion is precisely the idolatrous temptation to be avoided. That is, if Christianity is a religion of actualizing existential truth, then these efforts to abstract from existence in the realm of objective orthodoxy are essentially anti-Christian.

And so just as Gert Westphaler's loquaciousness on the issue of workers' rights should not be confused with actually improving workers' conditions, a profession of Christian faith should not be confused with actually being a Christian. Which is not to say Kierkegaard is himself claiming to be an actual Christian—far from it. He is resisting the idealization of Christianity: this resistance is not for the sake of securing his own privilege as a true Christian over and against the orthodox frauds, but is for the sake of not allowing Christianity to become a bourgeois tool of oppression, class signification, or xenophobia: he is not claiming to be a Christian, but he is claiming that the elites' appropriation of orthodoxy and doctrine for their own self-interested purposes—just like Hegel's appropriation of "rationality" for his own Eurocentrism; just like Proudhon's appropriation of "eternal economic laws" for his own anarchism—is a thoroughly ideological, not Christian, project.

But even given that he is not claiming to be a Christian in his attack on Christendom, Kierkegaard risks a slippage here, because the talk of actual Christianity is different from the talk of rebelling against God: On the one hand, Kierkegaard announces a desire for truth and honesty at all costs—even if this means dismissing Christianity; on the other hand, he provides a defense of actual Christianity against its idealist and orthodox imposters. How can these two positions be squared? How can Kierkegaard claim that he is willing to rebel against God and also claim that his critique of orthodoxy is its anti-Christian nature, that is, its own rebellion against God? In other words, why would Kierkegaard care that these imposters are rebelling against God, if he himself is prepared to do so? Or, how can Kierkegaard claim that he is defending a true understanding of actual Christianity as not concerned with describing and preserving its difference from others, but also make this very point by describing and preserving the difference of actual Christianity against its others? From what grounds is Kierkegaard launching his attack on Christendom?

The response cannot simply be that Kierkegaard has no ground from which he critiques, or that he has leapt over any such ground. Such a response would, after all, also be available to those whom Kierkegaard critiques: anyone could simply say that their projects are absurd, that truth is subjective, that ground is a metaphorical philosopheme and that they prefer the metaphorical philosopheme of leaping, and so on. Such "relativism" is not what Kierkegaard is doing. In February 1855, Kierkegaard wrote a newspaper article titled "Salt." In it, he admonishes the Christian Danish elite of his day:

> If in the Christian view there is any difference for God, then the beggar is infinitely more important than the king, infinitely more important, because the Gospel is preached to the poor! But see, to the pastors the king is infinitely more important than the beggar. "A beggar, how will he help us?" You rag of velvet, did Christianity come into the world in order to have help from human beings, or in order to help them, the poor, the beggar, since the Gospel is preached to the poor? (*TM*, 44)

Rags of velvet, the infinite importance of a beggar—these are passionate charges and commitments, free of any irony or deferral. Clearly, Kierkegaard does not intend his project as a critique of the possibility of critique, as if the rejection of the actuality of the identity of thinking and being prevented any sort of normative commitment. Clearly, Kierkegaard is willing to passionately make definitive judgments concerning the content of Christianity. So, the Christian might be an idolater and the idolater might be a Christian, and Kierkegaard might be willing to rebel against God, but none of this means that Christianity does not have a determinable content: "Because Christianity is not a doctrine, it holds true, as developed previously, that there is an enormous difference between knowing what Christianity is and being a Christian . . . To say that Christianity is empty of content because it is not a doctrine is only chicanery. When a believer exists in faith, his existence has enormous content, but not in the sense of a yield in paragraphs" (*CUP*, 380). That is, Kierkegaard is not nor has ever claimed to be a Christian—and he is not even sure he wants to be one—but he does know what a Christian is. That he can know Christianity without being a Christian is an effect of the distinction of knowing and existing earlier articulated. Kierkegaard has not and has never claimed to actualize the truth content of Christianity—which does not mean he does not know what that content is. Indeed, according to Kierkegaard, knowing this content is not difficult at all. The difficulty in being a Christian is not in the knowing, but in the existing: "Christianity is no doctrine; all talk of offense with regard to it as doctrine is a misunderstanding, is an enervation of the thrust of the collision of offense, as when one speaks of offense with respect to the doctrine of the God-man, the doctrine of Atonement. No, offense is related either to Christ or to being Christian oneself" (*Practice in Christianity [PC]*, 106). A theological engagement with Christianity should not be ordered to uncovering a hidden doctrinal truth, but toward better actualizing the demands of Christian existence. In that it demands a change in existence—a becoming Christian—Christianity "is not an intellectual but an ethical initiation" (*JN*, 2793).[47]

All of this is very consistent with Kierkegaard's existential dialectical materialism. On the one hand, truth must actually exist, and the person in truth must actualize this truth in his or her existence. In this way, it is not surprising that the truth of Christianity is the actual life praxis of Christians. Actual orthodoxy is orthopraxy. At the same time, an apparent tension—that Kierkegaard is willing to disobey God but passionately critiques those who disobey God—is addressed not ideally, as if Kierkegaard's positions could be squared with each other by sublating each within some higher conceptual apparatus, but materially: the actual, material demands of Christianity are such that Kierkegaard can be unsure if he wants to actualize them (that is, he is unsure if they are true) and also be absolutely certain that the elites have not.

And so Kierkegaard's rigorous methodological and theoretical observations lead to the general structural point that if Christianity has truth, this truth must actually exist. Returning to Pilate's questioning of Jesus, then, we can now say that Pilate should not have asked Jesus what truth is, but what he should truly do. Pilate provides an early example of a false engagement with Christianity: instead of asking what to do, Pilate puts Jesus on the cross—and washes his hands of it. But now, we can further specify this critique of Pilate: while it is the case that if Pilate was interested in truth he should have been interested in praxis and not ontology, it is also the case that he should not have needed to formulate this interest as an interrogative. That is, because Christianity is not a doctrine, Pilate did not need to ask Jesus to communicate some cognitive truth content. That content had already been given in advance and was the reason for Jesus's placement in front of Pilate to begin with.

Jesus does indeed communicate an answer to the question "what should I do?," but he does this through a non-semantic and non-intellectual form of communication. As Derrida notes, to ask for a communication is not necessarily to ask for a cognitive transmission of knowledge.[48] Kierkegaard is arguing the same: Jesus communicates not through a semantic or cognitive discourse, but through the actual praxis of his life. As actual, the content of Christianity is not something that is communicable through a philosophical treatise—here as everywhere, existence is irreducible to thought. The argument here is that Jesus's pedagogy—distinctly juxtaposed to Socrates's—is one of initiation into an orthopraxic community. Recall that, above, Kierkegaard, in his journals, wrote that Christianity is "not an intellectual but an ethical initiation." The full entry reads:

> Certainly, Christianity has never been—indeed, it has abhorred being—a mystery in the sense of existing only for a few brilliant minds who have become its initiates. No: God has chosen the lowly and the despised—but still there was no lack of initiation. It is not an intellectual but an ethical initiation, personality's enormous respect for inclusion in the Christian community, and this respect is not expressed in assurances and by making a fuss, but existentially, in action. (*JN*, 2793)

According to this, one enters into the true Christian community not through the proffering of assurances or doctrine, but through existential action. Such is the truth of Christianity, which reflects Kierkegaard's theoretical understanding of the relationship between the eternal and the temporal: the eternal, objective truth is found in an existential, orthopraxic community.[49] And so had Pilate asked Jesus, "what should I do?," his situation would have not been any closer to the truth: what he should have done was act as if he belonged to the praxical community Jesus had established, and, precisely by acting as such, actually belonged to it. The very act of formulating a discursive question is already an ideological displacement of the site of praxical decision: rather than ask Jesus how to behave, as if Jesus were a Socratic teacher possessing eternal secrets, one should act with Jesus in the praxis demanded by and in the Christian community.[50]

This understanding of Christianity as primarily orthopraxic—or, this reinscription of orthodoxy along the lines of orthopraxy—is demonstrated throughout Christian scripture, but nowhere more strikingly than in Matthew 19:16–24:

> And someone came to Him and said, "Teacher, what good thing shall I do that I may obtain eternal life?" And He said to him, "Why are you asking Me about what is good? There is only One who is good; but if you wish to enter into life, keep the commandments." Then he said to Him, "Which ones?" And Jesus said, "You shall not commit murder; You shall not commit adultery; You shall not steal; You shall not bear false witness; Honor your father and mother; and You shall love your neighbor as yourself." The young man said to Him, "All these things I have kept; what am I still lacking?" Jesus said to him, "If you wish to be complete, go and sell your possessions and give to the poor, and you will have treasure in heaven; and come, follow Me." But when the young man heard this statement, he went away grieving; for he was one who owned much property.
>
> And Jesus said to His disciples, "Truly I say to you, it is hard for a rich man to enter the kingdom of heaven. Again I say to you, it is easier for a camel to go through the eye of a needle, than for a rich man to enter the kingdom of God."

The rich man, foreshadowing Pilate, interrogates Jesus not about the truth, but about the good—that is, about another metaphysical "transcendental." Jesus immediately rejects the possibility of an ontological interpretation of the question: he does not want to address the question by philosophically clarifying what *is* the good. There is only one who *is* good—God—and this divine goodness has nothing to do with the praxical community that Jesus is establishing: Jesus tells the man to not concern himself with *being* good, but instead to commit to and perform a set of clearly articulated commands.[51] When the man claims that he has followed the commandments given, Jesus adds another, which proves too much: sell your possessions and give to the poor. Only upon completion of this task—which is never actually completed—can the rich man follow Jesus. That is, the following of Jesus is determined by action and coherence to clearly given praxical demands. It is not the case that the rich man could countersign doctrinal or orthodoxical positions and find himself included in the community by doing such. This sort of community would be ideal, grounded in propositions and cognitive adherence—but it would not be actual, and so it could not, according to the materialist existentialism Kierkegaard has developed, be rightly said to exist at all.

The same understanding of Christianity as an orthopraxic community is shown in the epistle of James, which is one of the most cited New Testament books in all of Kierkegaard's corpus, and which Kierkegaard claimed was his "favorite":[52]

> What use is it, my brethren, if someone says he has faith but he has no works? Can that faith save him? If a brother or sister is without clothing and in need of daily food, and one of you says to them, "Go in peace, be warmed and be filled," and yet you do not give them what is necessary for their body, what use is that? Even so faith, if it has no works, is dead, being by itself.
>
> But someone may well say, "You have faith and I have works; show me your faith without the works, and I will show you my faith by my works." You believe that God is one. You do well; the demons also believe, and shudder. (Jm 2:14–19)

As with the passage from Matthew, the profession of faith—precisely here, the profession of the orthodox proposition of monotheism—is not a sufficient, or even helpful, criteria for initiation into the Christian community. Whereas Kierkegaard claims that truth can never be known as distinct from lunacy, here the author of James writes that belief in God can never be known as distinct from the demonic: in both cases, material praxis, not ideal content, is decisive.[53] Or, as the author of James also writes: "prove yourselves doers of the word, and not merely hearers who delude themselves" (Jm 1:25).[54]

In both cases, the aspiring Christian is told that the initiation into Christianity is one of specific, material action. Such passages could be quoted at length (e.g., Matthew 7:21, which has Jesus say, "Not everyone who says to Me, 'Lord, Lord,' shall enter the kingdom of heaven, but he who does the will of My Father in heaven."). For Kierkegaard, all such passages are clear in intent and content—the difficulty, as always, is not in the understanding but in the doing:

> I open the NT and read: "If you want to be perfect, then sell all your goods and give to the poor and come and follow me." But scholarship helps us in our task of not wanting to understand, namely, not wanting to act accordingly . . . The New Testament is very easy to understand, but so far I have found tremendously

great difficulties in my own self when it comes to acting literally according to what is not difficult to understand. (JP, 2872)

That is, the act of reading scripture does not require advanced historical critical biblical scholarship.[55] Kierkegaard is defending a sort of naive first order reading that has more in common with Stephen Best and Sharon Marcus's "surface reading" than it does the "symptomatic" literary theories offered by Marxist, deconstructionist, or psychoanalytic critics with which he is more commonly associated.[56] While Kierkegaard's reading of philosophical texts are clearly deconstructive and rigorously theoretical, and while I have been at pains to show that Kierkegaard presumes a materialist methodology that leads to sustained and sophisticated ideology critique with Marxist affinity, his readings of the bible are intentionally surface level. When it comes to scripture, Kierkegaard is less a proponent of the "hermeneutics of suspicion" as he is suspicious of hermeneutics, or any other literary protocol, as such. For Kierkegaard, all such attempts to impose a hermeneutical-critical protocol of reading onto scripture serve the ideological function of withdrawing from the necessity of actualizing praxis. Kierkegaard writes to such an imagined hermeneut:

> If you happen to be a scholar, then please do see to it that in all this learned reading (which is not reading God's Word) you do not forget to read God's Word. "But," you perhaps say, "there are so many obscure passages in the Bible, whole books that are practically riddles." To that I would answer: Before I have anything to do with this objection, it must be made by someone whose life manifests that he has scrupulously complied with all the passages that are easy to understand; is this the case with you? God's Word is given in order that you shall act according to it, not that you shall practice interpreting obscure passages. (*For Self-Examination [FSE]*, 29)

Unlike Schmitt, who allegedly grounded his arguments concerning friendship and enmity on philological and historical research—shaky and questionable as it was—Kierkegaard intentionally avoids engagement with critical biblical scholarship, precisely because the bible does not tell him to engage with scholarship but to engage with the actual, material realities of his world. If reading the bible did not entail engagement with material actuality in this way, for Kierkegaard, it would not be true.

And so when applied to philosophical texts, Kierkegaard's privileging of existence leads to a rigorous theoretical critique of idealist philosophy. When applied to scripture, though, his existentialism does not encourage a deconstructive protocol, but instead an intentionally naive and first order type of surface reading. While the methods might appear different, both are guided by Kierkegaard's overarching concern for actuality and existence. When dealing with the complexities of Hegelian and Lessingian idealism, this concern articulates itself in an equally rigorous and complex manner—as was demonstrated in his discussion of the paradoxical nature of truth, for example. When dealing with the straightforward ethical commands of scripture, this concern articulates itself in an equally straightforward, yet still quite rigorous, manner. Kierkegaard uses two types of rigor—theoretical and praxical—both of which are ultimately concerned with defending the privileged position, now both theoretical and praxical, of material existence. Indeed, Kierkegaard rewrites an understanding of both theory and orthodoxy along the lines of an orthopraxy of material actuality. Far from resisting materialism, then, and far from offering mutually exclusive views of here religion and there politics, Kierkegaard is a materialist everywhere.

What has become clear, though, is that Kierkegaard does not believe that scripture is the only source for this orthopraxic content: remember that the Turk and the idolater might belong more truly to this orthopraxic community than does the orthodox Christian. The point is not that scripture has a monopoly on proper praxis, but that philosophy in particular and "thinking" in general cannot provide this material. Necessary praxis cannot be deduced from a priori logical axioms. An ugly broad ditch separates the two. In other words, it is impossible to know that praxis is helpful by measuring it against some independent philosophical or logical system—the argument is not just anti-Hegelian, but anti-Kantian: praxis concerns particular existences, not universal maxims.

What, then, are the specific criteria for involvement in this existential community? What practices are intended in this call to orthopraxis?

The next chapter will deal extensively with these questions. But to conclude this engagement with Kierkegaard, it can be noted that his answer is rather clear: Christian praxis is a commitment to improving the lives of the poor. As we've seen, he finds the command to give to the poor an example of one of the clearest in scripture. It is also likely that Kierkegaard—despite his suspicion of hermeneutics—is interpreting these biblical passages through an anti-capitalist frame. In his journals, Kierkegaard envisions an alliance between his existential understanding of Christianity, guided by an overarching concern for the poor, and communism:

The conflict concerning Christianity will no longer be a conflict about doctrine. (This is the conflict between orthodoxy and heterodoxy.) The dispute (occasioned also by the socialist and communist movements) will be about Christianity as a form of existence. The problem will be about loving one's "neighbor," attention will be directed toward Christianity's life, and Christianity will essentially accentuate conformity with his life. The world has gradually consumed those myriad illusions and partition walls by which people have ensured that the question was merely about Christianity as a doctrine. The rebellion in the world shouts: We want to see action! (*JN*, 450)

Elsewhere, Kierkegaard gives enough hints as to suggest familiarity with a socialist critique of capitalism: "The first barrel of gold, says the capitalist, will be the most difficult to gain; when one has that, the rest comes to itself" (*Christian Discourses [CD]*, 25).[57] This notion of the mystical self-production of capital—that it "comes to itself"—is of course essential in Marx's critique of political economy in *Capital*. And Kierkegaard also makes clear that possession of private property is antithetical to love of neighbor: "All earthly and worldly property is, strictly speaking, selfish, envious, its possession, envious or envied, is bound either way to impoverish others. What I have, no one else can have; the more I have, the less can anyone else have" (*CD*, 115). And for all of his talk of equality before God, Kierkegaard does claim, converging with Marx, that all of humanity can be split into "two great classes": "To be able to give and to have to receive is a way of dividing humanity into two great classes, and as soon as this difference is uttered in all its brevity, everyone is able to expand on it and to connect it with many happy or burdensome memories and with many joyful hopes or painful expectations as to what is to come" (*SW*, 45). From beginning to end, Kierkegaard identifies Christianity with a praxis for the improvement of the actual conditions of the poor and the dispossessed. To fight for the poor in this way is how one shows love of God. Indeed, such a struggle of the class of those who have to receive against the class who is able to give is to be waged in God's name: "If at a given time the forms under which one has to live are not the most perfect, if they can be improved, in God's name do so" (*Armed Neutrality [AN]*, 49).[58]

Ultimately, this is the only decision with which Kierkegaard is concerned, and it is the one decision that is unavoidable: to love God through those who need, or to hate God through those who have. A passionate commitment to the poor, actualized in existence, lived enthusiastically, is the truth that Kierkegaard yearns to actualize. Calculations, idealisms, ideological appeals to eternal truth, hermeneutics, and loquaciousness will all look to temper and displace this praxical demand, will all look to ideologically quell emancipatory praxis through concerns with orthodoxy, rationality, and reasonableness. To enthusiastically risk a decision against these powers for the sake of love for the poor is how one is initiated into the orthopraxic community:

> The world has no more knowledge of enthusiasm than a capitalist has of love, and you will always find that indolence and stupidity are primarily intent upon making comparisons and upon imprisoning everything in comparison's muddied 'realism.' Therefore do not look around; 'Greet no one on the way;' do not listen to cries or shouts which will trick you out of your enthusiasm and fool its power into laboring on the treadmill of comparisons. Do not let it disturb you that the world calls your enthusiasm crazy, calls it self-love—in eternity everyone will be compelled to understand what enthusiasm and love are (*Works of Love*, 108).

Chapter Five

God Is and Is Not Black

Black Theology, Marxism,
and the Relationship between Race and Class

Introduction

The previous chapter argued that Søren Kierkegaard articulated a dialectical materialist philosophy and a socialist politics informed by his deep existential commitment to Christian orthopraxy, which was read as itself a form of orthodoxy. While Kierkegaard's socialist commitments were clear, and while he clearly derived them from biblical precepts, Kierkegaard did not provide either a systematic normative political theology or an analytically rigorous critique of modern capitalist culture. Indeed, this lack of both systematic politics and analytical rigor was an important part of Kierkegaard's larger theological project: that the poor are poor is obvious, that they should not be poor is divinely commanded, and any complication of this situation can only be an ideological attempt at diverting proper praxis.

While wanting to maintain Kierkegaard's moral clarity and exigency, this final chapter will provide a more analytically careful reading of one especially important site of contemporary emancipatory struggle: the relationship between race and class. Building on James Cone's classical formulation of black theology, this chapter argues against ontological understandings of race and in favor of universalist anti-racist and anti-capitalist praxis. In a sense, direct engagement with the question of the relationship between race and class recapitulates this project's general argument in favor of an orthopraxical and revolutionary political theology responsive to the fall of metaphysics. Indeed, the question of race, and especially ontologized race, has been something like this project's "b-plot" from the very beginning: Schmitt's ontologization of transcendent sovereignty was, in material terms, an ontologization of Nazi race science, and so metaphysics and race proved inextricable for his project. This critique of metaphysics was then generalized through a reading of Derrida, whose own anti-essentialist position on race and racism remains an undertheorized dimension of his work.[1] Finally, Kierkegaard, while saying too little about race specifically, critiques idealism in such a way as to render any metaphysics, including racial metaphysics, directly antithetical to Christian praxis.

The first section of this chapter explicates an underappreciated dimension of Cone's project that has emancipatory potential: his epistemic privileging of self-determination. Epistemologically, Cone draws from the existentialist tradition to argue that Christian "truth" is determined by the self-determination of the oppressed and exploited. In short, the truth is that the oppressed and exploited should not be so, and so any action or claim is only "true" insofar as it promotes their self-determination. For Cone, the truth revealed by God is that all people should live lives of self-determination unfettered by material, social, and political limitations.

Yet, Cone recognizes that the impossibility of knowing "God" means that any theology that grounds truth claims in the identity of God and truth can only do so self-critically and provisionally—that is, riskily. Importantly, this risk is not just the philosophical one of making uncertain claims dependent on an uncertain metaphysics. More immediately, what Cone calls "the risk of faith" refers to the fact that acting according to an epistemology of emancipation will necessarily put one in conflict with societal power structures. Indeed, truth is determined by one's directness in addressing these structures, and so the extent to which one conflicts with the powerful becomes a measure of truth. While such a counter-cultural impulse was evident in Kierkegaard, counter-hegemonic praxis becomes a central Christian tenet in Cone's work.

While this articulation of truth as risky counter-hegemonic praxis is a potentially revolutionary theorization, Cone's implementation of it suffers from a lack of analytic clarity regarding the precise relationship between class exploitation and racial oppression and the methods of emancipation appropriate to each. While he tends to associate emancipation with self-determination, or "freedom," he rarely fills out the content of this demand. The chapter's second section, then, argues that Cone, especially in his first three works, implicitly associated "black" with "poor," and so anti-racism with anti-capitalism. An interrogation of these dyads directly relates to the debate concerning Cone's alleged "ontologization" of blackness. Responding to this charge, which is argued mostly convincingly by Victor Anderson and J. Kameron Carter, I will accept that Cone sometimes does use metaphysical categories for understanding blackness and sometimes does ontologize blackness. However, the impossibility of such an ontologization—there *is no such metaphysical thing as race*, because there is no such thing as a metaphysical concept, and so there cannot be an ontological category called blackness,[2] whiteness, redness, or whatever else—means that Cone's gestures toward metaphysics must obfuscate a more basic referent, which will have to be read. This is not to deny that something called "race" actually ideologically functions to explain oppressions, or that actual people do "believe in" race and so take is as motivational of behavior. The point is the much more limited one that, because there is no metaphysical, transhistorical substance called "race," any explanation of racial logics and racisms cannot itself be metaphysical: not metaphysics, but history and politics are the realms for both understanding and resisting racism.

I argue that this tension between metaphysical language and the impossibility of metaphysics as such points toward another fundamental tension within Cone's project: Cone articulates two tropics of blackness. On the one hand, blackness is a term that marks a position of structural oppression, and it is in this structural sense that Cone can say things like "being Black in American has very little to do with skin color."[3] Ultimately, this understanding of blackness as metonymic signifier calls for an explicitly anti-capitalist praxis that incorporates, but is not reducible to, anti-racism. On the other hand, blackness also sometimes refers to an ascriptive identity imposed upon people for phenotypical reasons largely having to do with perceived skin color. It is in this sense that Cone can write about things like "physical blackness" (*Black Theology and Black Power [BTBP]* 15) and can speak of the need to "accept the beauty of blackness" (*BTBP*, 18). This sense of blackness calls for explicitly anti-racist practices that might or might not include, but are never reducible to, anti-capitalism. While both senses of blackness coherently function within particular and circumscribed language games, and while political programs of anti-capitalism and anti-racism should each be pursued ruthlessly, Cone's ontologizing problems arise when the two senses cohere in the single, semantically overdetermined signifier "black." When this convergence occurs, structural oppression is read as necessarily inhering within the "physical blackness" of particular people. It is this convergence of the structural with the ascriptive that ontologizes the particular, historical, and contingent understanding of blackness as suffering. Concluding this section by reading historical census data concerning demographics and economic status, I historicize Cone's ontologizing tendencies by arguing that his association of black with poor does not account for growing economic disparities within, as well as between, ascriptive "races." In the political economy of the 1960s and early 1970s, Cone could more or less rightfully argue that anti-racism was a form of anti-capitalism. Now, though, with growing inequalities within ascriptively black communities, this assumption is less tenable, and so must be supplemented.

The chapter's third and final section argues that such a supplement is best pursued using the analytical tools of Marxist political economy. Importantly, Cone himself suggests this possibility, and so my suggested Marxist reinterpretation of Cone should be read as a building upon, and not a departure from, Cone's project. Cornel West's political theology—which is explicitly attentive to the relationship between race and class and rejects ontologized understandings of race—provides a possible Marxist clarification of Cone. West is able to provide an analytical political theology that engages both tropics of blackness without reducing or ontologizing blackness as suffering. Moreover, West's particular form of universalism demonstrates that Marxist political economy provides tools necessary for both anti-racism and anti-capitalism, without reducing either one to the other. For both West and Marx, anti-racism and anti-capitalism are understood as complementary but not identical in a sense that is analogous to the non-identical complementarity between racism and capitalism. Part of my argument here is that there is an anti-racist argument within Marx's work, and that this is made explicit in West's. My claim is not that socialism would necessarily lead to a post-racial society—as I demonstrate below, I do not hold this position. Nor am I promoting anti-capitalism as a replacement for anti-racism. Instead, my more basic point, drawing on West, is that Marxist political economy is a better tool for resisting racism than are essentialist approaches.

Before turning to that argument in earnest, it would be helpful to briefly position this anti-essentialist understanding of race and anti-racism in contrast to some popular contemporary formulations. My position, developed throughout this chapter, draws partly from the dialectical materialist and anti-metaphysical arguments articulated in this project's previous chapters, but also from Cone's axiomatic proclamations concerning the universal necessity of self-determination (which, through West, I read materially). That is, it considers anti-racism an axiomatic position. Anti-racism is not an ideal to be achieved but is a non-negotiable commitment. Implementing policies and defending norms grounded in this commitment will have revolutionary implications in a society that does not share this axiom. As Cone demonstrates, this simple axiom has the potential to also revolutionize epistemological and theological methodologies.

As will become important in the discussion of Cone's two tropics of blackness, this categorization of anti-racism as axiomatic differs from a socialist critique of capitalism, which is not axiomatic but is induced from historical and material analyses of particular forms of market economies and production schemes reliant on private property. As Marx's own abolitionist commitments demonstrate, while racism and capitalism have historically mutually reinforced each other, especially in America and its predecessor colonies since at least the seventeenth century, anti-racism is an axiomatic position that is both above and besides argument, while anti-capitalism is a non-obvious position that requires "scientific" study. Both anti-racism and anti-capitalism, though, are ultimately measured by material means and almost always overlap in their concrete commitments, for example in favor of the democratic production and control of goods; the abolition of police, jails, and Immigration and Customs Enforcement; and the smashing of predatory finance and banking. Any marginal position that adheres to one but not the other political program—for example, the endorsement of a socialist planned economy that excludes a racial underclass,[4] which would be anti-capitalist but not anti-racist, or the endorsement of a "black Wall Street," which would be anti-racist but not anti-capitalist—should be rejected, as total emancipation is possible only if both an axiomatic commitment to anti-racism and a scientific commitment to anti-capitalism are implemented without negotiation.

Importantly, and like Kierkegaard's critique of Gert Westphaler's loquaciousness, this axiomatic commitment to anti-racism also implies that calls for discussion, listening, dialogue, rethinking, conversations, hugging,[5] and so on are only ever ideological deferrals of positions that should be immediately implemented.[6] In the twenty-first century, any particular need to listen and dialogue is evidence only of years of an intentional deafness and isolation. Poor people and the racially oppressed, presumably, know that they do not want to be poor and do not want to be oppressed, and so do not need to listen to anyone to learn this. Of course, and as Cone's entire project demonstrates, there is always room for learning, escalating, and radicalizing. But this sense of dialogue—a nearly kenotic sense wherein the point of dialogue is to get beyond dialogue—is radically different from any colloquial or commonsense understanding of "dialogue."

This commitment to not listening anymore—the time for listening has passed—is antithetical to the dominant "race-relations," or "diversity," framework of racism, which is pointed toward in all these calls for discussion, listening, and so on. The race-relations framework thinks of racism as primarily a problem of bias against, discrimination toward, or oppression of one "race," typically black, by another, typically white.[7] As Stephen Steinberg shows, this race-relations framework has dominated the sociology of race from its institutional inception in the 1930s and achieved mainstream hegemony via government programs and publications such as the *Moynihan Report*[8] and the "Clinton Race Initiative."[9] Because of its attention to the relationship between ascriptive races, reliance on this framework typically leads to concerns with disparities in economics, health, education, and so on. Generally, this concern with disparities leads to a normative preference for representationally equitable diversity: Diversity becomes the solution to the problem of disparities.

Sara Ahmed[10] and James Thomas[11] each argue that the race-relations framework has achieved hegemonic status within the academy largely through its institutionalization in "diversity offices" and the like. A performance of petit bourgeois cultural capital (and, more and more, material capital), the discussion of diversity as solution to the problem of disparity, as Cedrick Michael-Simmons notes, displaces the actual site of violence: "If I were an employer, why wouldn't I want to hire a specialist to train workers to believe that their *own* identities and unconscious biases are the main sources of inequality, instead of exploitative workplace practices?"[12] Unfortunately, this displacement has been internalized in theological texts concerned with racism. Books such as *Can "White" People Be Saved? Triangulating Race, Theology, and Mission*,[13] and *Redisciplining the White Church: From Cheap Diversity to True Solidarity*[14] assume that the problem with racism is one of disparities and so follow closely the race-relations paradigm. *Can "White" People Be Saved?* begins by rehearsing the familiar statistics concerning pay inequalities between different ascriptive identities, and then claims that these economic inequalities "revolve around race." Swanson ostensibly distances himself from "cheap diversity" discourses but opts to substitute these discourses for one of "segregation." This theologization of what is mostly a bureaucratic and administrative discourse, in turn, functions to provide "activist" and "on the ground" credibility for advocates of the race-relations framework. That is, by internalizing race-relations arguments and then externalizing them through pastoral and ministerial care, the theology of race relations provides a post-facto justification and authority for the original dissemination of the race-relations framework.

From the perspective developed in this text's previous chapters, there are at least three problems with the race-relations framework, and so with the dominant theological discourse concerning race and anti-racism.

The first problem concerns these discourses' ambiguous relationship to capital. As Walter Benn Michaels argues, the race-relations framework substitutes a critique of the fact of inequality for a critique of lack of diversity.[15] This language of diversity, though, is categorically incapable of addressing economic inequality, and so does not address the need for anti-capitalism. Indeed, the race-relations framework's language of diversity, which is a possible response to the problem of oppression, is qualitatively different from the language of inequality, which is an analytic category that responds not to oppression, but to exploitation. "Economic diversity," although promoted by the institutions critiqued by Ahmed and Thomas, is nonsensical as an emancipatory project: the goal for an emancipatory politics is not the equal representation of poor and rich, exploited and exploiter, but of the total abolition of both the capitalistic structure productive of poor and rich and the systematic racism that feeds and is fed by capitalist structures. In other words, because of its preference for diversity discourses over inequality ones, the race-relations framework tacitly countersigns the acceptability of "disparities" caused by the market. A critique of the exploitative difference between poor and rich is displaced by, as opposed to supplemented with, a myopic attention to the internal differentiation of the poor. Finally then, and as Adolph Reed Jr. has commented, the race-relations framework, ostensibly anti-racist, serves the disruptive role within the proletariat formerly enacted by racism itself.[16]

Secondly, from a deconstructive and anti-metaphysical perspective, the race-relations framework too quickly accepts reified—that is, metaphysical and ideological—notions of race. Too often the race-relations paradigm, which has no anti-metaphysical critical impulse, accepts at face value colloquial and commonsensical understandings of race. This is a political problem because such pop-sociological framings are unaware of or unconcerned with the ideological and historical dimensions of these categories—and it is precisely these ideological and historical dimensions of race, not the empty metaphysical dimension, that needs to be addressed in order to smash the infrastructural possibility of racism as such. As womanist theologian and anti-racist activist Charlene Sinclair argues, "Blackness gives us more than a clue to the marginalized people in the United States; if probed deeply, it reveals the infrastructure that supports the alienating oppression of those at the bottom . . . Once this infrastructure previously hidden by the cloak of melanin is revealed, structural transformation, not merely recognition, becomes the imperative."[17] The race-relations framework—hoping for equal representation, lacking an anti-capitalist critique, and endorsing colloquial ontologized understandings of race—begins and ends with this cloak of melanin.

While Sinclair is attuned to the ways in which blackness covers structural injustice—and Cone will similarly focus on blackness—the same anti-metaphysical argument can and should be made in terms of whiteness. Here, the pertinent critique is against any metaphysical notion of whiteness in general and any construction of "whiteness" that adheres to a Platonic participatory metaphysics in particular: It is only with such a metaphysics—isomorphic, impossible, and so ideological—that an impoverished white warehouse worker forced by his supervisor to urinate in a soda bottle can feel some sort of ascriptive solidarity with, for example, Jeff Bezos. It is only through a metaphysical and essentialist perspective that this fictional worker and Bezos both participate in some metaphysical thing called whiteness. That is, it is also only through such a metaphysical perspective that Bezos and other capitalist oligarchs can be read by white workers as "racial friends" as opposed to "class enemies"—this substitution of racial fraternity for class enmity being one of racism's most enduring and pernicious effects. In this way, Martin Luther King's arguments concerning the deleterious effects of racism on white people should be understood as referring not only to the spiritual disease of enforcing racial hierarchy, but also to the material damage caused by the proliferation of racist, and so anti-solidaristic, practices. That notions as patently absurd and ontologically groundless as white supremacy, racial hierarchies, and so on have achieved some purchase on people's lived experience, especially when this purchase is harmful to white workers' material interests, is only further evidence of the need to critique the entire metaphysical-ideological enterprise from the infrastructural ground up: white racism should be rejected and resisted everywhere for both its dehumanizing and violent treatment of ascriptively black people and for its role in occluding the possibility of cross-racial class solidarity. All of which is to say: the metaphysical fiction whiteness—which has gained actual power along the lines of other deeply-reified fictions like money, property, and so on—is a problem for both anti-racism and anti-capitalism. The race-relations paradigm, which accepts at face value the ontological existence of "whiteness," even if understood through the lens of an historical ontology, cannot account for the full breadth of the category's depravity.

Thirdly, from a dialectical materialist perspective, and gestured toward directly above, this emphasis on disparities within the oppressed formally elides the problems of economic, health, education, and so on inequalities. That is: as of 2018, there were 38.1 million Americans in poverty. Of these, 20.8 percent, or roughly 7.9 million, self-identified as black. A focus on disparities would suggest that the problem here is that black people are overrepresented amongst the impoverished by roughly 8 percent, or 2.8 million people. From a materialist perspective, though, the immediate problem with these statistics is that 38.1 million Americans live in poverty.[18] While a critique of disparity is important for understanding and ultimately undoing this basic inequality, the race-relations framework encourages the substitution of this infrastructural critique with a diversity one. While the materialist perspective is sometimes critiqued as "reductionist" or "colorblind,"[19] it is important to note that the abolition of poverty would *disproportionately* benefit black people more than would a mere correction of current disparities. According to general population demographics, there "should be" 5.1 million black people living in poverty. A move toward this proportionate representation of the poor would, thus, require "lifting" 2.8 million black people out of poverty (and a lowering of 2.8 million whites into poverty). Instead, a total abolition of poverty according to a universalist anti-capitalist regime would "lift" 7.9 million self-identified black people out of poverty. The focus on disparities and a diversification solution, then, ultimately helps not only the poor in general, but also the black poor in particular, much less than would an overcoming of the possibility of economic inequality as such. In other words, not diversity offices but Marxist political economy, through its own anti-racist and anti-capitalist analyses and commitments, has the potential to actually resist both racism and capitalism, and so has the potential to improve the lives of both the racially oppressed and economically exploited. Anti-capitalisms that promote white supremacy and anti-racisms that promote capitalism—and I am arguing that the race-relations and structural-racism frameworks are examples of the latter—are both deeply antagonistic to this totally emancipatory Marxist critique, which I find explicitly in West and implicitly in Cone.

The Risk of Faith

J. Kameron Carter has described James Cone's ontology as an "I-Thou" ontology: "Because the I-Thou relationship is constitutive of existence and therefore of what it means to be—this is Cone's ontology, as I have cast it—the I-Thou relationship does not pass away."[20] That is, Cone begins with the simple premise that every person is an "I." This I-ness, though, is not recognized in exploitative and discriminatory relationships, which follow a model not of I-Thou, but of I-It. The correction of this I-It relationship into an I-Thou one is, according to Cone, the project of emancipation. To the extent that Cone is making an apodictic claim regarding how things really are—every person *is* an I—Carter's metaphysical rendering of Cone's position coheres. Yet, and as will become both a merit of and a problem within Cone's work, this metaphysical claim is also operative on existential and, most of all, theological registers. That is, while Cone is making a metaphysical claim here, he is doing so through reference to a theological position: For Cone, it is above all the incarnation of God in the person of Jesus Christ that both reveals and confirms the "I-ness" of each person. This is Cone's interpretation of the *imago dei*, and it is foundational for his project in general.

That this theologically-informed ontological claim has existential and political implications is made clear when Cone provides semantic content to his understanding of "I-ness" and to the *imago dei*. For Cone, the *imago dei* is primarily a declaration of freedom from externally imposed restriction, especially those that prevent or occlude the ability to pursue self-determination. That is, Cone is identifying freedom from oppression and freedom to create as divine attributes, and thus, by extension through the *imago dei*, as human attributes: "To be human is to be in the image of God—that is, to be creative . . . The image of God refers to the way in which God intends human beings to live in the world" (*A Black Theology of Liberation [BTL]*, 99).[21] And so the "I" that is recognized in Cone's I-Thou ontology signals the divinely-secured freedom to create free of external obstruction: "In order to be free, a person must be able to make choices that are not dependent on an oppressive system" (*BTL*, 102). And again: "A man is free when he can determine the style of his existence in an absurd world; a man is free when he sees himself for what he is and not as others define him. He is free when he determines the limits of his existence" (*BTBP*, 28).

And so Cone's theological axiom that every person is created for the sake of freedom has an intrinsic relationship to political praxis. Cone is reading the *imago dei* as meaning that the human person was created to freely determine his or her own "limits of existence." Understood in this way, the human person is not "free" in an internal or abstractly spiritual sense but *is* free as created in the image of the self-determining God. For Cone, then, there is an intrinsic relationship between theology understood as discourse about God and our understanding of quotidian human existence:

because humans image God, to talk about God is necessarily to talk about the material reality of humans.

As Cone himself notes, since the beginning of Christian theology, the *imago dei* has been subject to vast and mutually exclusive interpretations (*BTL*, 95–100). And so it is worth asking where and how Cone is settling on his understanding of the doctrine as implying self-determination. As I have shown above, the claim has a certain syllogistic coherence, wherein the transitive property seems to suggest that God's limitlessness implies humanity's. Yet, Cone is typically wary of such a procedure, preferring to speak, with Barth, of the absolute qualitative difference between God and creature (*BTL*, 51; *BTBP*, 37, 86), even if he sometimes suggests that Barth's emphasis on difference results in a God too far removed from historical projects (*God of the Oppressed [GO]*, 107).[22] Indeed, Cone more often speaks of the impossibility of knowing God *in se*. This apophatic commitment problematizes any easy analogy between God and creature, especially one articulated in typically metaphysical terms such as omnipotence.

When Cone does use analogical language to relate God and creature, he tends to do so in terms of what Carter calls an *analogia existentia* (*Race: A Theological Account [RTA]*, 171). For Cone, both God, as Jesus, and creature share in the struggle against exploitation and oppression. Importantly, this analogous relationship—both God and human resist exploitation, although in irreducibly different ways because God is not just a participant in the struggle for freedom but is also the creator of the possibility of freedom—exists purely because of God's decision to enter human history as oppressed. God takes on the role of freedom fighter, and so we can, in a phrase that will prove problematic, "become black with God" by likewise taking on this role. This association of God and struggle will become more important shortly, but for now the pertinent point is simply that the relationship between God and creature, for Cone, is one that takes place predominantly in history and in the very real and concrete historical project of emancipation. This is a relationship qualitatively different than the syllogistically accented transitive relationship described above.

All of which leaves the question open: If Cone says that the *imago dei* means that humans share in God's ontological freedom to create—that is, in the freedom of self-determination—but if Cone is both hesitant to use metaphysical language to refer to God *in se* and prefers to speak of the relationship between God and creature as one of a shared historical struggle, then from where does the important language of self-determination come? Although identifying influence is not my primary concern, it is a historical fact that the language of self-determination was prominent in the Black Power tradition to which Cone appealed. And not only self-determination, but also a resistance to integration, a penchant for nationalism, and a sympathy for "third world" anti-imperial resistances were all popular political motifs for both Black Power advocates and Cone.[23] Cone, for his part, would not deny this convergence between the political commitments of Black Power and the theological commitments of his own black theology. Indeed, such a convergence is the point of *Black Theology and Black Power*: "My concern is to show that the goal and message of Black Power is consistent with the Gospel of Jesus Christ. Indeed, I have even suggested that if Christ is present among the oppressed, as he promised, he must be working through the activity of Black Power" (*BTBP*, 48). The possibility of this convergence between radical secular politics and political theology is one of my major points in this text.

Yet, this convergence functions ambiguously in Cone's work. The convergence between ontological claims concerning self-determination and political ones is harbored, for Cone, by theology. In this sense, which for all of Cone's radicalism is, as Derrida argued, the classical sense, theology becomes the discourse that secures the identity of thinking and being—or, more specifically here, the identity of politics and ontology. As I will show shortly, Cone is aware of the risk that this identity runs and takes steps to account for it. Yet, despite Cone's awareness of this risk, this association of theology, ontology, and politics opens the possibility of the ideological ontologization of a too-particular understanding of blackness. This, in short, will be the charge levied against Cone by Victor Anderson. My point here is that this ontologization was prefigured from the very beginning of Cone's project, which begins with a theo-politically informed ontological axiom concerning self-determination. While Anderson will argue that this ontologization is a problematic element of Cone's work, and while my reading of Derrida's and Kierkegaard's deconstructive and existentialist critiques of metaphysics would likewise resist this ontologization, the close proximity Cone has established between ontology and politics, a proximity governed by theology, also potentially historicizes and so denaturalizes ontological claims. And so while Cone does display ontologizing tendencies from the beginning, and while he does sometimes revert to an ontologized language when speaking theologically, he also, from the very beginning, understands ontology in an explicitly political, historical, and contingent way. That his ontological axiom concerning self-determination is, if not informed by, at least intentionally convergent with the political positions of the Black Power movement is precisely what one would expect given my previous discussion of the actually material structure of all allegedly metaphysical decision. That is, Cone's ostensibly theologically informed ontological claims might always actually be informed by the particular political commitments of not God, but Stokely Carmichael. Yet, Cone demonstrates and sometimes even declares that this undecidability—who is working here? Stokely Carmichael or Jesus Christ? What's the difference?—*is* the proper relationship between theology, ontology, and politics. In this way, Cone's ontologizing tendencies—which are still worthy of critique for reasons articulated shortly—might avoid some of the problems of ideological metaphysical claims.

Before moving on to a closer look at the function of ontology in his political theology, it might be worth briefly differentiating Cone from one of the most prominent contemporary writers on the relationship between ontology and race, Frank Wilderson. Drawing widely from Orlando Patterson, Saidiya Hartman, Frantz Fanon, and others, Wilderson, one of Afropessimism's most prominent voices, argues that ontology itself—although he clearly has in mind a Heideggerian existential ontology—is essentially constituted by anti-blackness. That is, Wilderson argues that "human being" has always been constructed as excluding blackness, and so "blackness" articulates ontology's constitutive negation: "Whereas Humans exist on some plane of being and thus can become existentially present through some struggle for, of, or through recognition, Blacks cannot reach this plane" (*Red, White, and Black*, 38).[24] The history of western philosophy is not the history of the articulation of Parmenides's third fragment, as Derrida might have, but is instead the history of the denial of black humanity.

Most of Wilderson's work can be read as an articulation and elaboration of this basic conceit that humanity is constituted in and through the simultaneous exclusion and negation of blackness. From this, Wilderson draws several conclusions with which Cone and West would not agree. For example, given that the "human" is constitutively exclusive of blackness, Wilderson is deeply critical of all "humanist" emancipatory projects, including Marxism. Because Marxism is concerned with humans, it is, according to Wilderson, definitionally unconcerned with blackness. Indeed, Wilderson rejects any attempt to improve the material conditions of humans, because such attempts, again by definition, must be attached to this human, and therefore anti-black, world. In this way, socialists and other Marxists are not solidaristic allies in the quest for social justice but are "really no better than loyal opposition. This is true whether you're dealing with Bernie Sanders Democrats, or even socialists, in the US, or you're dealing with British radicals and African National Congress antiapartheid veterans in South Africa" (*Afropessimism and the Ruse of Analogy [ARA]*, 43).[25] Wilderson has no attachment to the human world, which he interprets as requiring his non-being. The solution is not to make the world better for humans but to radically abolish this human world altogether.

Despite his preoccupations with ontology, aspects of Wilderson's project do in fact cohere with this project. For example, Wilderson's commitment to revolutionary social change is not antagonistic to either Marxism or deconstruction. Nor is Wilderson's particular understanding of the unique structural role of blackness in racial logics at odds with what Marxist historians like Barbara Fields have to say about the origin of American ideological racism. However, I see at least two serious shortcomings in Wilderson's project.

First, his understanding of Marxist critiques of capitalism is severely limited, if not patently misguided. For Wilderson, Marxism belongs to a genus of redemptive humanist narratives, all of which follow the same basic structure: "The arc of an emancipatory progression which ends in either equality, liberation, or redress, in other words, a narrative of liberation, is marked by the three generic moments that one finds in any narrative: a progression from equilibrium (the spatial-temporal point prior to oppression), disequilibrium (capitalist political economy or the arrival and residence taking of the settler), and equilibrium restored/reorganized/or reimagined (the dictatorship of the proletariat or the settler's removal from one's land" (*The Black Liberation Army [TBLA]*, 4).[26] That is, in Wilderson's understanding, Marx articulates a "narrative of liberation" that calls for a restoration of some original, pre-capitalist equilibrium state. Needless to say, this is not Marx's position. In fact, Marx, in a text as basic as *The Communist Manifesto*, critiques those who wish to "roll back the wheel of history" as "reactionaries."[27] Wilderson's generic misreading of Marx on this question is unfortunate, because Marx's rejection of this logic of return is in fact important for understanding Marx's revolutionary desires, which ostensibly would align better with Wilderson's own revolutionary impulse.

Unfortunately, Wilderson's misreading of Marx is not accidentally hermeneutical, but extends to a deep misunderstanding of some fundamental Marxist notions. Wilderson is critical of all attempts to restore equilibrium, and so reads into Marx a desire for equilibrium. But this is not Marx's desire, and so Wilderson's generic critique of equilibrium politics falls short in its specific application to Marx. This shortfall seems to be the result of a basic and thorough misunderstanding, on Wilderson's part, of the Marxist critique of capitalism. For example, Wilderson describes capitalists in the following way: "Capitalists are the only ones with the capacity to accumulate surplus value" (*ARA*, 42). In a sense, Wilderson is not far off here. Capitalists are the "only ones" who "accumulate surplus value." But there is an important difference between the Marxist claim that some in the economy accumulate surplus value, and that we call these people capitalists, and that "capitalists are the only ones . . ." Wilderson's quote, especially read in conjunction with the previous critique of Marxism, implies that capitalists *accumulate surplus value because they are capitalists*. In this reading, there are—ontologically—a group of capitalists, and these people accumulate surplus value. Marx's point is the opposite. Capitalists are capitalists *because they accumulate surplus value*. Marx is defining a particular position within a particular social relation as capitalist, whereas Wilderson implies that social relations unfold according to the fact that there are capitalists. But, according to Marx, capitalists do not exist before capitalism; capitalists do not create capitalism. The opposite is Marx's view: capitalism creates capitalists.

The argument that capitalism precedes the existence of any one capitalist is analogous to arguments—developed shortly—that racism in some ways precedes the existence of race. This difference is the difference between analytically prioritizing political-economic structures (racism, capitalism) and analytically prioritizing reified ontological or ontological identities ("the capitalist," "blackness"). Which brings us to the second limitation facing Wilderson's project: his absolute embrace of ontology and ontological concepts prevents historical and political engagement with, and so overcoming of, ideological concepts. As Lewis Gordon notes, Wilderson's acceptance of and reliance on the notion that humanity is constituted through the exclusion and negation of blackness in fact reifies a racist understanding of humanity. That is, and putting aside the question of the claim's empirical accuracy, Wilderson accepts and embraces the racist notion that humanity excludes blackness. Rather than reject the premise, Wilderson rejects humanism. But, as Gordon, says, this raises an important political question: "Why must the social world be premised on the attitudes and perspectives of antiblack racists? Why don't blacks among each other and other communities of color count as social perspectives? If the question of racism is a function of unequal power, which it clearly is, why not offer a study of power, how it is gained and lost, instead of an assertion of its manifestations as ontological?" (32)[28] In other words, Gordon argues—correctly, in my view—that Wilderson has accepted as ontological that which is in fact a product of political power. This is not to deny that there is some sense of "ontology" according to which humanity excludes blackness—perhaps a Heideggerian-informed existentialist ontology that thinks of Dasein as inherently constituted by exclusion.[29] But it is to question what material benefit could possibly be gained through the introduction of ontological language into an analysis of what is fundamentally a political, social, and economic question. And Wilderson does *introduce* this language. As the last chapters have argued, Wilderson could not have possibly "discovered" these "ontological truths" out there in the world, but must have invented them, produced them in text; the world created racism, not ontology. This failure to engage the historically contingent nature of ostensibly ontological racial categories is a failure to engage race as ideology. In this way, and for whatever merits Wilderson's claimed revolutionary impulse might deserve, his project of Afropessimism is a basically conservative one that in fact disavows—openly—any prescriptive materialism: "Afropessimism is not a politics, in part, because the politics that arise from modernity's treatises of Human liberation (e.g., Marxism, feminism, postcolonialism, Indigenism) are all constructed by two scaffolds—one of which is conspicuously absent from Afropessimism. Those two scaffolds are description and prescription" (*ARA*, 42). Afropessimism is "not a politics" because it intentionally avoids any prescriptive program, which must, through its humanism, ignore the plight of black people (or as Wilderson sometimes has it, black "sentient beings"). Wilderson is consistent on this point. He writes, for example, that "political discourse is inherently anti-Black," and so "politics have no purchase" on black life. Wilderson disavows, or claims to disavow, politics.

This raises a couple of important questions. First, and as my critiques of ontology have argued throughout, Wilderson's embrace of ontology—which, in Wilderson's case especially, is an embrace of ideology—is unavoidably an embrace of a particular politics. There is no ontological non-politics. In this case, Wilderson's embrace of racial ontology reinscribes—and does not claim to undo and intentionally does not try to replace—the very politics that such an ontology ideologically harbors as its secret: a capitalist politics that looks to undermine interracial working-class solidarity. Until he demonstrates otherwise, this anti-solidaristic politics is the politics of both Wilderson and the racist humanists he critiques. Because of this ideological reification of a fractured proletariat, I fail to see how Wilderson's embrace of racial ideology will lead to a revolutionary overthrow of the current capitalist global order in any way.

Which leads to another important question left unanswered by Wilderson. To the above point, Wilderson might retort that a (humanist) overthrow of capitalism is not his goal, because such an overthrow alone would fail to revolutionize the humanism of the world as such, and, worse, would in fact reinscribe an allegedly anti-black socialist humanism. But such a retort raises the question: what exactly is the world that Wilderson wants to overthrow? The human one, of course, but without a properly historical, social, political, and economic description of this "world," Wilderson's reader is left with only vague ontological claims about the world: the world is human, non-black, Being, and so on. As I have been arguing throughout this book, the sense of none of these metaphysically tinged words is clear or self-obvious, and each is in need of material specification. Left without a critique of the underlying political and economic infrastructure of this allegedly ontological white world, Afropessimism not only chooses not to offer such a specification, but also cannot do so. At best, Wilderson can offer an idealist pedagogy:

> If we can help Black people to stay, as Saidaya Hartman says, "in the hold of the ship," that is, to stay in a state of pure analysis, then we can learn more about the totality and the totalizing nature of Black oppression. And then, move into a conversation about what is to be done, realizing that our language and our concepts (post-colonial, Marxist discourse) are so much a part of other peoples' problems, problems that can be solved, that we'll really never get to the thing that solves our problem—because it's already there in Fanon: the end of the world—because at least if we don't have a strategy and tactics for this end of the world, at least we will not have altered and corrupted our space of pure analysis to make it articulate with some kind of political project.[30]

Wilderson claims to want to avoid articulating a political project because it would alter and corrupt "our space of pure analysis." Instead of this political corruption, Wilderson prescriptively offers the usual tropes of race-relations paradigms: conversation, realizations about language, learning, and so on. Leaving aside the unbelievable claim that the oppressed need to be taught by Afropessimists about the totality of their oppression—it seems to me that the oppressed are aware of the fact—one should be reminded of Kierkegaard's critique of Gert Westphaler: as the world exploits and kills, Wilderson teaches and converses. Despite what Wilderson claims, his decision to choose conversation and pedagogy over politics is, in what reminds us now of Schmitt's critique of the liberal fetishization of discussion, a thoroughly political act. In that he denies the political implications of his decision—that is, in that Wilderson denies that his alleged rejection of politics is in fact an endorsement of an ideal bourgeois politics of discussion and pedagogy—Wilderson's ontological anti-politicism is thoroughly ideological.

In short, this project—and Cone's project—is one of *political* theology. Wilderson claims to dismiss politics, and so Afropessimism and the sort of revolutionary political theology I am after might seem to move as parallel lines on different planes, never intersecting. But, as I hope to have shown, ontology and politics are not disparate or dissociable discourses. Ontology is an ideological cover of politics: in this case, Wilderson's racial ontology is an ideological covering of the particular material mechanisms that created racism in the first place. And so Afropessimism is not just a unique, aesthetic discourse concerning black non-being. It is also a species of the genus of essentializing and ideological racial discourses that this chapter—following Cone, following West, following Marx—argues against. Despite his protestations to the contrary, Wilderson does offer a prescriptive program: pedagogy. What he does not offer is a radical politics that could actually change—never mind "end"—the world. Myopically concerned with ontology, Wilderness cannot do so.

This question of ontology and politics will return in this chapter's next section. For now, I want to refocus on the novel and potentially radical effects of Cone's onto-theo-political commitment to the axiom of self-determination—whatever its motivation and whatever its source. In *Black Theology and Black Power*, Cone relies on Albert Camus's theorization of the absurd to articulate the political effects of this ontological axiom. Cone notes that, for Camus, "the absurd" is neither the world nor the person, but instead arises in the encounter of the person with the world (*BTBP*, 11). The locating of the absurd in the relationship between world and person allows Cone to both maintain his ontological commitment concerning freedom and the *imago dei* while recognizing that these ontological and theological truths are not empirically manifest in the world. This empirical contradiction with an ontological truth is, according to Cone, constitutive of the black condition: "It is not that the black man is absurd or that the white society as such is absurd. Absurdity arises as the black man seeks to understand his place in the white world. The black man does not view himself as absurd; he views himself as human. But as he meets the white world and its values, he is confronted with an almighty 'No' and is defined as a thing. This produces the absurdity" (*BTBP*, 11). The white world's resistance to black self-determination means that the white world subjects black people to I-It, as opposed to I-Thou, relationships. In his less metaphysical moments, Cone will contrast the presence of this I-It structure not with the ontological affirmation of the I-ness of black people, and so with the ontological truth of the unavoidability of I-Thou relationships, but with a futurally oriented utopian political critique concerning what "ought to be": "Truth is a question not only of what is but of what ought to be. What is, is determined by the existing societal relations of material production, with the ruling class controlling the means of production as well as the intellectual forces which justify the present political arrangements. What ought to be is defined by what can be through the revolutionary praxis of the proletarian class, overthrowing unjust societal conditions" (*GO*, 38). His use of the category of "truth" means that Cone is not simply contrasting political reality with ontological reality. He is doing this, of course: one of the productive dialectics throughout Cone's work is that between empirical reality and ontological reality. Black, poor, and exploited people ontologically are people, even if they are not treated as such. Cone will never waver on this, and he considers it a basic, important, and inarguable axiom. Yet, as mentioned above, if Cone stopped here he would be subject to deconstructive criticisms concerning the distinction between thinking and being, as if Cone were only concerned with allowing an ontological structure—and one that, given empirical injustices, could only be considered a fiction—to ideally critique empirical reality. This is not what Cone is doing. Instead, Cone is here claiming that the "truth" is that black, poor, and exploited people *ought to be* treated as they really are—as I's.

Cone most directly articulates the relationship between this actualizing epistemology and the discipline of theology in *A Black Theology of Liberation*. It is here that Cone declares that "there is no real speech about God except in relationship to the liberation of the oppressed" (88) and that "whatever theology says about God and the world must arise out of its sole reason for existence as a discipline: to assist the oppressed in their liberation" (4). This understanding of theology as a discourse of assisting the poor and oppressed in their quest for self-determination is consistent not only with Cone's reliance on the *imago dei*, but also with his understanding of Jesus as primarily God's incarnated declaration that God is on the side of the oppressed in general and, in the American context, the side of poor blacks in particular (*BTL*, 125–30). Moreover, this affirmation that true theology has its "sole reason for existence" in the assistance of liberation helps us reread Cone's initial interpretation of the *imago dei*: now with this understanding of theology as necessarily pro-liberation, Cone's translation of God's omnipotence into an affirmation of human self-determination reads less problematically metaphysical than it might have initially. The theological claim of omnipotence, Cone now makes clear, can never have been anything but a statement concerning the liberation of the exploited and oppressed. *A Black Theology of Liberation* extends this program of an emancipatory reading of theological categories in chapters on the theological motifs of revelation, God, Jesus, the human, and the church.[31]

While Cone is by no means the first to argue that theology should or does serve emancipatory ends (and that it should but does not is part of Cone's institutional critique), his project is marked by its interpretation of emancipation according to the norm of self-determination. That is, Cone's epistemology does not make the formal argument that truth is actual or needs to be actualized in order to be true, nor does it adopt the left-liberal position that the poor and exploited should be granted some sort of preferential privilege or treatment when making praxical decisions. Cone's point is much stronger: the truth is, everyone has a (theological, ontological) right to self-determination. This right must be primary, and so cannot be denuded by or translated into any ethical regime that does not take this axiom of self-determination as determinative. The failure of some Christians to oppose slavery, to free the poor from bondage, and from treating all people as I's, that is, the existence of what Cone calls "white Christianity," is the result of not internalizing the axiom of self-determination. "Christian ethics" must be, but has not been, thought with constant and unique reference to the oppressed's occluded self-determination: "Theologians of the Christian church have not interpreted Christian ethics as an act for the liberation of the oppressed because their views of divine revelation were defined by philosophy and other cultural values rather than by the biblical theme of God as the liberator of the oppressed" (*GO*, 183). No philosophical morality and no "cultural values," which must include juridical regimes, can determine the validity or normative weight of any ethics. Indeed, given the predominance of exploitation, a subservience to dominant philosophical moralisms and cultural mores is a sure sign of a reactionary ethics—that is, an ethics against the liberation of the oppressed. Cone is arguing for a radical rejection of any and all norms, laws, politics, and ethics that do not begin and end with the right of self-determination.

Throughout his project, Cone applies this standard unremittingly, and sometimes with controversial if not intentionally provocative results. Consider, for example, Cone's treatment of the question of revolutionary violence's relationship to the Christian ethic of nonviolence: "Violence is not primarily a theoretical question but a practical question, and it should be viewed in the context of Christian ethics generally and the struggle of liberation in particular" (*GO*, 180). For Cone, any analysis of violence that begins with anything but the axiom of self-determination must be misguided. Such misguided analyses would include those ostensibly Christian ethical programs that take as axiomatic not freedom, but instead nonviolence.[32] In the concrete, this task entails beginning not just with the formal principle of self-determination, but specifically with those people whose self-determination is occluded—variously in Cone, the poor, blacks, and, more encompassingly, "the oppressed." The poor, black, and oppressed, not philosophers, not theologians, not judges, and certainly not professional-managerial-class "race-relations" administrators, determine the truth about violence and liberation: "In dealing with the question of violence and black people, Black Theology does not begin by assuming that this question can be answered merely by looking at the Western distinction between right and wrong. It begins by looking at the face of black America in the light of Jesus Christ. To be Christian means that one is concerned not about good and evil in the abstract but about men who are lynched, beaten, and denied the basic needs of life" (*BTBP*, 141). Allowing the self-determination of the oppressed to guide his ethics, Cone turns Nietzsche on his head. For Nietzsche, "slave morality" involves the reactionary substitution of a "good-evil" moral matrix in place of an "aristocratic" moral matrix of "good-bad." The slave, for example, is denied the freedom to pursue self-determination. For aristocratic morality, which is based on sentiment, this denial would be "bad." In slave morality, which reacts against aristocratic sentiment and so is a morality of *re-sentiment,* the denial of self-determination becomes "good" in contrast to the "evil" of the slave master who denies this self-determination. And so that which is originally considered "bad" by aristocratic morality is, through the process of slave morality ressentiment, revalued as "good." Likewise, that which is "good" according to aristocratic morality, for example actualized self-determination, is read as "evil" by slaves.[33]

Cone's study of actual American chattel slave morality, especially read through his absolute privileging of the right of self-determination, totally undermines Nietzsche's configuration. Central to Nietzsche's account is the notion that slave morality is resentful and reactionary: a social situation is imposed, and a reaction against this situation and the seeming impossibility of resistance leads to a valorization, a making "good," of what should be, according to aristocratic norms, "bad." Cone disputes this rendering of slave morality as reactionary by noting slaves' active resistance to their oppression. The tenets of slave morality were not formed in reaction to aristocratic noble values but were instead inspired by a need and desire for self-determination. For example, concerning theft, "black slaves made a distinction between 'stealing' and 'taking.' Stealing meant taking from a fellow slave, and slave ethics did not condone that. But to take from white folks was not wrong, because they were merely appropriating what was in fact rightfully theirs" (*GO*, 192). A similar ethical logic guided an endorsement of deception and lying if done for the sake defending slaves' lives and wellbeing. In these cases, Cone is not arguing that the slaves begrudgingly accepted the pragmatic necessity of stealing and deception. Such a rendering would maintain a negative moral connotation. Much more strongly, Cone is arguing that, for the slaves, stealing and deceiving were *good* because they worked toward and promoted self-determination. While theft and deception occurred in a context of violent oppression and so resisted others, the judgment that these activities were good occurred independently of the ideological machinations of master morality. The actual site of reactionary morality is found not in this endorsement of theft and deception but in the master's morality constructed to deny the slaves' right of self-determination. In short, "slaves did not feel themselves bound to white morality" (*GO*, 192).

In the case of slave violence, Cone frequently makes positive statements concerning slave rebellions and the killing of slave owners. Nat Turner and John Brown are heroes, unambiguous heroes, in Cone's telling. The black abolitionist minister Henry Highland Garnet, who "even argued that it was both a political and Christian right that slaves should rise in revolt against their white masters by taking up arms against them," is approvingly cited more than a few times (*BTBP*, 96; *BTL*, 36–37; *GO*, 29, 48, 141, 176, 178, 196, 220). Perhaps most powerfully, Cone critiques Theo Lehmann's interpretation of slave spirituals as promoting otherworldly, as opposed to this-worldly, liberation. For Cone, such a reading fails to account for "the role of spirituals in resurrections in which many whites were killed" (*The Spirituals and the Blues [SB]*, 134n37).[34] Indeed, for Cone, black theology originated in these acts of divine violence: Black theology "came into being when the black clergy realized that killing slave masters was doing the work of God" (*BTL*, 27). Moreover, what is needed now is not a domesticating move away from this founding violence. Instead, given the persistence of oppressive violence, Cone considers it a "sin" to "try to understand enslavers, to love them on their own terms." Rather than understand and love oppressors, "the oppressed now recognize their situation in light of God's revelation, they know that they should have killed their oppressors instead of trying to love them" (*BTL*, 54).

This is all consistent with the axiomatic foundation and argumentative thrust of Cone's entire project. In a phrase that could have been written by any number of controversial but ultimately emancipatory revolutionaries—including Fidel Castro ("history will absolve me")[35] and Ernesto Guevara ("a people without hate cannot triumph over a brutal enemy")[36]—Cone summarizes his position: "In the moment of liberation, there are no universal truths; there is only the truth of liberation itself, which the oppressed themselves define in the struggle for freedom" (*BTL*, 106). Killing slave masters is the truth of God because the truth of God is that the oppressed should be set free. Cone is arguing for a radical and complete revaluation of all morals according to the highest value of emancipation as measured by the norm of self-determination.

Because of its centrality to not only Cone's ethics, but also indeed to his entire theology, any engagement with Cone that styles itself sympathetic should not domesticate, explain away, or ignore Cone's radicalism on this point. Such is the approach taken by, for example, D. Stephen Long in his *Divine Economy: Theology and the Market*.[37] After suggesting that "black theology" "could easily resemble fascism," Long argues that, actually, "it is unclear that black theology advocates any possible employment of violence based purely on its effectiveness" (170). Long continues:

> Cone's own defense of violence could be construed as consistent not with Luther's voluntaristic conception of warfare (which seems ineluctably to lead to Clausewitz) but with that of Thomas Aquinas, who argued for the legitimacy of tyrannicide if it furthered the common good . . . And the "any means necessary" that Cone asserts has primarily to do with "selective buying, boycotting, marching, or even rebellion." He does suggest that "all acts which participate in the destruction of white racism are Christian," but he also maintains that it "is not possible to speak meaningfully to the black community about liberation unless it is analyzed from a Christian perspective which centers on Jesus Christ." (170)

Long's concern here seems to be to convince moderate Christians that Cone's calls for violence are not as radical as they might seem—that, actually, Cone is a Thomist, that "any means necessary," means boycotts, and that, perhaps, the depiction of anti-racism as definitionally Christian is a rhetorical ploy by which Cone can "speak meaningfully to the black community." The problem here is not only that Long directly contradicts Cone, who clearly and explicitly positions his ethics as anti-Thomist,[38] but also that Long reinscribes Cone—or a domesticated version of him—within the left-liberal "status quo" that Cone so forcefully resists. In doing so, Long has to impose erasure on Cone's fundamental privileging of self-determination: whether or not "violence" is necessary—or, whether or not an act is violent according to a Christian ethic if violence still means something bad, regrettable, unfortunate—is precisely determined "purely on its effectiveness" at promoting and defending self-determination.

Moreover, this downplaying of Cone's radical commitment to self-determination simultaneously exaggerates the radicalness of Cone's demands and underestimates the severity of the crisis to which Cone is responding. That the rather mundane content of Cone's demands—to be treated as a human—could demand killing is evidence of the depth of racism and exploitation in America. Cone juxtaposes a small ask—to be treated as a person—with a radical consequence—killing—and so shows the asymmetry at play: the exploiters will fight to the death in order to maintain their hegemonic structures. In this sense, Cone reads John Brown, Nat Turner, and other martyrs not as aggressors, but as individuals who decided to live out self-determination whatever the consequences—even if they involve violence: "This is Black Power, the power of the black man to say 'Yes' to his own 'black being,' and to make the other accept him or be prepared for a struggle" (*BTBP*, 8).

But as the fates of Nat Turner and John Brown show, such a living out of self-determination is a risky, sometimes fatal, endeavor. Cone is aware of and does not shy away from this risk: living a free life in an oppressive society will necessarily cause conflict, as one's life becomes both a symbolic judgment and a material resistance to the powerful. This sense of physical risk—the risk of martyrdom—is the primary sense Cone intends "risk" in *Black Theology and Black Power*. There, and working from the axioms articulated so far, Cone writes that "theology is not an intellectual exercise but a worldly risk" (*BTBP*, 84). This is because the task of theology is not (only) the production of discursive analyses of emancipation, but instead a "worldly" project of it. Because God's truth is that the poor shouldn't be poor, that the oppressed should be set free, and that all should have a right to self-determination, any discourse that does not produce real emancipatory fruits cannot be considered true. Cone is completely aligned with Kierkegaard on this point: it is one thing to say that God is for the poor, it is quite another to join the poor in their fight for freedom. Theology without this praxical element, for Cone, is white theology.

Important there is that Cone's discussion of the emancipatory thrust of theology inherently expands beyond the narrow confines of institutional theological discourse. Cone's claim is a universalist one. For Cone, God did not say that theologians should fight for the poor, but more generally that the poor should be free. It is in this derivative sense of reflection on God's command that theology is necessarily an emancipatory project, but so too, in Cone's rendering, ought to be every discourse. Politics, economics, hard sciences, trades, literature, quite literally everything: all of this should be directed for the sake of the emancipation of the poor, which is the truth of God.[39]

This demand to join the oppressed in their struggle for freedom again associates Cone more with the radical revolutionary tradition than it does the boycotts, dialogues, and marching suggested by Long and the race-relations framework. Cone is more Che Guevara than Robin DiAngelo. Where Guevara writes, "in a revolution one wins or dies, if it is a real one" (*Che Guevara Reader [CGR]*, 386), Cone writes, "when the Spirit of God gets hold of a man, he is made a new creature, a creature prepared to move head-on into the evils of this world, ready to die for God . . . To be possessed by God's spirit means that the believer is willing to be obedient unto death" (*BTBP*, 58–59). Where Guevara writes that "to die under the flag of Vietnam, of Venezuela, of Guatemala, of Laos, of Guinea, of Colombia, of Bolivia, of Brazil—to name only a few scenes of today's armed struggle—would be equally glorious and desirable for an American, an Asian, an African, even a European,"[40] Cone writes that "it seems not only appropriate but necessary to define the Christian community as the community of the oppressed which joins Jesus Christ in his fight for the liberation of humankind" (*BTL*, 3). Cone cites Stokely Carmichael, not John Lewis. Cone writes not about marching, but about Molotov cocktails: "We know, of course, that getting rid of evil takes something more than burning down buildings, but one must start somewhere" (*BTL*, 26).

All of this is morally and logically consistent with Cone's original emphasis on the *imago dei,* his I-Thou ontology, and his understanding of truth as the actualization of the poor and oppressed's self-determination. In order to dispute Cone on this point of violence and radicalism, or on the associated point of survivalism as compared to risky emancipation, one would need to either dispute his original premises or demonstrate how this radicalism does not follow. However, as I have demonstrated with respect to Long, such a reinterpretation of Cone will always risk a downplaying of the depth of American racism and exploitation. Instead of arguing against Cone on the point of violence, then, or instead of domesticating Cone by reinscribing him within a bourgeois race-relations framework, I accept that his theology is radical, provocative, and emancipatory unto death. Yet, even within his own framework and self-understanding, there is room to sharpen and specify Cone's presentation. While Cone consistently affirms the absolute epistemic privilege of emancipation, he also repeatedly affirms that his analyses as to the specific contents of both emancipation and oppression are open to revision. That is, while Cone is absolutely clear that the oppressed should be emancipated "by any means necessary" (*BTL*, 48, 104; *GO*, 172), he is also clear that the question as to which of these "means" is in fact "necessary" remains open: "Since God's will does not come in the form of absolute principles applicable for all situations, our obedience to the divine will involves the risk of faith" (*GO*, 190). That is, Cone has established an axiomatic politics that presupposes the truth that the oppressed should be emancipated. But he has not established a concrete politics by which to enact this emancipation. He is open to violence but has not divinized violence in a "fascist" way, because he is open to "violence" only if it contributes to the emancipation of the oppressed. And so Cone places the reader in a rather uncomfortable, if not downright aporetic, situation: the poor must be liberated by any means necessary, but the reader of Cone does not yet know what those means are. This situation is what Cone intends by the risk of faith, the need to act without knowledge of the outcome, and without knowledge of what action is required: "Ethics in this context is a terrible risk, an existential and historical burden that must be borne in the heat of the day" (*GO*, 202).

Ontological Blackness?

Victor Anderson's charge that Cone ontologizes blackness is, by now, well known.[41] In short, by ontologization Anderson has in mind any discourse that identifies a substantial essence. Ontological blackness, Anderson argues, is the discourse that articulates an essentially suffering black identity. In such a discourse, suffering and blackness are interchangeable and transferable, perhaps even synonymous, with each other. In Anderson's reading, these essentialist discourses serve to alienate actual black people. This alienation is the result of an asymmetry between the essentialized ideals of blackness—especially black masculinity and black genius, defined as creative expression of some black virtue (resistance, struggle, perseverance, again masculinity) formed in reaction to oppression—and the lived experience of black people. That is, ontological blackness's identification of blackness with a suffering substance erases all those who existentially identify as black and yet not with this ontological substance named black suffering.

According to Anderson, Cone's project follows these general ontological contours. Important here is Anderson's critique that Cone, despite his own self-presentation, is not actually grounding his theology in "black experience." Instead, Cone is ontologizing some particular experience and then hermeneutically privileging this ontological category as a means by which to interpret all "black" experience: "For Cone, the culture of black survival and black revolutionary consciousness constitute ontological schemes for interpreting the existential meaning of blackness" ("Black Ontology and Theology" ["BOT"], 397). In this way, Cone is ostensibly "defining black existence by black experience," but is not open with the fact that these governing experiences are both carefully curated and unnecessarily given ontological status.

In responding to this charge, and in looking to go "beyond" it (*RTA*, 159), J. Kameron Carter has argued that Anderson does not engage carefully enough the particularly theological, or "pseudotheological," component of Cone's ontologizing. According to Carter, the properly theological problem with Cone's ontologization is its immanentization of the transcendent: "The breakthrough in Cone's thought unravels in that his program unwittingly reinscribes the aberrant theology (or pseudotheology) of modern racial reasoning. This occurs insofar as Cone's ontology disallows transcendence and thus recapitulates the inner logic of modern racial reasoning" (*RTA*, 158). In making this critique, Carter is primarily concerned with the ways in which Cone's reliance on Paul Tillich's existential ontology, and so by extension Heidegger's existential ontology, has led to a reduction of the transcendent otherness of God. Operating with a univocal understanding of being, Cone is incapable of accounting for the "covenantal," that is racially impure and so anti-racist, character of Christ. Without an account of Jesus's covenantal flesh, Cone is unable to overcome his ontologized understanding of race, which now signifies an immanent understanding of race. Against such immanence and univocity, Carter argues that "what is needed is a vision of Christian identity that calls us to holy 'impurity' and 'promiscuity,' a vision that calls for race trading against the benefits of whiteness so as to enter into the miscegenized or mulattic existence of divinization" (*RTA*, 192).

While I agree with his assessment that Cone's ontological language draws from Tillich's existential ontology—and that this reliance might present its own unique set of problems—and while I countersign Carter's efforts to establish an anti-essentialist understanding of race, Carter's reinterpretation of Anderson's critique ultimately softens Anderson's critical edge. Anderson is correct that Cone, at least sometimes, identifies blackness and suffering. It is unclear to me, contra Carter, that a proper accounting of transcendence and "covenantal flesh"—to say nothing of "miscegenized or mulattic existence," categories that seem to multiply, not undo, racial logics—would necessarily alleviate these potential problems. Nor is it clear how a "vision" of these categories would allow one to "enter into . . . the existence of divinization." Carter seems to be implying here that racism and oppression are matters of improper ontology, that exploitation is the result not of power and material interests, but of bad vision. Indeed, to argue that Cone's identification of blackness with suffering is the result of a Tillichian existential ontology, and not some material experience, Carter must rely on a philosophical idealism against which his own preoccupations with flesh and history would suggest. That is, while Cone might be receiving the concept of an "ontological symbol" from Tillich, this does not mean that Tillich is determining Cone's particular identification of blackness with suffering—indeed, Tillich does not talk about blackness, and so cannot be determinative for Cone on this issue. Some other material must be informative. In this sense, a diachronic genealogical accounting of Cone's ontology, which Carter provides, cannot explain the particular synchronic content of this ontology. Moreover, if my previous arguments that all ontology masks a prior non-metaphysical decision are correct, then Cone's ontology—which both Anderson and Carter detect—must have a non-ontological referent or must somehow signify a non-ontological content. Identifying this non-ontological referent is this section's task.

In the previous section, I argued that Cone axiomatically declares the absolute right of self-determination. The question here is: What is the "self" that Cone intends when he makes this axiomatic declaration? In the most general sense, this self is simply "the oppressed." In *God of the Oppressed*, Cone claims that Jesus is "the liberator of the oppressed" (*GO*, 74, 82); the liberation that Jesus the liberator enacts happens when "the oppressed realize their fight for freedom" (*GO*, 127); this freedom, in turn, is "defined by the oppressed" (*GO*, 135). Similar claims are made throughout Cone's corpus. Yet, the fact remains that Cone often specifies "the oppressed"—that is, makes clear who is oppressed—in two related but ultimately non-identical ways. Sometimes, the oppressed are poor. Sometimes, the oppressed are black.

Perhaps surprisingly given their more straightforwardly racial titles—although, as I will argue, given historical political-economic realities, not surprisingly at all—Cone's tendency to speak in terms of class was more pronounced in his early texts. Consider the following passage from *Black Theology and Black Power*, which clearly identifies the poor as the emancipatory subject of self-determination:

> Jesus had little toleration for the middle- or upper-class religious snob whose attitude attempted to usurp the sovereignty of God and destroy the dignity of the poor. The Kingdom is for the poor and not the rich because the former has nothing to expect from the world while the latter's entire existence is grounded in his commitment to worldly things. The poor man may expect everything from God, while the rich man may expect nothing because he refuses to free himself from his own pride. (36)

And a few pages later, in the same text:

> God unquestionably will vindicate the poor. And if we can trust the New Testament, God became man in Jesus Christ in order that the poor might have the gospel preached to them; that the poor might have the Kingdom of God; that those who hunger might be satisfied; that those who weep might laugh. If God is to be true to himself, his righteousness must be directed to the helpless and the poor, those who can expect no security from this world. The rich, the secure, the suburbanite can have no part of God's righteousness because of their trust and dependence on the things of this world. (45)

Cone even puts on God's voice to say: "I became poor in Christ in order that man may not be poor" (*BTBP*, 46). The sentiment is repeated throughout *A Black Theology of Liberation* ("The kingdom is for the poor," [107, 121]) and *God of the Oppressed* ("the phrase 'all are oppressed' can only be understood from the perspective of the poor," [137]). In these same texts, however, Cone also identifies the emancipatory and privileged subject not with "the poor," but with black people. In these moments Cone writes that "to be free is to be black" *(BTL,* 108), that "black people must use blackness as the sole criterion for dialogue" (*BTBP,* 148) and that "the blackness of God means that God has made the oppressed condition God's own condition" (*BTL,* 67).

Cone suggests a reconciliation of these two positions by metonymically relating them. The pertinent passage appears early in *A Black Theology of Liberation*:

> We cannot describe God directly; we must use symbols that point to dimensions of reality that cannot be spoken of literally. Therefore to speak of black theology is to speak with the Tillichian understanding of symbol in mind. The focus on blackness does not mean that only blacks suffer as victims in a racist society, but that blackness is an ontological symbol and a visible reality which best describes what oppression means in America . . . Blackness, then, stands for all victims of oppression who realize that the survival of their humanity is bound up with liberation from whiteness. (8)

And so these differing claims as to the identity of the emancipatory subject—poor, black—are not meant, in Cone's logic, to compete with or exclude each other. Rather, Cone is suggesting that we read his use of "black" and "blackness" "symbolically." It is such a symbolic—really, metonymic—usage that allows Cone to write passages like the now famous conclusion to *Black Theology and Black Power*: "Being black in America has very little to do with skin color. To be black means that your heart, your soul, your mind, and your body are where the dispossessed are. We all know that a racist structure will reject and threaten a black man in white skin as quickly as a black man in black skin. It accepts and rewards whites in black skins nearly as well as whites in white skins" (*BTBP,* 151). Other instances of this metonymic use of blackness are found throughout Cone's oeuvre. For example, in *God of the Oppressed* we read that Jesus "is black because he was a Jew" (*GO,* 123). Here, blackness is metonymically substituting for any marginalized group, as the particularity of both Jewishness and blackness are meant to metonymically refer to generic oppression. And again, "in America," Cone says, "God's revelation on earth has always been black, red, or some other shocking shade, but never white" (*BTBP,* 150). Such a claim could only be coherently read from within the metonymic hermeneutic Cone describes above: Jesus is "red" or "black," but never white, because "red" and "black" represent particular manifestations of violent oppression in America—indigenous genocide and chattel slavery. It is in response to the continuation and persistence of the racist oppression of black people that Cone identifies Jesus, who is always with the oppressed, with blackness. In this sense, Jesus is black *because* black people are oppressed. Jesus is black because blackness metonymically represents oppression, and not for any ontological reason.

In such a structure, Cone's use of racial categories is best understood as a metonymic generalization of a particular—and particularly pernicious—site of oppression. Cone is universally against all structures that limit or oppose self-determination, and this universalist position is particularized in and through Cone's anti-racist commitments. A particular empirical oppression—racism—is read against an axiomatic universalist commitment to self-determination, and the discrepancy between what is and what should be is critiqued. Such is one tropic of blackness in Cone's work, and it explains the freedom with which he translates "black" as "poor," and vice versa: Blackness signifies an oppressed structural position.

While such a structural approach has the advantage of avoiding what Ivan Petrella calls *monochromatism*—the belief, which Petrella finds throughout liberation theology but especially in black theology, that color, not social position, should be both epistemically and soteriologically privileged—it faces at least two important challenges.[42]

The first challenge concerns the transhistoricism of any structural approach to racism.[43] For Cone, Jesus is both red and black, but never white; blackness stands for victims of oppression, but only those who conceive of their oppression as "bound up with a liberation from whiteness." And even when Cone is thinking explicitly in terms of class interests, he relies on the antagonistic category of whiteness: "Either we side with oppressed blacks and other unwanted minorities as they try to redefine the meaning of existence in a dehumanized society, or we take a stand with the President or whoever is defending the white establishment for General Motors and US Steel" (*GO*, 201). By associating General Motors and US Steel with the "white establishment," and not with the corporate oligarch class, and by thus identifying white as the antithesis of not only red and black but also worker and poor, Cone ensures that his structural analysis is always anchored in antagonism to whiteness. Thus, while Cone's use of blackness is not ontological in the sense of transhistorical—Cone never claims that blackness exists outside of history, but argues that it is the product of European modernity (*BTBP*, 16)—his understanding of whiteness is both transhistorical and overbroad.[44] It is only by a trick of racecraft and participatory metaphysics that a seventeenth-century colonist, a factory line worker at GM, a highly paid executive at GM, and a twentieth-century white supremacist can all occupy the same structural location in an analysis of oppression. Incidentally, this same trick allows the "white" worker at GM to find some sense of shared, racial accomplishment in the earnings of the "white" executive. But in order to overcome the exploitative poverty—both white and black—that Cone wants to overcome, the white worker must see the white boss as a class enemy, not a racial friend. Such a possibility is foreclosed by Cone's transhistorical identification of "whiteness" as occupying a dominant place in the generic structure of oppression. In this sense, and contra Anderson, the racial ontological category at work in Cone's project is less "the blackness that whiteness created" as it is the whiteness that whiteness created. This use of whiteness would have to be rejected for reasons both normative—we should not countersign, even for the sake of critique, false and ideological categories created for the sake of oppression—and theoretical—there can be no transhistorical, metaphysical category of whiteness because there can be no transhistorical, metaphysical category.

The second challenge this structural approach faces is its relatively unconvincing phenomenology of racism. In daily life, race does not function as a structural location, and, contra Cone's claim that "blacks are those who say they are black, regardless of skin color" (*BTL*, 69), the oppression imposed upon black people is largely due to their status in an ascriptive category that does at least somewhat relate to "skin color." Race as an identity is given, not chosen. This recognition that race is an ascriptive and so not a descriptive category—which Cone's structuralism argues, as "black" comes to describe a structural location—is important for addressing Anderson's critique of an ontological identification of blackness and suffering. Not only does this ontology imply that language is descriptive of a pre-linguistic realm—where "black" describes the ontological reality of "black" suffering—but it also imposes arbitrary and often alienating distinctions within the ascriptive group. Consider historian Touré Reed's critique of Ta-Nehisi Coates's praise for Barack Obama. Coates lauds Obama for "downloading black culture . . . for living black, for hosting Common, for brushing dirt off his shoulder during the primaries, for marrying a woman who looked like Michelle." According to Reed:

> For Coates, Obama's blackness is derived not from legal or cultural frameworks that classify people with his parentage as black;

Obama's blackness is wed to his embrace of specific consumer tastes, dating choices, idiomatic expressions and, ultimately, swag. To be sure, Coates sees the aforementioned markers of racial authenticity as outgrowths of a common experience. But African Americans whose experiences deviate from what Coates sees as "the black experience" are not really black. Indeed, while Coates lauds Obama for his decision to embrace black culture, he describes the former president as less black than another African American Chicago politician, mayor Harold Washington. To be clear, Coates sees Obama as less black than Mayor Washington because Obama's experiences do not conform to Coates' view of "the black experience" (*Toward Freedom [TF]*, 124).

Against this view that the performance of something called black culture renders one black, Reed argues that "since race is an ascriptive category, Obama is unquestionably black, in my view, irrespective of his personal predilections or behavior" (*TF*, 139). In my view, Reed's position is unquestionably more phenomenologically correct than is Coates's. On a quotidian level, it is purely an imposition based on phenotype that causes suspicious looks, distrust, street crossing, wallet clutching, and any other instantiation of the mundane yet exhausting slew of racist practices, to say nothing of more egregiously violent displays of racism such as police brutality, lynching, forcible evictions, and so on. In these instances, the practitioner of a racist act cannot possibly be deciding whether or not someone is black based on their structural location relative to oppression or their adherence to an alleged black culture—they know none of this information. And so a structural view does not account for the empirical realities of racist practices. Moreover, by identifying blackness with a particular cultural script, the structural view performs the essentialization of particularities that rightfully troubled Anderson. Thus, while the structural view might seem to be a less essentialist and less metaphysical regime than an ascriptive approach, and this because race and color are (allegedly) dissociated, it ends up retaining reference to some essentialized characteristic. The structural view, not the ascriptive one, essentially identifies "black" with "suffering."

Cone, while typically claiming to follow a structural-metonymic approach, does often implicitly rely on this ascriptive understanding. For example, he writes that "there is little evidence that whites can deal with the reality of physical blackness as an appropriate form of human existence" (*BTL*, 15) and that "the black experience is only possible for black persons"

(*BTL*, 26). While this latter reference to black experience might tend toward Coates's cultural reification, Cone is clear here that something outside of culture—"black persons"—governs the possibility of living "black experience." This governing agent, moreover, seems to have to do with "physical blackness." Cone even suggests that the ascriptive quality of race is so intricately connected to "physical blackness" as to call for a sort of nationalist withdrawal or separation: "Until white America is able to accept the beauty of blackness, there can be no peace, no integration in the higher sense. Black people must withdraw and form their own culture, their own way of life" (*BTBP*, 18). While I do not think this program of withdrawal is ultimately coherent with Cone's distinctly political emancipatory program, the pertinent point here is that Cone has black people forming "their own culture" after their withdrawal. Culture, in this instance, is the effect and not the cause of oppressions based on ascriptive group belonging. This logical structure is repeated and clarified when Cone claims that "the black community is an oppressed community primarily because of its blackness" (*BTL*, 126).

This ascriptive blackness is the second tropic of blackness in Cone's project. Independently, each tropic is internally consistent. And although I have argued that the ascriptive approach is ultimately more phenomenologically accurate, it might well be the case that the structural approach offers more possibilities for cross-racial solidarity—as evidenced by Cone's repeated applauding of John Brown. Recognizing various merits and demerits of both tropics might suggest the adoption of a bricolage approach, pulling from one or the other discourses depending on occasion. This, more or less, is the approach suggested by Timothy McGee. For McGee, Cone's ambiguity "marks his refusal to allow a stabilizing operation to operate unchecked in both racial and theological discourses. In fact, for Cone, theology becomes another iteration of whiteness precisely when it functions as a kind of regulatory or stabilizing discourse" ("Against [White] Redemption" ["AWH"], 547). That is, Cone's ambiguous use of the signifier black—in McGee's rendering, Cone employs sometimes "literal" and sometimes "symbolic" uses of blackness—is meant to rhetorically destabilize "white" attempts at stabilization or regulation. In this way McGee argues, against Anderson, that Cone actively resists reinscribing "the blackness that whiteness created" by actively avoiding reinscribing any regulated or stable understanding of blackness.

The problem with this approach is twofold: First, McGee primarily reads and defends Cone's ambiguous use of "black," but is not attentive to the related ambiguity concerning the identity of the emancipatory subject. Perhaps there is some rhetorical merit to "destabilizing" racial discourse, but there is also surely merit in identifying the actual subject of emancipation, and this identification is rendered difficult when blackness remains ambiguously overdetermined. Ultimately, especially when asking the question as to the emancipatory subject, the emphasis on and celebration of ambiguity undermines Cone's sharpness, radicalness, and moral clarity. When Cone has raised the stakes as high as he has—where the identity of the emancipatory subject has total moral and epistemological privilege—then an unambiguous and unflinching commitment as to the identity of the political actor is both necessary and unavoidable. In other words, McGee has utilized the ambiguity found in Cone's work as a way by which to avoid making the necessary praxical decision as to whose experience and whose self-determination is to be privileged.

This decision is necessary because, despite Cone's sometimes synonymous treatment of them, black and poor are not identical. This non-identity of blackness and poverty relates to the second problem with McGee's applauding of Cone's ambiguity: while McGee wants to prevent "whiteness" from imposing a stabilizing or regulating regime onto Cone's work, he is inattentive to the governing forces already at work within Cone. Above, I argued that Cone's axiomatic endorsement of self-determination, which is operative throughout his political theology, cohered with the political norms of the Black Power movement. While Cone might theologically ground his appeals to self-determination in a doctrine of divine omnipotence, it is undeniably the case that Cone's language was shared by his political interlocutors. A similar historical, contingent influence is, I suggest, at work in both Cone's ambiguous employment of blackness and his ambiguous identification of the emancipatory subject.

The two mutually reinforcing ambiguities that I have described each contribute to an implied association of blackness with poverty and whiteness with wealth. Occasionally, as with Cone's discussion of General Motors, this implied association becomes explicit.[45] When Cone wrote *Black Theology and Black Power* in 1969, this association of black and poor had more empirical support than it does in 2020. This is because Cone's early texts were not in a position to comment on or deal with the exorbitant wealth inequality that has proliferated inside black America over the past couple of decades. This growing inequality within the "black community" poses a problem for Cone's project in two ways: First, median black wealth, in America, has risen substantially since the writing of Cone's early works. This alone makes an identification of blackness with poverty difficult. Secondly, the growing wealth disparity in black America has forced a stronger decision between a racial nationalism that cuts across class divisions and a class solidarity that cuts across ascriptive racial groups. Importantly, and as this chapter's next section will argue, this decision between racial and class solidarities *does not at all* imply a decision between anti-racism and anti-capitalism—indeed, quite the contrary.

On the one hand, since the publication of Cone's first works, the black middle class has grown in ways Cone did not anticipate. In 1969, only 28 percent of black Americans had completed high school. By 2015, that number was 88 percent (in the same time, white high school graduation rates increased from 51 percent to 93 percent).[46] The percentage of black American college graduates has risen from 5 percent to 23 percent (white graduation rates have risen from 10 percent to 36 percent) ("Demographic Trends and Economic Well-Being"). Likewise, black median adjusted household income has nearly doubled since the writing of Cone's text, from $24,700 in 1967 to $43,00 in 2014 ("Demographic Trends and Economic Well-Being"). Black poverty rates have decreased from 34.7 percent to 21.8 percent. Black infant mortality and life expectancy—measures of quality of life and access to material care—are down 67.4 percent and up 11.5 years, respectively.[47]

At the same time, these absolute material gains were not equitably shared amongst black people. While the percentage of black Americans earning over $100,000 per year in adjusted dollars has grown from 3 percent in 1969 to 15 percent in 2016, 46 percent of black Americans still earn less than $35,000 per year.[48] Moreover, in 1969, 26.9 percent of black Americans earned under $15,000 per year; by 2018, that number had fallen only to 19.2 percent.[49] In 1968, the median black American's income placed her at the 25th percentile in annual income nationally. By 2018, that number had risen to the 35th percentile. This relative increase up the income ladder, though, was more than offset by the much larger growth in income disparity between the median earner and the poor: In 1968, a person at the 35th percentile earned 69 percent of the national mean. By 2016, that number had fallen to 49 percent of the national mean. That is, while the median black American improved her position relative to other racial groups, this relative improvement masks a larger decrease in wealth relative to the median earner.[50] In absolute terms, this means 3.03 million more black Americans live in extreme poverty today than when Cone wrote *Black Theology and Black Power*. Yet, 6.39 million more black Americans make more than $100,000 per year now as compared to the time of Cone's writing. There are both more poor and more wealthy black Americans now than then.

My point here is the narrow one that both the median economic situation of black Americans has improved since Cone's early texts and that the suffering of the poorest black Americans has worsened since the same time. This inter-racial wealth disparity means that Cone's 1960s and 1970s penchant for freely translating "black" with "poor," and vice versa, is not credible in the 2020s. All of which is to say, in 1968, especially in the socialist-friendly Black Power milieu in which Cone was writing, an endorsement of black self-determination could be read as an endorsement of self-determination of the poor, where "black" referred to but did not exhaust the referential breadth of "poor." This possibility means that Cone's synonymous treatment of black and poor could always have masked an implicit privileging of neither black nor poor per se, but instead of the black poor, oppressed and exploited, in particular. In this way, rather than an intentional ambiguity meant to rhetorically destabilize white hegemonic conceptions of blackness, Cone's two tropics of blackness did not problematize each other in Cone's writing because they did not represent two materially different realities. Such an understanding of universal emancipation as determined by the particular dual-oppressions of the black poor would nicely bring together the various ambiguities in Cone's text, as well as represent a unified political program of both anti-racism and anti-capitalism. However, such an interpretation of Cone would mean that Cone did not write a black theology of liberation, but instead a black poor theology of liberation. Such a theology would specify blackness economically and would specify poverty racially: Race and class, racism and capitalism, would be resisted within a single political-theological program. Cone would be a critic, not an adherent, of the structural racism and race-relations frameworks.

However, although this ordering and clarifying of the relationship between his two tropics can be imposed onto Cone's texts, Cone himself does not offer such a solution. In his political-economic situation there was no need for him to do so: Cone's penchant for easily translating between these two tropics of blackness—and the associated two identifications of the emancipatory subject—was governed by the contingent, historical moment in which Cone originally structured his program. It was a moment in which blackness could reasonably signify poverty, and could do so without making this signification explicit. Yet, the late-20th and early 21st centuries have seen an aggravation of income inequality in the globe generally and in black America in particular. This aggravation has brought about a new political economic moment, and so has made the once-easy convertibility of black and poor no longer possible. Cone did not adequately adapt his double-tropic structure for this new political-economic reality. And so a different discourse, one capable of addressing not only disparities between "races" but also within "races," is needed.

For a Marxist Anti-Racism

In 1980, Cone wrote a paper for Michael Harrington's Institute for Democratic Socialism titled "The Black Church and Marxism: What Do They Have to Say to Each Other?"[51] In it, Cone provides his most sustained treatment of the relationship between black liberation theology and Marxist political economy. He begins with a sort of apology for his lack of engagement with socialism in general and Marxism in particular: "It was an intellectual failure on my part that I did not deal with Marxism and socialism when I wrote *Black Theology and Black Power* which was published in 1969. Neither did the issue of socialism appear in my *A Black Theology of Liberation* and *God of the Oppressed*" ("BCM," 4). Cone is not being quite fair to himself here. *God of the Oppressed*, for example, includes a six-page section titled "Feuerbach, Marx, and the Sociology of Knowledge" (*GO*, 36–42). In this section, Cone countersigns the classic Marxist formulation that the ruling ideas of an epoch are the ideas of the epoch's ruling class to ask "what is the connection between dominant material relations and the ruling theological ideas in a given society?" (*GO*, 39). From this generally Marxist philosophical critique, Cone goes on to proclaim that truth is always interested and partial. Thus, "the assumption that theological thinking is objective or universal is ridiculous" (*GO*, 41). All of this coheres quite nicely with Cone's total epistemological privileging of the self-determination of the oppressed.

Cone is also incorrect that he "did not deal with Marxism and socialism when (he) wrote *Black Theology and Black Power*." In fact, this text contains some of Cone's most orthodox Marxist arguments, some of which might be considered reductionist by both the later Cone and by those working from within his liberal reception. On the Civil War and abolition, Cone writes that "the north could appear to be more concerned about blacks because of their work toward the abolition of slavery. But the reason is clear: Slavery was not as vital to their economy as it was to the south's" (*BTBP*, 76). Cone again argues that racial emancipation and segregation have economic motives when, in this same text, he writes that "when whites saw that it was no longer economically advantageous to worship with blacks, they put blacks out of their church as a matter of course" (*BTBP*, 104). Finally, Cone says that "the ghetto" exists "to further the social, political, and economic interests of the oppressor" (*BTBP*, 36). While none of these claims—and others like them that can be found in *A Black Theology of Liberation*[52]— mention Marx specifically, each one relies on a sort of political-economic logic much more at home with Marxism and contemporary Marxist historiographies of slavery than with the potentially reductionist structuralism of the race-relations framework.[53]

In these early moments Cone argues that economic interests and power inequalities, more so than structural racism, are ultimately responsible for the origin and perpetuation of not only chattel slavery but also contemporary racial injustices and inequalities. Yet, in the 1980 article on Marx, Cone complicates his position on this question of the causal priority of economics. On the one hand, he still argues that the Marxist position is analytically correct. On the other hand, he worries that such an economic emphasis is bad strategy, that it puts off more than calls in. For Cone in 1980, the Marxist infrastructure-superstructure dyad is analytically correct, but politically less than helpful: "When Marxists have been forced to face the question of race, they have always made it secondary to the economic question and the class struggle. While this may be scientifically correct, the way in which Marxists put forward their perspective on race and class is usually offensive to the victims of racism" ("BCM," 6). It is important to read this hesitation in accordance with Cone's epistemological privileging of emancipation. Doing so clarifies Cone's argument: He is not arguing that the Marxist critique of the economic foundation of slavery is incorrect, that blackness is a transhistorically oppressed category whose very essence involves subjection, or anything of the sort. He is not even arguing that Marxists were once correct, but that now racism has taken on a life of its own. Cone's interest is not in disputing the analytic accuracy of Marxist analyses, which he endorses and perhaps independently endorsed even before he read Marx on the topic of slavery. Instead, Cone is merely asking what political purchase such a critique has in a normative program of total self-determination. Ultimately for Cone, the "truth" of Marxism is not found in its analytic accuracy but in its worth as a tool for emancipation.

So, despite this hesitation, how does Cone value Marxism's use as an emancipatory tool? Quite highly. As his infrastructural economic arguments suggest he would, Cone writes that "I do not think that racism can be eliminated as long as capitalism remains intact" ("BCM," 5).[54] The overthrowing of capitalism becomes an explicit political program for black theology, and Cone is at pains to spread the recognition of this program.

In a moment that might read as out of touch in the contemporary context, which is rightfully wary of implicit Eurocentrisms, Cone goes so far as to argue that the black church's lack of engagement with Marxist theory is one of racism's deleterious effects. The passage deserves to be quoted at length:

> Black churchpeople need to take this critique (the Marxist critique of capital) seriously. We can say that in the history of our struggle, the oppression of black people was so extreme in every segment of our community that there was no opportunity for a comprehensive scientific analysis of American society, including a critique of capitalism and a consideration of socialism. Blacks were not a part of a European intellectual class but the descendants of African slaves. They simply responded to the most pressing contradiction in their historical experience: namely slavery and racism. They did not define their struggle as being against capitalism per se, and they did not recognize the need for a revolution as defined by Marxism. Blacks wanted to end racism as defined by slavery, lynching, and Jim Crow laws. Now, however, we have a small group of black intellectuals in the church and in other areas of black life who can provide the necessary leadership. They can and should offer black people a critique of capitalism and an alternative vision of social existence ("BCM," 8).

And so Cone believes that a Marxist critique of capitalism is essential to overcoming racism in America, but that its presentation, which seems to minimize the importance of racial justice, has been "offensive" to black Americans in general and black Christians in particular. It is unclear if Cone considers himself one of the "small group of black intellectuals" who "can and should offer black people a critique of capitalism," but it is clear that he supports such an effort. Which is to say, Cone is arguing here that Marxist anti-capitalism must become a more attractive tool for black liberation than it historically has been. Yet, this becoming does not entail a shift in the material content of Marxist analysis, but instead an increased openness from Marxists to the questions and particular concerns of black people and a complementary openness from black skeptics of Marxism regarding socialism as an alternative "social existence."[55] Possibly echoing Fred Hampton, Cone declares the need to "take a stand against capitalism and for democratic socialism, for Karl Marx and against Adam Smith, for the poor in all colors and against the rich of all colors, for the workers and against the corporations" ("BCM," 9).[56]

What is needed, then, is a Marxist critique of capital that epistemologically privileges its political use as a tool for total emancipation. More specifically, Cone is arguing here that Marxism must position itself in such a way that it appeals to people who identify racism, not capitalism, as the most pressing and immediate form of oppression in their lives. Above, I suggested that Claudia Jones and Barbara Smith's Combahee River Collective offered responses to this challenge. For them, the Marxist response to anti-racism was a universalizing of Marxist programs. In response to a perceived neglect of black women by Marxist organizations, Jones and Smith each argued that a truly Marxist program would universally include all materially oppressed people—including, of course, black women. In this sense, Jones and Smith offer a Marxist criticism of Marxists, and so strengthen the relationship between anti-racist and anti-capitalist commitments. For both, the response to racism is not race relations, but more Marxism.

Shortly, I will argue that Cornel West provides an articulation of Marxism's anti-racism that responds to Cone's call for a politically "true" Marxism. Before doing so, though, it is worth briefly responding to Cone's claims that "white socialists seem to be white first and socialists second" ("BCM," 3) and that "many liberal white-led groups were inclined" to "preserve class solidarity at the expense of racial justice" (*The Cross and the Lynching Tree [CLT]*, 46).[57] Undoubtedly, there have been white socialist racists and white socialists who did not consider anti-racism to be a truly socialist project. For example, the once-Marxist historian Eugene Genovese, although he became a conservative later in life, responded to the fact of Marx's abolitionism by absurdly criticizing "the retreat of Marx, Engels, and too many Marxists into liberalism."[58] Of course, this response is only possible because Marx did in fact maintain a strong abolitionist perspective. Marx's writings on the American Civil War are illuminative on this matter.[59]

Although typically neglected by both Civil War historians and Marxist theorists, Marx's writings on the American Civil War provide some of the most explicit articulations of Marx's anti-racist position. For Marx, the Civil War was predominantly a war over slavery. Rejecting both federalist and geo-political interpretations—according to which, respectively, the war was either an ideological battle between federalist and republican political theories or a proxy war between England and France—Marx argued that the war was explicitly and truly fought over slavery. Rather than a war for secession, according to Marx, the southern planter class was primarily interested in expanding the scope of slavery into both the northern and the newlyfounded midwestern states. Writing during the war, Marx writes that a confederate victory would result in "not a dissolution of the Union, but a reorganization of it, a reorganization on the basis of slavery, under the recognized control of the slaveholding oligarchy."[60] Indeed, and against reductionist interpretations like Chantal Mouffe's, for whom Marx was only concerned with factory production, Marx argues that "Direct slavery is as much the pivot upon which our present-day industrialism turns as are machinery, credit, etc. Without slavery there would be no cotton, without cotton there would be no modern industry. It is slavery which has given value to the colonies, it is the colonies which have created world trade, and world trade is the necessary condition for large-scale machine industry . . . Slavery is therefore an economic category of paramount importance."[61] And so rather than constrain his analyses to industrial production understood as trade unionist factory production, Marx contends that slavery stands in the center of nineteenth-century global capitalism. That is, slavery abolitionism was a critical and axiomatic tenet of Marx's anti-capitalist program: for communism to come, slavery had to go. Indeed, slavery's centrality to global capital made the American Civil War the front line of the international workers' revolution. Marx says as much in a letter, unsolicited and unreturned, to Abraham Lincoln:

> The working classes of Europe understood at once, even before the fanatic partisanship of the upper classes for the Confederate gentry had given its dismal warning, that the slave-holders' rebellion was to sound the tocsin for a general holy crusade of property against labor, and that for the men of labor, with their hopes for the future, even their past conquests were at stake in that tremendous conflict on the other side of the Atlantic. Everywhere they bore therefore patiently the hardships imposed upon them by the cotton crisis, opposed enthusiastically the proslavery intervention of their betters—and, from most parts of Europe, contributed their quota of blood to the good cause.[62]

In this same letter, Marx makes clear that racism from white workers, especially northern industrial workers, toward black slaves had worked to prevent a socialist revolution. The war, Marx thought, had the potential to create a sense of class solidarity between white workers and the soon-to-be-freed black slaves. Yet, Marx remained concerned that state-capitalist interference and persisting white racism would occlude such solidarity. For this reason, Marx levied particularly harsh criticism toward racist American whites. This is especially true of Irish-Americans, who as immigrants, Marx thought, should be better allies of black slaves. Where the Irish should have seen a class friend, they instead saw a racial enemy: "The Irishman," Marx writes, "sees in the Negro a dangerous competitor" (*Marx and Engles Collected Works, volume 19 [MECW 19]*, 264).[63] Upon the abolition of legal slavery, it is this ideological sense of racial competition amongst the working class that would prevent socialist revolution.

Against this racial fracturing of the proletariat, Marx demands an axiomatic anti-racism. Writing five months after Robert E. Lee's surrender, Marx warns Lincoln that any tolerance of racism or racial inequality would not only undo the war's potential gains but would also damn America to a future of violence: "Let your citizens of today be declared free and equal, without reserve. If you fail to give them citizens' rights, while you demand citizens' duties, there will yet remain a struggle for the future which may again stain your country with your people's blood . . . We warn you then, as brothers in the common cause, to remove every shackle from freedom's limb, and your victory will be complete."[64] All of which is to say that whatever the personal views of historians and polemicists writing under the banner of Marxism, it is clear that Karl Marx was a passionate and committed anti-racist who held these positions axiomatically. Part of responding to Cone's call to articulate the anti-racist character of Marxist anti-capitalism is surely a *ressourcement* of these decidedly anti-racist positions.

Cornel West's Political Theology

Cornel West works out of this anti-racist Marxist tradition in order to develop an explicitly anti-racist and anti-capitalist political theology, and does so in a manner consistent both with Cone's epistemological privileging of the oppressed and with Cone's emphasis on the riskiness of faith. More, West's project is decidedly anti-metaphysical in a way consistent with both Derrida's and Kierkegaard's critiques of metaphysics.[65] Finally, West accounts for Cone's two tropics of blackness in a way less ambiguous and more analytically careful than Cone's own approach.

Among theologians, West's most influential work is his *Prophesy Deliverance! An Afro-American Revolutionary Christianity (PD)*.[66] It is in this text that West, building on and specifying for the black American context George Mosse's *Toward the Final Solution: A History of European Racism*,[67] develops his genealogy of white supremacy. West's genealogical aim is to "give a brief account of the way in which the idea of white supremacy was constituted as an object of modern discourse in the West," and he approaches this aim by interrogating the "discursive conditions for the possibility of the intelligibility and legitimacy of the idea of white supremacy in modern discourse" (*PD*, 47–48). Importantly, by revealing the conditions of possibility of white supremacy, West is able to discuss and criticize racism without positing an ontological black subject. In this way, West's genealogy is more Nietzschean than Foucauldian; indeed, elsewhere West criticizes Foucault's methodology for what he sees as its still Kantian emphasis on the constitution of subjectivity. According to West, Foucault's "Kantian questions lead him to downplay human agency, to limit the revisability of discourses and disciplines and thereby to confine his attention to a specific set of operations of power, i.e., those linked to constituting subject" (*The American Evasion of Philosophy [AEP]*, 225).[68] West is decidedly not interested in a Foucauldian genealogical construction of the development of black or white subjects. Quite the opposite is the case: the creation of black and white subjects, for West, is an effect of material and discursive productions of white supremacy. That is, West argues that the material and discursive structures of European modernity, which themselves respond to the material interests of a European capitalist class and the epistemological interests of a European scientific elite, create the possibility of race as a modern category. This critical attention to the development of a hegemonic racist discourse productive of race allows West to avoid some of the ontological traps, especially those relating to whiteness, that problematized Cone's project.

Specifically, West argues that the scientific and philosophical structures of European modernity, especially in the subjective idealism of Descartes and the preoccupation with organization and classification of Linnaeus, "promotes and encourages the activities of observing, comparing, measuring and ordering the physical characteristics of human bodies" (*PD*, 48). This penchant for classification, in turn, was informed by, on the one hand, the classical Greek aesthetic privileging of lightness, and on the other hand, cultural biases that read European mores as more civilized than others. The result is a scientific, cultural, aesthetic, and philosophic discourse that "prohibited the intelligibility and legitimacy of the idea of black equality in beauty, culture, and intellectual capacity" (*PD*, 48). Discursively, blackness was created for the sake of securing the possibility of hierarchical thought. An attention to these discursive productions demonstrates the way in which phenotype is always already interpreted in extra-biological terms and can help explain how discrimination on "racial" grounds is possible. For West, capitalist economic forms alone are not enough to explain this possibility (*PD*, 49). The development of capitalism required a proletariat class but did not require that this class be subject to racial divisions. Some other explanatory mechanism—still rooted in history, not ontological myth—becomes necessary to explain this development, and West argues that the discursive productions of European modernity offer such an explanation. In critiquing these discursive structures, West aims to show that "the everyday life of black people is shaped not simply by the exploitative (oligopolistic) capitalist system of production, but also by cultural attitudes and sensibilities, including alienating ideals of beauty" (*PD*, 65). These alienating "attitudes and sensibilities" might serve the ideological function of reifying perceived racial differences—where the white worker is taught to alienate the black worker; that is, is taught to privilege racial enmity over class solidarity—but also operate on a relatively independent level of quotidian racist practice. When the white worker has no material power over the capitalist class, it is to such discursive "power" over black people that he turns. When his entire philosophical matrix is implicitly informed by an organizing and hierarchical logic, such a turn to discursive power serves not only to establish some level of supremacy over non-white others, but also works to confirm the credibility of the white worker's own self-understanding: the fact that the white worker "knows" that the black worker is of an inferior race itself becomes proof of this superiority. This ideological feedback loop, which is the structure of white identity, would be threatened by black power—material or discursive—and so the white person is encouraged to quell all practices in this direction. And so, as was the case with Schmitt, a racist discursive structure can quickly acquire material force—often with deadly and violent results. In this sense of a multi-layered false consciousness, wherein an economic infrastructure and a discursive superstructure mutually inform and aggravate each other, a vulgar Marxist reduction of the discursive to the material, for West, "is not wrong; it is simply inadequate" (*PD*, 49).

And so West demonstrates that the association of ascriptive and metonymic forms of blackness, which remains ambiguous in Cone, has been historically produced: the association of phenotype and economic status is a historical and contingent one. This emphasis on historicism means that West's elevation of discursive productions as necessary explanatory components in the formation of racism should not be read as a retreat from Marxist materialism, but as an expansion of historical materialism to extra-economic spheres. Following Marxist theorists of culture like Raymond Williams, Theodor Adorno, and Antonio Gramsci, West holds that culture and cultural norms are not abstract and free-floating phenomena, and are certainly not ontological ones, but are instead material productions that require agents, power, and interests. For the purpose of developing an orthopraxical political theology responsive to the deconstruction of metaphysics, and especially one responsive to the need for an anti-racist Marxism as propounded by Cone, this reliance on historical and material analyses—West refers to his style of genealogy as "a genealogical materialist analysis" (*The Cornel West Reader [CWR]*, 261)—is important because West's locating of truth in historical material processes places him firmly within a critical pragmatic tradition—West calls it "prophetic pragmatism"—that understands philosophy as essentially, not accidentally, political.

West clarifies his understanding of the relationship between anti-metaphysics and prophetic pragmatism in the following passage: "The claim is that once one gives up on the search for foundations and the quest for certainty, human inquiry into truth and knowledge shifts to the social and communal circumstances under which persons can communicate and cooperate in the process of acquiring knowledge. What was once purely epistemological now highlights the values and operations of power requisite for the human production of truth and knowledge" (*AEP*, 213). As I indicated above, this methodology is at work in West's genealogy of white supremacy, which begins not with ontological categories or essential truths, but with a thick historical description of particular actors, arguments, structures, and interests. The "truth" of white supremacy is found in its particular and contingent historical productions—indeed, it is from within operations of power that all truth is produced. This radically contextual and historical epistemology neatly coheres with my previous arguments concerning the ideological structure of all metaphysics. There, my point was not just that all metaphysics necessarily fail—they do, and Derrida showed this—but also that, because of this necessary failure, all ostensibly metaphysical truth claims have to be obfuscations of some non-metaphysical position. And so Schmitt's ontological racism was not only theoretically falsifiable, but also ideologically masked an existential commitment to fascistic antisemitism. West's point here is that all truth claims—and Derrida would be in agreement that truth as such is a metaphysical gesture, perhaps the metaphysical gesture par excellence—depend upon what he calls "operations of power." In such a critical scheme, the philosopher becomes responsible for detecting, revealing, and resisting political interests and powers at work in the construction of truth claims. This critical posture toward all truth claims was what allowed West, acting as a philosopher in this prophetic pragmatist sense, to both demonstrate the artifice and contingency of white supremacy and show the work performed by white supremacy for particular, capitalist, scientific, and political interests.

But if truth is always responsible to particular interests and operations of power, then the philosopher needs the analytical tools necessary for not only logical or theoretic, but now also political critique. Here, too, the determination of which tools are necessary is the product of historical development. For West—and for Cone, although in a more hesitant way—*the* most powerful analytic tool for unmasking operations of power is the Marxist critique of capitalist political economy. This is not because of some preternatural privilege of Marxism or dogmatic commitment on the part of West. Rather, Marxism is privileged as an analytical tool because it offers the best means for critiquing the economic infrastructure that ultimately makes possible not only racist practices but also interpretations of these practices. That is, Marxism, as a political critique of philosophical and pseudo-philosophical productions, is capable of critiquing both aspects, the apparent and the infrastructural, of the ideological structure of metaphysics: both racism and its underlying political economy are critiqued by Marxism.

And so West's historical materialism not only adds analytical clarity and historical specificity to Cone's approach—which, as I have shown, does in fact account for the particular history of American anti-black racism, but does not always account for the historically constructed nature of whiteness—but also provides a strategy for resisting interpretations of Cone dependent on the race-relations framework. Recall that above, I argued that the race-relations framework—and I have suggested that certain idealizing receptions of Cone fall within this framework—critiques racism on racism's own terms. That is, the race-relations framework argues against explicitly racial injustices such as wealth disparity, but lacks the analytical tools and political will necessary for a critique of the possibility of wealth inequality as such. West has provided the means by which to resist these readings, which are unconcerned with the relationship between ideological reifications and their underlying infrastructural supports.

Prophetic pragmatism, then, is explicitly anti-racist in a way that is critical of the actual structural conditions of possibility of racism. In this sense, West's prophetic pragmatism responds to Cone's call for a politically useful, that is attractively anti-racist, Marxism. Unlike race-relations approaches that are explicitly anti-racist but ultimately only better integrate the ascriptively oppressed into capitalist exploitation—and so only respond to one tropic of blackness in Cone's work—prophetic pragmatism presents itself as a double critique of the ideological structure of all racisms: ascriptive oppressions should be fought and resisted both because of their inhumanity and because of their role in disrupting class solidarity.

This emphasis on class solidarity as itself an anti-racist practice was implied in the early Cone's metonymic tropic of blackness—according to which one could "become black" by fighting with the poor—but was never made explicit. By the time of *The Cross and the Lynching Tree*, though, this metonymic association between blackness and poverty had weakened, and so too had Cone's openness to class solidarity as a form of anti-racism. Cone had become increasingly concerned that a class-solidarity politics did not account for the particularity of black suffering. Again, West's historical materialism offers a response to this challenge. First, West is in agreement with Cone that any "colorblind" valorization of the proletariat misses the very proletarian racism that is partly responsible for the group's continuing inability to revolt against the capitalist class. West is clear that "the proletariat itself is a construct that is shot through with all kinds of divisions, cleavages, heterogeneities and so on" (*CWR*, 224). West's earlier discussion of the reactionary problems caused by white proletarian racism—it is a critique that mirrors Marx's criticism of Irish anti-black racism almost perfectly—demonstrates that these "divisions, cleavages, heterogeneities, and so on" are weaponized by the capitalist class to maintain the proletariat's exploitation. Yet, West is also clear that the divisions intrinsic to the proletariat are mirrored by divisions intrinsic to any ascriptive identity group, including black people. As early as 1987, West writes about the "increasing class division" within black America, and about the "significant black middle class, highly anxiety-ridden, insecure, willing to be co-opted and incorporated into the powers that be, concerned with racism to the degree that it poses constraints on upward social mobility" (*CWR*, 284). Moreover, West is attentive not only to these racial differences within the proletariat and class differences within ascriptive racial groups, but also to the ways in which "feminist, gay, lesbian, and ecological modes" of oppression intersect with all of the above.

Yet, ultimately, these various forms of oppression do not all follow the same logic, and West argues that we should be wary of the ways in which capital interests can mask themselves as anti-racist, anti-homophobic, green, and so on. It is for this reason that West argues that, given precisely this multiplicity of oppressions, and given that "the majority of humankind experiences thick forms of victimization" (*CWR*, 370), "Marxism today becomes even more important" (*CWR*, 222). While ascriptive oppressions call for equality—and West fights for equality everywhere—the emancipatory logic of Marxism calls for a total restructuring of the economic infrastructure that undergirds all of these various forms of oppression. In short, capitalism *exploits*, while racism, sexism, homophobia, and so on *discriminate*. "Once we lose sight," West writes, "of the reasons why the working people, the working poor and the very poor, find themselves with very little access to resources—once we lose sight of that, which was analyzed by the Marxist tradition, once we lose sight of this, then we have little or no analytical tools in our freedom fight" (*CWR*, 222). The role of the prophetic pragmatist is to resist all suffering, but to do so by using particularized ascriptive suffering as a "springboard" for a revolutionizing of the capitalist structure that both feeds off and feeds inter-proletariat discriminations (*CWR*, 504).

So far, I have described West's anti-racist Marxism in primarily philosophic terms—albeit terms that are philosophic in the prophetic pragmatic, which is to say primarily political, sense with which West is consciously working. The question remains, though, as to the relationship between West's politics and his Christian faith commitments. For Cone, the incarnation of God in Jesus Christ reveals God's absolute epistemic and political privileging of the right of self-determination for the oppressed. Although West argues that his anti-metaphysical historical materialism is implied by Christian apophaticism, he makes no such Christocentric move.[69] Indeed, West criticizes Cone's Christocentrism as "too thick."[70] And again, while West believes, like Kierkegaard, that the bible makes strong and clear commands to alleviate the plight of the poor, he also looks to incorporate "the progressive possibilities of all secular ideologies" (*CWR*, 359) and does not believe that Christianity is a necessary starting point for any emancipatory politics (*CWR*, 370).

What role, then, does Christianity play in West's program? The question is especially pointed given that West's Christianity is one free of any metaphysics and totally non-necessary for emancipatory political praxis. For West, Christianity is a matter of neither metaphysical truth nor moral suasion but is instead a matter of sanity. His reflections on the issue are some of the most moving of his corpus:

> On the existential level, the self-understanding and self-identity that flow from this tradition's insights into the crises and traumas of life are indispensable for me to remain sane. It holds

> at bay the sheer absurdity so evident in life, without erasing or eliding the tragedy of life. Like Kierkegaard, whose reflections on Christian faith were so profound yet often so frustrating, I do not think it's possible to put forward rational defenses of one's faith that verify its veracity or even persuade one's critics. Yet it is possible to convey to others the sense of deep emptiness and pervasive meaninglessness one feels if one is not critically aligned with an enabling tradition. One risks not logical inconsistency, but actual insanity; the issue is not reason or irrationality, but life or death. (*AEP*, 233)

And again:

> My prophetic outlook is informed by a deep, historical consciousness that accents the finitude and fallenness of all human beings and accentuates an international outlook that links the human family with a common destiny; an acknowledgement of the inescapable yet ambiguous legacy of tradition and the fundamental role of community; a profound sense of the tragic character of life and history that generates a strenuous mood, a call for heroic, courageous moral action always against the odds; and a biblically motivated focus on and concern for the wretched of the earth that keeps track of the historic and social causes for much (though by no means all) of their misery. (*CWR*, 359)

Of course, West's religious commitments are not mere psychological tools. They are, after all, commitments: "Of course, the fundamental philosophical question remains whether the Christian gospel is ultimately true. And, as a Christian prophetic pragmatist whose focus is on coping with transient and provisional penultimate matters yet whose hope goes beyond them, I reply in the affirmative, bank my all on it, yet am willing to entertain the possibility in low moments that I may be deluded" (*AEP, 233*). West is here admitting that the fight for emancipation, for him, would be an impossible one were it not for a hope in justice that seems possible only with God. Overwhelmed by the perniciousness of capital and seemingly infinite oppressions, despaired by our lack of progress, haunted by the realist knowledge that death will come before the revolution, angered that none of this is necessary, surrounded by needless and heavy suffering, West, tragically but hopefully, turns to God for life. His is a Christianity free of metaphysical escapism or delusion, attuned sensitively to secular misery, committed to liberating the exploited and freeing the oppressed—that is, it is a Christianity in love with the wretched of the world, and it is that which allows West to believe another world is possible. It is a possibility without metaphysical assurance. Without this metaphysical security, and with the tragic knowledge of his necessary mortality, West must pursue justice and must fight capital knowing that he does so "against the odds." He is in complete agreement with Cone on this point, as both agree that the truth is we must fight for freedom even if the truth is that we will lose. This, then, is the praxical and revolutionary decision they make, and with which we are charged: For freedom; that is, for Marxism.

Now, Cone ends his article on the black church and Marxism with this: "Perhaps what we need today is to return to that good old-time religion of our grandparents and combine with it a Marxist critique of society" ("BCM," 10). The construction and defense of such a political theology has been the goal of this project. When my grandmother, once a nun, lost her son, she said he was still with us. A few days later, a penny rolled from under the couch, and she said, Look, there's Mark. The good old-time religion of my grandparents is not metaphysics. It is similar, I think, to Derrida kissing his shawl. It is also similar, I think, to Cone dreaming of Molotov cocktails flying in as if from heaven. In his last words, Jesus told the disciples to go and teach what he had commanded, and he assured them, "lo, I am with you always, even to the end of the age." Eternally, he promised: Solidarity forever.

Conclusion

St. John Brown

The previous chapter argued that James Cone and Cornel West articulate orthopraxical and revolutionary political theologies responsive to the fall of metaphysics in general and ontologized racism in particular. In that sense, Cone and West exemplify the sort of political theology for which this project argues: their political theologies have anti-racist, anti-capitalist, and non-metaphysical commitments. That the details remain sometimes fuzzy—that, as I said in my reading of Cone, we are committed to fighting for justice by any means necessary but do not necessarily know what the necessary means are in advance—does not signify a lack of rigor. Rather, such an indeterminable position, wherein a politics is necessary but not known, is the necessary effect of any political theology committed to emancipation without metaphysical security.

Shortly, I will offer a brief reading of the abolitionist John Brown. Doing so will demonstrate the potential radical and revolutionary consequences of an orthopraxical and revolutionary political theology. Before doing so, though, it is worth briefly recapitulating the argument so far:

In the project's introduction, I present the project's thesis: after the Derridean deconstruction of metaphysics and the Marxist critique of it—and the similarity of the critiques proved important throughout this book—the only theology worth pursuing is an orthopraxical and revolutionary one. It is only such a theology that can avoid reinscribing theology as ideology—idealist, metaphysical, and reactionary programs are always only ideological.

Carl Schmitt might have offered such a radical political theology. Indeed, for many on the contemporary left, Schmitt does just that. However, my reading of Schmitt demonstrated that Schmitt's ostensible radicalism ideologically obfuscates an underlying reactionary political theology. Far from offering a radical form that could be detached from this reactionary political theology, Schmitt's entire project is an ideological argument against democracy in general and Marxism in particular. This argument is "ideological" in that Schmitt appeals to metaphysical divinity and transcendent sovereignty in order to authorize these reactionary political commitments. The problem with Schmitt's program for an emancipatory left, then, is not only his valorization of capitalism and antisemitism, but is also his divinization of these horrors.

Schmitt's particular decisionistic structure—where the actual political decision occurs under the ideological cover of an ostensibly metaphysical one—is generalized in my reading of Jacques Derrida. Here, we see that there is no and can be no metaphysical decision, because there is no and can be no such thing as metaphysics. This is because all metaphysics must rely on some transcendental signified that both controls and is outside of semiotic referring and signifying. But precisely as both controlling, and so related to, but outside, and so independent of, signifying, such a transcendental signified is impossible. Moreover, this deconstruction of the possibility of a transcendental signified quickly reveals a deconstruction of reference and signification as such: not only are transcendental signifieds a fake, but so too is any signified held to purely present determined meaning. Every signified is always already a signifier.

The unavoidable fact of this interminable referring without transcendental security is what Derrida means when he says that there is no outside text. Without an outside text, though, theology in particular suffers: without a transcendent logos responsible for securing the meaningful relationship of signifier and signified, without a transcendent logos responsible for securing the identity of thinking and being, theology, which names this transcendent signified/logos "God," cannot credibly claim the truth. For some, such as Martin Hägglund, this deconstruction of truth requires and promotes a "radical atheism." For others, such as John Caputo, this deconstruction of metaphysics is both made possible by and engages in a religious "passion for the impossible." In this latter view, far from employing an atheistic methodology, deconstruction is itself a sort of religion. In my view, however, both the atheist and religious interpretations of Derridean deconstruction fail to engage the most radical element of Derrida's project: the deconstruction of the identity of thinking and being. With this identity deconstructed, theology understood as true, metaphysical discourse about God is surely impossible. Indeed, all metaphysics is impossible. Yet, this theoretical critique, precisely by rupturing the identity of thinking and being, does not itself preclude the possibility of God—and even less does it preclude religious faith. Indeed, only with metaphysical necessity deconstructively rendered impossible is religious faith possible. This sort of faith, however, would need to live materially, would need to concern itself with praxis over dogma. Such a faith might be found in Derrida's relationship to his tallith.

Ultimately, Søren Kierkegaard and James Cone each offers a similar sort of praxical religion, while also offering a politically revolutionary component perhaps less clearly articulated in—but surely not absent from—Derrida. Yet, any turn to the religious here should be careful to avoid reinscribing the pretense of necessity, as if only a theological or religious frame can offer a credible response to the challenges of postmodernity. Such a gesture is offered by John Milbank and his "radical orthodoxy" theology. For Milbank, secularism necessarily endorses a "violence" and a "nihilism" because it lacks the proper "peaceful" ordering made possible by a transcendent dimension. Without transcendence, Milbank argues, we are left with only competing claims to power, wherein difference implies antagonism. Against this rather bleak view of the secular world, the Norwegian author and essayist Karl Ove Knausgaard describes a secular longing for the world that promotes love and peace. For Knausgaard, the imposition of transcendence onto the world of immanence is itself a violent gesture: Knausgaard wants to belong to this world, with all of its grittiness and quotidian failures, even as he wants to improve this world. A religious interpretation, for Knausgaard, would necessarily relativize this world, and so would fetter his pursuit for worldly love. With this sort of secular desire, it is Milbank's insistence on ontology and transcendence, not anti-metaphysical "nihilism," that introduces violence. This possibility of a secular rejection of the religious—the possibility of a decision for the secular—must always remain credible if faith is to remain possible and not necessary.

While Knausgaard opts for secularism, his fellow Scandinavian Kierkegaard opts for Christianity—at least sometimes. This sort of Christianity, though, ends up looking a lot more like both Derrida's deconstruction and Knausgaard's secularism than it does Schmitt's Christianity. This is true on at least two accounts. First of all, Kierkegaard's philosophy theoretically mirrors Derrida's project through its own deconstructive gesture: where Derrida deconstructs the identity of thinking and being, Kierkegaard deconstructs the identity of "reality" and "actuality." Reality, for Kierkegaard, refers to the ideal "truths" of thinking. Reality is the domain of idealism. Actuality, on the other hand, refers to what actually happens. Something can be ideally "true," but so long as it remains unmanifested in existence, it will never actually be true. There is actually nothing outside existence. And so Kierkegaard's deconstruction, which resembles Derrida's, brings him into contact with a thinker like Knausgaard, for whom, like Kierkegaard, truth is a thing of the world.

Importantly, though, Kierkegaard is not here offering a romantic praise of worldliness or, as some of his politically motivated critics have it, of inwardness. While his philosophy is a materialist one in this sense of valorizing existence, Kierkegaard populates this materialist structure with a decidedly anti-capitalist, if not revolutionary socialist, content. For Kierkegaard, such a politics is obviously prescribed by the bible. Any deferral or avoidance of these obviously anti-capitalist biblical precepts, in turn, can only ever be a sign of ideological idealist subterfuge. The truth, for Kierkegaard, is that one must join and fight with the poor against exploitation. This is far from Schmitt's metaphysical capitalism-racism.

Finally, this orthopraxical and anti-capitalist political theology is further specified by James Cone, who, in turn, is supplemented by Cornel West. Cone continues this project's interest in articulating a non-metaphysical understanding of truth by relativizing all truth claims according to an orthopraxic privileging of emancipation. For Cone, much like for Kierkegaard, the truth is that the exploited should not be exploited and that the oppressed should not be oppressed. Something is true only to the extent that it supports this orthopraxic, revolutionary demand. His emphasis on actual material change makes of Cone a necessary and helpful critic of essentializing "race relations" and "diversity" frameworks of anti-racism, of which Afropessimism is one. For Cone, and for the sort of political theology developed in this project, these anti-racist frameworks too easily rely on ontologized accounts of race and racism. While clearly opposed to Schmitt's reactionary politics—he is a racist, and these frameworks are anti-racist—this reliance on metaphysics should and does disturb the sort of materialist politics that interests Cone. After all, because ontology can only ever ideologically obfuscate an underlying material decision, these ontologizations must be read critically in order to reveal the infrastructural work they do. In the case of the race relations framework, I argue that racial ontologizations serve the ideological function of disrupting cross-race class solidarity. That is, some contemporary anti-racist projects support—intentionally or not—capitalist ends. For Cone, such a pro-capitalist anti-racism simply will not do, because such measures fail to live up to the measure of total emancipation.

At this point of identifying and resisting these two distinct but related forms of violence—racist oppression and capitalist exploitation—Cornel

West becomes a necessary supplement to Cone. It is West, more so than Cone, who is able to carefully hold distinct while simultaneously addressing these two violences. In doing so, West relies on a "prophetic pragmatism" that looks much like Kierkegaard's materialist existentialism and Cone's epistemological privileging of the oppressed. For West, the primary task of philosophy is to critique the power imbalances that cause and the interests that motivate particular truth claims. Truth is always constructed—not only textually, but also politically (which is not to say that Derrida's emphasis on text was apolitical but is to show the opposite: that Derrida's emphasis on text was always indissociable from the political). With this understanding of philosophy and theory as serving political ends, West fully understands and addresses the ideological structure of all metaphysics. Schmitt was doing politics but pretended to do philosophy. West accepts that all philosophical pretense will likewise involve political decisions and decides to render explicit that terrain. The philosopher, then, for West and for this project's trajectory, becomes a political actor and critic.

But is it theology? Is it political theology? For West, his project is religious—if not theological—in that he personally relies on a groundless faith in his fight for justice. Religion is not necessary for this project: a Knausgaardian secularism remains possible and credible. But, West argues, religion—specifically for him, a heavily apophatic and Kierkegaardian Christianity—is deeply helpful. It is a faith in God, and a love of others that West reads as religious, that allows him to continue a pursuit for justice despite the knowledge that death will come before the revolution. Knowledge here, against all metaphysics, does not dictate practice. In fact, quite the opposite: West, and others like him, fight despite the knowledge, the "truth," that their fight will likely come up short.

In sum, this project constructively argues the following: a theology responsive to the fall of metaphysics should be an orthopraxic and revolutionary political theology. Such a theology cannot rely on ontologized categories, racial or otherwise (Schmitt). Indeed, it cannot rely on metaphysics or ontology at all because no metaphysics is ever possible (Derrida). Not relying on metaphysical security in its fight for justice, this political theology should always leave open the possibility of an actual secularism, which, contra Milbank, is far from necessarily violent (Knausgaard). While this secularism is necessarily possible, one can always metaphysically and groundlessly decide to choose Christianity—however, doing so comes with a set of rather stringent orthopraxic demands (Kierkegaard). In particular, a Christian political theology ought to universally decide against both capitalism and racism (Cone). Without the security of metaphysical surety, one might find in religion a source of unique hope, a source of inspiration that cries out: another world is possible (West).

Granted, so far my readings have been primarily of texts in the narrow and standard sense. With the exception of appeals to social science, economics, and history in especially the project's first and last chapters, my method has been primarily deconstructively textual. Yet, I have relied on deconstructive reading—accented by a certain Marxist materialism—to argue for the necessity of material engagement in actual existence. Political theology is not primarily—or even—getting right the history of ideas. It is certainly not idealism. A truly orthopraxic and revolutionary political theology decides to resist and struggle in material reality, in this world. As I have shown, it might produce theories—the deconstruction of thinking and being; an epistemology of actualization; an epistemological privileging of the oppressed and exploited—but the role of theories is to be understood in the Marxist sense: "The weapon of criticism cannot, of course, replace criticism by weapons, material force must be overthrown by material force; but theory also becomes a material force as soon as it has gripped the masses. Theory is capable of gripping the masses as soon as it demonstrates *ad hominem*, and it demonstrates *ad hominem* as soon as it becomes radical. To be radical is to grasp the root of the matter."[1] The question concerning theory, as both Cone and Marx have it, is whether or not a theory is radical enough as to grip the masses. Important here is that an attractive theory should not rely on ideological appearances. Any political theology that leaves intact the exploitative infrastructural regime of capital is not a credibly emancipatory one. The appeal of revolutionary theory is meant to convert the working class—a class *for the capitalists*—into the proletariat—a class *for itself.*

What, then, is the relationship between a rejection of metaphysics and an embrace of theories—which are not so much groundlessly "decided" as they are discovered in the text of the world of which there is no outside? Again, Kierkegaard provides the crucial link: the first revolutionary decision is surely to revolt, but this revolt ought to be understood as a leap. Recall that for Kierkegaard, one never has a good reason—only bad ones—to make the leap of faith. It is not until after the leap is made that something like religious sense can be found. Indeed, the truth of religion, for Kierkegaard, is that one must first leap. Importantly here, any sense or coherence that is discovered while leaping will always remain interminable, undecidable, "objectively uncertain." More than uncertain, such insights and commitments will appear outright mad from the outside. If they did not seem mad, then a leap would not be necessary.

This embrace of madness, where praxis and theory, where activity and passivity, where implementation and passion all implicate each other, is how we should understand the life and work of John Brown. Brown is most remembered for his 1859 raid on Harper's Ferry, a Confederate arms depot. But Brown's work as a committed abolitionist did not begin in 1859. Brown had not only been a prominent activist in the New England abolitionism scene for years—where he gained the friendship of Harriet Tubman, Frederick Douglass, and Henry Thoreau, among others—but had also launched several violent attacks on slave owners and plantations throughout the 1850s. Brown's raid on Harper's Ferry is not a one-off event, the effect of a madman's acute manic episode, but is instead continuous with a life committed to justice—whatever the cost, and by any means necessary.[2]

This question of insanity has often framed the conversation concerning Brown. As Ted Smith notes, the frame of the question seems to assume a dichotomy between pure violent insanity, on the one hand, and rational freedom fighting, on the other.[3] Interestingly, one's assessment of Brown's mental health does not necessarily imply a value judgment on his violence either way. For example, the claim that Brown was insane seems to have achieved its formal narratological structure when it was introduced by Asahel Lewis, a newspaper editor and friend of Brown's, as a defense for Brown during the abolitionist's trial.[4] Likewise, Henry Alexander Wise, Virginia's governor at the time of Brown's raid, was committed to the notion that Brown was not a "madman," but instead a "fanatic."

For his part, Brown is as clear as possible: "I am not insane, nor have I ever been" (*John Brown Speaks [JBS]*, 102). While not wanting to rely on a defense of insanity—which would undermine the decisiveness with which Brown led his life according to emancipatory ends—Brown is aware of the paradoxical difficulty, the catch-22 scenario, of proving his own sanity. To this end, Brown's defense is both brilliant and seemingly informed by a distinctly apophatic sensibility: "My observation teaches me that insane people know more on all subjects than all the rest of the world. I am not of that opinion in regard to myself . . . Insane persons, so far as my experience goes, have but little ability to judge of their own sanity; and, if I am insane of course I should think I know more than all the rest of the world. But I do not think so." (*JBS*, 102–103).[5] Brown's claim is that he cannot be considered insane, because he exhibits epistemic humility.

With this defense, Brown approaches something like the aforementioned tension between decisive action and the acceptance of received theory. The analogy becomes more sharp when considering the fact that Brown's appeal to epistemic humility is not an ironic gesture on his part. Instead, Brown always and everywhere relativizes and contextualizes his personal political and theological commitments. Brown's claim that he does not know much is one of the most common motifs of his life. While citations and examples could be provided ad nauseam, one particular moment captures Brown's generally apophatic outlook particularly well. After his arrest, and while he was held in a Virginia prison, David Eichelberger, editor of Charlestown's *Independent Democrat* journal, submitted a list of interview questions to Brown. Searching for a means to situate Brown within the contemporary political arena, Eichelberger asks Brown, "to what political party do you belong?" To which Brown, in writing, replies: "To God's party. (I think)."

With this parenthetical "I think," Brown recognizes, accepts, and leaps into absolute metaphysical indeterminacy. Brown belongs to God—he thinks. And to belong to God is a very simple thing—he thinks. Brown reflects on scripture and notes that it "teaches me that all things whatsoever I would that men should do to me, I should do even so to them. It teaches me, further, to 'remember them that are in bonds, as bound with them.'"[6] Receiving these commands, Brown has simply "endeavored to act up to that instruction" (*Speech to the Court*). For this reason, because Brown has simply followed that word of God, he "believes that to have interfered as I have done—as I have always freely admitted I have done—on behalf of His despised poor was not wrong, but right" (*Speech to the Court*).

Where Kierkegaard spoke of the Christian need to simply read and follow biblical precepts, Brown simply did read and follow biblical precepts. But he always does so with the full knowledge that he lacks full knowledge. Brown is, quite literally, "ready to die" for "the God of the oppressed and the poor" (*JBS*, 74), but is not entirely sure that he belongs to God's party. He is only sure that he thinks he does. All of which is to say, an "I think" separates the hope that Brown is following God from the sure knowledge that he is. An "I think" separates metaphysical assurance from hope. Thinking, here not metaphysical but purely existential, thinking about the meaning of his life, thinking about losing his life, in other words, allows for Brown's faith. Brown has faith because his thinking might be wrong—which also means Brown's faith is that his thinking is true. Thinking does not and has never secured knowledge, but disrupts it—only the insane have knowledge, to know is insane—and so creates a rupture between self and world that can only be overcome through action. Faith, thinking faith, allows Brown to leap, quite literally leap and run and hide and crawl and limp, into revolution.

Brown is a saint because Brown decides to fight for abolition—against capitalism, against racism—without any metaphysical assurance of either correctness of belief or surety of outcome. But if, as Marx would have it,

Brown's saintly life is to remain sufficiently attractively radical as to grip the masses, then his life must be presented in all of its radical tension. As Kierkegaard would have it, only with this tension—only with the real possibility that Brown is insane—is a decision for Brown possible. It is a decision with which Brown himself, like Abraham, is faced. On the one hand, Brown is unquestioning in and totally committed to his project for emancipation. The day before his execution, Brown writes: "Today is my last day upon Earth. Tomorrow I shall see God. I have no fear, I am not afraid to die" (*JBS*, 93). This is the confidence of a martyr who belongs to God's party. At the same time, Brown, in the solitude of his cell, awaiting his death, reflects on annihilation, and seems to accept the possibility that his death will permanently mark his departure from the world he still somehow loves. His prison bible marks and underlines Revelation 13–14: "And cinnamon, and odors, and ointments, and frankincense, and wine, and oil, and fine flour, and wheat, and beasts, and sheep, and horses, and chariots, and slaves, and souls of men. And the fruits that thy soul lusted after are departed from thee, and all things which were dainty and goodly are departed from thee, and thou shalt find them no more at all." This is the somber reflection of a martyr who thinks that he will never know if he belongs to God's party.

This undecidable position—God or not, God's party or not—is neglected by every metaphysics that ideologically feigns to decide the truth in advance. This undecidable position is also neglected by the capitalist's "invisible hand," and this is an invisibility that ideologically covers a fist, as well as the racist's ontologizing myths. But it is also from within this indeterminacy that Derrida turns to his shawl, that Knausgaard holds his daughter's hand, that Kierkegaard leaps, and that Cone prays for a Molotov cocktail. For although or because metaphysical assurance is philosophy and theology's violent founding myth, these thinkers—these actually existing individuals—have decided that the despair of a life lived under capital is best fought, not accepted. Modernity's capitalism and racism, under the mythical cover of metaphysics, challenge any orthopraxic and revolutionary political theology in all of the ways discussed throughout this project. John Brown, and all of the saints, heroic and mundane, secular and religious, successful and failed, Che Guevara and Fred Hampton and Jesus Christ, and the millions of permanently secret revolutionaries whom posterity has not remembered and never will, all of these saints lived lives whose radicalness cannot help but grip. Theirs is a grip that challenges as it welcomes. Theirs is a grip that holds on to solidarity through their deaths, which, depending on our decisions, can be, but always might not be, redeemed.

Notes

Introduction

1. John Brown receives extensive treatment in this project's conclusion.

2. On Paul's universalism: Alain Badiou, *Saint Paul: The Foundation of Universalism,* trans. Ray Brassier (Stanford, CA: Stanford University Press, 2003). On his messianism: Giorgio Agamben, *The Time That Remains: A Commentary on the Letter to the Romans,* trans. Patricia Dailey (Stanford, CA: Stanford University Press, 2005).

3. Jeffrey Robbins, "Alain Badiou and the Secular Reactivation of Theology," *Heythrop Journal* 55.4 (2014): 612–619.

4. Karl Marx, *Capital: A Critique of Political Economy,* trans. Samuel Moore and Edward Aveling (Moscow, Russia: Progress Publishers), 47–48. Accessible at https://www.marxists.org/archive/marx/works/download/pdf/Capital-Volume-I.pdf.

5. For more on this disagreement, see: Sven-Eric Liedman, *A World to Win: The Life and Works of Karl Marx,* trans. Jeffrey Skinner (New York, NY: Verso Books, 2018), 59–68.

6. As this sentence might make clear, I do not adhere to any distinction between "the political," understood as the pure fact of an antagonistic realm as Schmitt might have it, and "politics," understood as a particular commitment to particular material interests within the realm of "the political." This distinction is also an important one for Chantal Mouffe, as discussed below. But Mouffe's belief in the separability of "the political" from "politics" is precisely what prevents her from seeing the extent to which anti-Marxism informs Carl Schmitt's entire project. More simply, and as I illustrate through the example of Schmitt, I do not believe that a discussion of "the political" is possible without doing "politics." I do not know what "the political" without reference to politics could mean, and I don't think such a use is possible except as ideological.

7. For Parmenides's thinking of the relationship between thinking and being, and for this thinking's importance for the metaphysical tradition, see Martin Heidegger's *Early Greek Thought,* trans. David Krell and Frank Capuzzi (Manhattan, NY: Harper and Row, 1985), especially pages 79–101.

8. Slavoj Žižek, *Less Than Nothing: Hegel and the Shadow of Dialectical Materialism* (New York, NY: Verso Books, 2013), especially pages 53–69.

9. For the importance of this philosopheme in what he agrees should be called metaphysics, see Eric Perl's *Thinking Being: Introduction to Metaphysics in the Classical Tradition* (Leiden, Netherlands: Brill, 2014).

10. Philippe Lacoue-Labarthe, "The Fable (Literature and Philosophy)," trans. Hugh Silverman, *Research in Phenomenology* 15 (1985), 43–60. The claim is obviously not meant chronologically: philosophers have existed after Nietzsche, but this does not mean Nietzsche did not close the text of philosophy.

11. The complication that Derrida introduces, which will become important in chapters two and three, is the question of what sense "fiction" might have outside of its dichotomous positioning relative to "metaphysics," which might very well create "fiction" as a means of self-differentiation.

12. Michael Marder, *Groundless Existence: The Political Ontology of Carl Schmitt* (New York: Continuum, 2010).

13. For more on Žižek's understanding of ideology, see his *The Sublime Object of Ideology* (New York, NY: Verso Books, 2009).

14. For more on this sort of ideological abuse of feminism, see Serene Khader's *Decolonizing Universalism: A Transnational Feminist Ethic* (Oxford University Press, 2019).

15. For example, Alberto Toscano's "The Open Secret of Real Abstraction," *Rethinking Marxism* 20.2 (2008), 273–287.

16. My reading of Marx's critique of capitalist political economy is immensely informed by David Harvey's *Companion to Marx's Capital: The Complete Edition* (New York, NY: Verso Books, 2018).

17. Claudia Jones, "An End to the Neglect of the Problems of the Negro Woman!" Accessible at: https://palmm.digital.flvc.org/islandora/object/ucf%3A4865.

Chapter One

1. *Telos 71* (1987) and *Telos 73* (1987). Table of contents for both are accessible here: http://journal.telospress.com/content/by/year/1987.

2. But she is by no means the only one. See, for example, Matthew Gayetsky's "Partisans in Empire, or, Carl Schmitt as Revolutionary?" *Theory and Event 18.4* (2015), wherein Gayetsky writes that "Schmitt offers a rough outline for those forms of subjectivity which can act in opposition to Empire." Or Banu Bargu's "The Predicaments of Left-Schmittianism," *South Atlantic Quarterly* 113, 4 (2014),:713–27. Bargu's account is more sympathetic to Marx than is Mouffe's. Drawing on Jodi Dean's *The Communist Horizon* (New York, NY: Verso Books, 2018), Bargu argues that the "formalism" of "the Schmittian point that the political is based on a fundamental antagonism" can be "injected . . . with an economic analysis and normative

orientation that is derived from Marxism" (717). While I agree that the Marxist distinction between proletariat and capitalist—or Dean's distinction between "the 1% and the rest of us"—appears to structurally resemble Schmitt's distinction between friend and enemy, my reading of Schmitt argues that he is not at all a formalist. That is, his "formalism" cannot be "injected" with a different content because his formalism is always already deeply imbued with an ontologized pro-capitalist and antisemitic content. I support Bargu's and Dean's attempt at re-politicization, but only insofar as this politicization is distinctly inspired by Marx, not Schmitt. For example, only the overlooking of Schmitt's deeply anti-Marxist commitments can allow for Bargu to write that the "paradoxical but productive convergence of the far Right and the far Left and invites deeper reflection on this current of thought" (726). There cannot be any convergence between Marxism and anti-Marxism on the point of Marxism, and so I fail to see how the inclusion of Schmittian logic or rhetoric adds anything—material or intellectual—to Bargu's or Dean's emancipatory projects. All of this is to say nothing about left criticisms of Schmitt, especially by Slavoj Žižek, for whom Schmitt is a "formalist" (my reading disagrees, insofar as I argue that Schmitt is motivated primarily by material interests) and Giorgio Agamben (for whom Schmitt basically misunderstands the fictive nature of sovereignty).

3. Chantal Mouffe, *For a Left Populism* (New York, NY: Verso Books, 2018).

4. Curiously, Mouffe has little to say about the storied tradition of anti-racist and decolonial Marxists who found in Marx plenty of resources for overcoming ostensibly extra-economic forms of oppression. For more on this, see Kevin Anderson's *Marx at the Margins: On Nationalism, Ethnicity, and Non-Western Societies* (Chicago, IL: University of Chicago Press, 2010).

5. Chantal Mouffe, *On the Political* (Abington, UK: Routledge, 2005).

6. Along these same lines, Susan Buck-Morss turns to Schmitt as a corrective to "Marxian preoccupations with the global economy" that allegedly do not address "the specifically political nature of global power—political in the old-fashioned, institutional sense of the word, meaning sovereignty, legitimacy, violence, and war." See: "Sovereign Right and the Global Left," *Cultural Critique* 69 (2008): 145–71.

7. Of course, Schmitt "inscribes" this antisemitism in a structural and hidden sense: a naive reader of *Political Theology* might not know that they are reading the work of an antisemite. But, as I will argue shortly, this does not change the fact that antisemitism informs Schmitt's ideological use of concepts like "sovereignty," "decision," and so on. Precisely as an ideologue—and a clever one—we would not expect Schmitt to declare his antisemitism openly in his academic works (although, as we will see, his private writings are a separate matter).

8. Chantal Mouffe, "Post-Marxism: Identity and Democracy," *Society and Space* 13 (1995): 259–65.

9. Mouffe makes clear that, in her view, Marx's economic essentialism and actually existence socialism's reliance on this essentialism lead to just this sort of totalitarianism. See her "Post-Marxism Without Apologies," *New Left Review* 166 (1987).

10. As will become important in the next chapter, this prioritization of internal differentiation of any alleged identity over the inter-dichotomous difference that articulates the oppositional sense of any dichotomy is what distinguishes Derridean deconstruction from hermeneutical philosophy.

11. For more on the fascist privileging of unity, see Robert Paxton's excellent *The Anatomy of Fascism* (New York, NY: Vintage Books, 2005), as well as my "Notes on Christian Fascism," in *The Human in a Dehumanizing World* (Ossining, NY: Orbis Books, 2022), 96–106, where I provide an overview of some common understandings of fascism. For more on contemporary fascism's tendency to "other" foreigners, see Laziridis et al's *The Rise of the Far Right in Europe: Populist Shifts and "Othering,"* (London, UK: Palgrave Macmillan, 2016). Finally, for more on how essentialized identities and othering work together within fascist regimes, see Shane Burley's "Four Aspects of Contemporary Fascism," *Anarcho-Syndicalist Review* 73 (2018): 24–25.

12. Of course, Derrida and Marx are never far behind. Schmitt's ideological appeals to the ontological "unity" of the state serve the polemical function of denying class differentiations internal to the state.

13. Mark Neocleous, "Friend or Enemy? Reading Schmitt Politically," *Radical Philosophy* 79 (1996): 13–23.

14. Oswald Spengler, *The Decline of the West: An Abridged Edition*, trans. Charles Atkinson, eds. Arthur Helps and Helmut Warner (Oxford, UK: Oxford University Press, 1991).

15. Karl Barth, *The Epistle to the Romans*, trans. Edwyn Hoskyns (Oxford, UK: Oxford University Press, 1968), 28.

16. Gopal Balakrishnan, *The Enemy* (New York, NY: Verso Books, 2002).

17. Carl Schmitt, *Dictatorship: From the Beginning of the Modern Concept of Sovereignty to the Proletarian Class Struggle*, trans. Michael Hoelzl and Graham Ward (Cambridge, UK: Polity Press, 2014).

18. Conservatives seem more cognizant of this metaphysical dimension in Schmitt—and find in it a virtue. See: Renato Cristi, "The Metaphysics of Constituent Power: Schmitt and the Genesis of Chile's 1980 Constitution," *Cardozo Law Review* 21.5 (2000): 1749–76.

19. That Schmitt appears here to be criticizing Marxism's devaluation of the individual might give the impression of a liberal critique. Indeed, the relationship between liberalism, individualism, Marxism, collectivity, sovereignty, and fascism will remain an opaque cluster in Schmitt's work. I will attempt to treat this opacity when discussing *The Concept of the Political*.

20. For more on Schmitt's use of metaphysical categories like transcendence, substance, and ideality, especially as they relate to his theory of the state, see William Rasch's *Carl Schmitt: State and Society* (Lanham, MD: Rowman and Littlefield, 2019).

21. Carl Schmitt, *Politische Theologie* (Berlin, Germany: Duncker & Humblot, 2015), unpaginated.

22. All biblical quotations refer to the New American Standard Bible.

23. Joseph Cardinal Ratzinger, *Faith and Politics: Selected Writings* (San Francisco, CA: Ignatius Press, 2018), unpaginated.

24. See, for example, Stefan Rohrbacher, "The Charge of Deicide," *Journal of Medieval History* 17.4 (1991): 297–321.

25. For historical treatments of Schmitt's relationship to ordoliberalism, see: Werner Bonefeld, "Authoritarian Liberalism: From Schmitt via Ordoliberalism to the Euro" *Critical Sociology* 43.5 (2017): 747–61; Michael Wilkinson, "Authoritarian Liberalism in Europe: a Common Critique of Neoliberalism and Ordoliberalism," *Critical Sociology* 45.7 (2019): 1023–34; William E. Scheuerman, "The Unholy Alliance of Carl Schmitt and Friedrich A. Hayek," *Constellations* 4.2 (1997): 172–88.

26. See, Renato Cristi: *Carl Schmitt Authoritarian Liberalism: Strong State, Free Economy* (Cardiff, Wales: University of Wales Press, 1998).

27. Wolfgang Streeck, *How Will Capitalism End?* (New York, NY: Verso Books, 2016).

28. As will become clear, the sovereign is also a part of this legal order. Indeed, that the sovereign must occupy both a transcendent and an imminent place within Schmitt's political theology articulates one of the most ideological moments of Schmitt's text: he can and does play both sides of this tension depending upon political exigency.

29. Samuel Weber, "Taking Exception to Decision: Walter Benjamin and Carl Schmitt," *Diacritics* 22 (1992): 5–18.

30. The challenge for a political theology of decision credible in postmodernity will be to accept the appearance of Schmitt's decisionist critique of indecisive democracy—that democracy permanently defers decision, and so permanently depoliticizes politics—while rejecting its real and hidden fascist sympathies. Schmitt, then, puts the political left in the unusual position of agreeing with an ideological appearance while critiquing said appearance's infrastructural logic. For now, this strain can only be gestured toward.

31. For more on Benjamin's complex, but ultimately undeniably critical, relationship to Schmitt, see Marc de Wilde's "Meeting Opposites: The Political Theologies of Walter Benjamin and Carl Schmitt," in *Philosophy & Rhetoric* 44.4 (2011): 363–81.

32. Slavoj Žižek, "Carl Schmitt in the Age of Post-Politics," in *The Challenge of Carl Schmitt*, ed. Chantal Mouffe (New York, NY: Verso Books, 1999), 18–37.

33. Paul Hirst agrees with my view that this privileging of unity is fascistic in nature, especially for Schmitt: "What led him to collaborate with the Nazis from March 1933 to December 1936 was not ethical nihilism, but above all concern with order . . . Schmitt's doctrine thus involves a paradox. For all its stress on friend-enemy relations, on decisive political action, its core, its aim, is the maintenance of stability and order." See: "Carl Schmitt's Decisionism," in *The Challenge of Carl Schmitt*, ed. Chantal Mouffe (New York, NY: Verso Books, 1999), 7–17.

34. Giles Deleuze and Felix Guattari, *Anti-Oedipus: Capitalism and Schizophrenia*, trans. Helen Lane, Mark Seem, and Robert Hurley (London, UK: Bloomsbury Academic, 2004), 166.

35. Carl Schmitt, "Der Begriff des Politischen," *Archiv für Sozialwissenschaft und Sozialpolitik* 58.1 (1927): 1–33.

36. Carl Schmitt, *Der Begriff des Politischen* (Berlin, Germany: Duncker & Humblot, 1932).

37. Jacques Derrida, *The Politics of Friendship*, trans. George Collins (New York, NY: Verso Books, 2006).

38. Again we should note that these purifications of the political serve to further Schmitt's ordoliberal impulse: the state should not only be kept free of undue economic influence, but should also allow economic markets the freedom to work unfettered by democratic claims at redistribution.

39. Presumably, such a demand can be justified by the pro-market mandates of ordoliberal thought: the friend is the friend of free markets, and the enemy is the democratizing Marxist.

40. Carl Schmitt, *Glossarium: Aufzeichnungen aus den Jahren 1947 bis 1958*, eds. Gerd Giesler and Martin Tielke (Berlin, Germany: Duncker & Humblot, 2015), 14.

41. My discussion of Cone will argue that racial ontology must be rejected *tout court*. Racial ontology is an essential, not accidental, element of Schmitt's thought. Contemporary leftist politics that appropriates this ontology reinscribes fascist thought at its most vicious, antisemitic apogee. These attempts are inescapably reactionary, because the ontologization of race can only impose ontological division onto the political and social reality of cross-racial class solidarity.

42. Unfortunately, it is an error repeated and uncommented on by Schmitt's English translator and editor.

43. Warren Carter, *Matthew and the Margins* (London, UK: T&T Clark, 2000).

44. Ulrich Luz, *Matthew 1–7: A Commentary*, trans. Wilhelm Linss (Minneapolis, MN: Augsburg Fortress, 1989).

45. Gerhard Kittel, *Theological Dictionary of the New Testament: Volume 2*, trans. Geoffrey Bromiley (Grand Rapids, MI: Eerdmans Publishing Company, 1965).

46. Jeffrey Robbins, *Radical Democracy and Political Theology* (New York, NY: Columbia University Press, 2013).

47. This internal disruption of racial ontology will be discussed in more depth in this text's final chapter.

Chapter Two

1. This is the strategy pursued, for example, by Ted Smith, in his *Weird John Brown*: "(Schmitt) is right to open up a space for deliberating about sovereignty. But his own candidate for filling that space can only be described as idolatrous . . . In using the structure of theological thought to open up a space outside the rule of

law, but then losing any politically relevant sense in which theology can be outside or other to the order of human history, Schmitt opens the door to political theologies that would put humans, individually and collectively, in the role theologies have traditionally set aside for God" (65).

2. Jean-Luc Marion, *The Idol and Distance,* trans. Thomas Carlson (New York, NY: Fordham University Press, 2001). See also page 24 of this text, wherein Marion relies on chapter 17 of Acts to argue that "philosophers" have "purified (idolatry), that is, having conceptualized it."

3. Jacques Derrida, *Dissemination,* trans. Barbara Johnson (Chicago, IL: University of Chicago Press, 1981).

4. Jean-Luc Marion, "Thomas Aquinas and Onto-Theo-Logy," in *Mystics: Presence and Aporia,* eds. Michael Kessler and Christian Sheppard (Chicago, IL: University of Chicago Press, 2003), 38–74.

5. For a treatment of Heidegger's own involvement in the double-fake structure of metaphysical—or, in his case, at least ontological—decision, see Slavoj Žižek, *The Ticklish Subject: The Absent Center of Political Ontology* (New York, NY: Verso Books, 2009), 3–77.

6. For an overview of this relationship, see John Betz, "After Heidegger and Marion: The Task of Christian Metaphysics Today," *Modern Theology* 34.4 (2018): 265–97.

7. Jason Alvis, *The Inconspicuous God: Heidegger, French Phenomenology, and the Theological Turn* (Bloomington, IN: Indiana University Press, 2018).

8. Kevin Hector, *Theology without Metaphysics: God, Language and the Spirit of Recognition* (Cambridge, UK: Cambridge University Press, 2011).

9. For a brief overview and critique of this standard argument, see Steven Shakespeare, *Derrida and Theology* (London, UK: T&T Clark, 2009), 5–7. Yet even Shakespeare, who is aware of the artifice of this distinction, cites *Of Grammatology,* the text to which most of my attention will be aimed, only a handful of times. Given that *Of Grammatology* states that theology is *the* obstacle to grammatology, this relative oversight is unfortunate, if understandable given the restrains of Shakespeare's text.

10. Clayton Crockett, *Derrida after the End of Writing: Political Theology and New Materialism* (New York, NY: Fordham University Press, 2017). Crockett fully endorses the standard view that there is a shift in Derrida's work: "Derrida's philosophy works mostly within the motor scheme of writing. At a certain point, however, during the late 1980s and early 1990s, this cultural-intellectual-technological scheme of writing evolves into a motor scheme that Malabou describes as one of plasticity . . . there is a kind of transition from an intellectual motor scheme based on writing in a broad sense to one based on what Derrida sometimes characterizes in terms of the machinic, teletechnology, or technoscience" (1–2). While recognizing that a shift in motifs does occur between Derrida's early and later works, it should be noted that this shift is far from absolute: For example, Derrida critiques ethnocentrism in the very first pages of *Of Grammatology* his earliest lecture on *la différance* engages negative theology.

11. Hans Boersma, "Iraneaus, Derrida, and Hospitality: On the Eschatological Overcoming of Violence," *Modern Theology* 19.2 (2003): 163–80.

12. Andrew Shephard, *The Gift of the Other: Levinas, Derrida, and a Theology of Hospitality* (Eugene, OR: Pickwick Publications, 2014).

13. *Derrida and Negative Theology*, eds. Harold Coward and Toby Foshay (Albany, NY: State University of New York Press, 1992).

14. Ian Almond, "Derrida and the Secret of the Non-Secret: On Respiritualizing the Profane," *Literature and Theology* 17.4 (2003): 457–71.

15. *Divinanimality: Animal Theory, Creaturely Theology*, ed. Stephen Moore (New York, NY: Fordham University Press, 2014), especially pp. 17–36.

16. Some notable exceptions to this trend are typically found in the earlier theological receptions of Derrida—works published in large part before the English translations of Derrida's "later" works were available, and, in some cases, works published before Derrida's later works. For example, Mark C. Taylor's initial reception of Derrida as a source for theology dealt extensively with writing and grammatology—although perhaps Taylor's penchant for wordplay reduces some of the analytical rigor of Derrida's own contributions to the topic. Taylor's classic treatment of the topic is *Erring: A Postmodern A/theology* (Chicago, IL: University of Chicago Press, 1984). Kevin Hart's *The Trespass of the Sign: Deconstruction, Theology, and Philosophy* (Cambridge, UK: Cambridge University Press, 1990), although still partly guided by Heidegger's concerns, offers extensive and careful treatment of these "early" Derridean themes. While Hart's engagement with the early Derrida is exemplary, he ultimately reinscribes deconstruction within the tradition of negative theology. This move ultimately denudes the radicality of deconstruction's anti-theological critique.

17. For example, Mark Fisher, who was not a theologian but who is influential in contemporary postmodern theology, conceived of Derridean "hauntology" as a sort of positive force: "Haunting can be seen as intrinsically resistant to the contraction and homogenization of time and space. It happens when a place is stained by time, or when a particular place becomes the site for an encounter with broken time." A closer reading of hauntology according to the logic of the trace developed in Derrida's early works would not have led to this understanding of hauntology, which suggests that "haunting" "happens." Derrida's more immediate point with the discussion of hauntology is that all ontology is always already a fake, is conjured. The object to be studied as (a) *being* in any ontology must be conjured up, and so can only ever be a spectral entity. This is a critique of hauntologies posing as ontologies. Derrida is not, as Fisher suggests, endorsing some notion of ghosts disrupting the present; rather, the "present" is always already self-deconstructing, is never an entity nor a being and so is never the object of ontological—only hauntological—study. This reversal and subsequent misreading, where Derrida's object of deconstructive critique is somehow taken as his normative position, was also seen in the previous chapter's discussion of Jeffrey Robbins's pseudo-Derridean endorsement of "the politics of friendship." See Mark Fisher, "What is Hauntology?" *Film Quarterly* 66.1 (2012): 16–24.

18. This difference between the reality of thought and the actuality of existence will be explored in depth in this project's engagement with Kierkegaard.

19. Jacques Derrida, "Circumfession," in *Jacques Derrida*, trans. Geoffrey Bennington, ed. Geoffrey Bennington (Chicago, IL: University of Chicago Press, 1993).

20. John Milbank, *Theology and Social Theory: Beyond Secular Reason* (Hoboken, NJ: Blackwell Publishing, 2006).

21. For an overview of this difference between Derridean deconstruction and Gadamerian hermeneutics—that deconstruction finds indeterminacy in text and that hermeneutics finds indeterminacy residing between text and reader—see Ernst Behler, "Deconstruction Versus Hermeneutics: Derrida and Gadamer on Text and Interpretation," *Southern Humanities Review* 21.3 (1987): 201–23.

22. On the misreading of Derrida as promoting only negation, see Derrida's "Letter to a Japanese Friend," wherein Derrida explains that and why deconstruction is "not a negative operation." From *A Derrida Reader: Between the Blinds*, ed. Peggy Kamuf (New York, NY: Columbia University Press, 1991).

23. Aristotle, *On Interpretation*, Section 1 part 1.

24. Derrida is reacting against this identification of writing with fallenness and sin. For Derrida, writing is not sinful because there was never a pre-textual or pre-inscribed Edenic utopia. As will become more important in this project's next chapter, Derrida's anti-sin position problematizes John Milbank's critique of Derrida. For Milbank, Derrida and other "nihilists" have assumed an ontology of violence, wherein the truth of all language and all meaning is violence. Indeed, according to Milbank, for Derrida "violence is what there is to be known" (*Theology and Social Theory*, 314). As should be clear, though, Derrida is arguing against what he sees as the classical identification of writing with violence. Later in *Of Grammatology*, Derrida will speak of an originary violence, but this is in an expanded and generalized sense meant to undo—through affirmation and hyperbolization—the classical claim that writing is violence. There, it is as if Derrida is saying: You say writing is violence? Fine, then everything is violence. This same reversal-through-affirmation structure is at work in Derrida's claim that there is no outside text, which is discussed in depth below. For more on Milbank's critique of Derrida, see *Theology and Social Theory* (Hoboken, NJ: Wiley-Blackwell, 2006), esp. pp. 309–17. For a rigorous critique of Milbank's reception of Derrida, see: Marika Rose, *A Theology of Failure: Zizek against Christian Innocence* (New York, NY: Fordham University Press, 2019), esp. pp. 37–44. In this text, Rose convincingly argues that Derrida enacts a "radicalization" of Christian apophaticism—this opposed to Milbank's monolithic construction of "Christianity" that makes of Derrida a fundamentally anti-Christian nihilist.

25. Derrida leaves open here the possibility of a rethinking of distance from God not according to sin, but to prayer and adoration. Such would be one form of Marion's argument. As I will argue in this chapter's final section, Derrida's position does not preclude this positive valuation of distance, but it does preclude a structure that looks to use this distance for the sake of maintaining an identity of thought and being. The question of distance, sin, and prayer would then turn

not primarily on how distance is thought, but more generally on the possibility of writing "distance" outside of text.

26. This project's chapter on Kierkegaard will present an entirely different understanding of truth as existential.

27. It is also the logic of hyperessentialism that Derrida finds in Dionysius's negative theology. A full discussion of Derrida's relationship to negative theology is not possible in a footnote, but his major argument in those discussions does not radically differ from what I am developing here. In terms of negative theology, Derrida worries that the purification and rarefication of language is performed for the sake of securing a higher purity. The hyper-being that Derrida finds in Dionysius would still be subject to the generalized account of writing developed here: God could not be a transcendental signified, and God as hyper-being is no different. That negative theology apparently strips language of its descriptive capabilities does not change this necessity. Nor does such a program dissociate being from thinking: like Augustine's program, what is known in negative theology, according to Derrida, is God as unknowable. The link between thinking and being that allows for reference is not fundamentally challenged: even when speaking of a learned ignorance, negative theology speaks of controlling the relationship between language and its outside, God. The question would then always be, what authorizes this control? See: Jacques Derrida, "How to Avoid Speaking: Denials," from *Derrida and Negative Theology*, eds. Harold Coward and Toby Foshay (Albany, NY: State University of New York Press, 1992), 73–143.

28. John Betz has argued that Christian theology is not primarily interested in the coherence of the signifier and the signified in any sign. Rather, Christian theology operates with an analogical metaphysics wherein all of creation functions as a sort of fallen, incomplete, and improper signifier of God. In this way, creation partakes in the divine without immediate or direct access to the divine. Creation is then somehow a part of, and so somehow refers to, the creator, but the creator always and everywhere exceeds creation. But this program does not alleviate Derrida's concerns. Rather, it illuminates them: Betz's analogical metaphysics makes of God the only signified. That God is the ultimate transcendental signified is not an argument against Derrida, because it is Derrida's primary argument in *Of Grammatology*. Whereas Betz sees this locating of God in the transcendent as a cure to metaphysics' perceived ills, Derrida sees it as the source of metaphysics' problems. As Betz notes, the ultimate question concerning the relationship between metaphysics and theology is this: "to what extent is theology qua theo-*log*, as 'reasoned speech' about God, even possible?" It is precisely this "about," this structure of reference, which, as allegedly secured by God, is critiqued by Derridean deconstruction. Of course, and importantly, the claim that reference is only ever a reference of future reference is not quite the same as the claim that one cannot speak about God—this will be clarified in this chapter's final section. However, by reinscribing the signifier/signified structure within the creature/creator relationship, Betz's metaphysics does

ultimately conceive of God as an impossible transcendental signified, that is, as a fake. See: John Betz, "Theology without Metaphysics? A Reply to Kevin Hector," *Modern Theology* 31.3 (2013): 488–500. For more on Derrida's critique of analogy—which is a figure, and is textual, and so cannot be used to secure reference to an outside text—see Derrida's "White Mythology: Metaphor in the Text of Philosophy," in *Margins of Philosophy*.

29. In this sense, the condition of the impossibility of a transcendental signified, of an absolute and present truth, is the condition of possibility of writing and life. Against Pickstock, for whom Derrida is "a necrophiliac," Derrida's rejection of the sovereign and arresting power of the would-be transcendental signified is an affirmation of life. See: Catherine Pickstock, *After Writing: On the Liturgical Consummation of Philosophy* (Wiley-Blackwell, 1997), esp. pp. 101–114.

30. One could question even this determination: "And death, to what does that refer?" Among other texts, Derrida takes up this question in "Rams: Uninterrupted Dialogue—between Two Infinities, the Poem," from *Sovereignties in Question: The Poetics of Paul Celan* (New York, NY: Fordham University Press, 2005). In "Rams," Derrida argues that the possibility of death makes possible friendship: it is only with the knowledge that friendship is finite and asymmetrical, that one will die before the other, that one can pledge friendship to the other. Only if I know you might die first can I promise to carry you beyond death. And so despite this suggestion in *Of Grammatology*, and despite what Hägglund will have to say shortly, even the question and possibility of death seems to find itself in text.

31. Geoffrey Bennington, "Deconstruction and the Philosophers (The Very Idea)" *Oxford Literary Review* 10½ (1988): 73–130.

32. Derrida could have written that there is no inside text, either. The point is not that language is a prison from which we cannot leave. Rather, the critique of an "outside" should also be read as a critique of the structure that depends on a distinction between outside and inside. The notion that there could be a pure immanence of text—of anything—is totally foreign to Derrida's project. Indeed, in "Outwork," the opening essay of *Dissemination*, Derrida explicitly rejects it: "To allege that there is no absolute outside of the text is not to postulate some ideal immanence, the incessant reconstitution of writing's relation to itself. What is in question is no longer an idealist or theological operation which, in a Hegelian manner, would suspend and sublate what is outside discourse, logos, the concept, or the idea. The text *affirms* the outside, marks the limits of this speculative operation, deconstructs and reduces to the status of effects all the predicates through which speculation appropriates the outside" (35).

33. For more on the difficulties of Spivak's translation, see: Geoffrey Bennington, "Embarrassing Ourselves," *LA Review of Books* (March 2016).

34. "The abolition of religion as the *illusory* happiness of the people is the demand for their *real* happiness. To call on them to give up their illusions about their condition is to call on them to *give up a condition that requires illusions*. The

criticism of religion is, therefore, *in embryo, the criticism of that vale of tears* of which religion is the *halo*. Criticism has plucked the imaginary flowers on the chain not in order that man shall continue to bear that chain without fantasy or consolation, but so that he shall throw off the chain and pluck the living flower. The criticism of religion disillusions man, so that he will think, act, and fashion his reality like a man who has discarded his illusions and regained his senses, so that he will move around himself as his own true Sun. Religion is only the illusory Sun which revolves around man as long as he does not revolve around himself." Karl Marx, *A Contribution to the Critique of Hegel's Philosophy of Right*. Accessed: https://www.marxists.org/archive/marx/works/1843/critique-hpr/intro.htm#05.

35. John Caputo, "The Return of Anti-Religion: From Radical Atheism to Radical Theology," *Journal for Cultural and Religious Theory* 11.2 (2011): 32–116.

36. Martin Hägglund, "The Radical Evil of Deconstruction: A Reply to John Caputo," *Journal for Cultural and Religious Theory* 11.2 (2011): 126–50.

37. Martin Hägglund, *This Life: Secular Faith and Spiritual Freedom* (New York, NY: Pantheon Books, 2019).

38. John Caputo, "Looking the Impossible in the Eye: Kierkegaard, Derrida, and the Repetition of Religion," *Kierkegaard Studies Yearbook* (2002): 1–25. See also Caputo's *The Prayers and Tears of Jacques Derrida: Religion Without Religion* (Bloomington, IN: Indiana University Press, 1997), especially the book's concluding chapter (331–39), wherein Caputo writes: "What is this passion for the impossible if not the passion for God, for 'my God,' even if one were rightly to pass for an atheist?"

39. Jacques Derrida, "Sauf le nom," from *On the Name*, trans. David Wood, John Leavey, and Ian McLeod; ed. Thomas Dutoit (Stanford, CA: Stanford University Press, 1995), 35–89.

40. Richard Kearney, *Strangers, Gods, and Monsters: Interpreting Otherness* (Abington, UK: Routledge, 2002).

41. Although, Derrida has answered the question, and not in the way Kearney suggests. When asked by Mark Dooley if he considers himself an atheist, especially in light of the oft-quoted assertion that he rightly passes for an atheist, Derrida replies: "I don't know. I don't know whether I am or not. Sometimes it depends on the moment or the hour." The honesty of the answer belies the latent dogmatism in both Hägglund's atheism and Caputo's pseudo-theism. See: "The Becoming Possible of the Impossible: An Interview with Jacques Derrida," in *The Essential Caputo: Selected Writings* (Bloomington, IN: Indiana University Press, 2018), 44–54.

42. Graham Ward, "Review: *The Prayers and Tears of Jacques Derrida*," *Modern Theology* 15.4 (1999): 504–507.

43. This interpretation of Derrida, which depends upon a distinction between "revealability" and "revelation" and a privileging of revealability, leaves Derrida susceptible to critiques of escapism. Robyn Horner, whose "real point is that locating God in the absolute future, even if this promotes a kind of generally ethical or even religious impulse, is insufficient to sustain faith of any sort—even

faith so unspecified as Derrida's might be. No thinking of God can be meaningful without a thinking of revelation, for faith is a response to how God has passed in the past as much as a desire for God to come in the future," makes just this critique. Caputo's interpretation gives credibility to this critique but, as I hope to show especially in the chapter's next section, the opposite interpretation of Derrida is possible: Derrida does not forbid faith but makes it possible through a dissociation of thinking and being. See: Robyn Horner, "Theology after Derrida," *Modern Theology* 29.3 (2013): 230–47.

44. Žižek finds in Caputo's dismissal of the possibility of any particular faith, and especially in his dismissal of the possibility of a Kierkegaardian absurd, a dismissal of Christianity at large. For all of his talk of the impossible, Caputo is only ever at best able to approach religion ironically, with his "fingers crossed": "The paradox of Christian Incarnation: in Christ, this miserable individual, we see God himself . . . The properly Christian choice is the 'leap of faith' by means of which we take the risk to fully engage in a singular instantiation as the Truth embodied, with no ironic distance, no fingers crossed. 'Christ' stands for the very singular point excluded by Caputo: a direct short circuit, identity even, between a positive singularity and the divine Event. Caputo professes his love for Kierkegaard—but where here is the central insight of Kierkegaard's *Philosophical Fragments,* his insistence on the central paradox of Christianity: eternity is accessible only through time, through the belief in Christ's Incarnation as a temporal event?" (*The Monstrosity of Christ,* 258). That is, by foreclosing the possibility of paradox, by rejecting the possibility that the messiah might "actually show up," Caputo robs faith of its truly passionate potential.

45. John Caputo and Gianni Vattimo, *After the Death of God* (New York, NY: Columbia University Press, 2007).

46. Slavoj Žižek and John Milbank, *The Monstrosity of Christ* (Cambridge, MA: MIT University Press, 2009), 260.

47. While Žižek uses Altizer as means by which to distance himself from Caputo, a closer reading of Altizer on the question of politics might have left Žižek wanting. In particular, Altizer's claim that Marxism is a "consequence of the secularization of Christianity," and this because of Marx's reliance on Hegel, is a bit of idealist historiography that Žižek's insistence on materialism would dispute. For my purposes here, while I recognize some rhetorical and thematic similarities between my deconstruction of the identity of thinking and being and Altizer's death of God theology, a key difference marks our projects as ultimately opposed: For Altizer, radical politics is made possible because of the death of God. For me, following Derrida and Marx, secularism and a radical politics—secular or not—is in no way is the result of a theological development. As especially the next chapter will make clear, I am interested in pursuing a materialist, orthopraxical, anti-capitalist politics. Such a politics is available to believers and atheists, and so does not much rely on "death of God" discussions.

48. *Given Time: 1. Counterfeit Money,* trans. Peggy Kamuf (Chicago, IL: University of Chicago Press, 1994).

49. "Signature Event Context," from *Margins of Philosophy,* trans. Alan Bass (Chicago, IL: University of Chicago Press, 1982).

50. "Autoimmunity: Real and Symbolic Suicides," trans. Pascale-Anne Brault & Michael Nass, from *Philosophy in a Time of Terror,* ed. Giovanna Borradori (Chicago, IL: University of Chicago Press, 2004).

51. "Taking a Stand for Algeria," *College Literature* 30.1 (2003): 115–23; *Rouges: Two Essays on Reason,* trans. Pascale-Anne Brault and Michael Nass (Stanford, CA: Stanford University Press, 2005).

52. *The Gift of Death & Literature in Secret,* trans. Wills (Chicago, IL: University of Chicago Press, 2008).

53. Aristotle, *Metaphysics,* Book IV, 1003a.

54. For example, Bernard Longeran argues that "liberation" from structures of oppression is only possible if individuals order their ethical projects (Lonergan prefers to speak of ethics and not politics) by a religious commitment. Responding to the "problem" of the possibility of ethical living, Lonergan writes: "The solution has to be a still higher integration of human living. For the problem is radical and permanent; it is independent of the underlying physical, chemical, organic, and psychic manifolds; it is not met by revolutionary change, nor by human discovery, nor by the enforced implementation of discovery . . . Only a still higher integration can meet such requirements. For only a higher integration leaves underlying manifolds with their autonomy yet succeeds in introducing a higher systematization into their nonsystematic coincidences. And only a still higher integration than any that so far has been considered can deal with the dialectical manifold immanent in human subjects and the human situation" (*Insight*, 655). In such a view, the "manifolds" of life must be "integrated" religiously if they are to adequately respond to the problem of oppression. Hägglund's argument is that such "integration," if it is necessary, is possible totally secularly. One's commitment to any cause can order and integrate the "underlying manifolds," which I take to refer to specific existential projects—that is, if "integration" is even a helpful ethical category, a claim that any deconstructive reading could question. See: Bernard Lonergan, *Insight* (University of Toronto Press, 1992). Similar arguments concerning the religious or theological underpinning of secular projects are found in the radical orthodox figures already addressed, and by Charles Taylor, especially in *A Secular Age* (Cambridge, MA: Belknap Press, 2018). Hägglund's demonstration that deconstruction leaves open the possibility of a secular politics perhaps explains why Derrida serves as something of a villain for both Taylor and the radical orthodoxy movement.

55. In this sense, Žižek's critique of Caputo—from note 29 above—could also be read as a critique of Hägglund. Neither Caputo nor Hägglund allow for the possibility of God entering time, and so both foreclose the possibility of a passionate

and paradoxical faith. That both Hägglund and Caputo argue that "God" has to do strictly with eternity is just another example of the similarity of their respective projects.

56. Jacques Derrida and Richard Kearney, "On the Gift: A Discussion between Jacques Derrida and Jean-Luc Marion, Moderated by Richard Kearney," from *God, The Gift, and Postmodernism,* eds. John Caputo and Michael Scanlon (Bloomington, IN: Indiana University Press, 1999).

57. See Hägglund's discussion of Augustine in *This Life,* pp. 69–124. Here, Hägglund argues that Augustine's purported love for God dissimulates a prior love for Monica.

58. Richard Kearney and Jacques Derrida, "Terror, Religion, and the New Politics," *Debates in Continental Philosophy: Conversations with Contemporary Philosophers* (New York, NY: Fordham University Press, 2004).

59. "A Silkworm of One's Own (Points of View Stitched on the Other Veil)," trans. Geoffrey Bennington. *Oxford Literary Review* 18.12 (1996): 3–66.

Chapter Three

1. John Milbank, *Theology and Social Theory* (Hoboken, NJ: Wiley-Blackwell, 2006).

2. See Adam Kotsko, "So What Was Our Problem with Radical Orthodoxy?" (accessible at: https://itself.blog/2015/09/17/so-what-was-our-problem-with-radical-orthodoxy/) and Joshua Ralston, "Islamophobia and the Comeback of Christendom" (accessible at: https://www.abc.net.au/religion/islamophobia-and-the-comeback-of-christendom-riposte-to-adrian-p/10099132). See also Milbank's "Sovereignty, Empire, Capital, Terror," *South Atlantic Quarterly* 101.2 (2002), wherein Milbank, apparently unconcerned with or oblivious to decades of orientalism literature, shifts his critical attention from Duns Scotus toward the "Oriental thought" of Avicenna. Or, more troubling, see his review of Taylor's *A Secular Age*—"A Closer Walk on the Wild Side," *Studies in Christian Ethics* 22.1 (2009): 89–104—wherein Milbank seems to suggest that Mohammad was a "crazed religious enthusiast" and explicitly claims that Muslims "believe in thousands of hidden angelic and spiritual forces." Throughout the review, Platonism, not Islam, associates with Christianity and Judaism.

3. Mary-Jane Rubenstein, "Onward, Ridiculous Debaters," *Political Theology* 10.1 (2009): 125–29.

4. Daniel Horan, *Postmodernity and Univocity: A Critical Account of Radical Orthodoxy and Duns Scotus* (Philadelphia, PA: Fortress Press, 2014).

5. Donald Nielson, "Review of *Theology and Social Theory*," *Sociological Analysis* 53.4 (1992): 468–70.

6. Neither the Oxford *Handbook of Sociology of Religion* (2011) nor the Cambridge *Handbook of Sociology* (2017) mention Milbank at all.

7. John Milbank and Adrian Pabst, "The Meta-Crisis of Secular Capitalism," *International Review of Economics* 62 (2015): 197–212.

8. James K. A. Smith, *Introducing Radical Orthodoxy: Mapping a Post-Secular Theology* (Ada, MI: Baker Academic, 2004).

9. Michael Bruno, *Political Augustinianism* (Philadelphia, PA: Fortress Press, 2014).

10. For an overview of these histories, see Talal Asad, *Formations of the Secular: Christianity, Islam, Modernity* (Stanford, CA: Stanford University Press, 2003). Asad's text provides some of the same genetic arguments as does Milbank's but does so without reinscribing a Christian apologetic.

11. But even here we should be wary of relying on concepts of continuity, or else "history" and "historicity" become themselves transcendental signifieds. For a post-structural critique of the historical philosopheme of "continuity," see Derek Attridge, "Language as History/History as Language: Saussure and the Romance of Etymology," *Peculiar Language: Literature as Difference from the Renaissance to James Joyce* (Routledge, 2004, 90–126). In short, a phenomenal appearance today does not imply the continuity of some essential substance over time, and so cannot be causally explained by reference to some original past. As Renata Adler puts it: Speedboat: "I am not technically a Catholic. That is, I have not informed or asked the Church. I do not, certainly, believe in evolution. For example, fossils. I believe there are objects in nature—namely, fossils—which occur in layers, and which some half-rational fantasts insist derive from animals, the bottom ones more ancient than the top. The same, I think, with word derivations—arguments straining back to Sanskrit or Indo-European. I have never seen a word derive. It seems to me that there are given things, all strewn and simultaneous. Even footprints, except in detective stories, now leave me in some doubt that anyone passed by." *Speedboat* (New York Review Books, 2013), 42.

12. *My Struggle Book 1: A Death in the Family*, trans. Don Bartlett. Farrar, Straus and Giroux, 2013; *My Struggle: Book 2: A Man in Love*, trans. Don Bartlett. Farrar, Straus and Giroux, 2014; *My Struggle: Book 3: Boyhood*, trans. Don Bartlett. Farrar, Straus and Giroux, 2015; *My Struggle: Book 4: Dancing in the Dark*, trans. Don Bartlett. Farrar, Straus and Giroux, 2016; *My Struggle: Book 5: Some Rain Must Fall*, trans. Don Bartlett. Farrar, Straus and Giroux, 2017; *My Struggle: Book 6: The End*, trans. Don Bartlett and Martin Aitken (Brooklyn, NY: Archipelago, 2018).

13. Jonathon Sturgeon, "Buddies with Time: Why Knausgaard Really is Like Proust," *Flavorwire* (April, 2015), accessible at: https://www.flavorwire.com/515987/buddies-with-time-why-knausgaard-really-is-like-proust.

14. *Autumn*, trans. Ingvild Burkey (London, UK: Penguin, 2017); *Winter*, trans. Ingvild Burkey (London, UK: Penguin, 2018); *Spring*, trans. Ingvild Burkey (London, UK: Penguin, 2018); *Summer*, trans. Ingvild Burkey (London, UK: Penguin, 2018).

15. *So Much Longing in So Little Space: The Art of Edvard Munch*, trans. Ingvild Burkey (London, UK: Penguin Books, 2017).

16. With Fredrik Ekelund, *Home and Away: Writing the Beautiful Game,* trans. Don Bartlett and Sean Kinsella (New York, NY: Farrar, Straus and Giroux, 2017).

17. See J. Hillis Miller, "'Don't Count Me In': Derrida's Refraining," from *For Derrida* (New York, NY: Fordham University Press, 2009), 174–90; and Emily Eakin, "Derrida: The Excluded Favorite," *New York Review of Books* (March 25, 2013).

18. Or as the narrator of Knausgaard's *A Time for Everything* puts it: "Everything belonged in the category of dead things, but some dead things were alive." *A Time for Everything,* trans. James Anderson (Brooklyn, NY: Archipelago, 2009), 193.

19. "What is the world? Where does it come from? What is the meaning of life? Where does this meaning come from? Who am I? These questions, which are more important than all the rest, no one knows the answers to. That truth is beyond reach of the insights of science, whose movements in this respect perhaps most of all resemble those of a clown who as he bends down to pick up his hat ends up kicking it even farther away" (*Inadvertent,* 77).

20. Fredric Jameson, "Itemised," *London Review of Books* 21.8, 2018.

21. "I have no idea what writing is. That's true! The more I write, the less I know about what it is that makes something good. I normally think, you know, this is complete shit. And I sent it to my editor or someone else, and sometimes they say, 'No, this is alive.' Maybe two or three months later I can see that it was good. But I don't know why. Really, I've developed a method, which is being in the present, sitting here, drinking some coffee, thinking of a memory. That's the only way I know how to write. I don't know how to write a novel. But I know that, if I just try, something might happen." From "Karl Ove Knausgaard Looks Back on 'My Struggle,'" *New Yorker* (March, 2018), accessible at: https://www.newyorker.com/culture/the-new-yorker-interview/karl-ove-knausgaard-the-duty-of-literature-is-to-fight-fiction.

22. "There is always a religious beyond the ethical, which nonetheless grounds every ethic not reducible to the naturalistically pre-ethical. To be horrendously summary, one could say that ethics, like politics for Péguy, begins in the mystical and is exceeded by that which must nonetheless engender some sort of ethical practice in order to be authentic." "Wild Side," 95.

23. Karl Ove Knausgaard, "My Saga: Part 1," *New York Times Magazine* (March 1, 2015).

Chapter Four

1. The possible tension between a scriptural norm and a deconstructive rejection of truth regimes will be addressed throughout this chapter.

2. To date, there are only a few substantial studies that might support my argument. Two come from Jamie Aroosi: *The Dialectical Self: Kierkegaard, Marx, and the Making of the Modern Subject* (Philadelphia, PA: University of Pennsylvania Press, 2018) and his "The Causes of Bourgeois Culture: Kierkegaard's Relation to Marx Considered," *Philosophy and Social Criticism* 42.1 (2016): 71–92. Aroosi

argues against the typical story that places Kierkegaard and Marx in an antagonistic relationship. For Aroosi, the two are better understood as offering complementary responses to the problem of modern alienation. I would like to go further, and argue not that Kierkegaard and Marx are complements, but that their political projects more nearly converge entirely. The other study worth mentioning in this regard is Eliseo Pérez-Álvarez's *A Vexing Gadfly: The Late Kierkegaard on Economic Matters* (Princeton, NJ: Princeton University Press, 2009). In my view, Pérez-Álvarez's account unequivocally demonstrates the extent to which Kierkegaard held anti-capitalist positions. To that end, *A Vexing Gadfly* has not received the attention it deserves in Kierkegaard studies. That said, Pérez-Álvarez's project does not attempt a theoretical reading of "the early Kierkegaard," and so does not attempt to demonstrate the intrinsic connection between Kierkegaard's philosophical, theological, and economic positions. That is, Pérez-Álvarez convincingly shows that Kierkegaard the person harbored leftist political positions, but does this without substantially engaging Kierkegaard's theoretical works.

3. All citations are from György Lukács, *The Destruction of Reason,* trans. George Palmer (Chadwell Heath, London: Merlin Press, 1980).

4. All citations are from Theodor Adorno, *Kierkegaard: Construction of the Aesthetic,* trans. Robert Hullot-Kentor (Minneapolis, MN: University of Minnesota Press, 1989).

5. For an excellent overview of Adorno's reading of Kierkegaard, see Roland Boer, "A Totality of Ruins: Adorno on Kierkegaard," *Cultural Critique* 83 (2013): 1–30. Boer's argument that Adorno associates theology with ideology, and so finds in Kierkegaard's theology a pro-capitalist apologetic, is similar to the reading I gave of Derrida's anti-theology.

6. George Novack, *Understanding History,* accessed: https://www.marxists.org/archive/novack/works/history/ch12.htm, unpaginated.

7. Tom Carter, "A Closer Look at Kierkegaard," *World Socialist Web Site*, accessed: https://www.wsws.org/en/articles/2006/04/kier-a17.html.

8. When looking for a religious interlocutor, Hardt and Negri prefer St. Francis of Assisi. See Hardt and Negri, *Empire* (Cambridge, MA: Harvard University Press, 2001), 413.

9. Slavoj Žižek, *The Parallax View* (Cambridge, MA: MIT Press, 2009).

10. Slavoj Žižek, *The Puppet and the Dwarf: The Perverse Core of Christianity* (Cambridge, MA: MIT Press, 2003).

11. The series consists of twenty-one volumes, some of which are further broken into multiple "tomes": https://www.jonstewart.dk/krsrr.html.

12. In Stan's view, psychoanalysis is a "Marxian tradition." Additionally, dialectical materialism is held to be "unusual, if not sophistic." This is unfortunate, because the trope that Marxists are unusual and sophistic psychoanalysts is a common one in antisemitic discourses.

13. Leo Stan, "Risible Christianity? Kierkegaard vs. Žižek," *Toronto Journal of Theology* 28.2 (2012). See also Leo Stan, "Slavoj Žižek: Mirroring the Absent God," in *Kierkegaard's Influence on the Social Sciences,* ed. Jon Stewart (Farnham, UK: Ashgate Publishing, 2011).

14. Saitya Brata Das, *The Political Theology of Kierkegaard* (Edinburgh, Scotland: Edinburgh University Press, 2020). The Lowith citation, which is popular, is from Karl Lowith, *From Hegel to Nietzsche* (New York, NY: Holt, Rinehart, and Winston, 1964), 151. On this front, Gregor Malantschuk writes that "It is more accurate to say that this (the anti-communist manifesto) came later with *Works of Love.*" From Gregor Malantschuk, *Controversial Kierkegaard,* trans. Edna Hong and Howard Hong (Waterloo, ON: Wilfrid Laurier University Press, 1980).

15. George Pattison, *The Philosophy of Kierkegaard* (Montreal, QC: McGill University Press, 2005).

16. Jacob Taubes, *Occidental Eschatology,* trans. David Ratmoko (Stanford, CA: Stanford University Press, 2009).

17. *Truth Is Subjectivity: Kierkegaard and Political Theology,* ed. Sylvia Walsh Perkins (Macon, GA: Mercer University Press, 2019), 90.

18. Søren Kierkegaard, *Concluding Unscientific Postscript to Philosophical Fragments,* trans. Edna Hong and Howard Hong (Princeton, NJ: Princeton University Press, 1992).

19. *CUP,* 335.

20. To claim that "Kierkegaard" wrote this sentence should not be taken to elide the rhetorical and theoretical importance of the pseudonymous trope. The possibility of the distinction between Kierkegaard and any pseudonym will be important for my argument. That is, I do think it is both possible and important to separate the pseudonyms—whom Kierkegaard uses to frame arguments and to demonstrate possible shortcomings of arguments—from Kierkegaard himself. However, in following convention, and because it is actually the case that Søren Kierkegaard, and not Johannes Climacus wrote these words, I will typically cite Kierkegaard and not the pseudonyms. Yet, following the Derridean rejection of privileging originality, I do not hold that Kierkegaard's arguments are necessarily stronger than the pseudonyms' simply by virtue of Kierkegaard's material actuality (to the extent that any identity is actual!). That privilege has to be argued, not assumed.

21. Søren Kierkegaard, *Philosophical Fragments,* trans. Edna Hong and Howard Hong (Princeton, NJ: Princeton University Press, 2013).

22. It is worth noting that neither Kierkegaard nor any of the pseudonyms ever use a Danish phrase that could credibly be translated as "leap of faith." The invention of the phrase invents an ambiguity in the use of "of," suggesting that faith provides or has ownership over the leap—this is purely accidental, because the English phrase is a "translation" of a Danish phrase that never was. That a translation can invent that which it is translating in the very process of translation

is one example of the logic of the fetish construct to be critiqued shortly. It is also worth noting that this notion is really, from the beginning, two: the leap discussed by Climacus is the leap necessary in order to "leap" over Lessing's ditch between history and eternity. This leap is considered with the formal and a priori problem of philosophically defending faith. The sort of leap discussed by Silentio, on the other hand, makes no reference to Lessing, but instead references Abraham. The problematic here is not formal and philosophical but is more obviously existential and actual. For a careful and helpful overview of some of these distinctions, often passed over in secondary literature (such as by the Marxists named above), see M. Jamie Ferreira's "Faith and the Kierkegaardian Leap," in *The Cambridge Companion to Kierkegaard*, eds. Alastair Hannay and Gordon Marino (Cambridge, UK: Cambridge University Press, 1997).

23. Søren Kierkegaard, *Fear and Trembling and Repetition*, trans. Edna Hong & Howard Hong (Princeton, NJ: Princeton University Press, 1983). The text has become a sort of *locus classicus* for the topic of Kierkegaard and religion. But this is a relatively new development: in his lifetime, Kierkegaard sold only 250 copies of the text. It sold barely more than that in the eight decades after his death. Indeed, according to Google Books Ngram Viewer, the book was rarely cited before the mid-1930s, and did not grow to its current popularity until the 1940s. Its relative success in the '30s is likely due to the Jewish-French philosopher Jean Wahl's *Études Kierkegaardiennes*, which largely introduced Kierkegaard to Europe. This European engagement with Kierkegaard grew in the '40s, as the French existentialists, most of all Camus and Sartre, developed Wahl's work. Around the same time in Germany, Kierkegaard received a decidedly anti-humanist treatment by Martin Heidegger. Heidegger, however, was less concerned with the drama of *Fear and Trembling* and more concerned with the existential analytics of Kierkegaard's *The Concept of Anxiety*. The text's popularity has also benefited from its relatively early translation into English and publication in the Princeton University Press *Kierkegaard's Writings* series—*Fear and Trembling* was the sixth of twenty-seven manuscript volumes, plus twelve volumes of journals and notebooks, published by Princeton. Regardless of the recency of its popularity, the text has undoubtedly become canonical, and any engagement with Kierkegaard and religion is expected to address it. I will do so, but only minimally. The reasons for this will become clear, but for now they can be summarized like this: the pseudonymous nature of the text gives the impression that the arguments expressed are Kierkegaard's, but they are not. As I will show in my reading of *CUP*, Kierkegaard uses his pseudonyms to ironically perform arguments that resist propositional framing in straightforward philosophical treatises. That is, Kierkegaard does not always write what he means, and any treatment of *Fear and Trembling* should account for that. As they often do not, the text carries baggage, a thick history of misguided interpretation (some of which I will address)—none of which I want to cosign. For more on Kierkegaard's 1930s reception, particularly among Wahl's Jewish

milieu, see Melissa Fox-Muraton, "Faith in the Mode of Absence: Kierkegaard's Jewish Readers in 1930s France," *Kierkegaard Studies Yearbook 2016,* 189–216.

24. Carl Schmitt, *Political Theology,* trans. George Schwab (Chicago, IL: University of Chicago Press, 2006). But it is far from clear that Schmitt's endorsement from Kierkegaard, even this caricaturized Kierkegaard, is coherent. On this point, see Geoffrey Bennington's excellent *Scatter 1: The Politics of Politics in Foucault, Heidegger, and Derrida,* especially pages 193–97. Bennington demonstrates that Schmitt's lack of engagement with the Kierkegaardian notion of repetition—which is central to the passage that Schmitt misleadingly paraphrases—complicates the relationship between the singular and the universal in a way totally absent in Schmitt's overtly ontological account.

25. Because Kierkegaard did sign some texts under his own name throughout his career, because he could always do so and had no necessary reason not to do so, the choice to use a pseudonym is always something of a decision in the sense I have developed.

26. John Climacus, *The Ladder of Divine Ascent,* trans. Norman Russell (Mahwah, NJ: Paulist Press, 1982).

27. For more on this distinction, see Gabriel Ferreira da Silva, "Kierkegaard on the Relations between Being and Thought," *Kierkegaard Studies Yearbook 2015,* 3–20. da Silva ends his article with this tantalizing suggestion: "If theoretical access to Virkelighed as such is forbidden, it follows necessarily that the domain in which one can deal with it must be something else" (19). The second section of this chapter argues that this "something else" is found in a materialist political theology.

28. Critical realists and similarly aligned philosophers might rebuke Kierkegaard's near synonymous treatment of "ideality" and "universality." Yet we should remember that, for Kierkegaard, universality does not imply eternity or changelessness, and certainly does not imply trans-historicism. As his reading of Christianity shows, the opposite is the case: the universal is always only given through the particular, through existence, through writing in the Derridean sense. And so we must be careful here. As I argue throughout this chapter, to claim that thinking is *ideally universal* is not to claim that it is *actually universal.* Kierkegaard's argument that thinking is ideal and universal is a critique of metaphysics, not a description of it.

29. Ludvig Holberg, *Seven One Act Plays,* ed. Henry Alexander (Princeton, NJ: Princeton University Press, 1950).

30. That Schmitt tried to construct just such a politics of truth, and that Schmitt was decisively guided by an anti-Marxist, and so anti-materialist, polemic, only further suggests the materialist interest in rejecting this sort of identitarian philosopheme.

31. Kierkegaard extends the critique to the entire relationship, or nonrelationship, of philosophy and existence: "Even if a man his whole life through occupies himself exclusively with logic, he still does not become logic" (*CUP,* 93).

32. Karl Marx, Letter to Pavel Vasilyevich Annenkov, December 28, 1846, retrieved: http://hiaw.org/defcon6/works/1846/letters/46_12_28.html. The content of this letter was later incorporated in Marx's 1847 text, originally written in French, *Misère de la philosophie*. As will become clear in this text's conclusion, the relationship between "theory" and "praxis" is not as straightforward in Marx as this passage might imply: Marx's point here is to critique the trans-historicism and Platonism of Proudhon's political economy; it would be a mistake to general from this an argument that concepts do not do material work as such. At the least, a Marxist reading of ideology would be impossible without the recognition that concepts and theories can and do have material force.

33. Karl Marx, *The German Ideology Part 1: Feuerbach, Opposition of the Materialist and the Idealist Outlook*, retrieved: https://www.marxists.org/archive/marx/works/1845/german-ideology/ch01b.htm.

34. The relationship between Kierkegaard and Marx receives a treatment that is more subtle than those cited above in Sylviane Agacinski's *Aparté: Conceptions and Deaths of Søren Kierkegaard*, trans. Kevin Newmark (Gainesville, FL: University of Florida Press, 1988), especially pages 207–15. However, Agacinski's reading does cosign the prevailing view that, on the one hand, Kierkegaard and Marx are in agreement in that there is an "adversarial relation" between "the religious and the political orders," but that, on the other, the difference between Marx and Kierkegaard is that Marx identifies with and privileges the political, and Kierkegaard the religious. However, Agacinski does complicate this association of Kierkegaard with religion over and against politics. She does this by recognizing that both Marx and Kierkegaard can be in agreed critique of bourgeois Christianity: "The destruction of Christianity by a politicized Church or by a so-called religious State is therefore just as easily denounced from Kierkegaard's point of view as from Marx's" (212). But even here, two things should be noted: First, as will become clear in the chapter's next section, Kierkegaard does not reject a politicized church. Indeed, he wants one. What he rejects is a reactionary and capitalist church. Second, and related, such a framing of Marx as resistant to a "religious state" too quickly accepts a modern, metaphysical, and orthodoxical understanding of "religion." It is that modern religion, and not the religion of Thomas Müntzer, for example, whom Marx admiringly cites in *On the Jewish Question*, that is opposed to a left political project.

35. Jean-Paul Sartre, *Existentialism Is a Humanism*, trans. Carol Macomber (New Haven, CT: Yale University Press, 2007): "Man first exists: he materializes in the world, encounters himself, and only afterward defines himself. If man as existentialists conceive of him cannot be defined, it is because to begin with he is nothing. He will not be anything until later, and then he will be what he makes of himself. Thus, *there is no human nature since there is no God to conceive it*" (22, emphasis mine).

36. For Camus, Kierkegaard is ultimately unable to live with absurdity; he "wants to be cured." The turn to religion is this attempt at a cure. See Albert

Camus, *The Myth of Sisyphus,* trans. Justin O'Brien (New York, NY: Alfred A. Knopf, 1955), esp. p13.

37. John Caputo, *How to Read Kierkegaard* (New York, NY: W. W. Norton & Company, 2008).

38. Martin Hägglund, *This Life: Secular Life and Spiritual Freedom* (New York, NY: Random House, 2019).

39. In his *The Philosophy of Kierkegaard*: "we will be chary of simply identifying Johannes de Silentio's praise of Abraham with Kierkegaard's having taught that Abraham was right to do what he did. Rather, Kierkegaard might be read as asking us simply to consider how, if we once concede that situations analogous to this do arise in the lives of individuals seeking to live the moral life, we ourselves might act in such a pass" (132).

40. Søren Kierkegaard, *The Moment and Late Writings,* eds. Edna Hong and Howard Hong, trans. Edna Hong and Howard Hong (Princeton, NJ: Princeton University Press, 1998).

41. Søren Kierkegaard, *Spiritual Writings,* ed. George Pattison (New York, NY: Harper Collins, 2010).

42. Søren Kierkegaard, *Journals and Papers, Volume 3,* eds. Edna Hong and Howard Hong; trans. Hong & Hong (Bloomington, IN: Indiana University Press, 1999).

43. Boris Groys, *Introduction to Antiphilosophy* (New York, NY: Verso Books, 2012).

44. Søren Kierkegaard, *Practice in Christianity,* trans. Edna Hong and Howard Hong (Princeton, NJ: Princeton University Press, 1991), 205.

45. This happens in actuality—all the time. For example, Hillary Clinton, in 2014, writing of her vote in favor of the war in Iraq: "I thought I had acted in good faith and made the best decision I could with the information I had" (*Hard Choices*, 127). The description of faith and decision as determined by information is as un-Kierkegaardian as possible.

46. Carl Schmitt, *Concept of the Political,* trans. George Schwab (Chicago, IL: University of Chicago Press, 2007).

47. Søren Kierkegaard, *Journals and Notebooks, Volume 7,* eds. Alastair Hannay et al. (Princeton, NJ: Princeton University Press, 2014). The role of "ethics" in Kierkegaard is ambivalent and sometimes inconsistent. Some works, such as the second volume of *Either/Or* valorize ethics over and against aesthetics: without ethical guidance, aesthetic passion is fleeting, and so the aesthetic stage of life gives rise to the superior ethical. Other texts, such as *Fear and Trembling,* seem to critique ethics and impose the same sort of teleological critique (the advancement of one stage to the other) to the ethical stage as *Either/Or* imposed on the aesthetic stage. Yet other texts, notably *The Concept of Anxiety,* distinguish between Christian ethics ("second ethics") and non-Christian ethics ("first ethics"). While a "Christian ethics" seems impossible given the arguments of *Fear and Trembling,*

Kierkegaard's notebooks do suggest that, ultimately, this dual-ethics program is the one he actually held. For a helpful guide to some of these different uses of ethics, see Roe Fremstedal, "Kierkegaard's View on Normative Ethics, Moral Agency, and Metaethics," in *Blackwell Companion to Kierkegaard*, ed. Jon Stewart (Hoboken, NJ: Wiley Blackwell, 2015), 113–25.

48. See especially "Signature Event Context," from *Margins of Philosophy*, trans. Alan Bass (Chicago, IL: University of Chicago Press, 1982).

49. In words familiar to this argument, Kierkegaardian "truth" accepts that the "truths" of metaphysics have, in actuality, always been the truths of material existence. In other words, these truths cannot be secured or discovered through the ideal mandates of thought; the actuality of being cannot be deduced conceptually. On this front, Kierkegaard is totally in agreement with the Derridean notion that faith—we could say, faith that is truly faith—is only possible outside of metaphysical knowledge (because metaphysical knowledge itself is impossible).

50. This resistance to dialoguing with Jesus stands in sharp contrast to late twentieth century currents in especially Catholic hermeneutic theology that spoke of religion as a sort of "conversation." Such a conversational approach would entirely obfuscate the need for decision via its perpetual deferral—by definition, conversations are interminable. For an example of this hermeneutering of theology, see Frederick Lawrence, "Grace and Friendship: Postmodern Political Theology and God as Conversational," in *The Fragility of Consciousness: Faith, Reason, and the Human Good* (Toronto, ON: University of Toronto Press, 2017).

51. For Kierkegaard, ontology and existentialism only cohere—which is another way of saying actuality and thinking only identify—only in the person of God: "Existence itself is a system—for God, but it cannot be a system for any existing spirit" (*CUP*, 118).

52. For an overview of Kierkegaard's use of and deep appreciation for James, see Richard Bauckham, "James in Modern and Contemporary Contexts," in *James: Wisdom of James, Disciple of Jesus the Sage* (New York, NY: Routledge, 1999), 158–208. And also Kyle Roberts, "James: Putting Faith to Action," in *Kierkegaard and the Bible: Tome II: The New Testament*, ed. Jon Stewart (Farnham, UK: Ashgate, 2010).

53. Kierkegaard is aware that his reinscription of orthodoxy as a demand for orthopraxy, and the alignment with the epistle of James that this reinscription effects, places him in a minority position within his Lutheran tradition. Or, given Luther's known animus toward the epistle, places Kierkegaard in a place of confrontation with Luther. Kierkegaard, in an unusually diplomatic moment, decides against arguing with Luther directly, and instead addresses the issue indirectly. According to Kierkegaard, Luther decided that "in order to set things straight, James must be shoved aside." But, Kierkegaard says, if Luther was "in our own generation" he would surely say that "James must be drawn forward a little." Kierkegaard goes on to praise "Lutheran doctrine," which "is excellent, is the truth." However, despite this excellency, Kierkegaard wonders if "Luther—this man of God, this honest soul!—

overlooked or perhaps really forgot a certain something that a later age, especially ours, may perhaps stress only far too much." Namely, "that I am not an honest soul but a cunning fellow." That is, according to Kierkegaard, the doctrine does not address the needs and existential actuality of real individuals. Taken together—the claim that Luther was not of his generation, while elsewhere Kierkegaard writes that "you do not have the right to appropriate one word of Christ's, not one single word, you have not the slightest to do with him, you do not have the remotest fellowship with him if you have not become so contemporary with him in his basement that you, just like his contemporaries, have had to become aware of his admonition: Blessed is he who is not offended at me!" (*Practice in Christianity,* 37); the praise of doctrine, while the privileging of doctrine is ruthlessly attacked throughout Kierkegaard; and the suggestion that Luther does not address actual existences, while these are the only things Kierkegaard wants to address—all of this more than suggests that Kierkegaard's apparent devotion to Luther and protestantism masked a deep and serious critique of what he saw as some fundamental Lutheran positions. This possible antipathy toward Luther might also be evidenced by Kierkegaard's affinity with Marx, who above was seen to praise Luther's rival Thomas Müntzer. All quotations are from Søren Kierkegaard, *For Self-Examination,* trans. Edna Hong and Howard Hong (Princeton, NJ: Princeton University Press, 1990), 24–26. A similar critique of the excellency of doctrine not translating into existential praxis is given in Kierkegaard's journals: "The doctrine in the established Church and its organization are very good. But the lives, our lives—believe me, they are mediocre" (*Journals and Papers,* 6727).

54. On reading James as a description of "the actions or *praxis* that constitutes the faithful way of life," see Warren Carter & Amy-Jill Levine, "James," in *The New Testaments: Meanings and Methods* (Nashville, TN: Abingdon Press, 2013), 283–97.

55. On Kierkegaard's resistance to biblical scholarship, which he holds as unpassionate and so irrelevant to actual religious decision, see Lee Barrett, "Kierkegaard and Biblical Studies: A Critical Response to Nineteenth-Century Hermeneutics," in *Blackwell Companion to Kierkegaard,* ed. Jon Stewart (Hoboken, NJ: Wiley Blackwell, 2015), 143–54.

56. See Stephen Best and Sharon Marcus, "Surface Reading: An Introduction," *Representations* 108.1 (2009): 1–21. For a Marxist response to surface reading, see Russell Sbriglia, "The Symptoms of Ideology Critique; or, How We Learned to Enjoy the Symptom and Ignore the Fetish," in *Everything You Always Wanted to Know About Literature but Were Afraid to Ask Žižek* (Durham, NC: Duke University Press, 2017), 107–36.

57. Søren Kierkegaard, *Christian Discourses: The Crisis and the Crisis in the Life of an Actress,* trans. Edna Hong and Howard Hong (Princeton, NJ: Princeton University Press, 2009).

58. Søren Kierkegaard, *Armed Neutrality, and an Open Letter,* trans. Edna Hong and Howard Hong (New York, NY: Simon & Schuster, 1969).

Chapter Five

1. See Jacques Derrida, "Racism's Last Word," *Critical Inquiry* 12.1 (1985) and Derrida's rather biting reply to Anne McClintock and Rob Nixon's response to "Racism's Last Word": "But, beyond . . . (open letter to Anne McClintock and Rob Nixon)," *Critical Inquiry* 13.1 (1986). See also Derrida's 2003 keynote address at the University of California Humanities Research Institute's conference titled "tRaces: Race, Deconstruction, and Critical Theory," accessible at: https://www.youtube.com/watch?v=LfXdYefgKjw.

2. Possible alternative understandings of ontologized blackness will be treated shortly.

3. James Cone, *Black Theology and Black Power* (Ossington, NY: Orbis Press, 1997), 151.

4. This is essentially the Saudi Arabian model, as Saudi citizens benefit from a largely socialized welfare state wherein wealth is produced almost entirely by imported migrant workers.

5. Promoted as an anti-racist praxis by sociologist Rashawn Ray. See Ray's social media activism regarding the "American Strong Challenge."

6. The standard "anti-racist" reading list contains texts that emphasize this conversational nature of an allegedly anti-racist praxis: Carol Anderson, *White Rage: The Unspoken Truth of Our Racial Divide* (London, UK: Bloomsbury, 2017); Robin DiAngelo, *White Fragility: Why It's So Hard for White People to Talk about Racism* (Boston, MA: Beacon Press, 2018); Ijeoma Oluo, *So You Want to Talk about Race* (New York: Seal Press, 2019); Derald Wing Sue, *Race Talk and the Conspiracy of Silence: Understanding and Facilitating Difficult Dialogues on Race* (Hoboken, NJ: Wiley, 2016).

7. Stephen Steinberg, *Race Relations: A Critique* (Stanford, CA: Stanford University Press, 2007).

8. Accessible at: https://www.blackpast.org/african-american-history/moynihan-report-1965/. For a critique of Moynihan's reliance on the race-relations framework, see pp. 77–100.

9. Accessible at: https://clintonwhitehouse2.archives.gov/Initiatives/OneAmerica/PIR.pdf.

10. Sara Ahmed, *On Being Included: Racism and Diversity in Institutional Life* (Durham, NC: Duke University Press, 2012).

11. James Thomas, *Diversity Regimes: Why Talk is Not Enough to Fix Racial Inequality at Universities* (Lewisburg, PA: Bucknell University Press, 2020).

12. Cedrick Michael-Simmons, "I'm Black and Afraid of 'White Fragility,'" *The Bellows* June 2020, accessible at: https://www.thebellows.org/im-black-and-afraid-of-white-fragility/.

13. *Can "White" People Be Saved? Triangulating Race, Theology, and Mission*, eds. Love Sechrest, Johnny Ramirez-Johnson, and Amos Yong (Westmont, IL: IVP Academic, 2018).

14. David Swanson, *Redisciplining the White Church: From Cheap Diversity to True Solidarity* (Westmont, IL: IVP Academic, 2020).

15. Walter Benn Michaels, *The Trouble with Diversity: How We Learned to Love Identity and Ignore Inequality* (New York: Holt, 2007).

16. "The Bellows Conversation with Adolph Reed and Walter Benn Michaels," accessible at: https://www.youtube.com/watch?v=6SRSmufe-I4.

17. Charlene Sinclair, "Toward a Twenty-First Century Black Liberation Ethic: A Marxist Reclamation of Ontological Blackness" from *The Reemergence of Liberation Theologies: Models for the Twenty-First Century*, ed. Thia Cooper (London, UK: Palgrave Macmillan, 2013).

18. All statistics are from the US Census Bureau: https://www.census.gov/quickfacts/fact/table/US/PST045219.

19. Eduardo Bonilla-Silva, *Racism Without Racists: Color-Blind Racism and the Persistence of Racial Inequality in America* (Lanham, MD: Rowman & Littlefield, 2009). See also Bonilla-Silva's influential "Rethinking Racism: Toward a Structural Interpretation," *American Sociological Review* 62.3 (1997): 465–80. Bonilla-Silva represents a sort of middle position between the overt race-relations views I am critiquing here and my own more Marxist and deconstructivist position. On the one hand, Bonilla-Silva's structuralism aims to explain racism without necessary reference to "a long-distant past," and so avoids the problems of historical continuity/ahistorical essentialism discussed in this project's interlude. Likewise, Bonilla-Silva is intentionally more attuned to the material causes and effects of racism, and so styles himself, in a welcomed way, as a sort of Marxist response to the primarily discursive "racial formation" theory of Michael Omi and Howard Winant. On the other hand, though, and as Moon-Kie Jung notes, Bonilla-Silva ultimately considers the "racial structure" to be phenomenologically basic and so must "posit the ideological level as constitutive of, rather than external to, the racial structure" (Moon-Kie, 25). That is, Bonilla-Silva's program relies on a curious conception of an originary ideology—ideology is more typically thought of as derivative of an actual infrastructural reality. This reliance on an idiomatic understanding of ideology as basic to the social, and so as race as fundamental and non-derived, ultimately places Bonilla-Silva squarely in the tradition of race relations, albeit in a more sophisticated mode. As Moon-Kie again notes, Bonilla-Silva's reliance on the race-relations framework prevents him from taking a more global or world-systems perspective that would be more at home in a Marxist program. According to Moon-Kie, for Bonilla-Silva, the racial structure is "limited by the nation state" (Moon-Kie, 35). Consider American slavery, for example: Bonilla-Silva's structural approach reads American slavery through the lens of a racial struggle between whites and blacks. Such a reading is only possible given the total bracketing of the rest of the productive process: the cotton picked by black labor in the American south was manufactured by white labor in England. Without the wage labor of factories in England, American slavery—which used racism to cheaply produce cotton and did not use cotton to cheaply produce racism—would not have had any profitable value to plantation owners. This careful delineation of

the parameters of the racial structure—white/black, "social," statist—not only places Bonilla-Silva within the race-relations framework, but also introduces all of the associated problems with structuralism—arbitrary delineation, ahistoricism—made clear by mainly French poststructuralists like Derrida. Indeed, in Derrida's language, we could simply say that Bonilla-Silva's structural racism framework relies on the transcendental signified—impossible—of "racism." See: Moon-Kie Jung, *Beneath the Surface of White Supremacy: Denaturalizing US Racisms Past and Present* (Stanford, CA: Stanford University Press, 2015).

20. J. Kameron Carter, *Race: A Theological Account* (Oxford, UK: Oxford University Press, 2008), 189.

21. James Cone, *A Black Theology of Liberation* (Maryknoll, NY: Orbis Books, 2010).

22. James Cone, *God of the Oppressed* (Maryknoll, NY: Orbis Books, 2017).

23. See: Cedric Johnson, *Revolutionaries to Race Leaders: Black Power and the Making of African American Politics* (Minneapolis, MN: Minnesota University Press, 2007).

24. Frank Wilderson, *Red, White and Black: Cinema and the Structure of US Antagonisms* (Duke University Press, 2010).

25. Frank Wilderson, "Afropessimism and the Ruse of Analogy: Violence, Freedom Struggles, and the Death of Black Desire," from *Antiblackness*, eds. Moon-Kie Jung and Joao Vargas (Durham, NC: Duke University Press, 2021).

26. Frank Wilderson, *The Black Liberation Army & The Paradox of Political Engagement*, accessible at: https://illwilleditions.noblogs.org/files/2015/09/Wilderson-Black-Liberation-Army-the-Paradox-of-Political-Engagement-2013-READ-.pdf.

27. For more on this, see David Leopold's "Marx, Engels, and Other Socialisms," in *Cambridge Companion to the Communist Manifesto* (Cambridge, UK: Cambridge University Press, 2015), 32–49.

28. Lewis Gordon, "Thoughts on Two Recent Decades of Studying Race and Racism," *Journal for the Study of Race, Nation, and Culture* 24.1 (2018): 29–38.

29. This is the view articulated by Calvin Warren in his *Ontological Terror: Blackness, Nihilism, and Emancipation* (Durham, NC: Duke University Press, 2018).

30. Frank Wilderson, "We're Trying to Destroy the World," *Black Ink* (2018), accessible at: https://black-ink.info/2018/02/10/were-trying-to-destroy-the-world/.

31. In doing so, Cone relies on a recursive, even sometimes aphoristic, style. I am suggesting here that the axiom of self-determination is one of the central motifs by which Cone interprets his theological tradition. Other motifs, all related, would include Christ as liberator, the blackness of God, the unknowability of God, and the demand of freedom. Cone likely adopted elements of this style—wherein central motifs are recurrently used to interpret various data—from his deep reading of Barth, who used a similar style. See George Hunsinger, *How to Read Karl Barth: The Shape of His Theology* (Oxford, England: Oxford University Press, 1993).

32. And also would include libertarian political theorists who appeal to the so-called "non-aggression principle." The problem here would not only be that be

that the non-aggression principle actually functions to "aggressively" defend property rights (see Matt Zwolinski, "The Libertarian Nonaggression Principle," *Social Philosophy and Policy* 32.3 [2016]: 62–90), but also more simply that libertarians begin with something other than an undying commitment to self-determination. In short, Cone relativizes a position on "aggression" for the sake of defending self-determination, while libertarians relativize self-determination for the sake of resisting so-called aggression.

33. Friedrich Nietzsche, *The Genealogy of Morals and Ecce Homo,* trans. and ed. Walter Kaufmann (New York: Vintage, 1989).

34. James Cone, *The Spirituals and the Blues: An Interpretation* (Maryknoll, NY: Orbis Books, 1992).

35. Fidel Castro, *The Declarations of Havana* (New York: Verso Books, 2018).

36. A study of the relationship between Cuba and the Black Panthers, and so by extension Cone, is just outside the scope of this project. However, it should at least be noted that the Panthers' emphasis on self-determination was one shared by the Cuban revolutionaries. This association suggests the possibility of a more originally internationalist perspective to Cone's thought than is typically admitted, even by Cone himself. See Ruth Reitan, "Cuba, the Black Panther Party, and the US Black Movement in the 1960s: Issues of Security," *New Political Science* 21.1 (1999): 217–30. For the Cuban emphasis on self-determination, see Ernesto Guevara, "At the United Nations," in *Che Guevara Reader: Writings on Politics and Revolution* (Havana, Cuba: Ocean Press, 2003), 325–39, wherein Guevara argues that colonialism is a process of suppressing self-determination.

37. D. Stephen Long, *Divine Economy: Theology and the Market* (Abington, UK: Routledge, 2000).

38. "The problem of identifying Christian ethics with the status quo is also found in Augustine and Thomas Aquinas. While they differed regarding the role of faith and reason and theological discourse, they agreed that the slave should not seek to change his civil status through political struggle . . . For Thomas, slavery was a part of the natural order of creation. Thus 'the slave, in regard to his master, is an instrument . . . Between a master and his slave there is a special right of domination'" (*GO*, 182).

39. Cone's universalist understanding of emancipation fits well with Ivan Petrella's suggestion of "undercover" liberation theology. Petrella argues that theologians interested in liberation, precisely as interested in liberation, should look to imbue influence in secular spheres of knowledge and power. Liberation theology has been limited, Petrella argues, by its myopic attention to ecclesial and ministerial matters. This chapter's next section will move Cone's argument in this "undercover" direction. See Ivan Petrella, "Liberation Theology Undercover," *Political Theology* 18.4 (2017): 325–39.

40. Che Guevara, *Guerilla Warfare,* eds. Brian Loveman and Thomas Davies (Lincoln, NB: University of Nebraska Press, 2001), 174.

41. See not only the aforecited texts by Carter, Prevot, and Sinclair, but also Trevor Eppeheimer's "Victor Anderson's *Beyond Ontological Blackness* and James

Cone's Black Theology: A Discussion," *Black Theology* 4.1 (2006): 87–106; Timothy McGee's "Against (white) Redemption: James Cone and the Christological Disruption of Racial Discourse and White Solidarity" *Political Theology* 18.7 (2017): 542–59; and my "Black Hollyhock: Postmodernity in the Text of Black Theology," *Black Theology* 18.1 (2020), 75–94, some of which I draw on in what follows. For Anderson's critique, see not only his *Beyond Ontological Blackness: An Essay on African American Religious and Cultural Criticism* (New York: Bloomsbury Academic, 2016) but also his "Black Ontology and Theology," in *The Oxford Handbook of African American Theology*, eds. Anthony Pinn and Katie Cannon (Oxford, England: Oxford University Press, 2014).

42. Ivan Petrella, *Beyond Liberation Theology: A Polemic* (London UK: SCM Press, 2013), 84–100.

43. This is the challenge faced by Bonilla-Silva. Remember that for Bonilla-Silva, the "structural formation" of race means that every synchronic "society," and by "society" Bonilla-Silva intends primarily "state," is marked by an independent racial structure. While this racial structure is informed by and informs other social structures, Bonilla-Silva argues that racism maintains a structural autonomy and employs its own categories and contents. In this framework, racism, as has become somewhat of a trope, "has a life of its own." While this structural view has the advantage of not needing to rely on a transhistorical and essentialist understanding of any particular race—to be black or white in 2020 is not to be the same thing as to be black or white in 1820, never mind 220—it achieves this avoidance of one essentialism by recourse to another, namely, the essential continuity of "race" and "racism" as transhistorical structural realities. "Racism," then, is meant as a transhistorical signified: all racialized societies have some racial structure which receives its racial content through reference to the transhistorical reality of racism. If racism remains this self-referential and reductive, it cannot but be an empty universal category. If it has particular content, it must make reference to some other "structure," and so "racism" loses its status as transcendental signified. Again, this is simply the problem with any structuralism that does not account for the post-structural critique.

44. As has become well known in whiteness studies, the particular ethnic identifications that constitute "whiteness" have changed over time and continue to do so. I do not know if Cone was aware of this or not, but the point is besides the argument: Cone structurally identified whiteness as occupying an (and sometimes *the*) antagonistic point of his politically theology. As he says, God has been yellow, black, and red, but never white, because whiteness *as such*, and so regardless of its actual constitution, is opposed to liberation. The introduction of the as such is what marks his understanding of whiteness as transhistorical.

45. See also "White Christians see little contradiction between wealth and the Christian gospel" (*BTL*, 123) and "White western Christianity with its emphasis on individualism and capitalism as expressed in American Protestantism is unreal for blacks" (*BTBP*, 33).

46. "Demographic trends and economic well-being," *Pew Research Center*: https://www.pewsocialtrends.org/2016/06/27/1-demographic-trends-and-economic-well-being/st_2016-06-27_race-inequality-ch1-02/.

47. "Fifty Years after the Kerner Commission," *Economic Policy Institute*, accessible at: https://www.epi.org/publication/50-years-after-the-kerner-commission/.

48. "African American Earnings: 1967–2016," *Black Demographics*, accessible at: https://blackdemographics.com/households/african-american-income/.

49. "Income and Poverty in the United States," *US Census Bureau*, accessible at: https://www.census.gov/content/dam/Census/library/publications/2019/demo/p60-266.pdf.

50. "How Rising US Income Inequality Exacerbates Racial Economic Disparities," *Washington Center for Equitable Growth*, accessible at: https://equitablegrowth.org/how-rising-u-s-income-inequality-exacerbates-racial-economic-disparities/.

51. James Cone, "The Black Church and Marxism: What Do They Have to Say to Each Other?" *Institute for Democratic Socialism* (1980).

52. "And as long as black labor was needed, slavery was regarded as the only appropriate 'solution' to the 'black problem.' But when black labor was no longer needed, blacks were issued their 'freedom,' the freedom to live in a society which attempted to destroy them physically and spiritually" (*BTL*, 14).

53. For such histories, see the aforementioned *Racecraft* and Ellen Meiksins Wood's *Peasant-Citizen and Slave* (New York: Verso Books, 1989).

54. Cone is not arguing that the elimination of capitalism would bring about the elimination of racism, but that the elimination of racism would require the elimination of capitalism. For Cone, anti-capitalism is a necessary but insufficient condition for the promotion of anti-racism. This distinction is important because it allows Cone to avoid either race or class reductionism: He is not arguing that socialism would bring about a post-racial world. Nor is he arguing that anti-racism requires anti-capitalism. This latter point is the one made by Reed and Benn Michaels above: capitalism is flexible enough to incorporate anti-racism within itself.

55. Of course, Cone writes of an "alternative vision of social existence" and not more directly of an alternative social existence. This retreat from axiomatic commitments to a plea for imagination, so common in Cone's idealist reception but typically uncommon in Cone's texts, indicates that Cone himself, despite intellectually acknowledging that anti-racism is ultimately impossible without anti-capitalism, is perhaps one of the "black churchpeople" whose understandable preoccupation with "the most pressing contradiction" in their existence has prevented a complete acceptance of the necessity of socialism. That is, Cone never speaks of the need for a vision of black humanity. He accepts and forcefully declares black humanity, and the rest follows suit. Here, though, Cone shows a slight hesitation, introduces the trope of vision, and so does not quite make socialism an axiomatic commitment on the level of anti-racism.

56. The Hampton passage echoed by Cone: "We don't think you fight fire with fire best; we think you fight fire with water best. We're going to fight racism not

with racism, but we're going to fight with solidarity. We say we're not going to fight capitalism with black capitalism, but we're going to fight it with socialism." "Power Anywhere Where There's People," speech delivered at Olivet Church, 1969. Transcript accessible at: https://www.historyisaweapon.com/defcon1/fhamptonspeech.html.

57. While Cone references "liberal white-led groups," the context in which he does so—a critique of class-solidarity politics that preserve racial solidarity—demonstrates that he is in fact speaking of socialists, not liberals. This slippage only reflects Cone's adoption of the popular American vernacular according to which "liberal" means "leftist."

58. Eugene Genovese, *In Red and Black: Marxian Explorations in Southern and Afro-American History* (New York: Pantheon, 1971), 321. Genovese's apparently critical association of liberalism with abolitionism is just another example of the incredible semantic breadth the signifier "liberal" has acquired. Such a breadth is what allowed Schmitt to depict the Bolsheviks as liberals.

59. In this instance, it strikes me as important to separate Marx—who famously claimed that he, whatever he was, was not a Marxist—from the Marxist or, worse, socialist traditions. These groupings are too overbroad, both historically and theoretically, to carry much argumentative worth. One will always be able to find a racist socialist. This does not mean—this does not at all mean—that following a Marxist critique of capital is not the most effective way forward in promoting the emancipation and liberation of economically exploited workers in general and racially oppressed workers in particular. If Mouffe was correct that something in Marx was fundamentally incapable of addressing extra-economic oppression, then perhaps Marx would be a foe to anti-racist work. But as I tried to show in chapter one, and as I have argued here, the answer to the question of whether Marx is antithetical to anti-racism is unequivocally "no."

60. Karl Marx, "The Civil War in the United States," from *Marx and Engels Collected Works, volume 19* (Moscow, Russia: Progress Publishers, 1964), 51.

61. Karl Marx, "Letter to Pavel Vasilyevich Annenkov," from *Marx and Engels Collected Works, volume 38* (New York: International Publishers, 1975), 101–102.

62. Karl Marx, "Address of the International Working Men's Association to Abraham Lincoln, President of the United States of America," *The Bee-Hive Newspaper*, November 7, 1865, accessible at: https://www.marxists.org/archive/marx/iwma/documents/1864/lincoln-letter.htm.

63. And so again the friend-enemy distinction is read in ideological terms. In this sense, Schmitt's program was less a novel defense of Nazism as it was a participation in a long line of racist ideologies.

64. Karl Marx, "To the People of the United States of America," *Workman's Advocate*, October 14, 1865, accessible at: https://www.marxists.org/history/international/iwma/documents/1865/to-americans.htm.

65. "I'm a prophetic thinker without a thick metaphysics . . . I have a very strong antimetaphysical bent." From Cornel West, *The Cornel West Reader* (New York City: Civitas Books, 2000), 216.

66. Cornel West, *Prophesy Deliverance! An Afro-American Revolutionary Christianity* (Louisville, KY: Westminster John Knox Press, 2002).

67. George Mosse, *Toward the Final Solution: A History of European Racism* (New York: Howard Fertig, 1978).

68. Cornel West, *The American Evasion of Philosophy: A Genealogy of Pragmatism* (Madison, WI: University of Wisconsin Press, 1989).

69. "The paradox of the Christian tradition is that it precludes its own descriptions from grasping the truth; that is, the Christian notion of the fallenness of human creatures does not permit even Christian descriptions to be true. This is so, because, for Christians, Jesus Christ is the Truth and the reality of Jesus Christ always already rests outside any particular Christian description . . . Jesus Christ is literally the Truth, the Truth which cannot be intellectually reified but rather existentially appropriated by finite human beings with urgent needs and pressing problems" *(PD*, 98).

70. Cornel West, *Keeping Faith: Philosophy and Race in America* (Abington, UK: Routledge, 2012), 116.

Conclusion

1. Karl Marx, "The Introduction to Contribution to the Critique of Hegel's Philosophy of Right," accessible: https://www.marxists.org/archive/marx/works/1844/df-jahrbucher/law-abs.htm.

2. Several Brown biographies demonstrate this lifetime of commitment quite well. Among those, W. E. B. DuBois's *John Brown* remains especially important. Louis Decaro's *Fire from the Midst of You: A Religious Life of John Brown* (New York, NY: New York University Press, 2002) and David Reynolds's *John Brown, Abolitionist: The Man Who Killed Slavery, Sparked the Civil War, and Seeded Civil Rights* (New York, NY: Vintage, 2006) are also noteworthy in this regard.

3. Ted Smith, *Weird John Brown: Divine Violence and the Limits of Ethics* (Stanford, CA: Stanford University Press, 2015), 24–30.

4. Louis DeCaro, *John Brown Speaks* (Lanham, MD: Rowman & Littlefield, 2015).

5. It seems to me that Brown's commentary on so-called sanity could be relevant for debates in contemporary theory concerning mental health and illness, the psychiatrization of political marginality, the social construction of madness (Foucault), the inescapability of madness (Derrida), and so on. While interesting and potentially important, Brown's possible contribution to this subject can only be provisionally flagged here.

6. John Brown, *Speech to the Court,* November 2, 1859, accessible: https://nationalcenter.org/JohnBrown'sSpeech.html.

Bibliography

Adorno, Theodor. *Kierkegaard: Construction of the Aesthetic*. Translated by Robert Hullot-Kentor. Minneapolis, MN: University of Minnesota Press, 1989.
Agacinski, Sylviane. *Aparté: Conceptions and Deaths of Søren Kierkegaard*. Translated by Kevin Newmark. Gainesville, FL: University of Florida Press, 1988.
Ahmed, Sara. *On Being Included: Racism and Diversity in Institutional Life*. Durham, NC: Duke University Press, 2012.
Almond, Ian. "Derrida and the Secret of the Non-Secret: On Respiritualizing the Profane." *Literature and Theology* 17.4 (2003): 457–71.
Alvis, Jason. *The Inconspicuous God: Heidegger, French Phenomenology, and the Theological Turn*. Bloomington, IN: Indiana University Press, 2018.
Anderson, Carol. *White Rage: The Unspoken Truth of Our Racial Divide*. London, England: Bloomsbury, 2017.
Anderson, Kevin. *Marx at the Margins: On Nationalism, Ethnicity, and Non-Western Societies*. Chicago, IL: University of Chicago Press, 2016.
Anderson, Victor. *Beyond Ontological Blackness: An Essay on African American Religious and Cultural Criticism*. London, England: Bloomsbury Academic, 2016.
Anderson, Victor. "Black Ontology and Theology." In *The Oxford Handbook of African American Theology*. Edited by Anthony Pinn and Katie Cannon. Oxford, England: Oxford University Press, 2014.
Aristotle. *Metaphysics*. Translated by Hugh Tredennick. Cambridge, MA: Harvard University Press, 1989, accessed: http://www.perseus.tufts.edu/hopper/text?doc=Perseus:abo:tlg,0086,025:4.
Aristotle. *On Interpretation*. Translated by E. M. Edghill, accessed: http://classics.mit.edu/Aristotle/interpretation.1.1.html.
Aroosi, Jamie. "The Causes of Bourgeois Culture: Kierkegaard's Relation to Marx Considered." *Philosophy and Social Criticism* 42.1 (2016): 71–92.
Aroosi, Jamie. *The Dialectical Self: Kierkegaard, Marx, and the Making of the Modern Subject*. Philadelphia, PA: University of Pennsylvania Press, 2018.
Balakrishnan, Gopal. *The Enemy: An Intellectual Portrait of Carl Schmitt*. New York, NY: Verso Books, 2002.

Bargu, Banu. "The Predicaments of Left-Schmittianism." *South Atlantic Quarterly* 113.4 (2014): 713–27.
Barrett, Lee. "Kierkegaard and Biblical Studies: A Critical Response to Nineteenth-Century Hermeneutics." in *Blackwell Companion to Kierkegaard*. Edited by Jon Stewart. New York, NY: Wiley Blackwell, 2015.
Barth, Karl. *The Epistle to the Romans*. Translated by Edwyn Hoskyns. Oxford, England: Oxford University Press, 1968.
Bauckham, Richard. "James in Modern and Contemporary Contexts." in *James: Wisdom of James, Disciple of Jesus the Sage*. Abingdon, UK: Routledge, 1999.
Behler, Ernst. "Deconstruction Versus Hermeneutics: Derrida and Gadamer on Text and Interpretation." *Southern Humanities Review* 21.3 (1987): 201–223.
Benn Michaels, Walter. *The Trouble with Diversity: How We Learned to Love Identity and Ignore Inequality*. New York, NY: Holt, 2007.
Bennington, Geoffrey. "Deconstruction and the Philosophers (The Very Idea)." *Oxford Literary Review* 10 (1988): 73–130.
Bennington, Geoffrey. "Embarrassing Ourselves." *LA Review of Books*, 2016, accessed: https://lareviewofbooks.org/article/embarrassing-ourselves/.
Bennington, Geoffrey. *Scatter 1: The Politics of Politics in Foucault, Heidegger, and Derrida*. New York, NY: Fordham University Press, 2016.
Best, Stephen, and Sharon Marcus. "Surface Reading: An Introduction." *Representations* 108.1 (2009): 1–21.
Betz, John. "After Heidegger and Marion: The Task of Christian Metaphysics Today." *Modern Theology* 34.3 (2018): 265–97.
Betz, John. "Theology without Metaphysics? A Reply to Kevin Hector." *Modern Theology* 31.3 (2013): 488–500.
Boer, Roland. "A Totality of Ruins: Adorno on Kierkegaard." *Cultural Critique* 83 (2013): 1–30.
Boersma, Hans. "Iraneaus, Derrida, and Hospitality: On the Eschatological Overcoming of Violence." *Modern Theology* 19.2 (2003): 163–80.
Bonefeld, Werner. "Authoritarian Liberalism: From Schmitt via Ordoliberalism to the Euro." *Critical Sociology* 43.5 (2016): 747–61.
Bonilla-Silva, Eduardo. *Racism Without Racists: Color-Blind Racism and the Persistence of Racial Inequality in America*. Lanham, MD: Rowman & Littlefield, 2009.
Bonilla-Silva, Eduardo. "Rethinking Racism: Toward a Structural Interpretation." *American Sociological Review* 62.3 (1997): 465–80.
Brata Das, Saitya. *The Political Theology of Kierkegaard*. Edinburgh, Scotland: Edinburgh University Press, 2020.
Brown, Derek. "Black Hollyhock: Postmodernity in the Text of Black Theology." *Black Theology* 18.1 (2020): 75–94.
Buck-Morss, Susan. "Sovereign Right and the Global Left." *Cultural Critique* 69 (2008): 145–71.
Camus, Albert. *The Myth of Sisyphus*. Translated by Justin O'Brien. New York, NY: Alfred A. Knopf, 1955.

Caputo, John. *How to Read Kierkegaard*. New York, NY: W. W. Norton & Company, 2008.
Caputo, John. "Looking the Impossible in the Eye: Kierkegaard, Derrida, and the Repetition of Religion." *Kierkegaard Studies Yearbook* (2002): 1–25.
Caputo, John. *The Prayers and Tears of Jacques Derrida: Religion without Religion*. Bloomington, IN: Indiana University Press, 1997.
Caputo, John. "The Return of Anti-Religion: From Radical Atheism to Radical Theology." *Journal for Cultural and Religious Theory* 11.2 (2011): 32–116.
Caputo, John, and Gianni Vattimo. *After the Death of God*. New York, NY: Columbia University Press, 2007.
Carter, J. Kameron. *Race: A Theological Account*. Oxford, England: Oxford University Press, 2008.
Carter, Tom. "A Closer Look at Kierkegaard." *World Socialist Web Site*, accessed: https://www.wsws.org/en/articles/2006/04/kier-a17.html.
Carter, Warren. *Matthew and the Margins*. London, England: T&T Clark, 2000.
Carter, Warren, and Amy-Jill Levine. "James," in *The New Testaments: Meanings and Methods*. Nashville, TN: Abingdon Press, 2013.
Castro, Fidel. *The Declarations of Havana*. New York, NY: Verso Books, 2018.
Climacus, John. *The Ladder of Divine Ascent*. Translated by Norman Russell. Mahwah, NJ: Paulist Press, 1982.
Clinton, Hillary. *Hard Choices*. Stoughton, MA: Simon and Schuster, 2014.
Cone, James. The Black Church and Marxism: What Do They Have to Say to Each Other?" *Institute for Democratic Socialism* (1980).
Cone, James. *Black Theology and Black Power*. Ossining, NY: Orbis Press, 1997.
Cone, James. *A Black Theology of Liberation*. Ossining, NY: Orbis Books, 2010.
Cone, James. *The Cross and the Lynching Tree*. Ossining, NY: Orbis Books, 2011.
Cone, James. *God of the Oppressed*. Ossining, NY: Orbis Books, 2017.
Cone, James. *The Spirituals and the Blues: An Interpretation*. Ossining, NY: Orbis Books, 1992.
Cristi, Renato. *Carl Schmitt Authoritarian Liberalism: Strong State, Free Economy*. Cardiff, Wales: University of Wales Press, 1998.
Cristi, Renato. "The Metaphysics of Constituent Power: Schmitt and the Genesis of Chile's 1980 Constitution." *Cardozo Law Review* 21.5 (2000): 1749–76.
Crockett, Clayton. *Derrida after the End of Writing: Political Theology and New Materialism*. New York, NY: Fordham University Press, 2017.
da Silva, Gabriel Ferreira. "Kierkegaard on the Relations between Being and Thought." *Kierkegaard Studies Yearbook* (2015): 3–20.
Dean, Jodi. *The Communist Horizon*. New York, NY: Verso Books, 2018.
Deleuze, Giles, and Felix Guattari. *Anti-Oedipus: Capitalism and Schizophrenia*. Translated by Helen Lane, Mark Seem, and Robert Hurley. London, England: Bloomsbury Academic, 2004.
Derrida, Jacques. "But, beyond . . . (open letter to Anne McClintock and Rob Nixon)." *Critical Inquiry* 13.1 (1986): 155–70.

Derrida, Jacques. "Circumfession." in *Jacques Derrida*. Translated by Geoffrey Bennington. Edited by Geofrrey Bennington. Chicago, IL: University of Chicago Press, 1993.

Derrida, Jacques. *A Derrida Reader: Between the Blinds*. Edited by Peggy Kamuf. New York, NY: Columbia University Press, 1991.

Derrida, Jacques. *Dissemination*. Translated by Barbara Johnson. Chicago, IL: University of Chicago Press, 1981.

Derrida, Jacques. *The Gift of Death & Literature in Secret*. Translated by David Wills. Chicago, IL: University of Chicago Press, 2008.

Derrida, Jacques. *Given Time: 1. Counterfeit Money*. Translated by Peggy Kamuf. Chicago, IL: University of Chicago Press, 1994.

Derrida, Jacques. "How to Avoid Speaking: Denials." Translated by Ken Freiden. From *Derrida and Negative Theology*. Edited by Harold Coward and Toby Foshay. Albany, NY: State University of New York Press, 1992.

Derrida, Jacques. *Margins of Philosophy*. Translated by Alan Bass. Chicago, IL: University of Chicago Press, 1982.

Derrida, Jacques. *Of Grammatology*. Translated by Gayatri Spivak. Baltimore, MD: Johns Hopkins University Press, 1998 / *De la Grammatologie*. Paris, France: Éditions de Minuit, 1967.

Derrida, Jacques. *On the Name*. Translated by David Wood, John Leavey, and Ian McLeod. Edited by Thomas Dutoit. Standord, CA: Stanford University Press, 1995.

Derrida, Jacques. *Politiques de l'amitié*. Paris, France: Éditions Galilée, 1994 / *The Politics of Friendship*. Translated by George Collins. New York, NY: Verso Books, 2006.

Derrida, Jacques. "Racism's Last Word." *Critical Inquiry* 12.1 (1985): 290–99.

Derrida, Jacques. "Rams: Uninterrupted Dialogue—Between Two Infinities, the Poem." Translated by Thomas Dutoit and Philippe Romanski. From *Sovereignties in Question: The Poetics of Paul Celan*. Edited by Thomas Dutoit and Outi Pasanen. New York, NY: Fordham University Press, 2005.

Derrida, Jacques. "Signature Event Context." From *Margins of Philosophy*. Translated by Alan Bass Chicago, IL: University of Chicago Press, 1982.

Derrida, Jacques. "A Silkworm of One's Own (Points of View Stitched on the Other Veil)." Translated by Geoffrey Bennington. *Oxford Literary Review* 18.12 (1996): 3–66.

Derrida, Jacques. *Specters of Marx*. Translated by Peggy Kamuf. Abingdon, UK: Routledge, 1994.

Derrida, Jacques. "Taking a Stand for Algeria." *College Literature* 30.1 (2003): 115–123.

Derrida, Jacques, and Geoffrey Bennington. *Jacques Derrida*. Translated by Geoffrey Bennington. Chicago, IL: University of Chicago Press, 1999.

Derrida, Jacques, and Giovanna Borradori. *Philosophy in a Time of Terror*. Translated by Pascale-Anne Brault and Michael Nass. Edited by Borradori. Chicago, IL: University of Chicago Press, 2004.

Derrida, Jacques and Mark Dooley. "The Becoming Possible of the Impossible: An Interview with Jacques Derrida." in *The Essential Caputo: Selected Writings*. Edited by BK Putt. Bloomington, IN: Indiana University Press, 2018.

Derrida, Jacques, and Richard Kearney. "Deconstruction and the Other," from *Debates in Continental Philosophy: Conversations with Contemporary Philosophers*. Edited by Richard Kearney. New York: NY: Fordham University Press, 2004.

Derrida, Jacques, and Richard Kearney. "On the Gift," from *God, the Gift, and Postmodernism*. Edited by John Caputo and Michael Scanlon. Bloomington, IN: Indiana University Press, 1999.

Derrida, Jacques, and Richard Kearney. "Terror, Religion, and the New Politics." *Debates in Continental Philosophy: Conversations with Contemporary Philosophers*. Edited by Richard Kearney. New York, NY: Fordham University Press, 2004.

de Wilde, Marc. "Meeting Opposites: The Political Theologies of Walter Benjamin and Carl Schmitt." *Philosophy & Rhetoric* 44.4 (2011): 363–81.

DeWitt, Larry. "The Decision to Exclude Agricultural and Domestic Workers from the 1935 Social Security Act." *Social Security Bulletin* 70.4 (2010).

DiAngelo, Robin. *White Fragility: Why It's So Hard for White People to Talk about Racism*. Boston, MA: Beacon Press, 2018.

Eppeheimer, Trevor. "Victor Anderson's *Beyond Ontological Blackness* and James Cone's Black Theology: A Discussion." *Black Theology* 4.1 (2006): 87–106.

Ferreira, M. Jamie. "Faith and the Kierkegaardian Leap." In *The Cambridge Companion to Kierkegaard*. Edited by Alastair Hannay and Gordon Marino. Cambridge, UK: Cambridge University Press, 1997.

Fields, Barbara, and Karen Fields. *Racecraft: The Soul of Inequality in American Life*. New York, NY: Verso Books, 2014.

Fisher, Mark. "What is Hauntology?" *Film Quarterly* 66.1 (2012): 16–24.

Fox-Muraton, Melissa. "Faith in the Mode of Absence: Kierkegaard's Jewish Readers in 1930s France." *Kierkegaard Studies Yearbook* (2016): 189–216.

Fremstedal, Roe. "Kierkegaard's View on Normative Ethics, Moral Agency, and Metaethics." In *Blackwell Companion to Kierkegaard*. Edited by Jon Stewart. Hoboken, NJ: Wiley Blackwell, 2015.

Fukuyama, Francis. *The End of History and the Last Man*. New York, NY: Simon and Schuster, 1992.

Gayetsky, Matthew. "Partisans in Empire, or, Carl Schmitt as Revolutionary?" *Theory and Event 18.4*.

Genovese, Eugene. *In Red and Black: Marxian Explorations in Southern and Afro-American History*. New York, NY: Pantheon, 1971.

Groys, Boris. *Introduction to Antiphilosophy*. New York, NY: Verso Books, 2012.

Guevara, Ernesto. *Che Guevara Reader: Writings on Politics and Revolution*. Havana: Ocean Press, 2003.

Hägglund, Martin. "Beauty That Must Die: A Response to Michael Clune." *The New Continental Review* 15.3 (2015): 101–108.

Hägglund, Martin. *This Life: Secular Faith and Spiritual Freedom*. New York, NY: Pantheon, 2019.
Hägglund, Martin. *This Life: Secular Life and Spiritual Freedom*. New York, NY: Random House, 2019.
Hägglund, Martin. *Radical Atheism: Derrida and the Time of Life*. Stanford, CA: Stanford University Press, 2008.
Hägglund, Martin. "The Radical Evil of Deconstruction: A Reply to John Caputo." *Journal for Cultural and Religious Theory* 11.2 (2011): 126–50.
Hampton, Fred. "Power Anywhere Where There's People." Accessible: https://www.historyisaweapon.com/defcon1/fhamptonspeech.html.
Hardt, Michael, and Antonio Negri. *Empire*. Cambridge, MA: Harvard University Press, 2001.
Hart, Kevin. *The Trespass of the Sign: Deconstruction, Theology, and Philosophy*. Cambridge, England: Cambridge University Press, 1990.
Harvey, David. *Rebel Cities: From the Right to the City to the Urban Revolution*. New York, NY: Verso Books, 2012.
Hector, Kevin. *Theology without Metaphysics: God, Language, and the Spirit of Recognition*. Cambridge, England: Cambridge University Press, 2011.
Hirst, Paul. "Carl Schmitt's Decisionism." In *The Challenge of Carl Schmitt*. Edited by Chantal Mouffe. New York, NY: Verso Books, 1999.
Holberg, Ludvig. *Seven One Act Plays*. Edited by Henry Alexander. Princeton, NJ: Princeton University Press, 1950.
Holtz, Geoffrey. "Social Security Discrimination against African Americans: An Equal Protection Argument." *Hastings Law Journal* 48.1 (1996): 105–127.
Horner, Robyn. "Theology after Derrida." *Modern Theology* 29.3 (2013): 230–47.
Hunsinger, George. *How to Read Karl Barth: The Shape of His Theology*. Oxford, England: Oxford University Press, 1993.
Johnson, Cedric. *Revolutionaries to Race Leaders: Black Power and the Making of African American Politics*. Minneapolis, MN: Minnesota University Press, 2007.
Jones, Claudia. "An End to the Neglect of the Problems of the Negro Woman!" accessible at: https://www.newframe.com/from-the-archive-an-end-to-the-neglect-of-the-problems-of-the-negro-woman/.
Jones, William. *Is God a White Racist? A Preamble to Black Theology*. Boston, MA: Beacon Press, 1997.
Jung, Moon-Kie. *Beneath the Surface of White Supremacy: Denaturalizing US Racisms Past and Present*. Stanford, CA: Stanford University Press, 2015.
Kearney, Richard. "The Kingdom: Possible and Impossible." From *Cross and Khora: Deconstruction and Christianity in the Work of John D. Caputo*. Edited by Marko Zlomislic and Neal DeRoo. Eugene, OR: Wipf and Stock, 2010.
Kearney, Richard. *Strangers, Gods, and Monsters: Interpreting Otherness*. Abingdon, UK: Routledge, 2002.
Kierkegaard, Søren. *Armed Neutrality, and an Open Letter*. Translated by Edna Hong and Howard Hong. New York, NY: Simon & Schuster, 1969.

Kierkegaard, Søren. *Christian Discourses: The Crisis and the Crisis in the Life of an Actress*. Translated by Edna Hong and Howard Hong. Princeton, NJ: Princeton University Press, 2009.

Kierkegaard, Søren. *The Concept of Anxiety: A Simple Psychologically Orienting Deliberation on the Dogmatic Issue of Hereditary Sin*. Translated by Edna Hong and Howard Hong. Princeton, NJ: Princeton University Press, 1981.

Kierkegaard, Søren. *Concluding Unscientific Postscript to Philosophical Fragments*. Translated by Edna Hong and Howard Hong. Princeton, NJ: Princeton University Press, 1992.

Kierkegaard, Søren. *Either/Or, Part II*. Translated by Edna Hong and Howard Hong. Princeton, NJ: Princeton University Press, 1987.

Kierkegaard, Søren. *Fear and Trembling and Repetition*. Translated by Edna Hong and Howard Hong. Princeton, NJ: Princeton University Press, 1983.

Kierkegaard, Søren. *For Self-Examination*. Translated by Edna Hong and Howard Hong. Princeton, NJ: Princeton University Press, 1990.

Kierkegaard, Søren. *Journals and Notebooks, Volume 7*. Edited by Hannay et al. Princeton, NJ: Princeton University Press, 2014.

Kierkegaard, Søren. *Journals and Papers, Volume 3*. Edited by Edna Hong and Howard Hong. Translated by Edna Hong and Howard Hong. Bloomington, IN: Indiana University Press, 1999.

Kierkegaard, Søren. *The Moment and Late Writings*. Edited by Edna Hong and Howard Hong. Translated by Edna Hong and Howard Hong. Princeton, NJ: Princeton University Press, 1998.

Kierkegaard, Søren. *Philosophical Fragments*. Translated by Edna Hong and Howard Hong. Princeton, NJ: Princeton University Press, 2013.

Kierkegaard, Søren. *Practice in Christianity*. Translated by Edna Hong and Howard Hong. Princeton, NJ: Princeton University Press, 1991.

Kierkegaard, Søren. *Spiritual Writings*. Edited by George Pattison. New York, NY: Harper Collins, 2010.

Kittel, Gerhard. *Theological Dictionary of the New Testament: Volume 2*. Translated by Geoffrey Bromiley. Dulles, VA: Eerdmans Publishing Company, 1965.

Lawrence, Frederick. "Grace and Friendship: Postmodern Political Theology and God as Conversational." In *The Fragility of Consciousness: Faith, Reason, and the Human Good*. Toronto, ON: University of Toronto Press, 2017.

Lloyd, Vincent. "For What Are Whites to Hope?" *Political Theology* 17.2 (2016): 168–81.

Lonergan, Bernard. *Insight: A Study of Human Understanding*. Toronto, ON: University of Toronto Press, 1992.

Long, Stephen D. *Divine Economy: Theology and the Market*. Abingdon, UK: Routledge, 2000.

Lowith, Karl. *From Hegel to Nietzsche*. New York, NY: Holt, Rinehart, and Winston, 1964.

Lukács, György. *The Destruction of Reason*. Translated by Peter Palmer. London, England: Merlin Press, 1980.

Luz, Ulrich. *Matthew 1–7: A Commentary*. Translated by Wilhelm Linss. Minneapolis, MN: Augsburg Fortress, 1989
Malantschuk, Gregor. *Controversial Kierkegaard*. Translated by Edna Hong and Howard Hong. Waterloo, ON: Wilfrid Laurier University Press, 1980.
Marion, Jean-Luc. "Thomas Aquinas and Onto-Theo-Logy." In *Mystics: Presence and Aporia*. Edited by Michael Kessler and Christian Sheppard. Chicago, IL: University of Chicago Press, 2003.
Marion, Jean-Luc. *The Idol and Distance*. Translated by Thomas Carlson. New York, NY: Fordham University Press, 2001.
Marx, Karl. "Address of the International Working Men's Association to Abraham Lincoln, President of the United States of America." *Bee-Hive Newspaper*. November 7, 1865. Accessible: https://www.marxists.org/archive/marx/iwma/documents/1864/lincoln-letter.htm.
Marx, Karl. *A Contribution to the Critique of Hegel's Philosophy of Right*. *Deutsch-Franzoische Jahrbucher*, February 1844. Accessible: https://www.marxists.org/archive/marx/works/1843/critique-hpr/intro.htm.
Marx, Karl. Letter to Pavel Vasilyevich Annenkov, December 28, 1846. Retrieved: http://hiaw.org/defcon6/works/1846/letters/46_12_28.html.
Marx, Karl. *The German Ideology Part 1: Feuerbach, Opposition of the Materialist and the Idealist Outlook*. Retrieved: https://www.marxists.org/archive/marx/works/1845/german-ideology/ch01b.htm.
Marx, Karl. *On the Jewish Question*. Retrieved: https://www.marxists.org/archive/marx/works/1844/jewish-question/
Marx, Karl. *The Poverty of Philosophy*. Translated by Institute of Marxism Leninism. Retrieved: https://www.marxists.org/archive/marx/works/1847/poverty-philosophy/.
Marx, Karl. "To the People of the United States of America." *Workman's Advocate*. October 14, 1865. Accessible at: https://www.marxists.org/history/international/iwma/documents/1865/to-americans.htm.
Marx, Karl, and Frederick Engels. *Marx and Engels Collected Works, Volume 19*. Moscow, Russia: Progress Publishers, 1964.
Marx, Karl, and Frederick Engels. *Marx and Engels Collected Works, Volume 38*. New York, NY: International Publishers, 1975.
McGee, Timothy. "Against (White) Redemption: James Cone and the Christological Disruption of Racial Discourse and White Solidarity." *Political Theology* 18.7 (2017): 542–59.
Michael-Simmons, Cedrick. "I'm Black and Afraid of 'White Fragility.'" *The Bellows*. 2020. Accessible at: https://www.thebellows.org/im-black-and-afraid-of-white-fragility/.
Milbank, John. *Theology and Social Theory*. Hoboken, NJ: Wiley-Blackwell, 2006.
Moore, Stephen, ed. *Divinanimality: Animal Theory, Creaturely Theology*. New York, NY: Fordham University Press, 2014.

Mosse, George. *Toward the Final Solution: A History of European Racism.* New York, NY: Howard Fertig, 1978.
Mouffe, Chantal. *For a Left Populism.* New York, NY: Verso Books, 2018.
Mouffe, Chantal. *On the Political.* Abingdon, UK: Routledge, 2005.
Mouffe, Chantal. "Post-Marxism Without Apologies." *New Left Review* 166 (1987).
Mouffe, Chantal. "Post-Marxism: Identity and Democracy." *Society and Space* 13 (1995): 259–65.
Naas, Michael. "An Atheism that (Dieu merci!) Still Leaves Something to be Desired." *New Centennial Review* 9.1 (2009): 45–68.
Naas, Michael. *Derrida from Now On.* New York, NY: Fordham University Press, 2008.
Neocleous, Mark. "Friend or Enemy? Reading Schmitt Politically." *Radical Philosophy* 79 (1996): 13–23.
Nietzsche, Friedrich. *The Genealogy of Morals and Ecce Homo.* Translated and edited by Walter Kaufmann. New York, NY: Vintage, 1989.
Norris, Kristopher. "James Cone's Legacy for White Christians." *Political Theology* 21.3 (2020): 207–24.
Novack, George. *Understanding History.* Accessed: https://www.marxists.org/archive/novack/works/history/ch12.htm.
O'Connell, Heather. "The Impact of Slavery on Racial Inequality in Poverty in the Contemporary U.S. South." *Social Forces* 90.3 (2012): 713–34.
Oluo, Ijeonma. *So You Want to Talk about Race.* Cypress, CA: Seal Press, 2019.
Pattison, George. *The Philosophy of Kierkegaard.* Montreal, QC: McGill University Press, 2005.
Pérez-Álvarez, Eliseo. *A Vexing Gadfly: The Late Kierkegaard on Economic Matters.* Princeton, NJ: Princeton University Press, 2009.
Petrella, Ivan. *Beyond Liberation Theology: A Polemic.* London, England: SCM Press, 2013.
Petrella, Ivan. "Liberation Theology Undercover." *Political Theology* 18.4 (2017): 325–39.
Pickstock, Catherine. *After Writing: On the Liturgical Consummation of Philosophy.* Hoboken, NJ: Blackwell, 1997.
Prevot, Andrew. *Theology and Race: Black and Womanist Traditions in the United States.* Boston, MA: Brill, 2018.
Ratzinger, Joseph. *Faith and Politics: Selected Writings.* San Francisco, CA: Ignatius Press, 2018.
Reed Jr., Adolph. "Marx, Race, and Neoliberalism." *New Labor Forum* 22.1 (2013): 49–57.
Reed Jr., Adolph. "The Myth of Class Reductionism." *New Republic.* Accessed: https://newrepublic.com/article/154996/myth-class-reductionism.
Reed, Touré. *Toward Freedom: The Case Against Race Reductionism.* Verso Books, 2020
Reitan, Ruth. "Cuba, the Black Panther Party, and the US Black Movement in the 1960s: Issues of Security." *New Political Science* 21.1 (1999): 217–30.

Robbins, Jeffrey. *Radical Democracy and Political Theology.* New York, NY: Columbia University Press, 2013.
Roberts, Kyle. "James: Putting Faith to Action." In *Kierkegaard and the Bible: Tome II: The New Testament.* Edited by Jon Stewart. Surrey, UK: Ashgate, 2010.
Rohrbacher, Stefan. "The Charge of Deicide." *Journal of Medieval History* 17.4 (1991): 297–321.
Rorty, Richard. "Is Derrida a 'Quasi'-Transcendental Philosopher?" *Contemporary Literature* 36.1 (1995): 173–200.
Rose, Marika. *A Theology of Failure: Žižek Against Christian Innocence.* New York, NY: Fordham University Press, 2019.
Sartre, Jean-Paul. *Existentialism Is a Humanism.* Translated by Carol Macomber. New Haven, CT: Yale University Press, 2007.
Sbriglia, Russell. "The Symptoms of Ideology Critique; or, How We Learned to Enjoy the Symptom and Ignore the Fetish." In *Everything You Always Wanted to Know About Literature but Were Afraid to Ask* Žižek. Durham, NC: Duke University Press, 2017.
Scheuerman, William. "The Unholy Alliance of Carl Schmitt and Friedrich A Hayek." *Constellations* 4.2 (1997): 172–88.
Schmitt, Carl. *Concept of the Political.* Translated by George Schwab. Chicago, IL: University of Chicago Press, 2007.
Schmitt, Carl. *Crisis in Parliamentary Democracy.* Translated by Ellen Kennedy. Cambridge, MA: MIT Press, 1988.
Schmitt, Carl. "Der Begriff des Politischen." *Archiv für Sozialwissenschaft und Sozialpolitik* 58.1 (1927): 1–33.
Schmitt, Carl. *Der Begriff des Politischen.* Berlin, Germany: Duncker & Humblot, 1932 / *The Concept of the Political.* Translated by George Schwab. University of Chicago Press, 2007.
Schmitt, Carl. *Dictatorship.* Translated by Michael Hoelzl and Graham Ward. Cambridge, UK: Polity Press, 2014.
Schmitt, Carl. *Glossarium: Aufzeichnungen aus den Jahren 1947 bis 1958.* Edited by Gerd Giesler and Martin Tielke. Berlin, Germany: Duncker & Humblot, 2015.
Schmitt, Carl. *Political Theology II: The Myth of the Closure of Any Political Theology.* Translated by Michael Hoelzl and Graham Ward. Cambridge, UK: Polity Press, 2008.
Schmitt, Carl. *Political Theology.* Translated by George Schwab. Chicago, IL: University of Chicago Press, 2006.
Schmitt, Carl. *Politische Theologie.* Berlin, Germany: Duncker & Humblot, 2015 / *Political Theology: Four Chapters on the Concept of Sovereignty.* Translated by George Schwab. Chicago, IL: University of Chicago Press, 2006.
Sechrest, Ramirez-Johnson, and Amos Yong, eds. *Can "White" People Be Saved? Triangulating Race, Theology, and Mission.* Westmont, IL: IVP Academic, 2018.
Shakespeare, Steven. *Derrida and Theology.* London, England: T&T Clark, 2009.

Shephard, Andrew. *The Gift of the Other: Levinas, Derrida, and a Theology of Hospitality.* Eugene, OR: Pickwick Publications, 2014.

Sinclair, Charlene. "Toward a Twenty-First Century Black Liberation Ethic: A Marxist Reclamation of Ontological Blackness." From *The Reemergence of Liberation Theologies: Models for the Twenty-First Century.* Edited by Thia Cooper. London, England: Palgrave Macmillan, 2013.

Smith, Barbara. "Combahee River Collective Statement." Accessible at: https://www.blackpast.org/african-american-history/combahee-river-collective-statement-1977/.

Smith, Ted. *Weird John Brown: Divine Violence and the Limits of Ethics.* Stanford, CA: Stanford University Press, 2014.

Spengler, Oswald. *The Decline of the West: An Abridged Edition.* Translated by Charles Atkinson. Edited by Arthur Helps and Helmut Warner. Oxford, England: Oxford University Press, 1991.

Stan, Leo. "Risible Christianity? Kierkegaard vs. Žižek." *Toronto Journal of Theology* 28.2, 275–289 (2012).

Stan, Leo. "Slavoj Žižek: Mirroring the Absent God." In *Kierkegaard's Influence on the Social Sciences.* Edited by Jon Stewart. Farnham, UK: Ashgate Publishing, 2011.

Steinberg, Stephen. *Race Relations: A Critique.* Stanford, CA: Stanford University Press, 2007.

Streeck, Wolfgang. *How Will Capitalism End?* New York, NY: Verso Books, 2016.

Swanson, David. *Rediscipling the White Church: From Cheap Diversity to True Solidarity.* Westmont, IL: IVP, 2020.

Taubes, Jacob. *Occidental Eschatology.* Translated by David Ratmoko. Stanford, CA: Stanford University Press, 2009.

Taylor, Charles. *A Secular Age.* Cambridge, MA: Belknap Press, 2018.

Taylor, Mark C. *Erring: A Postmodern A/theology.* Chicago, IL: University of Chicago Press, 1984.

Thomas, James. *Diversity Regimes: Why Talk Is Not Enough to Fix Racial Inequality at Universities.* Lewisburg, PA: Bucknell University Press, 2020.

Uwe Hohendahl, Peter. *Perilous Futures: On Carl Schmitt's Late Writings.* Ithaca, NY: Cornell University Press, 2018.

Walsh Perkins, Sylvia, ed. *Truth Is Subjectivity: Kierkegaard and Political Theology.* Macon, GA: Mercer University Press, 2019.

Ward, Graham. "Review: *The Prayers and Tears of Jacques Derrida.*" *Modern Theology* 15.4 (1999): 504–507.

Warren, Elizabeth. "The Economics of Race: When Making it to the Middle Is Not Enough." *Washington and Lee Law Review* 61.4 (2004): 1777–99.

Weber, Samuel. "Taking Exception to Decision: Walter Benjamin and Carl Schmitt." *Diacritics* 22 (1992): 5–18.

West, Cornel. *The American Evasion of Philosophy: A Genealogy of Pragmatism.* Madison, WI: University of Wisconsin Press, 1989.

West, Cornel. *The Cornel West Reader.* New York, NY: Civitas Books, 2000.
West, Cornel. *Keeping Faith: Philosophy and Race in America.* Abingdon, UK: Routledge, 2012.
West, Cornel. *Prophesy Deliverance! An Afro-American Revolutionary Christianity.* Louisville, KY: Westminster John Knox Press, 2002.
Wilkinson, Michael. "Authoritarian liberalism in Europe: a common critique of neoliberalism and ordoliberalism," *Critical Sociology* 45.7 (2019), 1023–1034.
Wing Sue, Derald. *Race Talk and the Conspiracy of Silence: Understanding and Facilitating Difficult Dialogues on Race.* Hoboken, NJ: Wiley, 2016.
Wood, Ellen Meiskins. "Class, Race, and Capitalism." *Political Power and Social Theory* 15 (2002): 275–84.
Wood, Ellen Meiskins. *Peasant-Citizen and Slave.* New York, NY: Verso Books, 1989.
Žižek, Slavoj. "Carl Schmitt in the Age of Post-Politics." In *The Challenge of Carl Schmitt.* Edited by Chantal Mouffe. New York, NY: Verso Books, 1999.
Žižek, Slavoj. *The Parallax View.* Cambridge, MA: MIT Press, 2009.
Žižek, Slavoj. *The Puppet and the Dwarf: The Perverse Core of Christianity.* Cambridge, MA: MIT Press, 2003.
Žižek, Slavoj. *The Ticklish Subject: The Missing Center of Political Ontology.* New York, NY: Verso Books, 1999.
Žižek, Slavoj, and John Milbank. *The Monstrosity of Christ: Paradox or Dialectic?* Cambridge, MA: MIT Press, 2011.
Zwolinski, Matt. "The Libertarian Nonaggression Principle," *Social Philosophy and Policy* 32.3 (2016): 62–90.

Index

Abraham, 144, 146, 155, 227, 247n22, 251n39
Adorno, Theodore, 125–27, 212, 246n5
Afropessimism. *See* Wilderson, Frank
Agacinski, Sylviane, 124, 250n34
Ahmed, Sara, 172
Altizer, J. J., 85, 241n47
Alvis, Jason, 63
Anderson, Kevin, 231n4
Anderson, Victor, 169, 178, 192–94, 198–200
Anti-capitalism, 1, 2, 5, 9–10, 12, 14–17, 34, 125, 164, 167, 169–75, 202–03, 206–09, 219, 222. *See also* Capitalism
Anti-racism, 10, 15–16, 169–75, 189, 259n54, 259n55
   Marxism as, 204–09, 214, 222, 260n59
Antisemitism, 32, 47, 153, 231n7
Aquinas, Thomas, 1
   and Cone, 189
   Jean-Luc Marion on, 62
Aristotle, 6, 64, 68–74, 87
Atheism, 9, 29, 65, 75–76, 78, 82–84, 88–90, 93–96, 101, 117–18, 142, 220

Badiou, Alain, 2, 84

Barabbas, 31–32, 45
Barth, Karl, 25–26, 80, 177
Baudrillard, Jean, 103
Benjamin, Walter, 37
Bennington, Geoffrey, 73, 124
Bezos, Jeff, 174
Black power, 178, 190, 201, 203
Bodin, Jean, 26–27
Brown, John, 1, 5, 16–17, 146, 188–90, 200, 219, 225–27, 261n5

Capitalism, 2–4, 10–11, 19, 23, 33–35, 57, 60, 84, 124, 125, 165, 171, 173–75, 180–82, 203, 205–08, 211, 213–15, 222, 224, 227, 230n16, 250n34, 258n45, 259n54, 259n56. *See also* Anti-capitalism
Caputo, John, 12, 63–65, 77–88, 91–94, 96–97, 124, 138, 144–47, 220, 240n43
Carter, J. Kameron, 169, 175–77, 193–94
Carter, Tom, 126
Carter, Warren, 49
Castro, Fidel, 189
Christian fascism, 20, 24, 40, 57, 232n11
Class struggle, 11, 40, 53–54, 125, 205

Climacus, Johannes, 133–34
Clinton Race Initiative, 172
The Concept of the Political (Schmitt), 24, 30–42
Commissarial dictatorship, 26–27
Cone, James, 15–17, 57, 219
    and epistemology, 168, 185–91, 209, 215, 222–23
    and ontology, 167, 169, 175–79, 184, 192–95
    and revolution, 97, 191, 217, 221
    and the image of God, 177–78
    and two tropics of blackness, 171, 196–204, 214
    historical context of, 202, 211
    on violence, 187–89, 192, 256n32
    response to deconstruction, 13
    See also Marx, Karl
Cortés, Donoso, 31

Death, 45, 73, 76, 89, 102, 110–13, 191–92, 216, 227, 239n30
Derrida, Jacques
    alleged difference between early and late works, 63–64, 223, 235n10, 236n17
    and auto-deconstruction, 134
    and communication, 160
    and decision, 36–37, 66, 94–96, 98
    and his tallith, 98–99, 155, 217, 221, 227
    and ideology, 4, 61
    and Jean-Luc Marion, 61–62, 65
    and John Caputo, 65, 77–78, 81–84, 91–93
    and Karl Marx, 16, 67, 232n12, 241n47
    and Martin Hägglund, 65, 75–77, 87, 91–93
    and negative theology, 236n16, 238n27
    and race, 168, 254n1, 255n19
    and Søren Kierkegaard, 79, 92
    and the history of western philosophy, 179
    and the politics of friendship, 55
    and theology/metaphysics, 1–2, 3, 6–7, 9, 11–13, 28, 60, 62–63, 96–97, 118, 123, 128, 130, 143, 178, 209, 212, 220–22, 230n11
    and thinking and being, 14, 17
    and writing as deconstruction of metaphysics, 64, 66–75, 237n24, 238n28, 239n29, 239n32
    as Algerian, 66
    Chantal Mouffe's interpretation of, 22–23
    John Milbank's critique of, 103–04, 242n54
    on Carl Schmitt, 42, 51, 54, 123
    on God/faith, 94–96, 146, 237n25, 240n41
Decisionism, 12, 24, 38–39, 56, 59, 220, 233n30
Deconstruction, 6–9, 12–14, 17, 22, 55, 63–67, 75, 78–79, 82–83, 87–88, 94, 96–97, 101–02, 124, 127–28, 145–46, 163, 212, 219–21, 224, 236n16, 237n21. *See also* Derrida, Jacques
Deleuze, Giles, 6, 103, 234n34
Democracy, 22–24, 31, 33–34, 37, 87, 233n30
Dialectical materialism, 14, 53, 123, 126–27, 129–30, 170, 174
Dialogue, 15, 44–45, 171, 191
Dictatorship of the proletariat, 29, 34, 39, 57, 180
Différance, 7, 9, 77, 80, 94–96
Diversity, 15, 172–75, 222
Douglass, Frederick, 225
Durkheim, Emile, 103

Eichelberger, David, 226
Engels, Frederick, 29, 207
Eurocentrism, 157, 206
Existentialism, 14, 124, 138, 142, 162, 164, 223

Faith, 2, 10, 65–66, 78–79, 84, 89–90, 92–96, 99, 101–02, 116, 119, 131–33, 144, 146–47, 151–58, 162, 168, 192, 209, 216, 221, 223, 226. *See also* Leap of faith
Flesh, 110–11, 193–94
Foucault, Michel, 210, 261n5
French Revolution, 27, 29
Friend-enemy distinction, 11, 24, 44, 51–52, 56, 233n33

Gadamer, Hans Georg, 68, 237n21
Garnet, Henry Highland, 188
Genovese, Eugene, 207
God, 3–4, 13, 24–25, 27, 49–51, 59, 61–62, 64–66, 71, 74–78, 81–82, 84–85, 89–97, 101–02, 116–22, 141, 144, 146, 152, 155–59, 162, 165, 168, 176–77, 185–86, 190–91, 195–96, 215–16, 220, 226–27
Gospel of Matthew, 32, 47–48, 162
Guevara, Che, 16–17, 127, 146, 189, 191, 227, 257n36

Habermas, Jurgen, 44
Hägglund, Martin, 12, 65–66, 75–80, 83–94, 97, 101–02, 110, 118, 144–47
Hampton, Fred, 16, 146, 206–07, 259n56
Hardt, Michael, 126, 246n8
Hartman, Saidaya, 183
Harvey, David, 11, 230n16

Hector, Kevin, 63
Hegel, Georg Wilhelm Friedrich, 68, 71–73, 103, 108, 124–26, 139–40, 157
Heidegger, Martin, 7, 63–64, 193, 229n7, 235n5, 235n6, 235n7, 248n23
Hermeneutics, 65, 68, 163–64, 166, 237n21
Historical materialism, 37, 212–15
Holberg, Ludvig, 137–38
Hospitality, 64, 87–88
Husserl, Edmund, 71–72

Idealism, 2, 4–6, 9, 14–15, 25, 28, 29, 40, 67, 69, 94, 97, 124–30, 133, 136, 138–39, 141–42, 149–50, 157, 164, 166, 168, 183, 194, 210, 219, 221–22, 224
Ideology, 1, 8–9
and race, 182
existentialist critique of, 138
Imago dei, 176–77, 184–85, 191
Impossibility, 79–89, 91–94, 220
Isomorphism of thinking and being, 1, 5–8, 60, 65–66, 75, 88, 96, 99, 129–39, 178, 220, 241n43
Islamophobia, 104, 243n2

Jameson, Fredric, 114, 126
Jesus Christ, 14, 32, 49, 102, 152–54, 159–62, 176–79, 185–87, 194–97
Jones, Claudia, 11, 207
Judaism, 13, 50, 57

Kearney, Richard, 12, 63, 82, 95
Khora, 80–82, 85, 93–94–96
Kierkegaard, Søren, 14–16, 57
and the leap of faith, 134, 150–55, 224, 227, 241n44

278 / Index

Kierkegaard, Søren *(continued)*
  as deconstructive, 134, 146, 163, 178, 209, 221–22
  as materialist, 129, 139–42, 148, 159–60, 164, 167, 223
  as socialist, 164–66
  critique of Danish Christendom, 158
  John Caputo on, 82–84, 144, 146–47
  Karl Ove Knausgaard on, 116
  Martin Hägglund on, 145–47
  on Ludvig Holberg, 137–38
  on orthodoxy and orthopraxy, 143, 160–62
  on the eternal and the temporal, 131–33, 147–50
  on thinking and being, 130, 134–38
  on truth, 97, 143, 150–56, 159
  on Turks, 156–57
  See also Derrida, Jacques; Marx, Karl; Schmitt, Carl
King, Martin Luther Jr., 174
Kittel, Gerhard, 50–51
Knausgaard, Karl Ove, 13–14, 57, 97, 105–22, 155, 221–23
Kragh-Jacobsen, Svend, 137

Lacan, Jacques, 103
Leap of faith, 133, 224, 241, 247n22
Lee, Robert E., 209
Lehmann, Theo, 188
Lenin, Vladimir, 38, 127
Lewis, Asahel, 225
Liberalism, 15, 21, 26, 33–35, 45–46, 123, 207
Lincoln, Abraham, 208–09
Literature, 113–16, 119
Logos, 5–6, 17, 60, 64 71, 74, 94, 220, 239n32
Long, Stephen, 189–90, 192

Love command, 47–51
Lukács, György, 124–25
Luz, Ulrich, 49–50

Marder, Michael, 7
Marion, Jean-Luc, 12, 61–65, 90
Marx, Karl
  Afropessimist critique of, 179–83
  and Carl Schmitt, 28–33, 35–39, 46, 51, 53–54, 123, 220, 234n39
  and commodity fetishism, 2
  and Cornel West, 209–13, 215
  and deconstruction, 17
  and ideology, 8–9, 118
  and Jacques Derrida, 16–17, 60, 67, 74, 219
  and James Cone, 204–07, 217
  and Karl Ove Knausgaard, 119
  and Pierre-Joseph Proudhon, 140–41
  and post-Marxists, 230n2
  and prescriptive materialism, 9
  and race, 10, 11, 15–16, 170–75, 184, 207–09, 214, 231n4, 255n19, 256n27, 260n59
  and Søren Kierkegaard, 14, 123–30, 133, 136, 139, 142, 143, 146–48, 163, 165, 245n2, 250n34, 253n53
  and theory, 224, 226, 250n32
  and Thomas J. J. Altizer, 241n47
  and Young Hegelians, 4, 9
  Chantal Mouffe's critique of, 6, 19–23, 231n8, 231n9
  critique of capitalist political economy, 10, 165, 170
  critique of theology, 2, 5, 74, 118–19, 239n34
  critique of unity, 40
Materialism, 6, 8–11, 14–15, 25, 37, 54, 110, 112–13, 115–16, 123, 127, 138–39, 142, 164, 212–15.

See also Dialectical materialism;
Prescriptive materialism
McGee, Timothy, 200–01
Mental experience, 68–71
Messianism, 81, 83
Metaphysics
 as political, 1–3, 5, 24, 39, 57,
  61–62, 66, 123, 212
 deconstruction of, 1, 13
 definition of, 6–8
 Jean-Luc Marion and, 62
 religion and, 74
 theology as, 219
 See also Derrida, Jacques; Ideology;
  Marx, Karl
Metonymy, 8, 169, 196–97, 199,
 214
Michael-Simmons, Cedrick, 172
Milbank, John, 13, 67–68, 102–06,
 108, 112, 115–16, 120–22, 221
Mosse, George, 210
Mouffe, Chantal, 11, 20–24, 56,
 229n6
Moynihan Report, 172
Muslims, 48, 157, 243n2

Nancy, Jean-Luc, 63
Nazism, 50, 66, 168, 233n33
Negri, Antonio, 126, 246n8, 260n63
Neoliberalism, 33, 138
Nietzsche, Friedrich, 6, 187, 230n10
Novack, George, 126–27

Ochlos, 32, 36–37, 41, 84
Ontology, 7–8, 123, 141, 153, 175–
 76, 178–84, 193–94, 234n41,
 236n17
Ordoliberalism, 33–35, 53, 233n25,
 234n38, 234n39
Orthopraxy, 1, 5, 10, 15–17, 40, 83,
 97, 130, 159–60, 164, 167, 291,
 222–23, 252n53

Paradox, 79, 83, 97, 147–52, 164
Parmenides, 6, 179, 229n7
Pattison, George, 128, 145
Platonism, 2, 6, 49, 121, 174, 250n32
the political, 1, 21, 33, 40, 42–48,
 50–55, 56, 60, 66, 223, 229n6,
 230n2
Pontius Pilate, 31–32, 152–54, 159–61
Pope Benedict, 32
Postmodernism, 3, 16, 103
Prescriptive Materialism, 8–10, 182
Principle of noncontradiction, 65,
 87–88, 96, 119
Private property, 124, 139, 165, 171
Proletariat, 3, 10, 28–29, 34, 37, 39,
 57, 72, 142, 173, 180, 182, 185,
 209, 211, 214, 215, 224
Prophetic pragmatism, 213–14
Proudhon, Pierre-Joseph, 140–43, 157,
 250n32. *See also* Marx, Karl

Racism, 4, 10, 56, 169–75, 18–82,
 197, 203–15, 222. *See also*
 Anti-racism
Radical orthodoxy. *See* Milbank, John
Reality and actuality, 135–36
Robbins, Jeffrey, 2, 55, 236n17
Robespierre, Maximilien, 29, 127
Rousseau, Jean-Jacques, 66, 68, 73–74

Secularism, 13, 103–05, 120–22, 221,
 223, 241n47
Self-determination, 168, 170, 176–78,
 184–91, 195, 197, 201–03,
 256n31, 256n32, 257n36
Sermon on the Mount, 47–51
Sexism, 10, 215
Schmitt, Carl
 and "the political," 42–44, 46,
  51–53, 71, 107, 121, 229n6
 and antisemitism, 9, 47, 153, 212
 and dictatorship, 26–30

Schmitt, Carl *(continued)*
 and left-Schmittianism, 11–12,
  19–25, 219–20, 234n41
 and metaphysics, 7, 35, 54, 57,
  59–61, 69, 72, 96, 98, 129, 151,
  168, 222–23, 232n12, 232n20
 and ordoliberalism, 33–35, 53,
  233n25
 and Søren Kierkegaard, 36–37, 53,
  133–34, 155, 163, 249n24
 and sovereignty, 30–31, 36, 41, 57
 critique of Marxism, 9, 35, 37–39,
  53-5–56, 123, 129, 220, 249n30
 critique of parliamentarianism, 31,
  183
 on friendship and enmity, 45–47,
  55–56, 115, 136, 163, 230n2,
  260n63
 on loving enemies, 48–51
 on Turks, 157
 Slavoj Zizek's critique of, 38–40
 See also Antisemitism; Decisionism;
  Jacques, Derrida; Marx, Karl
Scotus, John Duns, 102, 243n2
Signifier, 67, 70, 72–73, 75, 77, 80,
 84, 238n28
Sinclair, Charlene, 173–74
Smith, Adam, 206
Smith, Barabara, 207
Smith, Ted, 225
Socialism, 15–16, 204–06
Socrates, 132, 149, 160
Sovereignty, 24, 26–46, 57, 59,
 233n28
Spengler, Oswald, 25–26
Spivak, Gayatri Chakravorty, 73–74,
 239n33
St. James, 2, 9, 162
St. Paul, 1–2, 120, 229n2
Stan, Leo, 127–28
State of exception, 24, 56
Steinber, Stephen, 172

Streeck, Wolfgang, 11, 34
Structural racism, 175, 196–99, 203,
 205, 255n19
Swanson, David, 172

Taubes, Jacob, 37, 129
Telos (journal), 19
Temporality, 76–77, 81, 83, 86
Thomas, James, 172
Thoreau, Henry, 225
Transcendental signified, 67, 71–73,
 75, 81, 84, 94, 96, 101, 103,
 238n27, 238n28. *See also*
 Deconstruction
Tropics of blackness, 169, 196–203
Truth, 13, 15, 17, 59–60, 64–65,
 69–75, 88, 94–99, 102, 113, 130,
 132–33, 136, 139–44, 147–62,
 168, 184–92, 212–213, 217, 220,
 222–23, 261n69
Tubman, Harriet, 225
Turks, 48, 156–57, 164
Turner, Nat, 188, 190

Veil, 98
Violence, 13, 50, 54, 66, 102–03,
 122, 172, 186–92, 221, 223

Walpurgis Night, 106–10, 120–21
Weber, Max, 103
Weber, Samuel, 36, 41
West, Cornel, 15–16, 170, 209–17,
 223
Westphaler, Gert, 136–39, 142, 157,
 171, 183
White supremacy, 9, 175, 189, 210–
 13
Wilderson, Frank, 179–84
Wise, Henry Alexander, 225

Žižek, Slavoj, 8, 38–40, 84–85,
 126–29, 231n2, 241n44, 141n47

www.ingramcontent.com/pod-product-compliance
Lightning Source LLC
Chambersburg PA
CBHW020640230426
43665CB00008B/256